P9-EEU-642

A Guide to Vocational Assessment

Please remember that this is a library book,
and that it belongs only temporarily to each
person who uses it. Be considerate. Do
not write in this, or any, library book.

A Guide to Vocational Assessment

THIRD EDITION

Paul W. Power

An International Publisher

8700 Shoal Creek Boulevard
Austin, Texas 78757-6897
800/897-3202   Fax 800/397-7633
Order online at http://www.proedinc.com

362.4
P887g
2000

© 2000, 1991, 1984 by PRO-ED, Inc.
8700 Shoal Creek Boulevard
Austin, Texas 78757-6897
800/897-3202   Fax 800/397-7633
Order online at http://www.proedinc.com

All rights reserved. No part of the material protected by this copyright notice may be reproduced or used in any form or by any means, electronic or mechanical, including photocopying, recording, or by any information storage and retrieval system, without the prior written permission of the copyright owner.

NOTICE: PRO-ED grants permission to the user of this material to make unlimited copies of the worksheets in Appendixes A through C for teaching purposes. Duplication of this material for commercial purposes is prohibited.

Library of Congress Cataloging-in-Publication Data

Power, Paul W.
    A guide to vocational assessment/Paul W. Power. —3rd ed.
      p. cm.
    Includes bibliographical references and index.
    ISBN 0-89079-786-2
    1. Vocational rehabilitation. 2. Disability evaluation.
  3. Vocational evaluation. I. Title.
HD7255.P68 1998
362.4'0484—dc21   98-19448
                                         CIP

This book is designed in Utopia and Goudy.

Production Director: Alan Grimes
Production Coordinator: Dolly Fisk Jackson
Managing Editor: Chris Olson
Art Director: Thomas Barkley
Designer: Jason Crosier
Print Buyer: Alicia Woods
Preproduction Coordinator: Chris Anne Worsham
Staff Copyeditor: Martin Wilson
Publishing Assistant: Jason Morris

Printed in the United States of America

2   3   4   5   6   7   8   9   10   04   03   02   01

For my wife Barbara, whose dedication and tireless work
for this project has made this third edition possible

Contents

Please remember that this is a library book, and that it belongs only temporarily to each person who uses it. Be considerate. Do not write in this, or any, library book.

Preface

This third edition is a product of 4 years of observing the changes in the vocational assessment field, identifying rehabilitation policy that continually influences client evaluation, and receiving feedback from assessment practitioners who have studied the earlier editions of this book. The combination of these elements has provided thoughtful insight into how a volume on vocational assessment can be more useful to rehabilitation professionals. In addition, increased attention is being given to such clients as persons with chronic mental illness, traumatic brain injury, and individuals with learning disabilities. More focused attention also is being directed to those individuals representing varied ethnic backgrounds. As a result, all of these populations demand a rethinking of traditional vocational assessment methods. New standards for psychological testing are being implemented, updated and renormed cognitive assessments are being used, and functional and situational approaches to evaluation are experiencing an increase in measurement sophistication.

This revised edition responds to the assessment needs of both multicultural populations and progressively recognized disability groups. Each chapter has been rewritten with material that represents more updated knowledge of the vocational assessment field. Models have been expanded, case studies have been changed, and several paper and pencil tests have been replaced by others that have been recommended because they are more readily available. Specifically, many of the chapters contain material explicitly written for either underserved populations or those for whom evaluation methods are still in the developing stage. Also, more attention is given to criterion-referenced assessment, the application of the Americans with Disabilities Act of 1990 (ADA) to evaluation issues, and the empowerment of the client through the vocational assessment process. In addition to the book's new chapter on computer-assisted vocational assessment, the discussion of transferable skills evaluation methods has been expanded. Further additions to the book include the following improvements:

1. enhanced attention to the role of the environment in assessment

2. a discussion of developed methods in employability and occupational handicap assessment

3. attention to varied learning styles, with an identification of appropriate methods

4. integration of culture-related issues throughout the volume

A reexamination of the definition of disability provides a context for many of the changes described in this book. Also—as was emphasized in the second edition—vocational evaluators must structure the assessment situation so that both evaluation and learning opportunities are created. The reason for this is the reality that few current measurement strategies and instruments are suitable for use with persons with severe handicaps who lack the skills or traits measured by popular assessment instruments. When assessments are structured in this manner, a person–environment assessment then becomes more feasible. However, so few fully developed assessment instruments that are currently available use a learning potential format in exploring vocational potential. The evaluator, consequently, must devise methods that are less traditional and yet can provide feedback on both employment possibilities and an individual's growth during the assessment process. As the rehabilitation process begins, the evaluator also should determine the client's behaviors in relation to those required of jobs that are available.

Through the case studies and accompanying questions in each chapter of this book, readers are invited to think critically and productively about numerous measurement-related issues. Readers are also encouraged to understand the difficulties of applying traditional evaluation methods to those with severe disabilities or those representing different ethnic groups. The reader is challenged to apply varied evaluation approaches to the complex issues that clients bring to rehabilitation. For example, readers are asked to apply the approaches of interest or personality assessment to those who are African American and who also have a severe disability.

Many reviewers have praised the two previous editions of this volume for including comprehensive material that assists in a thorough understanding of the evaluation process for clients with disabilities. Every effort has been made in this third edition to maintain that tradition. Readers will be exposed, however, to more current information about how one understands a person with a disability.

I would like particularly to express my appreciation to Norm Hursh of Sargent College, Boston University, for his careful review of the second edition, and for his insightful suggestions that helped shape this new edition.

Though several factors have influenced the thought and development of this revised edition, the overall purpose of this new volume is to encourage the rehabilitation professional to continue to act as an enlightened consumer. Evaluators need to assess the available measurement resources that apply to the population being evaluated, to examine carefully the normative data and the reliability and validity research efforts, and to corroborate with peers on the effectiveness of selected evaluation methods. This book will assist evaluators as they respond to those needs, thereby empowering clients to achieve their rehabilitation goals.

Introduction

This book explains how vocational assessment approaches can be used. Application of evaluation knowledge is based on understanding (a) the meaning of vocational rehabilitation, (b) current trends in rehabilitation practices that influence assessment approaches, (c) the role of assessment in the rehabilitation process, (d) a current conceptualization of vocational evaluation, (e) the target areas and components of vocational assessment, (f) the need for a personal philosophy of assessment that lays the base for everyday practice, (g) the different roles that can be adopted by the rehabilitation professional during assessment, and (h) expected competencies for the counselor as an evaluator. Each of these areas is discussed in this introduction.

REHABILITATION: MEANING, SCOPE, AND THE ROLE OF ASSESSMENT

As we approach the 21st century, our overriding view of rehabilitation is that it is a process of restoration—a way to help an individual achieve practical goals, self-dependence, and personal satisfaction. Rehabilitation is not only problem-centered, but it is also focused on adjustment. Moreover, rehabilitation aims at reducing disability conditions that restrict activities or cause handicaps; developing competencies necessary for adequate role performance in family, social, and occupational areas; and helping a person to participate in the life of the general community. Rehabilitation can also be viewed as a process of remediating a skills deficit. Anthony (1980) believed that:

> The goal of rehabilitation is to assure that the person with a disability possesses those physical, emotional, and intellectual skills needed to live, learn, and work in his or her own particular community. (p. 7)

Rehabilitation, consequently, has more than one goal, despite the fact that for decades many professionals believed that rehabilitation efforts should only be directed toward individuals who could be totally self-reliant in producing their income. Rehabilitation planning, moreover, identifies a person's strengths and builds on residual capacities. The ideas of rehabilitation have grown "into the concept of enabling a person to return to or to attain as much function and independence as possible" (Crowe, 1976, p. 30). It is no longer tied to manpower needs and is based both on productive output and productive living. As a result of this perspective, rehabilitation efforts are devoted to helping clients with handicaps become more productive until they are able to function adequately in varied settings. Vocational goals are still most important in rehabilitation, yet other functional outcomes are included. These can be activities of which a person is capable of engaging on a regular basis and that require the use of time, strength, and mental or physical faculties. Such activities might be, for example, sheltered employment (transitional or long-term, homebound employment), self-employment, employment by others, volunteer work, or programmed day tasks.

Anticipated changes in work and society have had an impact on rehabilitation efforts. Because advances in science and technology, jobs will be adapted in order to remain competitive in a global market. These advances and increased capability for job adaptation will open more employment opportunities for persons with a disability. Communication aids, better access to information, and better transportation can facilitate the viability of better paying job fields for persons with moderately severe disabilities (Vander Kolk, 1995). Because of these changes, it will be necessary to perform frequent job task analyses, to maximize the chances of successful job placement, and to explore through different evaluation approaches the client's ability to learn, cope with stress, and adapt to change. The scope of rehabilitation has widened to include clients who have severe disabilities and who cannot always fit into the traditional work structure of time and output. The recent increase of acceptable outcomes affects the extent of rehabilitation services delivery and necessitates that more relevant approaches for delivering these services be examined. This is particularly true of the role of assessment in the rehabilitation process.

The rehabilitation process is a form of social technology that assists clients as they make the transition from patient to rehabilitant. The traditional role usually is characterized as being dependent and passive ("You do it for me"), whereas current rehabilitant behavior emphasizes participating and initiating, with a dominant focus on residual strength and capabilities. If individuals with a disability are to achieve functional outcome, they must become rehabilitants. In other words, the rehabilitation process should help clients to become empowered, as well as to assume more responsibility for the achievement of appropriate living goals. This task not only depends on the person's ego strength, the attitude of family members toward rehabilitation, and the degree to which rehabilitation programs meet specific needs, but also on the quality and extent of the assessment early in the rehabilitation process. An evaluation that reaches out to involve the client in rehabilitation planning, emphasizing what the person *can do*— rather than the extent of his or her limitations—will considerably facilitate the client's achievement of worthwhile rehabilitation goals. Assessment, then, is a dynamic of the rehabilitation process as well as an integral part of the client's rehabilitation.

In the rehabilitation process, assessment typically is performed soon after the client makes a request for vocational services. If the person with a disability is referred to an evaluation center, he or she may wait for a considerable length of time because most centers have long waiting lists. Therefore, to keep clients motivated enough to pursue rehabilitation goals, rehabilitation professionals should conduct a beginning assessment that prevents any hopes of rehabilitation achievement from fading. An assessment performed soon after the initial client contact becomes the first step toward the development of an effective rehabilitation plan because it gives the person with a disability a renewed awareness of productive-oriented strengths and capabilities. This step often can become operationalized by using self-assessment procedures. This approach to assessment is becoming popular with agencies who have clients with the intellectual, physical, and emotional capacities to complete these evaluation tools.

CURRENT TRENDS IN REHABILITATION PRACTICE THAT INFLUENCE VOCATIONAL ASSESSMENT

Beginning in the 1980s, and receiving more attention in the 1990s because of federal legislation, consumer advocacy, population shifts, cost-effective policy developments, and technology advances, specific trends have emerged that influence the way vocational assessment is conducted. These trends, the implications of which will be discussed in the chapters of this book, are the following:

1. *A team approach to the vocational evaluation process, during which input is invited from medical and allied health professionals regarding the functional abilities of the client, is becoming increasingly prevalent.* Physicians, nurses, physical and occupational therapists, social workers, and psychologists may provide valuable information that can be integrated into rehabilitation planning. An interdisciplinary team approach allows for the effective use of information that can be translated into effective planning, implementation activities (e.g., placements, support services), and fulfilled vocational development for clients (Interdisciplinary Council, 1994).

2. *A focus on discrimination practices, especially in the areas of preemployment testing and screening, widens the scope of rehabilitation.* The Americans with Disabilities Act of 1990, as well as reauthorization legislation of this act, have addressed potential areas of discrimination, mandated when employment testing should be done, and described how testing must relate to the essential functions of the job. Title I of the ADA identifies the types of testing accommodations under three broad categories: testing medium, time limits, and test content (Bruyere & O'Keefe, 1994). Special accommodations for those with the specific disabilities of visual, hearing, and orthopedic impairments are also mandated.

3. *Increased attention is being given to the development of more appropriate assessment approaches for those representing different ethnic and minority groups.* These populations have been underserved, and most traditional evaluation methods have standardization data that is not relevant to specific subgroups of a community. Further, many well-used psychological tests contain a selection bias—namely, the test may have different predictive validities across groups. The fact that a test predicts the achievement of one selected population does not mean that it predicts appropriately that of another group, and assuming that it does so can result in content bias. In addition, the factor structure of a test may not be internally consistent (Walsh & Betz, 1995). Criterion-referenced

measurement, consequently, is increasingly becoming the assessment of choice for many evaluators. A criterion-referenced test is one in which scores are expressed in terms of the behaviors or skills achieved, rather than in terms of a comparison with other people.

4. *Rehabilitation counselors are increasingly engaging the client in the rehabilitation process.* Such involvement implies that the client is given more responsibility for developing rehabilitation plans, thus becoming a more active advocate for necessary services as well as the evaluation of his or her own role in implementing assessment results.

5. *The role of the environment when identifying barriers and facilitators to the client's overall life adjustment is now recognized as one of the key ingredients in exploring vocational potential.* Not only is there a greater emphasis on realism of the evaluation environment, but also consideration is given to adopting environmental characteristics to the client's unique abilities and limitations. Understanding factors such as external support resources and attitudes, expectations, and demands from the family, neighborhood, and workplace are important realities for a client's rehabilitation adjustment. It may not be the individual's disability, but handicapping conditions in a client's environment that may actually prevent career and employment adjustment. For the client's successful adjustment, environmental characteristics may have to be adapted to the person's unique abilities and limitations.

6. *Assistive technology has been developed to help persons with disability in education, personal mobility, communication, controls of the environment, recreation and leisure, and independent living.* This technology has also helped to make the assessment process more available to those with severe disability.

7. *Shorter time periods are not only being encouraged, but even mandated, for rehabilitation counseling, including the assessment steps of this process.* These expectations can influence the choice of evaluation approaches, as well as when and where evaluation is to be conducted.

8. *Assessment for most clients is now being viewed as developmental (leading to a career) rather than as static (completed once an entry level job is secured).* The medical course of certain disabilities, such as head injury and related neurological conditions, necessitate updated feedback on vocational planning, because one's condition may change. Also, clients move through different developmental stages, as identified in Figure 1.1. (found in Chapter 1), and client growth during these phases may demand more current information on the client's life adjustment and work-related capabilities.

A CONCEPTUALIZATION AND TARGET AREAS OF VOCATIONAL ASSESSMENT

Vocational assessment is a comprehensive, interdisciplinary process of evaluating an individual's physical, mental, and emotional abilities, limitations, and tolerances in order to identify an optimal outcome for the person with a disability or handicap. Evaluation is a method of acquiring information, a process to assist individuals in identifying their functional competencies and disabilities. It evaluates factors such as the individual with a disability's vocational strengths and weaknesses, which in turn can be found in the areas of personality, aptitude, interest, work habits, physical tolerance, and dexterity. Assessment is also prognostic because it attempts to answer questions such as whether a client will be able to work or what kind of productive activity the individual will be able to do. An added evaluation goal is to identify those services needed to overcome the functional disabilities that are barriers to successful performance.

Tests and assessment can be viewed as two, at times almost distinct, terms. Though both words convey the meaning that data is collected about persons, a test is a measuring device or procedure designed to identify specific variables about a client. Assessment is a more comprehensive process, and typically extends beyond obtaining a number to reflect the strength or absence, for example, of some personality trait. The interview can be an assessment tool; the *Sixteen Personality Factor Questionnaire* is a career-related test. Psychometric tests usually just add up the number of correct answers or the number of certain types of responses or performances, but assessment is often more interested in how the individual functions, rather than in simply the results of the functioning. If the counselor wishes to explore the client's ability to function in a work environment, the term *assessment* would be preferable to *testing* (Cohen, Swerdlik & Phillips, 1996).

In regard to understanding rehabilitation as an alleviation of a skills deficit, Anthony (1980) stated that the assessment process

> yields information about the disabled client's level of skills and the skill demands of the community in which he or she wants or needs to function. This information enables the rehabilitation practitioner to work with the client to develop a treatment plan designed to increase the client's strengths and assets or to identify an environment more suitable to the client's functioning. (p. 9)

The process of rehabilitation assessment, therefore, is mainly one of diagnosis and prediction, assisting both professionals and the client, in a relatively short time, to gain information concerning promising directions for client development. Evaluation can generate a course of action for individuals with disabilities that may range from competitive employment to effective productive activity within their own home. It can also be a way, through constructive feedback, to engage individuals in the rehabilitation process, as well as an effective approach to identify needed services. Although not all individuals are able to move toward competitive employment, different recommendations for all clients could be included within the goals of assessment.

In the process of vocational assessment, the word *comprehensive* is emphasized, for evaluation incorporates medical, psychological, social, vocational, educational, cultural, and economic data. When exploring a person's capabilities, the helping professional seeks information on such broad client characteristics as work interest, general intelligence, values, needs, transferable skills, physical capacity, work tolerance, and special aptitudes. Obtaining this information often requires the involvement of professionals or experts in several areas.

Information in rehabilitation assessment can be obtained both formally and informally. Informal assessment includes observing a person's behavior in a variety of situations, such as conversing with the client or getting information about the client from other sources. Formal assessment includes such processes as the structured interview, mental testing (e.g., intelligence, aptitude, ability, personality, and interest tests), selected work samples, job analyses, and situational assessments. The choice of an approach depends, of course, on the objectives for the assessment. No one of these methods can do everything in assessment because each deals with a specific, limited element of a multifaceted problem. When the rehabilitation professional understands each approach, he or she can then use or adapt it to provide optimal information for planning.

The interview is a person-to-person experience in which the professional obtains information relevant to rehabilitation goals. It can follow a structured or unstructured format, and is a way for the client to learn about his or her own strengths and weaknesses as well as to recognize those abilities and aptitudes that may facilitate or militate against training demands. It is often the most useful way for many severely disabled clients to learn the information needed for rehabilitation planning.

Psychometric tests have been used in assessment for many decades and are usually easy and relatively inexpensive to administer. Yet, their validity with people with disabilities and handicaps can be questioned. Testing accommodations may have to be made that can compromise the standardization data and the accuracy of measured results. If psychological testing is used for preemployment screening, this is not permissible under the Americans with Disabilities Act of 1990 (ADA). Most tests were normed on populations other than people with disabilites, and in a rapidly changing labor force, future job applicants may have very different characteristics from those that typified the standardization sample. Also, tests may be overemphasized and overgeneralized and may be erroneously viewed as evaluating the worth of people and their likelihood for future success (Cohen, Swerdlik, & Phillips, 1996). It is important to note that there are crucial differences between the demands of the test situation and the demands of the work or production situation (Neff, 1966). For example:

> In the test situation, attention, concentration, and motivation are maximized and under continuous control, while in the work situation these variables truly vary and are under very meager control. . . . Even with these difficulties, tests are widely used and are able to provide some very useful information for rehabilitation assessment purposes. (p. 684)

Work samples are close simulations of actual industrial operations that are no different in their essentials from what a potential worker would be required to perform on an ordinary job. Through performance on a work sample, tentative predictions about future performance can be made. This approach has a strong reality orientation and provides an opportunity to observe actual work behavior in a reasonably controlled situation. However, there are still unresolved problems of reliability and validity, and there is uncertainty as to the predictive efficiency of work samples.

The job analysis approach focuses on a description of the work to be performed, rather than on the characteristics of the worker. The work or task is observed very carefully, and detailed descriptions are written on what can be very complex activities. Although this method of assessment can be overanalytical, it is important to understand the detailed set of job requirements for a person whose potential for work is being evaluated. In the 1980s, the use of job analysis techniques by rehabilitation personnel and employers became common to screen out applicants. The focus of the 1990s, however, has shifted to job analysis and how it can be used to determine ways in which persons with disabilities can do work.

The situational assessments, like work samples, are based on an effort to simulate actual working conditions. The main orientation of the situation assessment, however, is toward work behavior in general. It asks questions such as: Can a person work at all and get along with coworkers? How does he or she work most effectively? What are his or her strengths and weaknesses as a worker?

A PHILOSOPHY OF EVALUATION

Approaches to effective assessment must be developed not only from acquired knowledge and continued experience, but also from a personal philosophy that embodies strong convictions about helping clients with disabilities. These convictions provide a direction to evaluation and represent assumptions that, in turn, generate attitudes toward how assessment will be performed. Often, the professional's attitudes regarding the assessment situation and the client can become more important than the content of the assessment itself. I have identified an assessment philosophy that has been formulated from working with clients of varied disability conditions. In order to develop an individual philosophy of vocational assessment, one should consider the following central issues of this philosophy:

1. *Assessment should be integrated into the counseling process and the continued interaction that takes place in rehabilitation between the professional and the client.* In other words, vocational assessment should be part of larger service delivery systems. Often, clients have the expectation that they must place themselves completely into the helping professional's hands to provide answers to finding a job or obtaining suitable training. This belief is expressed in statements such as, "I will put all the responsibility on you, and when you are through, you will be better able to tell me what I should do." If clients are

to feel better about themselves, they have to feel some sense of autonomy and control over their future. When vocational evaluation is integrated into the counseling process, clients are helped to identify and understand the attitudes and feelings about themselves that militate against successful living and employment. In counseling and vocational evaluation, limitations are recognized. More importantly, strengths that can be used for productive living can be discovered.

2. *During the vocational process, rehabilitation professionals must not only evaluate general employability factors (i.e., work habits, physical tolerance, intellectual and achievement levels of functioning, and the ability to learn), but also the client's social–emotional competence.* An individual's constellation of attitudes and behaviors may be more influential in determining future success than other work-related factors. People lose jobs primarily because of deficiencies in work behavior and not just because of skill deficits as such. For example, mental functioning should not be considered in isolation, but must be weighed with the person's motivational and personality structure. Assessment should take into account the social and cultural factors that have an impact on either achievement functioning or training. The individual's likelihood to function on future tasks is often based on personal attributes that have known predictive ability. Such traits can be the person with a disability's coping styles, motivation, relationship to others, understanding of self, manner of adjustment to disability, and ability to profit from experience.

3. *Persons with disabilities frequently magnify partial inadequacy to a totally negative view of themselves.* Consequently, the helping professional should conscientiously use esteem-enhancing efforts during assessment, particularly in the initial interview. The goal of the assessment process is not only to diagnose, but also to provide an opportunity to give positive feedback to clients. Such information can help individuals with a handicap achieve a renewed understanding of themselves as well as identify personal capabilities that they can use to generate productive outcomes.

4. *Assessment should include a multifactorial approach, which promotes the examination of a wide variety of client characteristics.* Intervention decisions in rehabilitation should not be based on a single attribute, such as educational or work achievement. Other factors (i.e., family network, adjustment style to disability, or social relationships) can be included to learn how an individual is going to adjust to work or similar productive situations. A more comprehensive exploration, then, demands both the broadening of the rehabilitation professional's knowledge of evaluation approaches and the integration of the client's interests, abilities, and other personality characteristics.

Vocational evaluation information, consequently, should be verified by using different methods, tools, and approaches. Using alternative methods to validate findings can often be achieved by (a) observing an individual's demonstrated behaviors; (b) using an individual's self-report or expressed statements; and (c) administering some type of survey, inventory, structured interview, or test (Interdisciplinary Council, 1994).

5. *As much as possible, the assessment process should be tailored to the client's individual needs and specific rehabilitation goals.* As Cohen, Swerdlik, and Phillips (1996) pointed

out, the evaluator, consequently, can reflect on such questions as: What information is needed? Does it seem likely that assessment can provide important information that is not available from other sources? What questions can be answered by assessment? and How will this client respond to or be affected by testing?

6. *What is good for the agency is not necessarily always beneficial for the client.* The dimensions of vocational rehabilitation have been expanded in the 1990s to include goals that make up transitional employment or more productive use of leisure time. Often, the agency has the view that unless a client can meet traditional employment demands, assessment is not going to be valuable. Broader expectations for what the client could possibly do can generate a more helpful attitude during assessment.

7. *Vocational assessment should not only be current, valid, and relevant, but should be an ongoing and developmental process in career development.* Individuals with disabilities may need evaluations of varying degrees given at different times over their career life span (Interdisciplinary Council, 1994).

The preceding beliefs have given a decided focus to my assessment efforts. They also influence the different roles that a rehabilitation professional may assume when performing an evaluation.

ROLES AND COMPETENCIES OF THE COUNSELOR DURING ASSESSMENT

When rehabilitation professionals begin to evaluate either the client's eligibility for services or capabilities for work-oriented productivity, they assume certain roles that will have an impact on the client. Each role conveys definite responsibilities. One of the primary responsibilities is to be a communicator, namely, someone who can establish a helping, interpersonal relationship with a client. This relationship should transmit empathy, trust, and the conviction that the rehabilitation professional is very willing to listen to the viewpoint and needs of the client. If such a relationship is established, then generally the client will respond readily by providing needed information that relates to the building of a rehabilitation plan.

The rehabilitation professional is also a provider of information. Feedback to clients should usually focus on what they can do, considering the limitations of the disability, and not what they cannot do. Each evaluation approach should be used to help clients understand their remaining strengths and how these strengths can be used either in the work sector or in avocational activities.

Another necessary role of the rehabilitation professional is that of a reinforcer. In attempting to cope with a disability, clients face many frustrations and setbacks. The reality of perceived failure could be an everyday occurrence. These perceptions and disappointments lower their self-concepts and contribute to their belief that there is probably not much opportunity to become a wage earner. The helping professional should take every chance during assessment to provide some needed feedback on the client's capabilities. For example, when persons with a disability reveal how a certain adjustmental problem was handled, the professional should give needed support, and even when the adaptive attempt failed, can compliment clients on the courage to discuss a disappointing experience.

Of course, one of the primary responsibilities during assessment is to be an evaluator—to know how to diagnose and then make predictive statements about rehabilitation outcomes. This role necessitates a comprehensive knowledge of diagnostic approaches, but more concisely, presumes that the helping professional understands human nature. The evaluator role also demands a knowledge of technology in such areas as adaptive devices. This knowledge includes the ability to select for each client the appropriate simulated experiences and specialized tests, as well as critical behaviors to be observed. Skill in rating and using observed behaviors to make recommendations for training and placement is also required (Vander Kolk, 1995). Acquiring all of this information is gained not only by standardized approaches to psychometric testing, but also by the professional's intuition, willingness to listen to what clients are saying, and understanding of what it means to experience a disability.

With diverse roles, there are different competencies that counselors should demonstrate when conducting rehabilitation assessment. They include, as stated by the Interdisciplinary Council (1994):

1. The ability to select, adopt, and develop methods and approaches that are useful in determining an individual's attributes, abilities, and needs.

2. The ability to use alternative methods and approaches that can be used to cross-validate information generated from other assessment sources.

3. The ability to conduct formal and informal behavioral observation strategies that can be integrated in a variety of settings.

4. The ability to collect and interpret ongoing data that can be used to promote successful transition through critical junctures of the individual's career development.

5. The ability to interpret vocational evaluation and assessment data in a manner that contributes to the total service delivery system. Vocational evaluation and assessment team members must be capable of synthesizing and reporting formal and informal data in a manner that promotes appropriate planning, appropriate goal setting, and coordination of needed support services.

6. The ability to function as an effective participant on an interdisciplinary team.

7. The ability to select, implement, and integrate evaluation and assessment approaches that are current, valid, reliable, and grounded in career, vocational, and work contexts.

CONCLUSION

The purpose of rehabilitation assessment is to plan a course of action. It involves exploring a person's strengths and weaknesses and discovering how the individual's potential for vocational adjustment can be enhanced (Wright, 1980). Approaches in assessment are never used to measure people themselves, but characteristics of people, such as verbal skills, self-confidence, and intellectual capacities. Assessment today must be undertaken in a context of legislation, consumer advocacy and involvement, environmental demands and influences, professional collaboration, ethnically diverse client populations, and assistive technology.

In vocational rehabilitation, it is important for evaluation to have a comprehensive perspective, for it considers the physical, intellectual, and emotional components of personality as well as the influence of the environment on an individual with a disability. The interrelationships of feeling, mental functioning, and body capabilities must always be considered. The most useful assessment approaches take into account all three of these dimensions, and the client's participation in the evaluation process is crucial to the success of any assessment approach. Helping people with a handicap to become productive implies that not only are various ways used to gain information about possible functioning, but also that the person with a disability has the opportunity to understand the diagnostic information in order to make educated decisions.

Questions that this book answers are as follows: What are the varied assessment approaches that can tap the client's intellectual and emotional resources? How can persons with disabilities become integrally involved in the evaluation process? What reasonable accommodations need to be made to assist those with severe disabilities to learn more about their career potential? How does the client's environment influence the identification of adaptive skills and motivation?

Perspectives in Vocational Evaluation

Vocational rehabilitation embraces many activities—assessment, counseling, job preparation, and job placement. Each has an integral part in what is called the rehabilitation process. As mentioned in the introduction to this book, the principal aim of this process is to assist clients in reaching productivity, especially in employment areas. Underlying both client development and the achievement of these goals is a comprehensive and current evaluation of the client's capabilities.

Client assessment is the first step and the vital link to all successful rehabilitation activities. Many of the mistakes made in job placement can be avoided if an appropriate and accurate evaluation is performed. Assessment can also become a stimulus to the reluctant rehabilitation professional who considers job placement an undesirable task. A knowledge of what the client can do often encourages the professional to look for job possibilities that are in harmony with this awareness.

The rehabilitation professional, however, usually sees the client some months after the occurrence of a chronic illness or disability. Clients bring much of their past, particularly in the areas of vocational functioning, to this encounter. They then look ahead to possible directions for a satisfying future. Figure 1.1 conceptualizes this process. As suggested, individuals frequently proceed through stages in their childhood, adolescence, and early adulthood before following a particular career direction. Ginzberg (1972), Super (1957), and Tiedeman (1961) formulated theories that identified this vocational development. Other theorists emphasized situational or economic issues as the facilitators for the development of career patterns. Whatever theory is followed, the client with a disability usually presents himself or herself as someone who has been functioning in some kind of vocational environment. Such predisability, work-related characteristics are not completely extinguished by the disability experience; rather, they serve as both guidelines for current functioning and foundation areas for renewed or further vocational development.

An exception to the sequence outlined in Figure 1.1 is persons who are born with a disability. Although their vocational development may be slower, they still have the same potential and, perhaps, the same vocational behaviors as persons who have a disability as a result of a traumatic experience. In contrast to the latter population, the

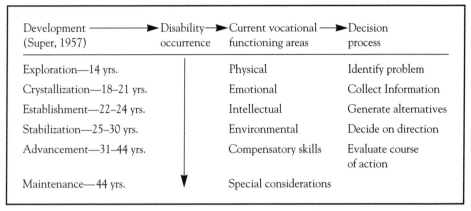

Figure 1.1. Predisability vocational functioning.

life of the individual with a congenital disability has not been suddenly disrupted by a traumatic, disabling event. Such an event breaks the adjustmental patterns that have been formed, although few persons handicapped since birth never adapt to their new limitations.

Table 1.1 shows a more elaborate model of vocational functioning, which establishes a broad framework for vocational assessment. The model specifies the areas that need to be identified in evaluation. It depicts an individual's possible vocational functioning at a fixed point in time, usually at the initial interview with a client. Any model, however, is developed from certain assumptions, and this model of vocational functioning is based on the following:

1. Work satisfaction depends on the extent to which individuals find adequate outlets for their abilities, interests, personality traits, and values (Super, 1957).

2. Occupations are chosen to meet needs. The occupation that is chosen is that field or area that the person believes will best meet the needs that most concern him or her (Hoppock, 1976).

3. An occupational choice is determined by the individual's socioeconomic level, age, abilities, personality characteristics, education, and available opportunities. The choice is also determined by (a) inner limiting factors such as limited physical abilities, limited mental capabilities, or scarce financial resources; (b) outer limiting factors such as lack of availability of relevant training resources or poor employment outlook; or (c) outer directing factors, such as perceived prestige of occupations and positive family and employee expectations for return to work.

4. A person's vocational preference, living situation, work environment, and self-concept change with time and experience, making occupational choice and adjustment a continuous process.

TABLE 1.1
Model of Vocational Functioning

Vocational Functioning	Vocational and Independent Living Tasks and Demands
Client Physical Characteristics	
General appearance	Work appropriateness Employment interview

Stamina and endurance	Work tolerance
	  Work full-time
	  Work part-time
	  Light physical activity
	  Sedentary work
	Work pace

General health status	Working conditions Current level of response to work location (hot, cold, humidity, noise, hazards, and other atmospheric conditions)
Vision and hearing	Work appropriateness and work conditions

Motor coordination
  Eye/hand/foot coordination
  Finger dexterity
  Mobility
	Work demands
	  Transportation
	  Mobility in work space
	  Self-care

Personal hygiene	Work appropriateness
Physical limitations	Ability to meet work demands Necessary job modifications
Client Intellectual Characteristics	
General level of knowledge	Self-knowledge Knowledge of work demands Awareness of entry requirements
Educational development	Level of possible training Language development and skills Mathematics and computational skills Level of reasoning

(continues)

TABLE 1.1 *(continued)*

Vocational Functioning	Vocational and Independent Living Tasks and Demands
Client Intellectual Characteristics *(continued)*	
Aptitudes	Communication demand
Verbal and speech	Complete employment forms
Numerical	Hold job interview
Spatial perception	Ability to abstract and calculate
Form perception	Measuring ability
Conceptual ability	
Work experience	Skills and competencies developed
Homemaking	Safety consciousness
Leisure time	Ability of person to return to former job
Avocational activities	Transferable abilities and skills to a work situation
Decision-making skills	Initiative in work areas
	Take opportunities for job and work development
Memory	Ability to retain instructions
	Training capability
Attention span	Ability to follow work directions
	Training capability
Work competencies	Attendance
	Promptness
	Speed of production
	Use of time
Interests	Preferred type of jobs
	Preference for certain types of work activities
Values	Perception of work for life functioning
	Work habits
	Expectations for self in job situation
Disability-related knowledge	Understanding of assets and disability limitations in relation to work
Adaptive Behavior	Ability to adjust to job requirements

TABLE 1.1 *(continued)*

Vocational Functioning	Vocational and Independent Living Tasks and Demands
Client Emotional Characteristics	
Mood and Temperament	Relations to supervisors and other people
Indifferent	Frustration tolerance
Apathetic	Adjustment to strains and pressures of work
Cooperative	environment
Eager	
Self-assured	
Interested	
Needs[a]	Change orientation
Responsibility	Adaptability
Security	Ability to take risks with self
Social status	Openness of alternatives
Variety	
Supervision/Authority	
Recognition	
Creativity	
Independence	
Achievement	
Good working conditions	
Advancement	
Autonomy	
Attitudes	Sense of responsibility
Toward self	Successful job performance
Toward others	Relationship with others
	Self-confidence in work situations
Motivation to work	Seeks rehabilitation goals
	Energy on job
	Achievement level
Adjustment to disability	Confidence in self as worker
	Accepts limitations
	Dependent or independent role
Personal and Environmental Coping Skills	Adjustment to the work environment

(continues)

TABLE 1.1 *(continued)*

Vocational Functioning	Vocational and Independent Living Tasks and Demands
Environmental Factors	
Family situation	Family members supportive of rehabilitation goals Family accepting of occupational choices Family recognizes client capabilities

Available financial resources
    Workers' compensation
        benefits
    SSI
    SSDI
    Primary source of support
	Current finances are sufficient to meet client needs
	Will occupation meet client financial needs?

Attitudes
    Employer
    Co-worker
	Acceptance on job

Accessibility
    Work site
    Community
	Availability of job opportunities

Community Factors
    Transportation
    Local economy
    Training opportunities
    Support network
    Housing
	Availability and accessibility to job opportunities

Client Special Considerations	
Medications	Attention, concentration, stamina, and safety on job
Aids	Transportation Can drive own car Can take public transportation Needs assistance for transportation
Certificates, licenses, or union membership	Job opportunity
Precautions	Job and work flexibility Job or work modification
Social skills	Work demands Relationship to others

[a]Lofquist and Dawes, 1969.

5. The experience of disability represents a transitional period in the sense that many behaviors common to the predisability state are gradually replaced.

6. The changes that the onset of disability precipitate frequently have traumatic implications for the family, organizational, or work system in which an individual is embedded.

7. Work itself may not be central to the lifestyle or aspirations of some persons, and, for many, it has connotations that repel rather than attract (Zytowski, 1965).

8. Prevalent career choices, which are primarily based on research studies using samples of boys and men, may not be applicable for girls and women. Although research that is more longitudinal in scope is needed regarding girls and women, current vocational practices should recognize the distinctive needs of women as well as minimize sex role bias.

9. Assessment can be a proactive tool to initiate change, rather than one that is used in a more passive, defensive way to insure that someone is not being "categorized" inappropriately (Sedlacek, 1994).

The content of the model in Table 1.1 is developed from various sources, including Hoppock (1976), Knefelkamp and Slepitza (1976), Lofquist and Dawes (1969), Super (1957), Hershenson (1990), and Farley, Little, Bolton, and Chunn (1993), as well as the author's own extensive professional experience in vocational evaluation. The model includes all people with disabilities—namely, those who were born with a disability and those who incurred the disability because of an accident or illness. The model also includes women. Most women are becoming a part of the labor force outside of the home, and many of them will acquire a disability and want to return as wage earners.

Unfortunately, there are almost no specific assessment techniques available for the vocational evaluation of ethnic groups (Helms, 1992). Because different minority groups have various experiences and ways of presenting their attributes and abilities, it is not likely that a single assessment approach or measure can be equally valid for each distinctive, ethnic group (Sedlacek, 1994). Vocational evaluation issues with these populations will be discussed in Chapter 3.

EVALUATING FOR SUCCESSFUL JOB PLACEMENT

This model of vocational functioning is particularly useful in job placement activities. The goal of helping clients obtain gainful employment should influence each step in the rehabilitation process. It begins at the time of the referral and first interview and extends through every step taken with the client, including the last follow-up contact. Assessment, training, and vocational or adjustmental counseling can each be carefully viewed in the perspective of placement. Over the years, job placement has maintained the viability and growth of vocational rehabilitation. At the same time, this activity in rehabilitation has created the most concerns for the rehabilitation professional and potential employers.

Many rehabilitation professionals view their job responsibilities as being mainly counseling or case coordination. Performing job development tasks or generating employer awareness about hiring persons with a disability is considered by many to be an unwelcomed activity. In turn, many employers today claim that clients referred to them for possible jobs are, in reality, not "job ready." Yet, one of the continuing facts in rehabilitation is that when a rehabilitation professional engages in job and employer development activities including vocational assessment and refers clients who have the immediate capabilities to hold a particular job, such jobs are usually obtained, even in a tight labor market.

Job placement is in itself a process within the overall rehabilitation process. Usually, the process of job placement includes client assessment, job development, employer development, client development, and follow-up. Vandergoot, Jacobsen, and Worral (1979) have conceptualized the rehabilitation process in a refreshing manner as "productivity enrichment, productivity realization, and career enhancement" (p. 17). Job placement is viewed as a central focus for each of these three components. Productivity enrichment, for example, includes information development, strategy development, and strategy implementation with such identified tasks as using occupational and labor market information, evaluating client skills and needs, establishing occupational goals, and using community resources. Underlying each component is the assumption that an appropriate assessment of the client's capabilities has been made.

Assuming that client assessment is the indispensable, initial step and the prime consideration for job placement, this evaluation should be perceptively, efficiently, and comprehensively conducted. It is a responsibility, moreover, that can frequently be performed by the rehabilitation professional whose primary job task is not work evaluation. Issues related to the assessment responsibility are discussed in Chapter 2.

The exploration for job placement can be structured in such a way as to allow the rehabilitation professional the opportunity to gain necessary information in an easily understood manner. This structure develops around the general concept of *work readiness*. There has been much confusion regarding the definition and application of work readiness (Vandergoot, 1982). Bitter (1968) believed that it is a general term relating to an individual's personal attributes in the world of work. But job readiness, he suggested, is more specific; namely, it is the extent to which an individual's qualifications fit the skill requirements of a particular job. Sinick (1969) distinguished *employability* from *placeability*. Employability refers to someone who possesses the requisite skills and work personality; placeability refers to the perceived attractiveness of an applicant to an employer.

The concepts of work readiness, employability, and placeability are terms useful to understand the process of vocational assessment as a beginning step for eventual client placement. Employability and placeability are components of work readiness. These concepts also provide a perspective for exploring those client characteristics needed to respond to labor market demands.

Work Readiness

Farley et al. (1993) define readiness as the "level of self-knowledge (interests, aptitudes, abilities, strengths, limitations, work values, needs, etc.) and knowledge of the work world or amount of occupational information (the nature of work involved in specific jobs, duties and requirements, education and training needed, where jobs are to be found, salary levels, outlook for the future, etc.) the individual possesses" (p. 9).

There are different methods for determining work readiness. The general approaches, which are explained in greater detail later in this book, include the following:

1. Analysis of work history
2. Analysis of educational and social data
3. Interviews with client and family
4. Medical and psychiatric consultation
5. Psychological testing
6. Work samples evaluation
7. Analysis of part-time or temporary work experience
8. Analysis of on-the-job training experience

Any one or a combination of these eight approaches can be used when determining either employability or placeability. There are more specific guidelines to follow when exploring job readiness.

Employability

During the initial interview, an assessment has to be made as to whether the client is ready for work. Although the model of vocational functioning presented earlier in this chapter provides a broad structure for assessment activities, more specific questions must be asked in order to ascertain whether an individual has the ability to meet the varied requirements of jobs and occupations. Walls, Zane, and Werner (1979) developed the *Vocational Behavior Checklist*, which identifies eight areas of employment-related capabilities. Bolton (1982) clarified these areas as described below, and they are quite useful for understanding employability issues.

Prevocational skills. The client's vocational interests and potential; knowledge about his or her need for work and what a job is

Job-seeking skills. Behaviors needed for locating and applying for employment, such as understanding ads and completing applications

Interview skills. Behaviors needed to conduct an effective interview with a prospective employer, including understanding the interview situation, responding, and asking appropriate questions

Job-related skills. Skills one should have to adjust to a job situation, such as following rules and adjusting to the work environment

Work performance skills. Behaviors of arriving at work on time, following instructions, working safely, using and caring for tools, and so on

On-the-job social skills. Getting along with others and constructively handling criticism

Union and financial security skills. Understanding and following company policies, such as obtaining pay, overtime, union functions, insurance, and benefits

Decision making skills. Ability to make choices for job opportunities and engage in vocational planning

From these areas, questions develop for assessing one's potential for employment.

Physical Questions

Is the client at the maximum level of physical capacity?

Can the client travel to and from a job? Use public transportation?

Can the client work a full workday? A full work week?

Can the client meet the physical demands of the kind of work sought (current level of performance in strength, climbing, stooping, reaching, talking, and seeing)?

Does the client understand the nature of his or her disability?

Is the client aware of activities and situations that would tend to aggravate the disability or impair general health, such as cold, heat, work location, humidity, noise, hazards, and atmospheric conditions?

Does the client recognize danger signs, like fatigue or coughing, that can be warnings that rest or treatment may be necessary?

Is the client aware of the need for periodic examinations or further treatment?

Is the client capable of living independently?

Would the client's personal appearance be acceptable to employers and coworkers? Poor personal grooming, dirty clothes, or inappropriate clothing are three major problem areas.

Does the client have a number of unfortunate personal mannerisms (tics, failure to maintain eye contact, etc.)?

Psychological Questions

Do the client and family accept the client's limitations?

Do the client and family recognize the client's capabilities?

Is the client sincerely motivated toward employment?

Can the client adjust to the strains and pressures of a work environment?

Does the client react appropriately to supervision?

Can the client get along with others, such as coworkers and supervisors?

Is the client a dependable worker in terms of attendance, promptness, and appropriate use of time?

Are the client's personality traits suitable for performing the usual job tasks?

Are there personal or social problems that might affect the client's performance on the job?

Does the client regularly engage in any antisocial or seriously maladaptive behaviors?

Occupational Questions

Are the client's aptitudes, skills, knowledge, and experience commensurate with current and future job requirements?

Can the client do the job; namely, what is the client's capability for productivity, speed of learning, and ability to do accurate and efficient work?

Is the client aware of wages and hours?

Do the nonmonetary, psychological rewards of working complement the client's needs, values, and long-range goals?

Does the client have an occupational goal; namely, is he or she oriented toward employment?

How does the client feel about work?

What jobs has the client held, for how long were they held, when did the client leave, and what were the reasons given by the client for leaving?

What aspects of the job were most satisfying to clients and why was this so?

Socioenvironmental Questions

Do the important people in the client's life accept the client as a worker?

Would the client's family be supportive of the client as a worker?

Is the client presently receiving monetary benefits because of the disability?

In defining vocational evaluation "as a comprehensive process that systematically uses work, either real or simulated, as the focal point for assessment and vocational exploration" (p. 1), Farley et al. (1993) developed an approach that focuses on vocational choice assessment and planning as integral to employability and identifies the following attributes as targets for evaluation strategies:

Vocational readiness
Aptitudes
Interests
Vocationally relevant personality factors
Work Temperament
Strengths and Limitations
Work Values and Needs

Important to the approach is for the client to select an appropriate and suitable occupational goal, and then devise a plan to achieve that goal. The client's involvement in this planning process is necessary, because the more knowledge the individual has about his or her personal traits, the more effectively the individual can participate in developing realistic goals (Farley et al., 1993). Furthermore, though their model focuses on person variables, environmental factors are not ignored and should be considered in the client's assessment. The environmental variables include such factors as *personal* (finances and family support); *community* (transportation, housing, service delivery programs, support network, local economy, accessible community, and training opportunities); *workplace* (employer attitude, co-worker attitude, accessible work site, and technology); and *general* (legislation, economy, benefits, and labor market trends) (Farley & Bolton, 1994).

The amount of exploration into employability-related concerns depends on the client's problems and needs, as well as the barriers that hinder productivity. Yet, it is not only the physical, psychological, occupational, and socioenvironmental areas that make the difference between readiness and lack of readiness for most types of employment. The attitudes and feelings of the client, as well as the attitudes of prospective employers and the expectations of available family members, are also important determinants of employability. An evaluation of job employability should include an assessment of clients' fundamental systems of values and their basic feelings and perceptions about themselves, especially as these feelings and perceptions relate to work. From this information, the professional can gain a beginning idea of the client's motivation. All in all, personality factors take on tremendous importance insofar as employability is concerned. During the evaluation, attempts must be made to assess how these attitudes affect performance and what, if anything, can be done about them (Forrest, 1963).

The determination of employability, consequently, can be identified largely during the initial client interview. The Arkansas Research and Training Center in Vocational Rehabilitation has developed a useful readiness instrument titled the *Employability Maturity Interview* (EMI) (Roessler & Bolton, 1987). The EMI is a 10-item structured interview developed to assess readiness for the vocational rehabilitation planning process. The EMI's main purpose is to identify those clients needing additional vocational exploration and employability services. Moreover, Marrone, Horgan, Scripture, and

Grossman (1984) provide a practical list of positive and negative indicators of client job readiness, especially employability, and these can be used during the assessment interview. These indicators are summarized and modified and are stated below.

Positive Indicators

1. The client has a work history that is recent, consistent, or both.

2. Work has a value to the client that he or she can express.

3. The client has a course of illness that is relatively predictable.

4. There is evidence that the client has cooperated in a physical or mental health treatment program.

5. The client appears to communicate a good impression of him- or herself physically, verbally, or both.

6. The client states that significant persons contribute life support to his or her vocational rehabilitation process.

Negative Indicators

1. The client consistently misses appointments without a good excuse.

2. The client doesn't express interest in vocational rehabilitation with work as a goal.

3. The client has no stable living situation or steady source of income.

4. Contingencies exist that interfere with vocational planning (e.g., court cases, child custody proceedings, etc.).

5. The family or significant others are heavily invested in the status quo. For example, they are satisfied with their current income or are insistent that the family member with a disability not return to paid employment.

6. The client is persistent in maintaining a strong, rigid interest in an unrealistic vocational goal.

Determination of Placeability

Placeability is the ability of the individual to meet the hiring requirements of employers, particularly as defined by personnel officers. An individual can be employable without being placeable—for example, a client who possesses many job-related skills, but is not able to obtain a job in a particular geographical area. Criteria for placement readiness include:

1. To what extent can the client participate in the job-finding process? Most chronically unemployed people fail to seek work with sufficient frequency. Interviewing the client should reveal the reasons for this failure, such as fear, lack of financial

need to work, and lack of a job goal. Job frequency probably does depend on job opportunities to some extent.

2. Does the client know and use sources of job leads?

3. Can the client develop a resume or a personal information packet?

4. Can the client satisfactorily complete a job application?

5. Can the client present himself or herself adequately in a job interview?

   a. Can the client make his or her capabilities clear to employers? Can the client account for problems, such as periods of unemployment? Most clients are handicapped in an employment interview by an inability to explain some of their problems in a manner that induces a prospective employer to overlook or accept such problems. Typical problems are age, history of institutionalization, history of lengthy unemployment, physical handicap, and poor work history (Walker, 1966). Also, an evaluation of whether the client can explain his or her skills to an employer is needed, because employers basically hire job applicants for skills that they are known to have. During the job interview, clients need to explain their skills, usually in a very brief period of time.

   b. Is the client reasonably free of mannerisms that annoy the employer? This area can be easily evaluated by simply looking at the client and deciding whether his or her personal appearance would be acceptable to employers and coworkers.

6. Would the client continue a job search if met with some rejections?

7. Would the client conduct him- or herself appropriately if starting work tomorrow?

An explanation of placeability also includes such job market factors as (a) unemployment rate in the client's skill area, (b) availability of jobs in the geographic area, (c) union requirements, and (d) wage requirements. During the evaluation process, the rehabilitation professional should always keep these factors in mind.

When considering the goals of either employability or placeability, an important consideration is the appropriate selection of an assessment approach. Seligman (1994) has identified several criteria to be used when planning career evaluation. They have been adapted for vocational rehabilitation and are as follows:

1. *What are the goals of rehabilitation assessment?* Though vocational behavior is multifaceted and involves many areas of human functioning, the evaluator should focus on areas that are relevant to vocational goals. Such a focus does not imply the necessity of exploring the way interests, abilities, and personality interact to influence life adjustment, career choice, and vocational goals.

2. *What information is needed to accomplish these goals?* In rehabilitation assessment, relevant information should include vocational interests, possible transferable skills, values, abilities, and personality characteristics. Because these factors are usually developed on diverse timetables, and because underlying characteristics of personality can

create a wider range of choices, individuals with different career patterns sometimes experience particular problems during the adjustment phases to a disability.

3. *How is the client likely to respond to and be affected by assessment?* Chapter 3 of this book identifies different types of clients who present themselves for vocational evaluation. Many of these clients can harbor anxieties about the assessment experience, and these should be addressed during the initial client interview. Such issues as motivation, alertness, length of the assessment, evaluator's ability to establish rapport, and the client's cognitive skills are to be considered with the client's capability to respond. Also, the interaction among setting, client, evaluator, and assessment materials is a dynamic one that is subject to a variety of influences.

4. *Are additional resources being used that may provide information otherwise collected by vocational evaluation approaches?* School or job records can be quite useful, as they provide knowledge about the client's academic and work history. During the client interview, information may be disclosed honestly that provides sufficient data about the client's functioning, thereby alleviating the need for further assessment.

PITFALLS OF THE ASSESSMENT PROCESS

Though vocational evaluation is a productive resource on understanding a client's living, learning, and working needs and capabilities, there are dangers that should be identified in order to prevent the assessment process from actually harming the person with a disability. Ethical guidelines are discussed in the next chapter, but apart from these standards, there are further expectations that need attention. Some of these are as follows:

1. Frequently an inaccurate or harmful label may be given to a client as a result of assessment (e.g., "unemployable," "unmotivated," or "borderline retarded"). This labelling not only damages one's self esteem, but also interferes with the necessary delivery of services. At times, people erroneously view tests as evaluators of an individual's worth or an absolute predictor of future success in employment opportunities.

2. If the evaluation process only focuses on one area of the client's functioning, such as specific, job-related capabilities, it can foster a narrow concept of abilities, thereby neglecting the client's strength in other areas. The concept of career includes many personality factors, and these need to be identified during the evaluation process.

3. Adequate safeguards may not be provided during the evaluation experience to ensure privacy. Information may be released to others without the client's permission. Also, the evaluation may cause uncertainty regarding how the assessment results will be used.

Assessment results have little meaning unless they are understood by the client and reflect an evaluation philosophy that is explained earlier in this chapter. Tests are imperfect and represent only a sampling of behavior. Rehabilitation counselors should remember that tests can be biased, and should make every effort to select measures that are appropriate to the culture and capabilities of the client.

CHAPTER 1 CONCLUSION

There are several perspectives to consider when planning rehabilitation assessment. Although the principal focus of any vocational evaluation should be the determination of job readiness, this focus is developed by an understanding of client characteristics, the concepts of employability and placeability, and those client and environmental factors that may be incremental or decremental to the client's eventual job placement. An awareness of all of these indicators lays the groundwork for the selection of appropriate assessment goals and the information needed to accomplish these objectives.

 ## CASE STUDY: JOSEPH

Joseph is a 36-year-old White male. He is applying for disability funds from a public agency and has been referred to you for vocational assessment. Supplemental information accompanying the referral includes a recent report from internal medicine at a local hospital. The client entered the hospital with low back pain as his primary symptom. During the client interview, the internist elicited a 3-year history that included numbness of the entire left side, headaches behind the left ear for 9 months, and stuttering speech for 6 weeks. Consequently, the internist requested a neuropsychiatric consultation, and the neuropsychiatrist diagnosed a probable conversion reaction but recommended further study.

An orthopedic consultant was called in, and he diagnosed a psychophysiological reaction—lower back syndrome. Because the diagnosis up to this point seemed to suggest a possible psychiatric problem, another psychiatrist was called in. He noted in his report that the client had not worked in 3 years and that he was chronically anxious. This psychiatrist's diagnosis described a passive–dependent personality, conversion reaction, and psychophysiological reaction that included multiple physical complaints in the past. The final diagnosis upon discharge from the hospital was "chronic anxiety reaction with hyperventilation syndrome" and "psychophysiological musculoskeletal reaction—low back pain." Therapy recommended was primarily symptomatic, with the use of drugs and physiotherapy. An attempt was made to explain to the client and his wife the nature of his illness. The client was instructed in the use of a plastic bag for rebreathing to control the hyperventilation attacks. Regarding the disability, the client was judged "status competent."

At the time of the disability examination, the client is found to be a rather heavyset man who looks older than his stated age. Throughout most of the examination, he sits looking at the floor, and his speech is characterized by constant stammering. He appears to have a passive–dependent attitude, occasionally weeping, but his tears reflect some real depression.

He states that approximately 3 years previously he was located in Georgia and was a district sales manager for a large insurance company. He is very proud of that fact, and frequently states that he "once made a lot of money." In a low, hesitant voice he states, "I'm getting better, I know I am; I'm going to be all right and make a lot of money again." But the client is very difficult to interview. His thoughts wander, he is circuitous in his thinking, and it is impossible to get any dates from him regarding his history. Rather than admit he cannot remember, he gives evasive answers. Important information emerges only tangentially and in a rather incoherent fashion. In response to a question about his previous employment, he states that "something happened" on the job, and that one day he "blew up and told them all to go to hell." He goes on to say that he does not know why he did that, and he wishes now that he had not done it.

As can be best determined, after walking off his job, the client spent the next 2 years at home and did not attempt further employment. His wife went to work at a factory job in order to support the family. There were two children, ages 16 and 11, who attended public school. The client had a personal physician and apparently went to him more than one time. On a mental status exam the client demonstrates a pronounced difficulty with memory. He could not remember how long he had been married, only that he got married sometime in the month of February. He cannot remember how long he went to high school, just that he graduated at some time. Several times he wishes that his wife were with him in the interview because she could answer questions that he cannot remember.

 ## Chapter 1 Case Study Questions

DIRECTIONS: With this information, please answer the following questions:

1. What do you perceive as *employability* capabilities and limitations of this client?

2. What type of vocational assessment would you conduct with Joseph? What problems do you foresee could arise during the evaluation with Joseph?

3. What do you believe are the particular placement problems with Joseph? What would you look for in determining placeability?

Issues for Developing Effective Vocational Assessment

The following issues are important to the task of rehabilitation assessment: (a) the particular role of the rehabilitation professional in vocational evaluation; (b) the varied ethical and legal issues in vocational assessment; (c) the criteria for client readiness, which include appropriate responses to the vocational assessment process and issues related to client empowerment; (d) the relationship between disability effects and the selection, administration, and interpretation of different tests; (e) the principles important in modifying tests when it might be necessary to encourage participation in the assessment process for those with disabilities; (f) an assessment battery for rehabilitation professionals; (g) the criteria to be used when either reviewing or critiquing a psychometric test or evaluation approach to be used with those with disabilities; and (h) a brief discussion on the importance of evaluating learning ability or learning style. These issues are presented in this chapter as building stones that constitute a foundation for effective assessment.

THE ROLE OF THE REHABILITATION PROFESSIONAL IN ASSESSMENT

As stated in the Introduction, this book is directed mainly to rehabilitation professionals and students in human services; its purpose is to help them develop basic vocational and rehabilitation skills or update their existing knowledge of client evaluation. Although many practitioners may believe that an early diagnosis of client strengths and work-related limitations is necessary, assessment does not make up a large part of their job duties unless they have been specifically trained as vocational evaluators. Fortunately, many allied health professionals are trained in diagnostic skills, which can be applied to exploring vocational goals.

The use of evaluation skills is based on the initial diagnosis, the available time to perform such an exploration, and the assessment knowledge of approaches and measures that can generate relevant information. The usual practice in most rehabilitation agencies is to purchase vocational diagnostic services. The waiting period for obtaining such information is often very long, causing some clients to lose interest in the rehabilitation process. Another possible limitation is that other evaluation resources may not be available. Roessler and Rubin (1982) explained that other assessment opportunities should be considered because many clients have a positive work history that does not require intensive vocational evaluation. If a person is not returning to his or her previous job, a brief vocational analysis can be conducted to identify other employment options. Also, understanding the client's productive-related strengths early and providing him or her with this information can often strongly motivate the client to achieve rehabilitation goals.

In rehabilitation, particularly in state vocational rehabilitation agencies, many cases are reopened after services in the rehabilitation process have been interrupted. Frequently, clients do not have to go through another extended vocational evaluation (depending on the circumstances), but an update of client employable strengths can be most useful. When the counselor has the ability to conduct such an exploration, he or she can use this assessment to expedite the achievement of rehabilitation goals.

The National Seminar on Competency-Based Rehabilitation Education in Atlanta in July 1978 indicated that rehabilitation counselors, as well as vocational evaluators, must be capable of developing a systematic evaluation plan and writing useful evaluation reports on clients (Rubin & Porter, 1979). Roessler and Rubin (1982) believed that counselors must be able to "manage" a comprehensive medical, psychological, and vocational evaluation of the client. The Interdisciplinary Council on Vocational Evaluation/ Assessment reiterates the idea that assessment information should be verified by using different methods, tools, and approaches because the process requires a collaborative approach to data collection and decision making (Schuster & Smith, 1994). An implication of this management is that the counselor must at least be able to understand the process of obtaining assessment data, recognize the diagnostic instruments used, and organize all of this information for client planning purposes.

The *independent living* movement in rehabilitation suggests a more active role for the rehabilitation counselor in evaluation functions. Although counseling is usually the only direct service provided in local rehabilitation offices, many assessment measures have been devised for use by rehabilitation professionals who work with severely disabled persons (Bolton, 1982). The "Functional Assessment Inventory" (Crewe & Athelstan, 1978) and the *Vocational Behavior Checklist* (Walls, Zane, & Werner, 1978) are two examples (Bolton, 1982). Boland and Alonso (1982) explained that in order to meet the demands of clients in independent living, counselors must have the knowledge and skills to develop and carry out highly individualized rehabilitation plans. Counselors also have to continually reassess their clients to determine new areas of need and then change their rehabilitation plans accordingly. Wright (1980) believed that rehabilitation professionals who work with individuals with severe disabilities often confront the demands of a basic evaluation. Their assessment includes determining functional limitations and capacities. The intake interview with people with severe disabilities necessitates the responsibility for knowing what specific independent listing services are needed for the particular client. But such a task presumes an ability to understand client capabilities, a necessary step for actually evaluating rehabilitation potential and goals.

Consequently, for varied reasons, rehabilitation professionals should help their clients acquire some useful knowledge related to productive rehabilitation capabilities. For many years, the opportunity to do this has been given primarily to those specially trained in vocational assessment. Although psychologists or vocational evaluators are credibly performing a very needed job, still other rehabilitation professionals could perform many vocationally related diagnostic activities. But these assessment duties cannot be performed without adequate knowledge of basic evaluation situations, particular approaches, and developed methods. Even then, the extent of the professional's assessment tasks is limited. For example, many areas of personality functioning or disabilities that relate to brain impairment demand specialized training and should only be evaluated by professionals who have expertise in these areas.

For the rehabilitation counselor, the amount of time that can be devoted to this task of evaluation is uncertain. Other case management functions are quite time-consuming. For professional, philosophical reasons that influence job responsibilities, counselors may hesitate to become involved in assessment tasks. Arguments about the role and function of the rehabilitation counselor have been going on for many, many years. Roessler and Rubin (1982) identified several studies that describe how rehabilitation counselors spend their time or view their jobs. The majority of time seems to be spent either in recording, report writing, clerical work, counseling, or guidance (Rubin & Emener, 1979; Zadny & James, 1977). All the research reports suggest that the rehabilitation counselor has a diverse job role (Rubin & Emener, 1979; Wright & Fraser, 1976).

Though job functions vary according to the rehabilitation setting and identified client goals, assessment tasks are integral to vocational rehabilitation planning. Many of the evaluator's roles that accompany these tasks are the following:

1. *Coordinator.* Many professionals, such as medical and allied health personnel, may be involved in a client's assessment, industry-based supervision (when situational assessment is used), and job coaching. Vocational evaluation programs based in schools are multilevel programs. At each level, the assessment process has different purposes and uses a variety of evaluation techniques and strategies. There may also be interfacing of the vocational assessment and special education processes, and Levinson (1994) believes that a school-based evaluation process may include local community agencies. This role implies, consequently, the receipt of information from other resources and the identification of support services. Such services may provide assessment services while helping the client develop personal and interpersonal skills.

2. *Counselor.* Establishing positive rapport with the client is crucial to effective vocational assessment. This facilitative relationship implies such skills as the ability to attend, listen, and respond to the needs, and perhaps unique cultural situation, of the client.

3. *Planner*. One of the outcomes of the client's evaluation is the development of appropriate plans for training, eventual job placement, or both. This planning process requires the evaluator to view and treat the client as an equal.

4. *Assessor*. Not only is the evaluator's task to understand the client's strengths and vocational capabilities, but also to determine life adjustment, employment needs, and priorities for rehabilitation services. In many agencies the helping professional must determine, through a standard set of guidelines, whether a potential client meets the eligibility criteria for rehabilitation assistance.

Although all of these functions suggest a variation in thought and research on the role and functions of many rehabilitation professionals, they do not eliminate the opportunity and necessity for helping the client to acquire important information for eventual rehabilitation planning. An understanding of productive and work-related capabilities is an integral part of this knowledge. These client goals bring about a challenge and, in many instances, a responsibility for the rehabilitation professional. The professional can be a physical or occupational therapist working in a hospital or clinic; a rehabilitation nurse or counselor who pursues private practice or is employed by a state agency, private firm, or large institution; or a social worker who is also assisting clients back to work. Regardless of the professional's situation, he or she can conduct many vocational assessment tasks with the training and motivation to perform the beginning evaluation. This book presumes the presence of motivation and is written to provide both basic and selected rehabilitation assessment skills.

LEGAL AND ETHICAL ISSUES IN VOCATIONAL ASSESSMENT

Matkin (1980) identified many important issues concerning the provision of evaluation services. He explained that

> problems with test use can be avoided or substantially reduced if care is taken to select devices which reportedly measure those traits to be evaluated. The evaluator should also be aware of the intended use for which the instrument was designed and avoid interpreting results in areas beyond the capabilities of the device. (p. 59)

Other significant guidelines (Matkin, 1980) are as follows:

1. *Caution must be exercised when depending on test instruments to provide information about client needs and traits*. The client's evaluation program should be carefully planned to avoid the overuse or indiscriminate use of testing. For example, instrument selection should be tailored to the needs of the client and tests designed specifically for certain disability groups should be used to ensure the accuracy of outcome scores. It is impor-

tant that the purpose of assessment and the explicit use of results must be made known to the client prior to evaluation. Specific orientation or information must also be provided to the client prior to and following the test administration so that the results of assessment may be placed in proper perspective with other relevant factors. The helping professional should ensure that instrument limitations are not exceeded and that periodic review and retesting are made to prevent client stereotyping (Rayman, 1990). In schools, for example, caution should be used especially when interpreting results. Decisions must be based on people's abilities and behavior rather than on a diagnosis or label.

2. *Vocational assessment may be used as both a descriptive measure of client functioning and as an indicator of potential.* When exploring client capability, the rehabilitation professional must examine the appropriateness of the testing instrument with regard to reliability, validity, and norming populations. One must proceed with caution when attempting to evaluate and interpret the performance of minority group members or other persons who are not represented in the norm group on which the instrument was standardized (Rayman, 1990). Sensitivity must be used when working with people from different cultural and linguistic backgrounds and with young people who have different types of disabling conditions. Matkin (1980) wrote: "The vocational evaluator is ethically obliged when reporting outcomes to indicate the reasons why clients fail to perform at average or above levels and ways for remediating the deficiency" (p. 59).

3. *The privacy of the client must be respected, and all information and materials obtained during the assessment process should be safeguarded.* Policy standards developed by the American Counseling Association (ACA) concerning the responsibility of users of standardized tests state that confidentiality of information and materials should be maintained (ACA, 1994). The policy also states that the client should be informed about who will receive the assessment information and under what circumstances it will be released. Test scores, moreover, should be released only to those persons qualified to interpret them. When making any statements to the public about tests and testing, consequently, the evaluator must give accurate information and avoid false claims or misconceptions. Special efforts are often required to avoid unwarranted connotations of such terms as IQ and grade equivalent scores or other technical scale names (Rayman, 1990).

4. *The client's needs and reaction to the assessment process should be carefully considered.* Environmental influences (e.g., room temperature, ventilation, restricted movement, or inappropriate language in the instructions) and client traits (e.g., sensory defects, inability to read, motivation level, lighting, or test-taking strategies) demand attention to ensure that "outcome measures reflect an accurate assessment of the evaluated traits" (Rayman, 1990, p. 60).

5. *Although a relatively long period of intensive training and supervised experience is required for the proper use of individual intelligence tests and most personality measures, a minimum of specialized psychological training is needed for educational achievement or vocational proficiency tests.* Different tests demand different levels of competence for administration, scoring, and interpretation. The helping professional must recognize the limits of one's competence and perform only those functions for which one is prepared. If the

evaluator, for example, is using computer-based test interpretations, then he or she should be trained in the construct being measured and the specific instrument being used prior to using this type of computer application (Rayman, 1990).

6. *Testing should only be used when necessary, and the rehabilitation professional should be aware of the proper use of testing and the specific instruments from which to choose.* Also, testing material should be stored in a secure place.

7. *Rehabilitation professionals involved in assessment should demonstrate competencies, not only in the understanding and interpretation acquired during the assessment and rehabilitation process, but also in knowledge of the world of work, familiarity with studies of human behavior, and an awareness of the limitations of test interpretation.* Rehabilitation professionals involved in assessment should periodically reexamine their own competencies, as well as keep abreast of current labor market trends, employment requirements for assorted occupations, and work modification techniques.

8. *Tests should be administered under the same conditions that were established in their standardization.* When tests are not administered under standard conditions or when unusual behavior or irregularities occur during the testing session, these conditions must be noted and the results designated as invalid or of questionable validity. When there is a need to modify tests to accommodate certain disability groups, attention should be given to appropriate assessment methods that do not compromise the validity and reliability of the test. Scores obtained from tests that are not reliable or valid do not reflect the effects of the individual's disability. As the issue of test modification becomes more important, it becomes necessary to consider whether and how tests could be modified (Gordon, Stump, & Glaser, 1996). The Americans with Disabilities Act of 1990 (ADA) reemphasizes the requirement for reasonable accommodations to the physical or mental limitations of persons with disabilities, including the appropriate adjustment or modification of examinations (Nester, 1994).

The types of testing accommodations are usually in three categories:

a. *Testing medium.* This refers to the use of a different method to present the same information. Large print, a reader, or audiotape can be identified as different ways to present the same information. However, it should be noted that changing a test from a printed version into a sign language version is a translation into another language, rather than simply a change of medium (Nester, 1994).

b. *Time limits.* With many individuals with disabilities, it is necessary to change a test's time limits. There is often the difficult problem of determining exactly how much extra time should be allotted so that the person with a disability is neither advantaged nor disadvantaged. Accommodation solutions may include eliminating (in specific circumstances) the use of timed power tests, exploring the opportunity to conduct empirical studies to determine appropriate time limits, or reporting two time scores (one that recognizes the test's published guidelines, and the other that allows for any modification due to the individual's physical or mental limitations).

c. *Test content.* While any change in test content needs to be consistent with the validity strategy on which the test was based, changes in test content can be divided into the following categories: (a) change in individual test questions; (b) change in the question type; and (c) change in the knowledge, skill, or ability that is being measured (Nester, 1994). Accommodations can be implemented according to these changes if another type of question exists to measure the same ability and if the skill to be tested can be evaluated in another manner (e.g., through an interview or through work experience requirements) (Nester, 1994). But changing or deleting a knowledge, skill, or ability is only justified if the helping professional has no appropriate way to measure these factors and he or she believes that the specific skill or knowledge area is not a job requirement for the person with a disability.

Very little is known, however, about the effects of deviations from standard test administration procedures (Gordon et al., 1996). Guidelines regarding accommodations typically are developed to accompany standardized tests or to be ordered separately (Ziezula, 1986). Further investigation into appropriate assessment accommodations, as well as the effects of test modification, is urgently needed.

CLIENT PREPARATION IN ASSESSMENT

Building on the assumption that rehabilitation workers perform some evaluation with their clients and also communicate effectively with them, a necessary step in the assessment process is to prepare the client for this involvement. (Preparing clients who are referred to outside agencies for vocational evaluation is discussed in Chapter 14.) Because the interview itself can be a valuable assessment resource (as explained in Chapter 4), no specific client preparation for the interview is needed.

After the professional decides to use standardized measures to gain more information for rehabilitation planning, he or she should prepare the client for this opportunity. The professional should (a) create a relaxed, nonthreatening atmosphere and (b) solicit the client's input for the particular goals of assessment. In other words, explaining the purpose of assessment and how it fits into the development of effective rehabilitation planning frequently helps the client to identify some personal goals for evaluation. For clients representing different ethnic minority groups, it is important to understand the individual's specific world view, which can include attitudes toward the assessment experience and learning more about oneself. Certain cultures have definite attitudes on inhibitions about being tested. The importance of learning more about and, especially becoming aware of, personal strengths should also be stressed. Such questions as, "How do you feel about identifying your capabilities and interests?" and "What particular information about yourself would you like to have?" can encourage the client's input. It is necessary to be aware of the client's level of understanding and the obstacles that might block his or her comprehension of these questions and the assessment process itself. Speech and hearing limitations, intellectual deficits, and the side effects of medication can present barriers to effective communication.

An important aspect of client preparation is the client's degree of readiness for the assessment process. Whether the client is ready for the steps following evaluation can be determined during the actual assessment, but readiness for any involvement in vocational and employment diagnosis should be identified during the initial interview. Several criteria that can be used to determine readiness are the following:

1. *Motivation.* A client's motivatation regarding participation in the assessment process is a determination that can be assisted by exploring the client's employment history, nature of disability, individual strengths according to self-report, and current interview behavior.

2. *Stability.* This criterion refers to the client's physical and emotional condition, including endurance capabilities for evaluation involvement. Such disabilities as head injury and other neurological traumas frequently necessitate long periods of recovery or exacerbation. Such conditions should be reasonably stabilized before any reliability of the career assessment process is achieved.

3. *Availability for assessment.* This criterion implies that accessible transportation is available for the client. It also includes the realization that sufficient time during the client's rehabilitation will be allotted to assessment demands.

4. *Expectations.* This presumes that significant others in the client's environment, such as available family members, have positive attitudes concerning the client's participation in vocational assessment. Negative attitudes toward the client's involvement from persons who have a decided influence on the client's life can undermine the evaluative process.

5. *Medication management.* When clients present themselves for vocational assessment, most individuals are taking some form of medication. Certain medicines may have an effect on the client's attention, concentration, and stamina. The helping professional should identify the client's medications and ascertain their effect on the assessment process.

6. *Client awareness.* This awareness includes an understanding of the goals of the evaluation process and the demands implied in different assessment tasks. Such awareness must also consider cultural factors that relate to rehabilitation services as well as attitudes toward the disability itself. Many individuals representing a cultural minority have definite ideas about sharing personal information with a helping professional who is not a member of one's ethnic group, or else may view the assessment process as another failure experience designed by the dominant culture. These perceptions should be identified and discussed as part of the client's evaluation preparation.

After acquiring client input and making a determination of client readiness, the vocational professional must make a decision about the sequence of tests that should be administered. This choice should not be made, however, until the rehabilitation worker decides what further information must be obtained after the initial interview, if the chosen test will be used for diagnostic purposes. My priority for providing standardized measures is for interest tests to begin the formal evaluation process. A number of these tests, appropriate for a wide variety of clients, are discussed in Chapter 6. Frequently, the client can take home an interest test after the initial interview, but the professional must be very careful about reliability and related test-taking issues, as discussed in Chapter 5.

Regardless of the sequence in which tests are administered, precautions should be taken. During testing, all possible distractions should be reduced and client fatigue minimized. Also, the client should realize that every effort must be exerted to do as well as possible. Of course, all clients experience anxiety and apprehension when taking any test. However, when the nature of the test, background information concerning the norm group, and relationship of the particular measure to the assessment goals are all communicated, this tension can be reduced. When clients are told about the confidentiality issues of assessment and are told that when taking an interest or personality measure, they are actually describing themselves *to* themselves, they often feel better about the evaluation. Also, questions from clients about a particular assessment measure should be solicited.

Client preparation is based on timely and knowledgeable communication from the rehabilitation professional. Understanding client needs and disability-related limitations, uses of a test, and factors that enhance the reliability of the client's involvement (e.g., rest, minimal distractions, control of anxiety, and best possible effort) can contribute to developing a relaxed, nonthreatening atmosphere. Such an evaluation environment can help to make the assessment experience a valuable one for the client.

The experience can also facilitate the client's sense of empowerment. Instilling client empowerment is now integral to the client's rehabilitation, and this is frequently achieved by (a) soliciting input from the client regarding career expectations and the most feasible way to attain these goals; (b) helping the client become aware of all the dynamics influencing rehabilitation and eventual adjustment; (c) taking control over certain assessment tasks, when possible; (d) learning decision-making skills when formulating plans emerging from assessment results; (e) gaining awareness of both inner-directed forces (e.g., intelligence, personality style, and related strengths) and outer-directed forces (e.g., positive expectations and contributions from others); and (f) participating as much as possible in the different assessment tasks, especially providing feedback about personal perceptions during the interpretation session of evaluation results.

RELATIONSHIP OF DISABILITY EFFECTS TO THE SELECTION, ADMINISTRATION, AND INTERPRETATION OF ASSESSMENT MEASURES

Even with careful preparation of the client, further considerations must be heeded when developing assessment plans. There is the ever-present possibility that evaluation, especially psychometric testing, may do more harm than good. Unless particular attention is directed to the choice of an appropriate test, the prudent use of administration procedures, and the enlightened interpretation of assessment results, the client and rehabilitation professional will have a decidedly negative experience.

Clients bring to rehabilitation opportunities a variety of individual traits, competencies, and limitations. They also bring a distinctive cultural background and individual expectations, attitudes, and values that emerge from one's ethnicity. Frequently, factors such as motivation, interests, ethnicity, and work tolerance may be just as important for reaching rehabilitation goals as qualities such as intelligence and learning-related aptitudes. Using standardized test instruments is not necessarily the best way for evaluating many of these client characteristics. Observation of the client in different settings, trial experiences in a job situation, and behavioral techniques can be better methods for understanding the person with a disability's rehabilitation potential. For example, a client who has a congenital disability may have had different life experiences than those of the populations on whom the standardized tests were normed. If this disability is present in someone who is African American, Hispanic, or Asian, then there is an added range of varied life experiences. The use of standardized, psychological measures, therefore, may not be appropriate for him or her, and other assessment approaches should be explored.

The inappropriateness of standardized tests for certain populations in rehabilitation is especially true when such measures are used only for exploring the person's potential for learning. The test performances of persons with severe disabilities are often affected by emotional issues and sensory and motor limitations. Comparing the person with a disability's performance on a particular test to that of the norm group used to standardize the measure (when the norm group did not have comparable limitations) is discriminatory.

Learning capability stimulates the question: How do people learn? Frequently, the selection of assessment approaches and the choice of specific psychometric tests depends on a person's learning style. Learning style models are based on the assumption that individuals have learning differences that are unique and need to be accommodated (Griggs, 1985). Not only does everyone have his or her own learning style, but each individual also has been taught tasks in a different manner. Some are more verbal and learn best through the written or spoken word. Others are more visual and need to see things through charts, pictures, or demonstrations. Still others do not master a task until they experience doing it. To evaluate the learning style preference of the client with a disability implies the importance of identifying specific strategies that will assist the individual to learn more about personal strengths and employment-related assets. A person's learning style may have to be assessed through a nonstandardized screening battery, which can generate particular, remediation information for the client.

When the purpose of evaluation is to understand the client's level of current functioning, the use of standardized measures may be justified. The rehabilitation professional wants to know how the client scores on the measure and how this compares with persons without a disability. The careful use of tests, particularly aptitude and achievement measures, is warranted because specific knowledge of the way a client's abilities or competencies compare with those of persons without a disability may be necessary for rehabilitation planning to be relevant. After all, the client may work with people who do not have a disability, and he or she has to meet their work demands. Information regarding both how the client will meet these demands and what will be needed in order to compete in a training or work situation is crucial when developing rehabilitation plans.

If the rehabilitation professional is aware of these issues and pays special attention to disability effects and their impact on the vocational assessment process, then evaluation can become a valuable opportunity for the client. In this perspective of awareness, the following factors should be considered when exploring evaluation approaches for a particular client. Many of these factors are similar to the readiness criteria stated earlier in this chapter.

1. Age of disability onset

2. Nature of physical and emotional limitations

3. Medication effects

4. Relationship of the client's life experiences to the content of the proposed evaluation measures

5. Learning style preferences

6. Educational experiences

7. Physical tolerance

8. The extent to which rehabilitation procedures have assisted the client in compensating for physical limitations

This exploration presumes, of course, that the rehabilitation professional is knowledgeable about the particular tests used in vocational assessment, and pays special attention to the nature of test items and the reliability of the testing situation. (These issues are discussed in Chapter 5.) Along with the eight factors identified above, particular concerns relating to disability effects (physical, emotional, and intellectual) must be addressed when considering the selection, administration, and interpretation of evaluation measures.

Physical Disability Effects

Physical disability effects include communication difficulties, such as visual and hearing impairments, and motor and orthopedic problems.

Selection

What is the verbal level of the test? What is the difficulty level of the concepts involved? How has the nature of the disability affected the range of life experiences to which the person with a disability has been exposed? Does a person with visual impairment have enough sight to handle large objects, locate test pieces in a work space, or follow the hand movements of the rehabilitation professional? Also, can this person read ink print effectively even though he or she may need large type? What is the extent of impaired manual ability?

Administration

To minimize client anxiety, the less involved and performance-type tests should be administered first. When possible, tests should be administered individually and in small blocks of time rather than in concentrated periods. Many clients with neurologic impairments, for example, may have a high level of distractibility. Also, many persons with physical disabilities, especially those with severe impairments, tire easily. Fatigue can be lessened by efforts to deal with communication difficulties during the testing process. Particular attention must be given to individuals with visual or auditory impairments. The professional should eliminate flickering lights, establish rapport so that the client feels free to tell the professional that he or she is tiring, and adjust time limits as necessary, realizing that such a change will affect the standardized scoring.

For many persons with severe disabilities, the manner of recording answers may have to be changed. For example, a client may have no use of either hand or, even with use of one hand, have great difficulty in correctly marking the answer space. The use of another person to record the answers or a specially designed answer sheet may be required.

Interpretation

(This subject is discussed in greater detail in Chapter 13.) Always communicate test results at the client's level of understanding. Give special concern to how the client's disability relates to influences on the test-taking process, such as transient emotional states, the deviation from the normative response, and why there is a deviation. Is there a deviation because of, for example, special disability factors, or is it because of developmental factors? In other words, the client's current functioning, as well as past experiences, are considered in the process of test interpretation.

Emotional and Intellectual Disability Effects

Emotional and intellectual disability effects can include organically based mental deficiencies; emotional states of long duration, such as grief and mourning, anger, depression, and denial; and emotional behaviors resulting from chronic mental conditions, such as varied forms of schizophrenia.

Selection

Attention should be given to the selection of assessment measures that are appropriate to the client's level of understanding, particularly his or her reading ability. Assessment measures that require a long period of time to complete should be avoided. Most clients with serious emotional and cognitive problems have low attention spans, and shorter tasks are certainly more appropriate.

Administration

If possible, administer the assessment measures individually. Group testing may provide too many distractions for emotionally disturbed persons, who may have difficulty understanding the test-taking procedures unless they are explained slowly, carefully, and individually. Particular attention should be given to whether the client understands the directions for taking a particular assessment measure. It is helpful if the professional asks the client to explain these directions after they have been communicated to this person with a disability.

Interpretation

As explained earlier, interpretation issues are discussed in Chapter 13. Feedback regarding test results is critical in vocational evaluation. The rehabilitation professional should make every effort to report information so that it is understood by the client. Persons with a disability must also be given a chance to express their feelings about this information. Frequently, the clients' rehabilitation expectations exceed their measured abilities, and the professional will have to spend some time dealing with this discrepancy.

Conclusions: Physical and Mental Disability Assessment

The preceding materials identify many selected issues that arise when clients with either a physical or mental disability approach the rehabilitation assessment situation. If the professional is aware that special problems (usually arising from disability-related limitations) can occur during evaluation, he or she can take a beginning step toward ensuring the credibility of the client's vocational assessment.

AN ASSESSMENT BATTERY

Table 2.1 outlines assessment tools that can be used when exploring rehabilitation goals with the client. Most of these measures or approaches are explained in later chapters of this book, but they are introduced here to give an overview of the varied ways in which information about a person with a mental or physical disability can be gained.

TABLE 2.1
Assessment Tools for Exploring Rehabilitation Goals

Type of Disability	Information needed about the person	Measures and Approaches
Physical Functioning		
	Current level of performance in strength, walking, stooping, reaching, talking, and seeing; current level of response to work location, cold, heat, humidity, noise, hazards, and atmospheric conditions	Medical records; Interview information and self-description; *Crawford Small Parts Dexterity Test*
Learning disability, emotional disturbance, mental retardation, hearing impairment, and cerebral palsy or orthopedic handicap		
All disabilities		*World of Work Inventory*
All disabilities, but special modifications needed for visual and hearing impairment and orthopedic handicap		*Purdue Pegboard*
Intellectual and Aptitude Functioning		
	Current level of reasoning, mathematics, and language development; specific capacities and aptitudes	Educational experience and records; Interview information and self-description; *Wechsler Adult Intelligence Scale–Third Edition* (WAIS–III)
All disabilities, but limited use with visual and hearing impairment		
All disabilities, but limited use with visual and hearing impairment		*Slosson Intelligence Test; Peabody Picture Vocabulary Test–Revised* (PPVT–R); *Revised Beta Examination; Raven Progressive Matrices; Quick Test; Shipley; Otis Lennon School Ability Test; Kaufman Brief Intelligence Test*
Designed more for visual impairment		*Haptic Intelligence Scale for the Adult Blind; Standford Kohs Tactile Block Design*

TABLE 2.1 *(continued)*

Type of Disability	Information needed about the person	Measures and Approaches
Intellectual and Aptitude Functioning *(continued)*		
All disabilities except hearing impairment and visual impairment		*Wide Range Achievement Test–Third Edition; Adult Basic Learning Examination* (ABLE); *Peabody Individual Achievement Test–Revised*
All disabilities except visual impairment; GATB might require modification for cerebral palsy, orthopedic handicap, mental retardation, and hearing impairment		*General Aptitude Test Battery* (GATB); *Nonreading Aptitude Test Battery; Differential Aptitude Tests; Flanagan Aptitude Classification Test; Bennett Mechanical Comprehension Test; Minnesota Paper Form Board–Revised*
All disabilities, but some modifications of each work sample may be necessary for some disabilities		Work samples
Emotional Functioning		
	Adjustment to different types of occupational situations	Verified work history; Interview information and self-description;
Learning disability; cerebral palsy; orthopedic handicap; hearing impairment		*Edwards Personnel Preference Schedule*
All disabilities except mental retardation and visual impairment		*Sixteen Personality Factor Questionnaire* (16 PF), Form E;
Mental retardation		*AAMR Adaptive Behavior Scales;*
All disabilities except mental retardation and visual impairment		*The Psychological Screening Inventory;*

(continues)

TABLE 2.1 *(continued)*

Type of Disability	Information needed about the person	Measures and Approaches
Emotional Functioning *(continued)*		
All disabilities except mental retardation and visual impairment; some modification for mental illness		*Tennessee Self-Concept Scale*
Interest Exploration		
All but visual impairment	Preference for certain types of work activities	*Reading-Free Vocational Interest Inventory*
All disabilities		*Wide Range Interest–Opinion Test;*
All but visual impairment		*Geist Picture Interest Inventory–Revised;*
All disabilities, if verbally presented		*Gordon Occupational Checklist;*
All disabilities except visual impairment and mental retardation		*Strong Interest Inventory* *Career Assessment Inventory*
All disabilities except visual impairment and mental retardation		*Kuder Occupational Interest Survey* *Ohio Vocational Interest Survey*
All disabilities except visual impairment and mental retardation		*The Self-Directed Search Interest Checklist*
All disabilities except persons with severe visual and/or hearing impairments	Learning capacities	*Learning Capacities Approach* (Rusalem & Malikin, 1976); *Ohio State University Approach* (Growick & Schmidt, 1988)
Function in Particular Areas (Employability and Placeability)		
All handicaps except visual impairment and mental retardation (much of this information obtained by a supervisor	Job readiness	Previous work experience Employability evaluation Employability information sheet Placement readiness checklist

TABLE 2.1 *(continued)*

Type of Disability	Information Needed About the Person	Measures and Approaches
Function in Particular Areas (Employability and Placeability) *(continued)*		
		Interview information and self-description
		Employability plan
		Job readiness scale
		Job readiness test
		Readiness planning checklist
Environmental (Family Situation and Financial Resources)		
	Influence of significant others	Interview information and self-description

CHAPTER 2 CONCLUSION

If the professional acknowledges the opportunity to gain needed information about a client's vocational capabilities and understands how disability limitations affect the evaluation process, a timely, relevant diagnostic experience for the person with a disability can be facilitated. Vocational assessment, of course, is done to obtain needed information. It is part of the overall rehabilitation process and, as an integral factor in the client's development toward rehabilitation goals, presents an invaluable chance for self-awareness and effective decision making. To achieve this effectiveness, the professional and client must work together. When the person with a disability is intimately involved in vocational evaluation and the professional is knowledgeable about the different ways to gain information about a client, the process will be meaningful. The following chapters of this book discuss how this evaluation experience becomes an important, unique step for the client to reach rehabilitation goals.

The following case study emphasizes the importance of both preparing a client for the evaluation opportunity and understanding how emotional and physical factors influence the way assessment is pursued with him or her.

 CASE STUDY: LOUISE

Louise is a 19-year-old Black woman who dropped out of high school in her junior year in order to take care of home duties. She has been diagnosed with dyslexia and has moderate hearing loss in the left ear. Louise is living with her mother, who, prior to 12 months ago, was successfully employed as an office receptionist and administrative assistant for a large retail firm in the Washington area. However, she became very ill 12 months ago, was forced to quit her job, and is only now recuperating from her illness. Her doctors have told her that she can return to work in 2 months, and apparently her previous employer will be happy for her return. Louise's father has not been living in the family home for 7 years, although her mother has not remarried. Extended family is available in the Washington area, and Louise claims that they "see each other quite often." Louise has one brother, age 21, who has a high school degree and is working in the retail sales field. He does not live at home at the present time.

Louise claims that when her mother became sick, family money became very scarce for a reason unknown to her. Louise only knows that her mother made it known that in some way Louise would have to help out with the finances as much as she could. Louise then decided to drop out of school, and was able to obtain simple, entry-type jobs to bring in some extra family income. She states to you during the initial interview that she was a C-average student in general high school subjects who liked school, yet claims that much of it was a struggle. Because of her dyslexia, and because she baby-sat after school to earn some extra money, Louise had difficulties in school. She now likes to spend time with her friends, and together they go to the malls or watch TV. She has not been dating anyone seriously.

Louise comes to you, the helping professional, to explore career options. She would now like to return to school, as her mother will return to work, but would also like to have a part-time job while she is going to school. She says she might be interested in college "if it would help my career, but I don't know what my career should be."

Chapter 2 Case Study Questions

DIRECTIONS: With this information, please answer the following questions:

1. As a rehabilitation worker, what opportunity would you have to perform any vocational assessment with this client? Could you use any standardized tests?

2. Presuming that Louise will return for some vocational assessment with you, how would you want to prepare Louise for this experience?

3. Considering Louise's disability and related factors such as culture, family, and learning style, what must you keep in mind as possible influences on the evaluation process?

Understanding the Client

There are a number of vital considerations when preparing vocational rehabilitation plans for clients. Among them are (a) the evaluator's understanding of the meaning of disability, (b) the results of vocational assessment, (c) employment opportunities, (d) existing training resources in the geographical area, (e) the feasibility of alternative goals when a full-time job is not possible because of physical or mental limitations, and (f) the need for client input to the plan itself. One of the most important ingredients in effective planning is the professional's awareness of both the differences between the terms impairment, disability, and handicap and specific client dynamics that can facilitate or impede the achievement of rehabilitation goals. The helping professional's perception of what disability, impairment, and handicap mean can influence the selection of assessment approaches. Impairment, according to the World Health Organization, is the loss or limitation of an organ of the body or mind, whereas disability is primarily of the individual who is impaired, and the solution to this problem is to eliminate, reduce, or compensate for the impairment (Acton, 1982). The Americans with Disabilities Act of 1990 (ADA) defines a disability as a physical or mental impairment that (a) substantially limits one or more of the major life activities of an individual, (b) has a record of such an impairment, and (c) is regarded as having such an impairment (Rubin & Roessler, 1995). Handicap is society's response to the impairment or disability (Acton, 1982). Disability, consequently, is an individual limitation to be overcome, and the definition only accounts for a minority of those who have a disability; it does not consider those who have chronic disease, severe learning disorders, speech or hearing limitations, or drug or alcohol abuse sequelae. However, the perception of disability is changing. This perception is now increasingly focusing on both the crucial role of the environment as it affects the individual's life adjustment and on a holistic perspective that includes an awareness of the rights of those with disabilities (Hahn, 1985). Environmental assessment approaches and multifaceted evaluation plans can respond to this expanded meaning of disability.

Concerning the specific client dynamics that can facilitate or impede the achievement of rehabilitation goals, a client's vocational rehabilitation is influenced by personality (DeNour & Czaczkes, 1975). Clients come for assessment with a wide assortment of distinctive vocational assets and problems, including certain emotional difficulties that represent barriers to productivity. Recognizing all of these factors is important in identifying what vocational evaluation approaches should be used for a particular client. This chapter explains such problems, assets, and emotional issues by describing typical clients in rehabilitation assessment. Client categories have been identified mainly by experience in working with rehabilitation clients throughout the years.

THE RESTORER–ACHIEVER

Restorer–achievers have usually incurred a disability after years of satisfying work. Generally, they are younger (ages 30–45), have a strong work ethic, and through working, have gained a sense of both stability and identity in their lives. Importantly, these persons believe they possess many work-related skills. Although they harbor feelings of loss because of disability-related limitations, they are anxious to return to work and are usually open to many job alternatives. They perceive their disabilities as a fact of life, an inconvenience, a cause of frustration, or a combination of these.

These clients can manage their own affairs, and typically come to a state or private rehabilitation agency for training or other remedial help (e.g., prosthetics or job leads). Unaware of the different resources that can assist them in their rehabilitation efforts, they seek information on how to reenter the job market. Although they are often suspicious about the kind of help the agency can offer, they are task-oriented, show much energy and motivation, and possess a positive attitude shaped by past experiences. They need and want the help that rehabilitation agencies can provide. These clients have many of the employable traits that are necessary to hold a job (e.g., psychological readiness, a work personality previously shaped by conscientiousness and competitiveness, and transferable job skills). What they particularly need from assessment is an awareness of transferable skills and abilities that can help them to regain employment, as well as support from the helping professional when planning rehabilitation goals.

Case Example: Matthew

Matthew, who worked for 8 years as the manager of a fast food restaurant, had a stroke while working. He is a 27-year-old African American who is a high school graduate. Matthew has been married for 6 years and has two children. He had been promoted quickly at the franchise because of his interpersonal skills, physical energy, and commitment to delivering excellent services. After hospitalization and cognitive retraining, he has decided to apply for vocational services at a state rehabilitation agency. Medical reports state that his physical limitations consist of left-side weakness, with little use of his left arm, no lifting capacity over 15 pounds, and a shuffling gait. Cognitive functions have now been restored, and prior to applying for vocational services he completed an English Composition course at a community college with the grade of B. He is eager to learn new tasks, although still sad about seeking another line of work. His wife is working as an accountant for the federal government. Disability-related benefits are being paid and he still sees himself as the main family provider. He views evaluation as an opportunity to identify new job-related capacities.

Issues To Consider

Assessment approaches for Matthew and similar clients should be challenging enough to explore optimal capabilities. The client's input should be solicited frequently during the evaluation, especially regarding personal feelings about performance on evaluative tasks. Soliciting such feedback conveys the professional's respect for the opinion of clients, helping them to become more involved in the assessment process. Such involvement might alleviate feelings of suspicion about the agency, and lead to greater independence and an increased sense of control.

THE AMBIVALENT CLIENT

Clients who have mixed feelings about returning to work represent one of the lingering thorns in the side of the rehabilitation professional. Because of a long period of medical recuperation, many individuals become accustomed to an inactive lifestyle, which gradually minimizes vocational responsibility. Ambivalent clients want to go back to work and believe they can return to their former job; deep down, however, they harbor the strong suspicion that it is not going to be possible. Many ambivalent clients are receiving workers' compensation payments. Often, paid employment provides these clients with little gain of income over insurance payments, and rehabilitation offers little incentive for renouncing secure, steady, and dependable payment (Schlenoff, 1979). Yet, these persons are frequently required to seek rehabilitation services. They are afraid of losing their newly gained benefits if they find a job, and such monetary compensation often fosters a dependence on these benefits. They view themselves as suffering individuals. They feel inept and unable to meet the standards of being productive. They are afraid to take risks and are particularly uncomfortable if their considerations about returning to work include competing for available jobs. Competition involves too many risks of failure. Generally, they show repeated expressions of an approach or avoidance conflict regarding employment and independence.

Ambivalent clients usually have attitudinal problems, including a pessimistic view about their occupational future. Surprisingly, however, when they are involved in the assessment process, they are usually cooperative and often willing to please the agency staff. These clients also actively pursue many assessment tasks and are anxious to learn about the evaluation results. At the same time, their actual job outlook is characterized by extreme caution, suspiciousness, and a reluctance to learn about their own capabilities.

Many ambivalent clients, moreover, are also undecided about their career or specific work goals. Because of disability experiences and compensation-related benefits, work is not a central part of their lives. They are hesitant to take the risk of making a commitment to eventual employment. These clients may be more concerned with adjustment demands and their own identity as a person with a disability than with a worker identity. After the disability trauma and continued medical rehabilitation, they may be unaware of their work-related strengths and possess little self-confidence in making decisions.

What often maintains this ambivalence is not only a suspiciousness of accepting employment, but also the realization of little continued satisfaction from previous work experiences. Ambivalent clients have seldomly viewed work as a desirable goal in life, and when they encounter rehabilitation opportunities, they become very uncertain, defensive, and confused. Disability gives them a convenient and socially acceptable excuse for continued hesitation to work.

On some occasions, clients may claim to have mixed feelings about rehabilitation, when in fact they are only being very cautious or feel suspicious of the evaluation process itself. They may associate assessment primarily with testing, and they may have poorly developed test-taking skills or a history of failing many tests in school. Consequently, they feel reluctant about going into a situation in which they might look bad or feel more inadequate than they really are. For many people with disadvantages, the most difficult part of any assessment is not the content (such as achievement tests or work samples), but the very fact they are being tested. Ambivalence can occur as a result of fear of failure; negative, reinforcing experiences in one's past; or a hostile attitude displayed by vocational evaluation staff toward minorities or those with handicaps. Clients may perceive that the rehabilitation professional either has a negative expectation toward them or really does not expect too much. In approaching an assessment situation, then, the client has a tendency to "freeze" as his or her values and way of life are challenged.

Case Example: Corey

Corey, a 23-year-old single White female, incurred a back injury while driving the delivery truck for a gourmet bakery chain. She was not responsible for the accident, but her injuries kept her in the rehabilitation hospital for 10 weeks. Corey has now been told that she will be unable to drive the truck, because the responsibility also necessitates lifting duties. The company is unable to place her in another position and is strongly encouraging her to take the generous disability-related compensation benefits and "travel and see the world for a few years."

The client has come for assessment to help her "find her way" regarding career goals. Corey states that she is a college graduate with an English major but has no interest in pursuing "anything related to that field." She also mentions that she did not "enjoy driving the bakery truck," and believes that she is lost, confused, and has no academic and career interests. Corey explains that she enjoys being distracted by friends who live in her apartment and spends a great deal of time on the phone and socializing. During the initial interview the counselor observed that Corey appears to have little self-confidence in making decisions and seeks other people to give her the answers she needs.

Issues To Consider

Generally, clients who have mixed feelings about whether or not to return to work need information about their capabilities, support in facing the unknown, clarification about their medical condition, and assurance that renewed opportunities can bring personal satisfaction. Alternatives to a life of dependency on disability-related benefits or opportunities for newly discovered self-esteem through work accomplishment should be indicated. This exploration of choice is usually more successful with younger clients. A reason for this difference is that the older worker with a disability tends to see disability payments as a much better alternative to the tediousness of employment, especially if his or her job brought little emotional gain. Because ambivalent clients have trouble finding direction in their lives, short assessments that give immediate, positive feedback to the client are necessary. Situational assessment, explored later in this book, is often the most valuable evaluative method to provide this feedback. Assessment should also explore measured interests, transferable skills, the client's locus of control, and possibly, the source for the fear of commitment. Any family issues can also be identified, as well as the client's level of self-esteem.

THE SECONDARY GAINER

Secondary gainers are clients who make no pretense about their desire to return to work. They usually go through an assessment experience because they are required to do so to receive continued disability-related benefits. Unlike ambivalent clients, secondary gainers are not even willing to cautiously try to find new work opportunities. They maximize the extent of work limitations resulting from a chronic condition, and many of these limitations are self-imposed.

The concept of secondary gain proves to be of particular concern with regard to clients who receive insurance payments. They generally have had little confidence in themselves as workers and now view the dependency role as a preferred style of living. Disability even strengthens the dependency. Family members may also encourage this dependence because they may unwittingly contribute to the person with disability's helplessness and inactive lifestyle. Both lowered family expectations regarding the performance of household responsibilities and exaggerated attention to the person's needs may further contribute to this dependence. The family attempts to make the person's life easier and less burdensome, and in doing so, not only meets the person's needs but also removes responsibilities related to home and family goals. Dependency then becomes a way of life, and the person with a disability is very comfortable in an existence of which needs are easily met and demands are minimal.

In an interview session during vocational evaluation, secondary gainers are often manipulative. They try to present their current life situation in such a way to solicit sympathy for their disability. There are also difficulties in establishing plans of action to meet any life responsibilities. They convey a lack of stability regarding future plans and little willingness to meet scheduling demands for medical, training, and counselor appointments during the rehabilitation process. Furthermore, these clients focus more on the negative aspects of their life. The secondary gainer may have had many negative experiences associated with work. Employment that is personally fulfilling has never been found, and now the disability provides an excuse for not working.

Many clients who have found a valuable secondary gain in dependency also have continued physical pain related to the disability. This is particularly true with workers who have injured their lower backs. These workers often display

> unusual postures, limps, patterns of inactivity, or a reliance on medication and prosthetic appliances to help control the pain. Ironically, reliance upon such methods often serves to maintain the disability process and in turn, reduces the probability of successful vocational rehabilitation. (Lynch, 1979, p. 165)

Pain becomes a dominating reality in their lives and precipitates such behaviors as fear, chronic complaining, depression, and dependency.

Surprisingly, the person's self-esteem is often not lowered because of the continued gratification for dependency needs. The role of having a disability becomes satisfying because it may force others to care for the client. Compensation benefits accruing for an injury also increase the reinforcement value of the sick role. These clients, consequently, have career and work readiness problems. They are quite reluctant to take on the role of worker. Regardless of their skills, aptitudes, and intellectual abilities, secondary gainers' prior experiences (e.g., physical pain, failure at jobs, poor academic performance, and complete dependence on family members) have negatively conditioned and inhibited them from assuming the worker role.

Case Example: Oscar

After discharge from the military service, Oscar obtained a job as a sorter with the post office. While coming to work one winter day, he slipped on ice, fell, and although proceeding to his "boring, dead-end job," went to his family doctor at the end of the day. During the examination, the doctor discovered other symptoms that eventually led, after specialized consultation, to the diagnosis of multiple sclerosis. Oscar was told that he could still work and generally maintain the pattern of his daily life. Instead, he decided to leave his job and seek compensation benefits to maintain an unmarried, very routine lifestyle. After a few months, he obtained these benefits because of his medical condition, and for the next 26 years did not seek or have regular employment. When he married, his wife worked, for she was anxious to pursue her own career as an elementary school teacher. Over the years, the compensation benefits grew. When he was eventually referred to evaluation for possible rehabilitation goals, he stated to the evaluator, "I never derived any pleasure from working." He went through the motions of assessment, but before its conclusion, called the evaluator to say that he felt his illness had become worse and he could not continue.

Issues To Consider

Another form of secondary gain is expressed by clients who want to maintain the status quo of an inactive lifestyle. Usually middle-aged people with good work histories, secondary gainers become injured and then resist any efforts for a return to the work sector. They are basically very angry at having disabilities, but the anger is suppressed and takes the form of reluctance. As the disability is perceived as a burdensome and unwelcome disruption on what was a stable, conservative lifestyle, they claim, "I've done my work already . . . I can't do anything more." Attempts to plan rehabilitation goals are resisted, and although they may come for assessment, they really do not want to be involved in evaluation and are most reluctant to follow through on any vocational plan. During work evaluation, they cannot organize effectively, and because of slowness and hesitancy, their assessment productivity is below competitive standards. These clients often claim they lack the physical energy to meet the job expectations of others.

During assessment, it is important to help these clients acknowledge their own remaining work capabilities, and gradually to assist them in recognizing their lifestyles of dependency and secondary gain. When reluctance to be involved in evaluative tasks is detected, the professional should communicate a concern and then explore the reasons for this hesitancy. This is done by reflecting the feelings of the client, describing the concept of secondary gain to the client, and providing the client with an understanding—for example, explaining that his or her reluctance to be involved or to return to work may be a fear of losing compensation or newly found family support. These clients should be involved in decisions for assessment planning and given as much responsibility as possible.

One of the assessment goals also should be to raise the client's level of expectations. Continued feedback on work-related strengths then becomes vitally important, as well as selected behavior modification techniques that may help one to gradually find satisfaction in the worker role. Even with these efforts, however, the prognosis for return to employment is generally guarded.

THE ANGRY RESISTER

Many clients who begin rehabilitation assessment with good work histories, motivation to work, and confidence in themselves as workers also display a "you-owe-me-something" attitude, or say, "I will go back to work, but only on my terms." Often, they bring a history of personality disturbances (Lynch, 1979). Predisability life situations were often troubling times, and their personality structures made it almost impossible to cope with their life problems. The occurrence of disability brings another source for inadequate coping. These clients believe that life owes them a lot, such as topflight rehabilitation services, the helping professional's total time and attention, or perhaps an exceptional compensation package. Frequently, in response to efforts aimed at helping them, angry resisters state, "Yes, but . . ." or they do not follow through with anything that has been suggested or agreed to (Pickman, 1994).

Overall, the main source of these clients' anger is their disability, which has caused the disruption of a stable lifestyle. These clients usually want to return to their former place of employment, but they may have had a job-related, handicapping accident, and the employer views the injured worker as

> incapable of functioning productively not only in that person's former capacity but in any capacity involved in the employer's business or operations. (Eaton, 1979, p. 61)

Such rejection affects the client's self-concept, and with this deterioration in self-esteem comes a hostility often projected toward others.

Another source of anger may be the perceived reality of different losses accruing from the disability situation. Because the onset of accidents is sudden, many disabled clients are unprepared to handle the physical, social, psychological, vocational, and financial implications of their injuries. They may no longer have control of their life situations and thus have lost their self-determination (Lynch, 1979). For many people with a disability, lingering anger is a sign of unresolved grief; perhaps they have never been given the chance to come to terms with their losses. These feelings of loss stimulate individuals to question their self-worth, and, in turn, they develop grandiose plans in order to counteract self-doubts. For example, these clients may want money to begin their own business, and often feel that this money is owed them because of their disability.

Other clients who can be typified as angry resisters are critical of rehabilitation possibilities, rigid in their own work expectations, and resistant to counselor suggestions. They express behavioral patterns that tend to turn people off, such as appearing late for counseling appointments or demanding too much of the counselor's time. During vocational assessment, they may ask for detailed reasons for every request that is made of them and are hesitant to cooperate with the counselor in reaching evaluation objectives unless such goals are in complete harmony with their own wishes. Consequently, what occurs during assessment is a conflict between the expectations of the client and those of the rehabilitation professional. Although this conflict may also occur with secondary gainers or those who are ambivalent about their own rehabilitation gain, angry clients are determined to have their vocational wishes followed.

Case Example: Felix

After operating his own auto parts business for 21 years—the business he had been running since age 27—Felix was diagnosed with multiple sclerosis. Depressed about the reality that he could lose many of his physical functions, he sold the business and decided to stay at home to take care of "family concerns." As a Hispanic male, Felix has always felt that family issues are an important priority for him. During his business career, he had spent a great deal of nonworking time with extended family living nearby. After he had spent 3 months at home, his wife encouraged him to seek vocational rehabilitation services because she wanted him to be a more active role model to his family. To please his wife, and to avoid perceptions of others that he is an inadequate male in the Hispanic culture, he made an appointment with a rehabilitation counselor.

During the interview, Felix stated that he could find a part-time job in a relative's liquor store, but that the job did not meet his expectations. He wanted to establish his own business at home and requested a considerable sum of money from the state rehabilitation agency to finance the beginning. When the counselor tried to convince him that such an investment apparently was not practical at that time, he responded, "This money is owed to me because I have paid taxes for a long time, and now I need some money so I can be independent and my family can be proud of me."

Issues To Consider

The rehabilitation professional needs to deal with the client's anger before any assessment can provide a reliable estimate of vocationally related capabilities. These clients should have the opportunity to ventilate their feelings. When employee rejection or unresolved grief has been identified, understanding from the professional can facilitate the client's involvement in evaluation tasks.

After this expression of feelings, the angry client should have an opportunity during assessment for short-term reality experiences that provide immediate feedback about his or her work potential. Work samples are often effective in achieving this goal. Importantly, the professional should not raise work expectations to an unrealistic level, promising these clients that better job opportunities will be available when it may not be so. Such false hope not only provokes anger and resentment from the client but also further inhibits the assessment process. The counselor should make every effort to establish a working relationship built on trust with the angry resister, because the client usually treats the professional as a service functionary. Such clients often put forth very little effort to establish a bond or connection with their counselor (Pickman, 1994).

THE CLIENT WITH DEVELOPMENTAL DISABILITIES

Many clients who present themselves for rehabilitation are functioning at a borderline or lower level of intelligence. They may have been in special education classes throughout their education, and when schooling formally concluded, remained at home. Overprotective parents or underdeveloped social skills become inhibiting factors to choosing opportunities that bring job possibilities. There has been no transition to the world of work.

Because these clients have never learned about the behavioral demands of working, they usually approach the assessment situation cautiously and anxiously. These behaviors typically are caused by ignorance, rather than by rejection of work itself. Because these clients have little self-confidence and are unaware of their employment-related assets, they are passive at the beginning of the rehabilitation process. At the same time, however, persons with developmental disabilities want to work but have no knowledge of their job usefulness. Also, when initially presenting themselves for vocational rehabilitation, they are cooperative but hesitant because of the unknown.

Both inexperience with work and the many years under close supervision of others have created dependency patterns that rarely include self-initiating behavior. Although their energy level and motivation may be high, clients with developmental disabilities have limited capacity to solve their own problems. These clients are almost exclusively outer-directed, and they look to rehabilitation as a resource that will lead them by the hand to job opportunities.

Case Example: Laura

Following completion of her high school special education classes, Laura was awarded a special certificate. Like her classmates, she wanted to seek work in her community, but her parents insisted that she stay at home and baby-sit with her younger brother and sisters. Because she had been limited to only a few, parent-chaperoned dates during high school, her parents were afraid that she was not mature enough for daily interaction with men in a job situation.

Laura stayed at home for 3 years until a social worker finally insisted that her parents allow her to see a rehabilitation counselor. During the interview, Laura was quiet, speaking only to answer questions and to express her wishes for a job in a soft, passive tone. Often during the interview, she mentioned that she had no idea of what would be expected of her in a job, yet said that she was very anxious to get out of the house and earn some money.

Issues To Consider

The assessment situation becomes an important beginning for individuals who are developmentally disabled because it can provide them with necessary feedback about job-related capabilities. They have been tested many times, and their perception of assessment might be of another failure situation. What often is more appropriate is situational assessment—that is, placement in an actual work environment in which persons with a disability can realistically explore their abilities and limitations. (This form of assessment is explained in Chapter 12.) Such an opportunity also provides a chance for behavioral exploration. These individuals have difficulty reaching their maximum skill-functioning levels because of behavioral limitations, most of which are derived from a lack of awareness about what is expected in a work situation. Whether a client is aware of such work behaviors as sustained attention to a task or promptness in returning from work breaks should be explored. Many of these persons become more employable when they acquire important job-keeping behaviors. Consequently, rehabilitation professionals approaching assessment with clients with developmental disabilities often find that a diagnostic picture obtained from an actual job situation can be more accurate than what is learned from paper-and-pencil measures. Through this assessment, the client gains a better understanding of his or her abilities and the demands of the working environment. Understanding establishes the groundwork for the worker's self-confidence and identity.

THE ISOLATED WORKER

Many clients referred to vocational rehabilitation have been institutionalized for many years. The de-institutionalization movement in mental health has facilitated the return to community living of thousands of persons with mental illness who otherwise would have remained in state hospitals. However, this movement brings distinct problems to rehabilitation. Usually, people with mental illness have not been taught the skills necessary to function appropriately in the community. Years of institutionalization have created dependency behaviors that inhibit the assessment process. Often combined with this passivity is a minimal amount of formal education, a feeling that opportunities for the future are quite bleak, and a lingering sense of inferiority. When confronted with an assessment situation, these clients usually do not say very much, often giving the impression that they have no demonstrated commitment to change and find it uncomfortable to take the risk of learning more about themselves and their abilities for work. During assessment, they generally give the impression of being bored.

Case Example: Evelyn

Evelyn, age 28, was placed in a state hospital after a severe nervous breakdown. Before her illness, she had worked successfully as a secretary but changed jobs every 2 years because she felt the job pressure was becoming too stressful. When her boyfriend of many years left her just before they were to get married, she began to experience hallucinations and delusions, and could not attend to her daily needs.

After 1 year of intense psychiatric treatment in the institution, Evelyn was referred to the hospital's workshop, where she worked 5 hours a day performing simple packaging tasks. For 6 months, she made enough progress to warrant the social worker to make arrangements for a community living situation. Upon settling into her new residence, Evelyn was referred for vocational rehabilitation. During the initial interview, she had difficulty establishing continued eye contact and never initiated any conversation. With her hands folded on her lap, she briefly responded to questions, occasionally explaining, "I am very anxious to work." She referred to her rejection by her boyfriend almost 2 years earlier, and expressed doubt as to whether any employer would hire her.

Issues To Consider

Many isolated workers want to work but are hesitant to take that first step to learn about themselves or understand realistic work demands. The assessment opportunity can be a valuable time to provide many of these clients with positive feedback about themselves. Assessment should be structured so that they can gain some helpful information about what they can do. Also during evaluation, they will need much support because their anxiety about meeting a new situation can seriously hinder personal effectiveness. Paper-and-pencil measures should be used minimally for diagnostic purposes, and more emphasis can be given to work samples and the initial interview as assessment tools. Moreover, a comprehensive assessment of the client should be acquired—namely, an understanding of the client's functioning in the living, learning, and working areas of his or her life. A client often needs to learn basic social, living skills before employability can be explored. The client who is unable to talk appropriately with people in a living environment is not going to be able to meet personal interaction demands in a job situation. Because living skills influence work responsibilities, a comprehensive approach to assessment generates information that will show the relationship of performance in living to skills in working.

THE CLIENT WITH CHRONIC MENTAL ILLNESS

Clients with a psychiatric impairment have a degree of disability that is usually much greater than is typically encountered in current vocational evaluation systems. The impairment manifests itself in pervasive and aberrant behaviors, feelings, and cognitions. When a person has a psychiatric disability, his or her deficits in psychobiological processes such as memory, attention, perception, and concept formation hinder social interaction. The socially limited person faces different problems than those who have physical disabilities (Murray, 1990). The disability itself may not readily be understood and may exhibit a broad range of variability in terms of the impact on the individual's functioning at any given time (Beley & Felker, 1981). Though the client may possess work-related assets, these may be masked by passive–dependent behaviors or extrapyramidal motor effects associated with long-term use of psychotropic medication (Beley & Felker, 1981). Also, there is rarely a permanent cure for mental illness. Though higher levels of functioning may improve, mental patients have the frequent tendency to regress (Anthony, Howell, & Danley, 1984). Vocational evaluation conclusions that represent one point in time can be misleading.

The vocational evaluation approach used with clients who have a psychiatric disability is only slightly different from the vocational intervention approach used with other persons with a disability. The important differences are in emphasis. More time is needed, for example, for those with mental illness to go through the process. More alternative vocational environments are needed to allow these clients the opportunity for reality-testing and exploration. Social and emotional difficulties may be more subtle and more easily ignored (Anthony et al., 1984), and approaches should be used to identify these problems. Murray (1990) notes that emerging developments in the evolution of persons with psychiatric disability, such as psychoeducation (combining educational objectives with assessment) and supported employment (providing clients with weekly feedback from a supervisor and a job coach in the form of functional assessment) are approaches that are being used to compensate for client deficits and ease the stress of assessment.

Before one undertakes vocational evaluation of a client with psychiatric disability, he or she should perform an in-depth assessment of the psychological dysfunction, an assessment that also focuses on the vocational implications of the client's disability (Beley & Felker, 1981). Unfortunately, existing psychometric instruments rarely provide normative data for this population. Although evaluators should still procure valid and reliable psychological information, they should use a multiple perspective approach to their own vocational evaluation. This evaluation should have a specific focus on an assessment of the environment in which a client wishes to function. Much time should be devoted to a determination of the client's needed skills and the environmental supports necessary to function successfully in a realistic work setting (Anthony et al., 1984). An effective vocational evaluation for clients who have mental illness builds on existing psychological information and incorporates, over a relatively long period of time, the social–environmental demands of an employment situation. Consequently, an evaluation that includes an identification of the client's functioning in a job environment provides an opportunity to learn client strengths and limitations that may not be revealed in a psychological assessment.

Because a vocational evaluation should be designed somewhat differently for those with psychiatric disability, Murray (1990) offers the following suggestions:

1. The evaluation should be administered in a patient and flexible manner that plans procedures to the particular stress-tolerance level of the client who needs continued encouragement.

2. The evaluator should have high expectations, because many people with psychiatric difficulties are able to achieve a higher level of functioning than has previously been expected.

3. Evaluate functional skills—namely, those generic work-related qualities such as dependability, attention span, work tolerance, speed, production, and attention to detail. Independent living capabilities are also important.

4. Evaluate social skills; to accomplish this evaluation, structured, simulated work sites are suggested. In these evaluations that can help to determine employment readiness, the focus of the social skills is on such behaviors "as the ability to get along with co-workers and supervisors, to communicate effectively, to behave in socially appropriate ways, to take instructions, and to be punctual, dependable, and flexible" (p. 152).

5. Emphasize situational assessment. This approach to evaluation can explore clients' on-the-job attitudes and behaviors because observation, which is the main technique for situational assessment, is necessary to gather information regarding attitudes, motivation, perseverance, and self-confidence.

To identify the complexity of issues that confront the professional who is assessing the vocational options of clients who have chronic mental illness, the following case of Bernard is described. It illustrates the chronicity of the illness and indicates the feasibility of vocational rehabilitation when a mental health regimen is used.

Case Example: Bernard

Bernard, age 26, has been hospitalized seven times in 9 years. His usual symptoms are thoughts of suicide, severe depression, anxiety in exacerbation, difficulty sleeping, loss of appetite, hallucinations, feelings of worthlessness, and hopelessness. Precipitation causes have varied. Mainly, they involved loss of therapists, increased interpersonal contact, increased exposure to heterosexual situations, and raised tension resulting from conflict between guilt feelings and sexual feelings. Diagnoses have ranged from chronic schizophrenia to obsessive–compulsive personality with depressive, hysterical, and paranoid features.

Bernard is White, single, intelligent, middle-class, suburban, educated (college degree in accounting), and in possession of job-related skills. He has been assigned within a hospital environment over the past years to both a therapist and a rehabilitation counselor; he has had four therapists and two counselors. Currently, he is seeing a therapist, but his counselor has retired from vocational rehabilitation. Presently, he is living alone in a furnished apartment, is regularly taking prescribed medication, has several friends, and for the first time in several years, has started to date. The therapist believes that Bernard is making progress in therapy and really is ready to look at preparing himself for employment. Overall, this man has received innumerable hours of psychiatric care, mainly accumulated as an outpatient, in which capacity he has been seen three times a week. The seven hospitalizations ranged from 2 months to 1 year in length. The client's mother and father are still living, and his father, a physician, retired 4 years ago. Bernard reports that he sees his parents infrequently. He has no brothers or sisters.

Issues To Consider

If vocational assessment is to be successful, then the evaluator must coordinate the planned evaluation activities with Bernard's therapist. Both professionals must work together, especially if the assessment process becomes too stressful. Feedback about Bernard's tolerance for the different evaluation tasks is necessary. Information about the current medication and how it could affect the client's performance during the evaluation experience may also be helpful. With Bernard's permission, the evaluator can also give progress reports to the therapist on the assessment process.

THE CLIENT WITH TRAUMATIC BRAIN INJURY

Brain injury is a relatively new disability category that has become recognized as a result of advancing medical technology. Between 400,000 and 600,000 Americans receive head injuries each year, and between 30,000 and 100,000 persons incur traumatic head injuries that result in disabilities severe enough to preclude returning to a normal lifestyle (Fayne, 1989). Of all age groups, 15- to 24-year-olds have the highest rate of head injuries, and the chief cause of head injuries is motor vehicle accidents (Zeigler, 1987).

Traumatic brain injury often results in a myriad of cognitive, behavioral, and physical disabilities. Cognitive disabilities can include varying degrees of short-term memory loss, difficulty in concentrating, problems in processing abstract information, decreased self-awareness and insight, poor retrieval of stored information, impairment of abstract reasoning, and impaired processing in planning, initiating, and carrying out actions. Physical and sensory disabilities can include impairments in speech, vision, hearing, fine and gross motor skills, and balance. Behavioral and emotional difficulties can result from a combination of specific neurological damage and feelings of frustration that come from having to cope with the overwhelming effects of the traumatic brain injury (Virginia Commonwealth University, 1989). These difficulties can include changes in mood and affect, feelings of vulnerability, lack of inhibitions, and inappropriate social behavior. Goal-formulation and problem-solving difficulties, as well as vocational–educational problems, also occur.

Musante (1983) believes that the approach to vocational evaluation and rehabilitation of this population is basically different—for several reasons—from other populations who may exhibit similar behaviors. Although psychological factors cannot be ignored, it has been suggested that an underlying organic component affects behavior, cognition, and emotions. Psychological testing alone may not reveal all of the deficits that will be seen in a work setting. Musante, in citing relevant research studies, explains that a major difficulty in evaluating persons with head injury is estimating the ability to function in view of the inconsistencies that are present. Other issues that concern professionals evaluating persons with traumatic injury are:

1. Expression of anger is a natural reaction to the evaluation process, compounded by emotional lability and impulsivity.

2. Inherent problems exist in using standardized tests and work samples with this population.

3. Nonstatic evaluations are needed over longer periods of time. In other words, techniques should be used within evaluation and work adjustment training programs to improve reading ability and abstract thinking. This can be approached in terms of generalized reading ability, as well as in reading and following instructions toward specific task completion (Musante, 1983).

4. Baxter, Cohen, and Ylvisaker (1985) believe that a client's appropriateness for formal assessment is based chiefly on three considerations. First, the client must not be seriously confused. If the individual is unable to orient to the task and remain so oriented, interpretation of results will be virtually impossible. Second, the client should have an attention span of 30 minutes or more to allow for meaningful testing sessions. Third, if the client is in a period of rapid recovery, extensive testing is usually not indicated. Brief screening instruments can be used to establish levels of functioning for program planning.

For the vocational evaluator, timeliness of referral and comprehensiveness of referral information are critical factors when working with individuals who have traumatic head injury. To benefit optimally from vocational assessment, as was suggested in number 4 above, such an individual should be medically stable and functioning at his or her optimal communication ability. Consequently, a current progress report from the individual's physician is critical. An individual who is referred prior to learning to compensate for difficulties common to this disability in areas such as memory, concentration, judgment, learning, perception, and organization may feel out of control and frustrated in the vocational evaluation setting (Fayne, 1989).

The following brief case example describes some of the hidden factors that can indicate a continued adjustment to employment. Though many clients who have experienced a traumatic head injury indicate a willingness to work, the lack of self-awareness can become a definite obstacle to achieving job adjustment.

Case Example: Gregory

Gregory is an 18-year-old adolescent who experienced a traumatic brain injury on his 17th birthday as a result of a serious car accident. His 17th birthday coincided with the day of his high school graduation. He was in a coma for 6 days. Following his injury, Gregory had continued difficulties with following instructions and concentration, and has had reduced mobility on his left side. Though his cognitive abilities are slowly improving, a psychologist states that Gregory is having difficulties with interpersonal relationships, in which he displays impulsive behavior and is confused about taking responsibility for his own actions. The psychologist considers him "at risk" for maintaining a satisfactory adjustment with peers.

Prior to the accident, Gregory was an excellent student and had been accepted into a prestigious university. He also worked part-time during high school at a delicatessen and was considered a "valued employee." During initial counseling with a vocational rehabilitation counselor, he explained that he believes he cannot enter college in the near future as, "I need to get my life stabilized, and I would like now to find a satisfactory job for at least 2 years."

Issues To Consider

With Gregory, the evaluator needs to receive an updated progress report from health professionals who are involved in their client's physical rehabilitation. Determination of readiness for the assessment process depends on this feedback. The evaluator should also consider at what point in Gregory's overall rehabilitation was the referral made for employment exploration. Because the traumatic head injury can have differential behavior and cognitive effects during the entire course of rehabilitation (namely, these deficits can suddenly improve), assessment may have to be repeated during Gregory's rehabilitation. A focus on the vocational training needs of Gregory may also be appropriate, because extensive training in work skills and related behaviors may be necessary before the rehabilitation professional considers employability.

THE CLIENT WITH A LEARNING DISABILITY

For the past 16 years, adults with a learning disability have been increasingly identified and have become the recipients of vocational rehabilitation services. Diagnosis of specific learning disabilities is a complex and controversial issue due to the extreme heterogeneity of persons with specific learning disabilities and the lack of a clear consensus on one definition of specific learning disabilities (McCue, 1989). Learning disabilities are a lifelong condition, but the manifestation of a learning disability varies over time based on the individual's age, developmental stage, and specific settings (Vogel, 1989). It is more likely, according to McCue, that a person experiences a type of learning disability that is characterized by a subgroup of symptoms. For example, an individual might have a variety of perceptual and spatial difficulties but have intact phonetic language skills. Assessment procedures vary accordingly, and should not be limited to available, formal standardized measures or to academic areas exclusively.

Though specific learning disabilities have been viewed primarily as a school or special education problem, the disabling aspects of a learning disability appear to be magnified as the individual is confronted by increasing and more complex demands of work, home, social, and community living (Hursh, 1989). Learning disabilities interfere with a range of activities important to getting and keeping a job. Individuals with these problems may have difficulties making a decision about appropriate and realistic career choices or completing job applications, or they may show cognitive and perceptual characteristics that often result in accidents, errors, inefficiency, attention problems, poor judgment, trouble being on time, or difficulty learning new tasks or task sequences (Kroll, 1984; Silberberg & Silberberg, 1978). Learning disability is an invisible disability, often misunderstood by employers or friends and always confusing to the individuals themselves. On the job, the worker may appear unable to concentrate, and be forgetful, disorganized, insolent, or rude; or sometimes he or she will just appear to "space out" (Hursh, 1989).

Regarding a definition of learning disabilities, regulations adopted by the Rehabilitation Services Administration (RSA) state that

> a specific learning disability is a disorder in one or more of the central nervous system processes involved in perceiving, understanding, and/or in using concepts through verbal (spoken) or written language or nonverbal means. This disorder manifests itself with a deficit in one or more of the following areas: attention, reasoning, processing, memory, communication, reading, spelling, writing, calculation, coordination, social competence, and emotional maturity. (U.S. Department of Education, 1985)

There are many important considerations concerning vocational assessment with those who have a learning disability. Information from vocational evaluation can be used to refine information regarding the functional impact of cognitive, behavioral, or emotional deficits. In fact, evaluation

> can be streamlined to address primarily those areas of potential difficulty as identified by cognitive tests. An individual who presents attention and memory problems in testing might be placed on vocational tasks that require various levels of competency in attentional and memory skills to determine the extent to which such deficits might impact on job performance. (McCue, 1989, p. 25)

The questions, consequently, that should be addressed in vocational evaluation are: (a) What, if any, is the functional limitation in employment that results from deficits in these areas (Vogel, 1989)? and (b) What kind of assessment should be conducted?

If possible, a comprehensive assessment should be done to identify all potential areas of deficit. Because individuals with learning disabilities can show a broad range of cognitive, behavioral, and emotional problems, relying on one specific battery might fail to identify an individual's specific disorder. The comprehensive assessment is accomplished through a combination of clinical and psychometric tools, which include (a) the clinical interview; (b) collection of historical data, such as developmental milestones or school records; (c) direct behavioral observation; and (d) norm-referenced tests. Because no established battery of tests exists that sufficiently addresses all of the cognitive, behavioral, and emotional domains required for a comprehensive assessment, assessment must be accomplished by combining a variety of instruments to cover required areas of functioning (McCue, 1989). McCue believes that this assessment should include the following:

1. *Psychoeducational assessment,* which focuses on the intellectual and academic manifestations of specific learning disabilities

2. *Psychological and neuropsychological assessment,* which address the cognitive, language, perceptual, motor, and emotional manifestations of specific learning disabilities

3. *Medical and neurological evaluations,* which focus on the medical and etiological considerations of the importance of assessment and treatment of specific learning disabilities

4. *Vocational assessment,* which addresses the functional manifestations of specific learning disabilities with respect to work

Because many adults, especially those with above-average cognitive abilities, have experienced difficulties in employment because of learning problems, these individuals will have spent much energy either on hiding these difficulties or developing compensatory strategies. These strategies allow the individual to minimize the effect of the disability on academic or job performance. Examples of compensatory strategies include using a dictionary to improve spelling or using a word processor to alleviate handwriting difficulties (Simpson & Umbach, 1989). Consequently, when clients are involved in evaluation tasks and do not have access to these aids, they may become quite anxious or even resistant to difficult tasks because of the fear of painful disclosure (Vogel, 1989).

The context of vocational evaluation and the length of time to conduct assessment are two variables to consider when assisting those with a learning disability. Also, an individual often hides learning-disability–related limitations or receives sympathetic treatment from others that can inhibit eventual, appropriate work adjustment. The following case of Scott illustrates some of these issues.

Case Example: Scott

Scott has been referred to you as a counselor because of his reported disruptive behavior and difficulties concentrating on the job. Scott replies, "I get so frustrated trying to do the jobs assigned to me in the factory." He is 23 years old, a high school graduate who barely finished high school because of low grades. According to Scott, "I am a very likable and good-looking person, and I think my teachers often gave me the benefit of the doubt." According to available school reports, Scott had particular problems with receptive language and with understanding relationships and associations.

Upon graduation, Scott immediately obtained a job in a local factory performing simple, assembly-like tasks. His work attendance had been excellent and he was well liked by supervisors. Work problems began to occur when, after asking for another pay raise, he was assigned to another department in which the jobs require the careful reading of instructions and the assembly of different shapes into an organized whole. Scott looks at you and states, "I wonder why I can't do this job."

Issues To Consider

With Scott, it is important to explore his understanding of the learning disability and what information has previously been given to him about its impact on his daily functioning. A focus of assessment can also include what accommodations need to be made in the workplace to respond to the limitations emerging from the learning disability.

THE CLIENT ON MEDICATION

Clients with mental or physical disabilities usually take some form of medication. Those with chronic conditions often receive a continued, regular dosage, either to alleviate pain or to counteract harmful symptoms that threaten active responses to daily life demands. For example, the chronic pain patient or chronic schizophrenic must take daily medication to minimize symptoms so that he or she can assume necessary living responsibilities. However, taking these drugs constantly can lead to a hypochondriac personality or produce harmful side effects during the assessment process.

Aside from the alleviation of pain, many drugs are taken by clients, especially those with chronic mental illness, to control symptoms that inhibit overall life functioning. For example, certain drugs can help keep disruptive behavior in check, minimize hallucinations, or prevent continued delusions. However, these drugs can also produce such side effects as drowsiness; confusion; a tendency toward confabulation, absurdity, and fluidity; and sometimes even the loss of depth perception.

Many clients who experience continued pain have become dependent on drugs to control their personal discomfort. Unfortunately, much of their attention focuses on their symptoms, and they often become egocentric, demanding, and prone to irritability. They view their life through the pain experience, and they are psychologically dependent on their medication.

During assessment, the counselor should determine how much the client's pain experience and the resulting medication have influenced his or her energy, motivation to reach rehabilitation goals, and relationships to others. Many chronic pain patients enjoy talking about their symptoms and the various remedies they choose to assuage the discomfort. Moreover, because of their medical condition, they usually have a pessimistic outlook toward rehabilitation and are even predisposed toward failure. They self-impose limitations (many of which are unwarranted) on their daily performances.

The interview in particular should be used as an assessment tool to ascertain not only motivation and energy level, but also mood and affect, coping resources, residual capabilities, and the ability to focus on goals. The manner in which clients talk about themselves reveals significant information about these factors. This information can be used to determine the client's willingness to be rehabilitated. The counselor should also discover when drugs were last taken, what they were, and how have they affected the client. If drugs have been consumed recently and a behavioral disturbance or change is noted, then the reliability of the assessment situation can be seriously compromised. The counselor may then have to delay assessment until a time when the client can respond more appropriately to evaluation measures.

Case Example: Beatrice

While working as a package handler and sorter for a large shipping firm, Beatrice fell and injured her back. After extensive physical therapy treatments, she was placed on medication to alleviate the occasional severe pain, especially in the evenings. She was assigned to lighter work by her previous employer, and necessary accommodations were made to prevent any reoccurrence of her injury. However, the medication tended to cause drowsiness in Beatrice, and when she attempted to reduce the dosage, she became irritable and found it difficult to get along with coworkers. She also realized that when talking with others she made frequent references to her physical condition. This disturbed her and she then decided to seek vocational counseling to find employment that would help get her mind off her pain and physical problems.

Issues To Consider

During the initial interview, the counselor should attempt to identify Beatrice's perception of her pain and the impact it has had on her daily life. The counselor could also explore whether the pain is a secondary gain factor. Her attitude toward her employment future could also be evaluated.

THE CLIENT RECOVERING
FROM SUBSTANCE ABUSE

Because of the emerging incidence of chemical and alcohol abuse, as well as the increasing recovery rate due to the large number of substance abuse treatment programs available, a significant number of recovering addicts are presenting themselves for vocational rehabilitation and career counseling. As specified by the ADA, these individuals are not eligible for vocational services unless they are at least actively in treatment. For the helping professional who is planning vocational assessment strategies, the focus of attention is both on the identification of factors that may cause a relapse, and on an awareness of client characteristics that may be used for vocational development, such as cognitive, emotional, and physical capabilities.

Fisher and Harrison (1997), citing the research of Gorski (1990), explain a recovery sequence of several steps. Each of these steps can suggest a direction for understanding what the client may need to successfully manage his or her drug rehabilitation. This information can be collected during an initial interview, and includes the following:

1. *Explore who the person is and discover which places and things may promote his or her chemical use.* Such information can be gained from a detailed social history, a reconstruction of the presenting problems, an exploration of any past recovery and relapse history (when available), and an identification of any lifestyle issues that are associated with relapse (Gorski, 1990).

2. *Identify self-defeating behaviors and mistaken core beliefs that may suppress painful feelings and encourage irrational thinking.* During the client's communication of his or her history of chemical abuse, causes for this behavior may emerge that relate to unresolved grief or the unwarranted conviction "that I am just no good."

3. *Explore the ways in which this client responsibly manages feelings and emotions without relying on the use of harmful substances.* An identification of coping behaviors used successfully to overcome difficult situations in the past, can heighten the client's awareness of personal resources to be employed when confronting a possible relapse situation.

4. *Determine which addictive-thinking patterns create painful feelings and self-defeating behaviors.* An in-depth review of the client's history of drug abuse, and the circumstances that prompted the abuse, should be conducted.

Skinstad (1998) identifies further criteria that can assist the evaluator during the interview process. These criteria include the following:

Recurrent substance use resulting in a failure to fulfill major role obligations at work, school, or home (e.g., repeated absences or poor work performance related to substance use; substance-related absences, suspensions, or expulsions from school; neglect of children or household)

Recurrent substance use in situations in which it is physically hazardous (e.g., when driving an automobile or operating a machine)

Recurrent substance-related legal problems (e.g., arrests for substance-related disorderly conduct)

Continued substance use despite having persistent or recurrent social or interpersonal problems caused or exacerbated by the effects of the substance (e.g., arguments with spouse about consequences of intoxication, physical fights)

An assessment of emotional, behavioral and cognitive capabilities, as well as work-related abilities, is discussed in several chapters of this book. Such evaluative approaches do not necessarily have to be specially tailored to the client recovering from substance abuse. Particular attention should be given, however, to the effect of continued drug abuse on the client's cognitive functioning and emotional strengths, with special attention being paid to the client's anger management skills. The following case illustrates these factors.

Case Example: Lewis

Lewis, a 27-year-old accountant, lost his wife of 3 years in a car accident 2 years prior to his self-referral for vocational assessment. His wife once worked with him as an accountant in a large, family-owned business. Soon after his wife's death, he began taking drugs, returning to a habit that he maintained when he was 17 to 19 years old, but had been in successful recovery from for 6 years. During the initial interview Lewis stated, "My wife was all I had . . . we had no children . . . she was killed from a head-on collision, and was not responsible for the accident. I am very angry, and I just can't shake my anger. I turned to drugs because they made me feel better. But a friend has put me into drug rehabilitation and I have been drug-free for 6 months." Lewis explains that he is looking for another career because "working as an accountant brings too many painful memories."

Issues To Consider

When working with Lewis, the evaluator should explore any self-defeating behaviors, the client's own awareness of responsibility to himself for any rehabilitation progress, coping behaviors that have managed successfully in the past any stimuli that could cause substance abuse episodes, and the effects of the abuse on the client's cognitive functioning. The client's environment concerning what factors reinforce drug abstinence, such as family and friends, could also be identified. Developing a trusting relationship with Lewis is important, because once Lewis is comfortable during the assessment process, he may be more willing to express his feelings and relate an accurate history of substance abuse behavior. The assessment process could also be quite helpful in assisting Lewis in identifying those skills and personality strengths that could be presented effectively during a job interview.

THE MINORITY CLIENT WITH A DISABILITY

The client's culture plays a large role in vocational assessment. A person with a disability brings specific attitudes to the evaluation experience. These attitudes reflect beliefs about the service delivery system, as well as perceptions about the meaning of assessment that have been shaped by the individual's culture and ethnic background. In fact, traditional approaches to vocational evaluation may be in direct conflict with values and rehabilitation views held by minority group members. The ethnic diversification that is occurring in many societies has stimulated considerable interest in developing alternative ways to understand the employment potential of someone for whom traditional evaluation measures have not been standardized using one's ethnic group. Many assessment tests are actually discriminatory to different minority members. There is a need, consequently, to identify guidelines that can assist an evaluator when working with a client representing a culture different from one's own. The following are several assessment guidelines to consider when developing evaluation plans:

1. The evaluator must be flexible when considering the most appropriate and effective way to explore the career potential of someone from an ethnic minority. This attitude includes an awareness of the cultural factors affecting career and employment, such as family, extent of acculturation and socialization, and perhaps an experience with institutional racism. The client's view of evaluation, and of the feasibility for developing long-range assessment goals, should be identified. The helping professional and client, consequently, must work together to define the assessment problem (Fouad, 1993).

2. In selecting standardized measures to be used in the evaluation process, one should give careful attention to (a) conceptual equivalence—namely, the similarity of meaning attached to behaviors or concepts by the evaluator and the client; (b) the validity of test translations when standard English is the second language of the client; (c) avoidance of test bias—making sure that test items are not more familiar to one group than to another, and that a test does not have differential predictive validity across groups; and (d) appropriateness of the norm group, the reference group for the instrument, for the client (Fouad, 1993).

3. Minority group members with a disability tend to show high anxiety in the assessment situation. They frequently believe that traditional evaluation tests represent unfairness of content, are liable for improper interpretation of scores, and have items that are often not related to the actual job requirements of a career (Doppelt & Bennett, 1967). They do not trust the use of tests, perceiving that tests have been used to maintain discriminatory practices (Sue & Sue, 1990).

4. In order to ascertain the impact that cultural values have had on the client's career assessment, the evaluation interview should include an exploration of the client's family history, individual educational and work history, assimilation into the dominant cul-

ture, and socioeconomic status. Individuals from several cultures may find it difficult to disclose such personal information because of ethnic-related values. The evaluator, consequently, should assist the client to become more comfortable. To achieve this, two suggested strategies may involve personal disclosure on the part of the counselor concerning professional training and reasons to enter a professional field, and clarifying the role expectations that a client may have for the evaluator (Prince, Vemura, Chao, & Gonzales, 1992).

5. Because of norming difficulties associated with many standardized tests when used with minority members, the evaluator may choose to use such nonstandardized instruments as short checklists, observational assessments, and behavioral evaluations (Fouad, 1993).

6. Because the evaluator needs to use considerable caution and judgment when determining the usefulness of a particular inventory for minority populations, both the language of a particular assessment measure and the client's test-taking attitude or response style must be identified. If the individual's primary language is not English, it would be appropriate to administer, if possible, the version of the inventory that corresponds to that person's language. However, it is necessary to review the technical accuracy of the translated version. Moreover, ethnic response sets may invalidate the results of some inventories. Sue and Sue (1990) believed that there may be a tendency among particular cultural groups to respond to an inventory with certain norms and expectations in mind. For example, on an interest inventory a client may show a pattern of not endorsing interests that reflect a separation from one's parents or that conflict with the values of one's culture (Prince et al., 1992).

In order to achieve equitable assessments for all, there is a need to think of evaluation measures differentially. The evaluator should attempt to develop and use the most valid approaches one can for all groups that can be operationally defined. Though there are few assessment techniques available for work with nontraditional groups, the evaluator needs to be diversity sensitive and plan appropriate assessment strategies that can reproduce useful information (Sedlacek, 1994). Many of the cultural issues explained in this chapter are implied with the following case example.

Case Example: Bob

Bob is a 29-year-old African American male who is married and has four children ranging in age from 2 months to 6 years. His wife does not work outside the home. He had worked as a maintenance man for a high-rise building for 7 years until he injured his back while working on the job.

In his evaluation, Bob presents several work problems, stating that because of his weight, which is in excess of 250 pounds, he has been restricted from climbing. This restriction jeopardizes his job because it prevents him from being able to perform all of his duties as a maintenance man. He states that when he was hired, his weight was in excess of the weight limit imposed by the management and federal standards, and argues that his weight should not matter now. The client has health insurance through a health maintenance organization (HMO), but was treated by a clinical psychologist with whom he bartered painting and carpentry work in exchange for clinical services. During medical rehabilitation for his back injury, a psychologist made a diagnosis of borderline personality disorder, complicated by being abused as a child by his alcoholic father.

The psychologist also got permission at the beginning of counseling to speak with the client's wife. The wife reported that the family was $20,000 in debt due to her husband's spending. Furthermore, she reported that the primary care physician has not paid them much credence because her husband was not that cooperative with his rehabilitation regimen. The primary care physician proposed further counseling through a local, community-based crisis service at the client's expense.

Issues To Consider

To avoid stereotyping or imposing the evaluator's value system on the client, the helping professional should act as a listener when encouraging Bob to share his expectations for assessment. The level of anxiety over the evaluation experience may be high, and methods other than standardized testing should be explored that could provide useful information for vocational planning. Communication with Bob's physician would be helpful, because his physical capacities associated with the back disability are an important part of the evaluation. Information from Bob's wife would be important, assuming that Bob gives the evaluator permission for this communication.

CHAPTER 3 CONCLUSION

These 12 different types of clients represent many of the varieties of people who present themselves for rehabilitation. Categorizing is one way to identify the many behaviors that clients show; such behaviors can either facilitate or deter progress to rehabilitation goals. The categories often overlap because many disabled persons display, for example, both angry resister and secondary gainer traits. Regardless of the way the professional understands client behaviors, however, most clients with a disability have strong inhibitions about going into an assessment situation in which they might look bad. They feel that assessment might show them as being more inadequate than they really are. Many clients also have negative expectations toward the counselor because they perceive that their counselor has negative expectations toward them. Professionals may have a low expectation for the rehabilitation success of their clients, and although such a feeling may be quite warranted, this attitude breeds distrust and apprehension.

For all clients who have a history of physical or mental disability, the most difficult part of the assessment phase of rehabilitation is not necessarily its content but the very fact that they must be evaluated. Fear of a strange situation, poor test-taking skills, inferior feelings, discouragement attributable to past failures relating to the disability, and perhaps a hostile attitude from the counselor might cause conflict and anxiety. Vocational evaluation can even be seen as a humiliation, a device for proving and exposing the client's limitations.

Client assessment, then, becomes an opportunity for professionals to ask themselves the following questions:

1. *Will my characteristics as a helping professional make a difference in the client's assessment performance?* The assessment process involves a complex interaction among the professional, the client, and situational variables. The manner in which rapport is established and maintained and the way the evaluator responds to the client's attitudes and feelings have a bearing on how successful the professional is in attempting to elicit a client's best efforts.

2. *How can I, as a professional, recognize and accept the client's fears, apprehensions, distrust, and skepticism?* By recognizing and accepting these perceived behaviors, professionals can begin to acknowledge the emotional rewards needed to give stimulus or meaning to the rehabilitation experience. Support, approval, and encouragement are important professional responses that become more meaningful to clients as they progress through the steps in the rehabilitation program. These responses also can help to increase the client's self-confidence.

3. *What can I, as a professional, do to enhance the reliability of the assessment situation?* In other words, what can be done to reduce anxiety and to generate mutual respect? The professional's beliefs about the expectations of the person with a disability can be the key to client trust and confidence. If the professional possesses high, positive expectations for clients, usually clients will respond accordingly and attempt to be open and provide as much energy as possible in the assessment situation. Paying attention to the client's emotional needs and listening intently to the client are tools that can help build mutual respect.

The answers to these questions influence the effectiveness of client assessment. Such questions pervade the entire assessment process and demand attention as professionals attempt to learn more information about their clients. Ways to respond to these issues in assessment, as well as formulate a comprehensive assessment approach to the different behaviors of clients, are discussed in the next chapters.

To assist the reader to become more aware of the different characteristics shown by clients with a physical and mental disability, the following case is presented with questions that may facilitate discussion.

CASE STUDY: MR. R.

Mr. R. is a White, fair-complected male of average height who appears somewhat over-weight. He was born December 18, 1952, in Wilmington, North Carolina. He is the youngest of three children—his brother is 6 years older and his sister is 11 years older. Their father worked for the postal service.

Mr. R. graduated from high school in July of 1971, reporting that he received "aver-age" grades during school with science and history as his best subjects. He played varsity football and during the last 2 years of high school was part of the work–study program. He went to school in the morning, was employed in the afternoon, and took electronics courses in the evening. Mr. R. mentioned that when he was in secondary school, his father told him that the family only had enough money to send one of the children to college and was going to send Mr. R.'s older brother. The brother went to the University of South Carolina and, after graduating, went to seminary and obtained a Master of Science degree in counseling and another degree in theology. According to Mr. R., the brother is pres-ently a minister in the largest Protestant church in a capital city in the South.

Upon graduating from high school, Mr. R. enlisted in the Army, because he "wanted an education and liked to travel." During boot camp, he attended night classes in medical science at the University of North Carolina. This continued for 10 weeks. The client was then notified that he had been selected for military intelligence school at Fort Davens. There, he was trained in espionage, surveillance, and investigative techniques. Mr. R. states that he was very happy to be selected for such work and enjoyed the school. He was then assigned to surveillance work in Vietnam, where he was selected as the "top man in a class of 30." He was then assigned to Officer's Candidate School and, upon graduating in 1973, was immediately assigned to Vietnam, where he was the intelligence officer for an artillery battalion. His duty was to direct support fire while in the field and direct B-52s to bomb enemy positions and villages where there were suspected Vietcong.

While on patrol during a late enemy offensive, the impact of an incoming shell blew Mr. R. off a bridge, and he landed in a gully 20 feet below. He remembers that, upon awakening, he couldn't feel anything from his waist down, but that after 4 days, he was able to get up and return to base camp where he was placed in bed for a week. His injury was diagnosed as a back sprain. While recuperating at base camp, he was walking outside with two buddies when an enemy rocket attack occurred, killing both friends. Mr. R. sustained shoulder and hand injuries. These injuries were diagnosed as sprains, and he was returned to duty. Because of the patient's continued complaints of back pain, he was returned to the United States and was eventually assigned as an intelligence officer to an Army unit in Tucson, Arizona. Mr. R. still complained of back pain and in September of 1975 was notified that he was going to be discharged. He left the military service in December of 1975 and, upon discharge, started looking for work. He states, "I applied for 67 jobs, but was turned down because of my back." Finally, he obtained a position in the Northeast United States as an assistant juvenile officer. He is very unhappy in this job and has come for vocational evaluation. He is married and has two children.

Chapter 3 Case Study Questions

DIRECTIONS: With this information, please answer the following questions:

1. What behaviors is this person showing that could be detrimental to obtaining accurate information from the vocational evaluation process?

2. According to the categories of clients identified in this chapter, to which category do you feel this client belongs?

The Interview as an
Effective Assessment Tool

The preceding chapter identifies different clients who present particular behavior-related problems and concerns for vocational evaluation. Just as effective rehabilitation planning begins with a thorough evaluation of the person's disability residual capacities, an assessment approach also should provide useful and reliable information for the rehabilitation professional. Unfortunately, traditional evaluation approaches are still frequently used in vocational assessment, and this can be unfair to the client. (Some of these issues are discussed in Chapters 2 and 3.) Many of the assessment instruments presently used are developed from theories that assume that certain client traits are unalterable. However, many aptitudes, abilities, and other so-called traits are not static; rather, they are influenced by the situational variables that surround a person's evaluation or learning experiences. The pattern of failure in the lives of many persons with disabilities, the negative influence of family members, or the stereotypic expectation from many rehabilitation professionals that certain clients cannot do well in evaluation can decidedly influence a client's response to evaluation. These attitudes can also inhibit a person with a disability's motivation or performance.

The interview is one approach among many assessment techniques that can provide meaningful information related to planning effective training programs for persons with severe disabilities. These programs usually focus on developing work-related skills and behaviors. Training variables can play an important role in evaluating the employability of persons with disabilities. These variables, such as motivation, ability to get along with others, the capacity to learn from previous experience, and attention to task, are not taken into account by traditional evaluation techniques. Assessment strategies that emphasize prediction and predominately measure general abilities, achievement, and aptitudes may be nonfunctional for many of those with severe disabilities. However, the interview can be used to identify the specific training needs of persons with disabilities (Menchetti & Rusch, 1988).

Because of the difficulty in using much of the standardized data to develop interventions that can make a significant difference in the individual's reaching rehabilitation goals, I use the interview as an evaluation tool. An *intake interview*, of course, is required in all rehabilitation agencies. Farley and Rubin (1982) defined this interview "as a conversation between a counselor and a client with a definite mutually acceptable purpose" (p. 39). The interview is a technique for gathering information by means of discussion. The purpose of the intake interview can differ according to the agency, but usually it serves to accomplish the objectives that follow.

1. *Develop rapport between the professional and client* (Farley & Rubin, 1982).

2. *Give the client necessary information about the role and function of the agency, available services, and client responsibilities* (Farley & Rubin, 1982).

3. *Help clients identify their own strengths and weaknesses, as well as recognize and become aware of personality traits, abilities, and aptitudes that may facilitate achieving rehabilitation goals.* Through nondirective problem exploration, reflection, and clarification of feeling for self-acceptance and insight, the client may gain self-understanding, which is a necessary goal for the rehabilitation process. This is particularly important for persons with disabilities who need to appreciate their residual physical, intellectual, and emotional assets. During medical treatment, attention usually focuses on the impairment or illness. Patients grow accustomed to focusing on what they cannot do. Interview feedback can help clients alleviate these perceptions and focus on more helpful knowledge about themselves.

4. *Help the client feel more comfortable about the rehabilitation process and help him or her gain a feeling of self-confidence.* As mentioned in the previous chapter, many persons with disabilities harbor anxiety or tension about the possibility of reaching rehabilitation goals. Dependency patterns may already have been developed, or an assessment situation during vocational rehabilitation can revive memories of previous failures in testing. This memory only stimulates added anxiety. The interview creates an opportunity for the professional to begin to ease the anxiety and provides a chance for the client to discuss particular fears about the rehabilitation experience.

5. *Provide the counselor with beginning information for vocational assessment planning and eventual rehabilitation training.* This information is acquired through directive exploration of factual data from the client's work history, academic records, family history, and any available test data. The acquisition of this information is integral to the interview process.

In addition to building relationships and providing information, the intake interview can be a valuable opportunity to generate necessary facts for rehabilitation planning. It is also a chance for the interviewer to help clients become aware of their own responsibility for making decisions when they learn additional information about themselves. Such a realization can help the person gain some control over the rehabilitation outcome, as well as gain a sense of empowerment. What is needed, however, is an interview structure to organize this information and facilitate this awareness for rehabilitation purposes.

This chapter presents a structure that gives the intake interview more of a diagnostic perspective. There are occasions when more than one interview meeting is needed in order to obtain the necessary information for planning purposes. Time considerations or the initial reticence of a client to disclose information can extend the interview beyond one session. Regardless of the time it takes to learn more about the client, the time itself (namely, the interview) is more evaluation-based (Roessler & Rubin, 1982). When using the intake interview as a diagnostic resource, there are two general steps—each of which depends upon the other: (a) conducting the interview itself and (b) using a structure to collect the information gained from this interview. Certain dynamics generate an effective interview. Also, if the interview is to be a valuable opportunity for a beginning evaluation of the client, a structure for organizing the facts must be identified. All of these issues are discussed in this chapter.

CONDUCTING THE INTERVIEW

There are many ways to conduct an interview. Choosing a method depends on what type of information is to be gained, the circumstances in which it is to be obtained, and the individual conducting the interview. An approach that I have used with clients with disabilities, especially those with severe handicaps, follows. It is important to note that interviewers learn about clients not only from what the latter say but also how they say it—including how, in general, they present themselves during the interview (Cohen, Swerdlik, & Phillips, 1996). Unless the rehabilitation professional develops a relationship with clients, the counselor cannot help these people with a disability feel better about themselves, recognize their productive capabilities, or control their own fears about future training or other rehabilitation opportunities. Experienced interviewers attempt to create a positive, accepting climate in which to conduct the interview. The process for developing this relationship basically includes two components: (a) contextual interviewing and (b) personal interviewing. Both of these concepts, described at length by Carkhuff (1969) and Anthony (1979), apply to the vocational evaluation process.

Contextual Interviewing

Contextual interviewing is concerned with both the environment in which the interview is conducted and the way the rehabilitation professional physically relates to the client. For example, it considers (a) the location of the professional's office, (b) privacy and confidentiality factors, (c) where the professional sits while interviewing, and (d) the number of distractions that are present in an office. For example, many interviews are conducted while the professional sits behind the desk, with the client in front. The desk represents a barrier to communication, acting as a distancing factor between two people. Clients usually feel very strange with this arrangement, and often feel more comfortable if the professional moves away from the desk. If this is not possible, then having the client sit beside the desk reduces some of this communication difficulty.

Also, having too many posters hanging in the professional's office can be very distracting. A few posters, if appropriately placed, can have a calming effect on the client and convey a personal dimension of the professional. However, if the office is a mini-museum (even if there is an interesting assortment of collectibles), the client may feel overwhelmed.

Another facet of contextual interviewing involves whether the rehabilitation professional takes notes or uses an agency's standard interview form to write comments while talking with a client. If possible, the client should complete this form before the interview itself. If this is not possible because of some functional limitation, the agency should assist the client. Before the interview begins, the professional should scan the form to discover any needed information that might be missing, while learning basic demographic facts about the individual. The professional should tell the client in advance if notes are to be taken during the interview. Clients often become cautious about revealing information if they do not understand how it is going to be used by the interviewer.

Contextual interviewing establishes a mood by creating an atmosphere in which people feel more comfortable and are reassured that they are receiving direct attention. The rehabilitation professional's office can be a form of communication that helps both to reduce the client's anxiety and to develop a good relationship during the interview. The warmth that is expressed by the office decor, the professional's placement in relation to the client, and the maintenance of privacy and confidentiality can promote communication between the interviewer and the person with a disability. Good interviewing is not only the result of the complex interplay of the rehabilitation professional, the client, and the purpose of the interview, but also is achieved by the setting in which it is conducted.

Personal Interviewing

During the interview the individual with a disability usually has a story to tell—a story with problems, conflicts, and perhaps unhappiness. This story may be wide-ranging in subject matter or narrowly focused on a particular area, depending on variables such as the nature of the referral question, the nature and quantity of available background information, the demands (with respect to time and the willingness or ability of the client to respond) of the particular situation, and the judgment of the interviewer (Cohen et al., 1996). The content of the interview, consequently, can vary from one situation to the next, and the tone of the interview as set by the interviewer may also vary. Interviews that are used as assessment tools in vocational evaluation are more exploratory, covering areas such as those identified in Table 4.1 later in this chapter. The interview should include the client's disability history and the current problems associated with life adjustment. Many rehabilitation agencies may require, however, more of a structured interview, in which all the questions that will be asked have been prepared in advance. For individuals with a disability, there are several issues, such as relationships to helping professionals, family expectations for return to work, and personal feelings related to the onset of the disability that may only emerge from an open-ended, wide-ranging interview format.

If the interview is to be used as an assessment approach, the rehabilitation professional must not only establish and maintain a good relationship with the client, but also stimulate the person with a disability to participate productively in the interview. Such productivity is frequently encouraged by an interviewer who is warm and accepting, conveys understanding to the client by verbal or nonverbal means, and who prefers to ask open-ended questions (Cohen et al., 1996). Also, the conversation must keep moving productively to achieve needed information. This entails communication, flexibility, control of the interview situation, organization of the information embedded in much of the interview conversation, and the processing of data according to interview goals.

Carkhuff and Anthony (1979) identified four communicative skills that, when used by the rehabilitation professional, can considerably enhance the effectiveness of the interview situation. These skills—attending, observing, listening, and responding—are fundamental and should be used throughout the entire interview session to help the client become involved.

Attending

This skill refers to the physical positioning of rehabilitation professionals as they talk with clients. It requires the counselor to establish eye contact and sit in such a way that both interest and attention are communicated to the client. Eye contact should be natural, direct without constituting a stare, and generally constant because frequent breaks in eye contact suggest inattention.

Observing

This means that the interviewer first watches for specific aspects of the client's appearance and behavior, and then uses this information to draw some careful inferences concerning the client's functioning (Carkhuff & Anthony, 1979). For example, when observing the client's use of eyes, grooming, changes in posture, and, in particular, changes in the positioning of the head and shoulders during the interview, the rehabilitation professional gains a beginning, tentative understanding of the client's interest and motivation in the assessment situation.

Listening

Like observing, listening can promote the client's participation in the interview and facilitate the disclosure of information important for rehabilitation planning. Listening implies attention not only to the client's verbal expression but also to the accompanying tone of voice, such as loudness, softness, and rapidity of speech. Listening also means that possible judgments about the client's behavior are suspended. It is very easy

to formulate attitudes about the client as the interview proceeds. At this stage of rehabilitation involvement, these perceptions can become obstacles to a genuine and reliable understanding of the client's functioning. By actively listening to what the client
is saying, the professional communicates continued concern which, in turn, often
prompts the client to discuss valuable information needed for rehabilitation planning.

Responding

In responding to the client's verbal messages during the interview, the rehabilitation professional is attempting to help the client become aware of his or her feelings, especially
those regarding the disability situation. The professional initially responds to verbal
content as the client expresses specifics relating to his or her immediate situation. The
professional then responds to the meaning that is inherent in the client's statements and
nonverbal behavior. Finally, as clients express the immediate feelings that each aspect
of the disability arouses in them, the professional promotes continued exploration of those
feelings by responding to them (Carkhuff & Anthony, 1979). The following is a suggested format for this development of responding:

**Responding to the content of the client's expression ("So you're saying . . ."
or "You're saying that . . ."):**

CLIENT: My family ignores me most of the time.

INTERVIEWER: You're saying that members of your family leave you alone.

Responding to the immediate meaning ("You mean . . ."):

CLIENT: I am very upset because my disability prevents me from enjoying life.

INTERVIEWER: You mean that you don't understand all your disability still allows you
to do.

**Responding to the immediate feelings ("You feel . . ." or "That can really
make you feel . . ."):**

CLIENT: I have tried many times to return to work but I just can't bring myself
to face my employer again.

INTERVIEWER: You feel anxious about what the employer might say to you.

The interviewer's responses during the interview should be frequently inter-
spersed with words that express feelings. The most direct way to introduce a response
to feeling is to use the opening, "You feel . . ." The rehabilitation professional can vary
the form of the response, as long as he or she includes a specific feeling, word, or phrase
that the client recognizes as interchangeable with the feeling expressed in his or her
own statements.

To promote a positive relationship between the client and interviewer, and to convey to clients that they are respected as persons, other techniques may have to be used. One approach is for the professional to immediately introduce himself or herself and then briefly explain the particular job of a rehabilitation professional. (Many persons are confused about job functions of rehabilitation counselors or vocational evaluators. They may believe that the professional's only responsibility is to get the person a job.) To help the client feel initially comfortable about the interview situation, the professional can ask, "Could you tell me why you feel you are here at this agency today?" Most clients usually respond to this question, and a small exchange helps both the professional and the client understand the purposes of the interview. During the beginning of the interview, therefore, there should be time for relationship-building and clarification.

With an awareness of these interpersonal skills and approaches, the rehabilitation professional also needs to determine at the beginning of the interview which topics should be emphasized and which areas are most critical to explore for eventual rehabilitation planning. Again, before the interview, the agency application form should be scanned to identify these areas. At times, however, the interview as an assessment resource might have to be conducted over several sessions. Such client disability factors as poor attention span or poorly developed communication skills may dictate a slower interviewing pace. Some topics, such as a criminal record or sporadic employment history, may be too sensitive for the client to introduce immediately. The professional may want to proceed cautiously, helping the client to discuss initially those topics about which he or she seems to be most comfortable. When the client believes that the interviewer can be trusted, he or she becomes more willing to reveal the sensitive, but necessary areas for rehabilitation assessment. Often, this takes more than one session.

ISSUES ARISING DURING THE INTERVIEW

Many other issues should be addressed during the interview if this dialogue is to be successful, providing the necessary information for rehabilitation planning. The following issues are particularly important: (a) the role of questions during the interview, (b) the timing of reinforcement, (c) the effective use of confrontations, (d) the use of silence, (e) the establishment of interview control, and (f) the awareness of certain processes that reveal information.

The Role of Questions During the Interview

Unfortunately, many interviews are conducted in a question-and-answer format in which the client replies to repeated inquiries from the professional. In order to gather needed information, broader responsiveness must be encouraged. Questions should be framed to invite exploration rather than a single "yes" or "no" response from the client.

The interviewer's questions should relate as closely as possible to the topic being discussed and flow from the immediate dialogue between the client and professional. Too often, questions are asked in order to change the subject when the helping professional becomes uncomfortable with the client's responses. Timing is also vitally important, because questions can inhibit a client from pursuing a subject further, especially if he or she discusses the more negative aspects of his or her work history or disability experience. Also, comments such as, "That sounds very interesting," or "It does take a lot of courage to look honestly at a person's background" are usually more conducive to soliciting information than questions that can be limiting.

To create a mutually understanding climate, seasoned interviewers tend to begin with open-ended questions, and then shift to closed questions, which obtain specific information (Cohen et al., 1996). Open-ended, indirect questions encourage the expression of ideas and information that might never be obtained by a direct approach. Using adroit, appropriate questioning can encourage the client to draw out his or her perceived strengths and assets. The following questions illustrate this point.

Direct Question

INTERVIEWER: Did you like that job?

CLIENT: Yes (or No).

Indirect Question

INTERVIEWER: What things did you like most about the job?

CLIENT: I thought the attitude of the supervisor toward his workers helped me do the job better.

The professional may receive several responses that contribute to understanding the applicant's motivation and interests. When probing for information, the counselor can use such beginning words as *how* or *why* to provide the client with a chance to be more flexible in his or her response. A tactful use of the word *what* can also solicit information, but the professional must then try to employ a reassuring manner and tone. An abrasive tone of voice immediately inhibits clients from talking. Many questions are asked too directly, causing the client to feel reluctant to reveal needed information. For example, "Why did you leave that job?" might be too direct. Instead, a more appropriate inquiry may be, "How did you happen to leave that job?"

The Timing of Reinforcement

One of the purposes of the interview is to facilitate responsiveness from the client. There are several ways to accomplish this goal, some of which concern relationship-building through effective communication skills. Other approaches focus on helping the client to talk more readily about the negative aspects of his or her background. Persons with a disability usually have encountered many personal failures or rejecting attitudes. Their self-concepts are often low, and they are understandably hesitant to talk about areas that might convey a negative impression. Low marks in school, the inability to hold a permanent job, and low-motivation in exploring productive opportunities are frequently difficult to reveal in an interview situation. At the same time, these issues should be discussed in order for the professional to identify possible obstacles for reaching rehabilitation goals.

The professional can attempt to make it as easy as possible for clients to talk about negative aspects of their backgrounds by playing down the importance of that information by some casual, understanding remark. For example, when the client begins to mention that he or she received low marks in school, the professional can compliment the person for having been able to recognize this difficulty and then face up to it. Rehabilitation professionals who give the slightest indication that their judgments are adversely influenced by unfavorable information will get no further information of this kind.

A skillful professional gives frequent "pats on the back" or verbal reinforcement, never openly disagreeing with a client on any point or giving the appearance of cross-examining. The technique of expressing agreement places heavy demands on facial expressions and general interviewing manners, including avoiding words that convey a negative meaning. For example, words like *weaknesses*, *faults*, or *liabilities* can be replaced by *shortcomings*.

Spontaneous comments by the professional create a favorable climate for conversation. These remarks provide some continuity to the client's verbal expression, as well as assist the client in revealing negative information. In fact, comments can often be used in place of questions. For example, the comment, "I can imagine there were some really tough problems in a job like that one," can be used instead of the question, "What were some of the most difficult problems you faced on that job?"

Also, by using such words or expressions as *and then*, *ummhmm*, and *right*, the interviewer provides at least minimal encouragement and at the same time helps the client feel more at ease during the interview.

Effective Confrontation

During the interview, the rehabilitation worker should identify contradictions in what the client is saying. The client might be setting very unrealistic goals in relation to his or her abilities or past experiences. He or she might also be employing defensive strategies that may block appropriate rehabilitation planning, such as denial or the projection onto others of his or her own anger. The professional wants to help the client identify and resolve these discrepancies.

Confrontation should only be used after a good client relationship has been established. There are many ways to confront a client. Comments should not include accusations, judgments, or solutions to problems. Carkhuff and Anthony (1979) suggested that using a format such as, "On the one hand you say (*feel, do*) . . . , and on the other hand you say (*feel, do*) . . . ," is only minimally threatening to the client because it focuses on an element of contrast that comes entirely from the client's own frame of reference.

The Use of Silence

Silences often occur during the interview, perhaps because clients are nervous, shy, or anxious about revealing information relevant to their disabilities. Silence is also a form of reluctance, which is discussed in a later section of this chapter. However, silences are often a positive form of communication, telling the professional that a certain subject is probably quite difficult to discuss. A client simply may have exhausted a particular subject and is waiting for the professional to suggest another topic area. Silences themselves should not become too long without an interviewer response. The following are some examples of responses in a silent situation:

"You feel uncomfortable to discuss this subject further."

"Perhaps we should change the subject . . ."

"It is difficult to talk about those areas of your life that remind you of failure and pain."

Many clients are silent during the interview because they have limited verbal skills, the result of functional limitations. In these instances, the interviewer has to be more directive in the interview situation, providing reinforcing statements like, "This is your first time in this agency and I can understand that it would be difficult to talk about yourself." The low-verbal client frequently finds it hard to elaborate on any topic suggested by the professional. Appendix A suggests a form to facilitate both interview conversation and the disclosure of needed information.

Controlling the Interview

Control of the interview means simply that the interviewer guides the client to talk about the topics necessary to explore appropriately vocational circumstances. Time is limited, and important information must be obtained in a relatively short period of time. The client, however, may want to talk about nonpertinent information or evade pertinent facts. But there are approaches that can help the interviewer to control this specific diagnostic session, without severely inhibiting the client's verbal expression.

1. *The helping professional must plan the interview carefully*. He or she needs to identify what information should be collected, while remaining cognizant of the client's limitations and thresholds.

2. *The interview should be initiated in a positive way*. Listening intently to the client's responses, asking open-ended questions, and providing information that indicates the

counselor's understanding of what the client is saying can each help to create a positive experience for the interviewee.

3. *The rehabilitation counselor must direct the focus of the interview.* Though many clients may be somewhat fearful of the interview situation—and their anxiety may interfere with their ability to communicate—the interviewer should keep the interviewee talking, staying on the topic about which the interviewer needs information. Repeating a critical word, phrase, or sentence that the client has just used, asking a related question that cannot be answered "yes" or "no," stating an area that you as an interviewer would like to hear about, and defining specifically what it is you want to know are all ways to help the client to remain focused.

4. *Though the helping professional should structure the interview situation, this does not mean that the interview cannot be meaningful and personal.* The professional can keep the conversation rewarding for the client by moving to a new, relevant topic at the moment the interviewee mentions it; providing a statement that allows a natural transition to take place when a change of topic is needed; attempting to refocus the client by alluding to an area that was previously discussed; and making a personal remark about something the client may have said or done.

Avoiding Hostility

Hostility may occur during the interview because of the interviewer's or the client's chronic stress; a conflict within the client because he or she faces two mutually exclusive choices; or a clash of opinions, viewpoints, or ethnic backgrounds. If the interviewer, however, accepts the client and allows him or her to vent appropriately some feelings, then this interviewer can often minimize the hostility. By acknowledging that the perceived conflict is a problem—without attempting to solve it for the interviewee—the interviewer can assure the client that this problem will be considered in one's vocational plans and that through this planning he or she can hope to decrease the stress. Each of these approaches may alleviate the client's hostility or anger.

Certain Interview Processes

During the interview, certain processes that occur between the rehabilitation professional and client can reveal information about the client's mental and emotional functioning. There are four areas that the professional should especially look for.

Association of Ideas

A client may be discussing some of the difficulties in finding a job and then switch suddenly to talking about his or her disability benefits and how they have alleviated many adjustmental problems. Thus, the client has probably indicated that the problem in finding a job is not isolated but is actually connected to receiving entitlement payments.

Shifts in Conversation

A sudden shift in conversation can indicate that clients feel that they are telling too much and do not want to reveal more information about that particular subject. Perhaps a client begins to talk about material that is becoming too painful to pursue, and decides to avoid further discussion. A sudden shift in topics during the interview should be responded to by the rehabilitation professional. Statements such as, "On the one hand you were talking about . . . and now you are discussing. . . . This is confusing to me and I wonder if you would clarify it," can encourage a response from the client.

Recurrent References

A client may repeatedly return to a certain subject. Such repetition often indicates a main focus of reference or the client's true feelings about a disability situation. Someone who continually mentions that his or her family is pleased that more time is spent now with family members than before the onset of the disability can be suggesting that it is really more rewarding to be at home than to return to employment. Frequent references should be explored by the professional, because they usually contain valuable information related to the client's motivation and expectations for rehabilitation evaluation involvement.

Inconsistencies or Gaps

A client may tell a story that is primarily straightforward but has unexpected gaps. For example, the person with a disability may carefully neglect to give any reasons for leaving the last job. Being alert to the possibility of such a gap, the professional can mildly confront the client with a statement exploring the reason for such inconsistency—for example, "As you were talking, I noticed that something seemed to be left out. Could you give me some idea of what this is?"

INTERVIEW ISSUES WITH
SELECTED POPULATIONS

Though the interview material explained in this chapter can usually apply to all populations with a disability, specific concerns arise with clients who are experiencing circumstances that require extra attention. Examples include, but are not limited to, those who (a) have chronic mental illness, learning disability, or the residuals of a head trauma; (b) represent varied ethnic backgrounds; (c) are injured workers who are not motivated to explore return-to-work options; (d) are classified as an "older worker"; (e) are adolescents involved in school-to-work or adult life transition; or (f) have been diagnosed with AIDS. As the rehabilitation process progresses, clients can become increasingly aware of cultural differences; negative attitudes toward returning to work; and their own physical, emotional, and intellectual limitations. These clients can show anxiety, irritability, even agitation, problems apparently born of frustration. Such problems may also be reactions to many experiences of failure, and vocational evaluation may highlight failure. Whatever symptoms the client may show, the rehabilitation worker must keep in mind certain guidelines that focus on conducting the interview.

1. *The skillful interviewer should try to shift the client's own perceptions of inadequacy (e.g., "I'm going to look bad during the rehabilitation process") to information-seeking, discovery, and problem solving.* To accomplish this goal, the rehabilitation worker should attempt to create a positive client–interviewer partnership during the assessment process. For example, the purpose of the interview, as well as the different steps to follow in the rehabilitation process, can be carefully explained. The client can be asked to explain the perceived difficulties he or she anticipates during this process, and to describe possible strategies for responding to or solving these problems. In this way, the evaluator may gain valuable insights while the client may realize that the interview and the succeeding steps in the rehabilitation process are significant (Vogel, 1989).

2. *When clients begin the assessment process, they usually have a specific set of expectations.* Koch (1998) believes that these initial expectations tend to be self-fulfilling and that discrepancies between expectations and what actually occurs in assessment can result in premature termination of evaluation. Expectations can be categorized as preferences (what one wants to occur) and anticipations (what one thinks will occur) (Koch, 1998). Expectations should be discussed at different times during assessment, because the discussion can both clarify role behaviors of the evaluator and client and suggest the type of assessment outcome.

3. *The interviewer should be quite literal and explicit when talking with a client who has brain injury or chronic mental illness.* Specific examples can be used to illustrate a question. For example, when asking the client, "Whom did you like best in your last job?," the evaluator could also describe what *like best* means.

4. *The interviewer should be encouraging to the client during the interview, calling attention to the person's assets and success.* Clients who may be aware of cognitive deficits frequently have problems with self-esteem. Identifying specific strengths of the client may facilitate the building of self-worth.

5. *With clients who have a learning disability or cognitive, emotional, and perceptual deficits, family background should be explored during the interview—with attention given to how the client perceives the family reaction to the disability.* The interview might explore the client's interpersonal relationships with other family members. When this information can be obtained, it could suggest possible areas of difficulty in a training or work situation. Also, such information may indicate possible obstacles to or resources for the client's vocational rehabilitation.

6. *An examination of previous records, when available, may be particularly helpful when collecting all the assessment information for rehabilitation planning.* Such records include neurological exam results and school and employment records.

7. *Especially for those with a learning disability or head injury, specific problems are created in vocational assessment.* Some of these problems can be administrative procedures requiring reading, multiple-step individual tasks, and the lack of opportunity to explore or fully understand performance expectations (Hursh & Kerns, 1988). With an awareness of these potential difficulties, the evaluator can inform the client of what further vocational assessment may involve, and how the difficulties can be minimized.

8. *With clients who are experiencing mental illness, it is especially important for the evaluator to include specific information.* Interview data must include such topics as type and frequency of medication, as well as involvement with a counselor, therapist, or community mental health agency.

9. *When interviewing persons with a disability who are from an ethnic background different than their own, helping professionals need to be aware of their clients' cultural background.* Language capability, work roles, cultural and religious beliefs, and available support systems should be considered. Racial and identity development should also be identified. Obstacles to career advancement such as the attitudes of significant others, discrimination in the workplace, and other barriers posed by the social, political, and economic system can be explored. Further areas that need to be explored are the client's level of acculturation and the way he or she identifies with his or her culture. The client's attitude toward seeking help about disability-related issues can also be important for rehabilitation planning. Among minority cultures, there are critical between- and within-group differences. Understanding these topics can be a starting point for understanding a client who represents a minority culture and who has a disability. Race and ethnicity are fundamental concerns in the delivery of rehabilitation services.

10. *Because many injured workers may show such behaviors as unwarranted dependency, passivity, and a reluctance to take any initiative for employment planning, the interviewer should be alert to client evasiveness.* Evasiveness can take such forms as changing the topic as soon as employment goals are mentioned, answering questions with questions, or using meaningless statements. The interviewer may have a better chance of soliciting needed information by using nondirective techniques, as well as stating that he or she really is interested in knowing about specific areas that affect the client's vocational plans.

11. *When the rehabilitation professional is working with students who have a significant disability, specific factors should be addressed during the screening interview.* The vocational evaluation procedures that have been integrated into educational settings typically involve a variety of personnel. In addition, school-based vocational programs primarily target disadvantaged students and students with mild and moderate disabilities for services (Levinson, 1994).

These programs are usually multilevel programs that use a variety of techniques to gather information. The content of the interview should include an exploration of needs, values, behavioral tendencies, work habits as shown in past employment, temperament, and social–interpersonal skills. This information should not be identified in isolation, but should be combined with psychological, educational, social, medical, and other data to provide a comprehensive picture of the student (Levinson, 1994).

CONCLUDING THE INTERVIEW

When the interview is to conclude because of time considerations or the rehabilitation professional's realization that needed information has been obtained, the client should be asked to indicate what has been learned during this particular interview session. Because the client may have difficulty reviewing this information, the discussion should be stimulated by pointing out one or more strengths that have been observed. For example, "Well, I have learned that you seem to get along unusually well with people, and this, of course, is a tremendous asset in any job situation."

It is important for the client to leave the interview feeling positive about the experience and understanding what is needed for successful achievement of rehabilitation goals. This feeling can be achieved through summarizing information that has been gained from the session. Again, the review focus should be on the client's identified strengths. The ideal interview represents a beginning for the client, providing a new awareness of identified strengths and a knowledge of the opportunities that rehabilitation offers. Also, the end of the interview is an important time to clarify any questions and discuss vocational evaluation arrangements.

A STRUCTURE FOR THE COLLECTION OF INTERVIEW INFORMATION

As the client talks about personal history, the disability, and its implications for his or her immediate life, the information that is generated is most important for rehabilitation planning. The key to using this information effectively is to have a structure for organizing interview facts. The structure of the interview can be an interview guide that the rehabilitation professional completes immediately following the interview, or a mental outline that the professional follows while talking with the client. (I have used the structure both ways.) After gathering the interview information in this framework, the professional can then begin to make rehabilitation plans.

Using the interview structure suggested in Table 4.1, Bordin (1943) has developed interview topics that can be useful in vocational assessment. Though identified over 50 years ago, the basic concepts still have remarkable relevance for the rehabilitation professional who needs brief guidelines during the assessment interview. The following is a brief explanation of Bordin's approach.

1. *Problem Appraisal*—identification of the person's problem, as well as motivation to change or assume responsibility for problem solution. Included in this appraisal is an

identification of the factors related to the career problem, such as the part that is played by the family in problem development and resolution, financial resources, marriage plans, and academic achievement.

2. *Personal Appraisal*—a picture of the client is obtained from a variety of demographic, psychometric, and social data, and should include an assessment of strengths as well as weaknesses, present status and functioning, and developmental history. This history includes the history of the onset of physical or mental disability, family background, early interests and abilities, and perhaps early vocational choices and plans.

3. *Prognostic Appraisal*—an evaluation of such factors as motivation for vocational assessment and the follow-through of vocational planning. This appraisal can also include an assessment of whether the evaluation should only focus on an identified problem, or could be extended to the identification of the client's potential to learn skills that solve other career problems.

The interview structure described in Table 4.1 includes 18 items of client functioning and their relationship to rehabilitation goals. Each item should be explored during the interview. The way each item relates to training or employment is listed in the right-hand column. Importantly, approaches for gaining this information from the client are suggested in the middle column.

Figure 4.1 shows the form that I use during the client intake interview. Some of the items listed follow those already identified in Table 4.1. As mentioned, the author completes this form after the intake interview or other needed sessions with the client. Then, this form is used when rehabilitation plans are developed (as discussed in Chapter 16 of this book). Relevant planning necessitates the use of this information, and it becomes an important step in rehabilitation planning.

CHAPTER 4 CONCLUSION

This chapter suggests ways for the interviewer to gain information about a client, especially when traditional assessment approaches are perceived as quite limited in providing the necessary data. Using the interview as an effective diagnostic tool requires the establishment of a positive, helping relationship between the client and interviewer. When this is achieved, both the interviewer and the client can begin to gain feedback that is crucial for rehabilitation planning.

The personal history of Felix illustrates how the interview can be used effectively in vocational assessment when either a specific structure or certain guidelines for obtaining information is followed. These guidelines are identified after the description of Felix. The following information was provided you by a graduate resident assistant who was given permission by Felix to share these facts with you.

(text continues on page 86)

TABLE 4.1
A Structure for Organizing Interview Facts

Items of client functioning	Approaches for gaining information about areas of client functioning	Relationship to training or employment
1. General appearance and behavior	Observe	Personal habits Appropriateness Work behaviors Neatness Relationship to coworkers Dependency Relationship to evaluator and future supervisors
2. Principal way of communicating	Listen to the way client talks about problems and himself or herself	Attention Comprehension and retention of instructions Reality contact
3. Mental processes and content	Observe the way the individual verbally constructs his or her life experiences; listen to the association of ideas, shifts in conversation, and inconsistencies and gaps in the conversation	Realistic expectations Judgment and problem-solving ability Reality contact Potential to learn work demands
4. Mood and affect	Observe nonverbal behaviors; listen to the client's affect as he or she talks; *Ask:* How are you feeling now?	Response to pressure Adaptability Emotional reaction to disability
5. Coping resources	*Ask:* What do you think you do best? What are the most difficult problems you have faced? How were they handled? Have you experienced a recent stress? How did you manage? How do you handle pressure on the job or at home? What is your present living situation?	Independent functioning Frustration tolerance Handling failure or setbacks Response to pressure Confidence/self-concept Adjustment and maturity
6. Orientation towards other people	Ask the client to describe the relationship with his or her coworkers. *Ask:* How do you feel when you are in social situations? Whose opinion do you see as valuable to you in your life planning?	Interpersonal skills Job-keeping behaviors Relationship with supervisor and coworkers Social acceptability

(continues)

TABLE 4.1 (*continued*)

Items of client functioning	Approaches for gaining information about areas of client functioning	Relationship to training or employment
7. Capacity for facing problems	*Explore:* What are the most difficult problems you have faced? How were they handled? What is your reaction to your disability? How do you handle unpleasant situations?	Job-getting behaviors Seeking of training opportunities Adjustment and maturity
8. Education and training experience	*Ask:* Tell me about what you have done best in school or any other training.	Skills and compentence Job alternatives
9. Social factors	*Ask:* Who is available to help you during vocational rehabilitation? Who does not support you?	Available support services Assistance in problem solving Identification of external barriers

10. Energy level	*Ask:* How do you think things can be different for you? What can you do about it? Are you willing to take risks to make changes? I would like to hear how you spend your time each day. Watch for recurrent references in the interview.	Motivation
		Identification with productive role
		Job-seeking behaviors
		Job-keeping behaviors
		    Regular work attendance
		    Promptness
		    Work production
		    Lack of time wasted

11. Goal-directedness	*Ask:* What type of work do you see yourself doing 5 years from now? What are you looking for in a career? What are you looking for in a job?	Growth and development
		Job objective behaviors
		    Seeks a vocational goal
		    Has an appropriate work objective

12. Strengths of client	*Ask:* What do you do well? What do you like about yourself? What do you feel are your strong points? What have you learned from your work experience?	Compensatory skills Confidence Job-keeping behaviors Relevance for work Sufficiency of work

TABLE 4.1 *(continued)*

Items of client functioning	Approaches for gaining information about areas of client functioning	Relationship to training or employment

13. Interests of client	Explore educational experience
	    Competencies
	    Particular difficulties
	    What was liked best
	Explore work experience
	    Special areas of interest
	    Special areas of competence
	    Major duties and responsibilities
	Leisure time and general interests
	Ask: What would be the ideal job for you?
		Training goals
		Job objective behaviors
		Job alternatives
		Readiness for work

14. Work history	*Ask:* What kind of work have you performed in the past?	Skills and competence Adaptability and adjustment Stability
15. Disability factors	*Ask:* Describe your present disability. How does it limit you? Are there any medications? What are the effects?	Performance Training selection and disability Transfer of skills
16. Outer-directing factors	*Explore:* family and peer expectations; perceived prestige of certain occupations; economic job market opportunities; available support services	Motivation
17. Outer-limiting factors	*Explore:* Presence of prejudicial attitudes; geographical opportunity; accessibility of training and work sites; family expectations; financial resources and current job market opportunities; available transportation; (other external barriers)	Opportunity for training and employment Motivation

18. Expectations	*Ask:* What would you like to accomplish as a result of participating in assessment? What do you think will happen during the assessment process? What kind of assessment services do you think you will receive?	Congruence between
		    assessment process and
		    client; motivation;
		    possible remediation
		    of incongruencies

Client Information Items	Comments	Training goals
Work history and experience		
Education and training experience		
Social factors		
Disability factors		
Principal way of communicating		
General appearance and behavior		
Mental processes and content		
Mood and affect		
Coping resources		
Orientation toward other people		
Capacity for facing problems		
Energy level		
Goal-directedness		
Strengths of client		
Interests of client		
Outer-directing factors		
Outer-limiting factors		
Expectations		

Figure 4.1. Client intake interview form.

 CASE STUDY: LUIS

Luis is a 19-year-old freshman attending a major university. He is the oldest of five siblings, all of whom currently reside at the family home 100 miles away from the university. Luis's father works as a delivery driver for a brewery and his mother is employed part-time as a housekeeper. Both parents have worked hard to make ends meet and have been instrumental in sending their eldest son to college.

Because of a birth injury, Luis has a withered left arm, and is right-handed with all necessary movements. He is the first in his entire family (including relatives) to have ever attended an institution of higher education. It is generally understood that the parents do not have the financial resources to send Luis's other brothers and sisters to college. If they are to make it, they will need to do it on their own or obtain help elsewhere. As a result, Luis found a part time job, without the knowledge of his parents, in order to secretly save money for his siblings' future education.

Luis obtained a B average in all subjects in high school, was apparently well-liked by his peers, and participated in many extracurricular activities, such as debating and writing for the school newspaper. During the last two quarters, Luis has been having extreme difficulties in his classes at college. Luis's inability to obtain grades better that C's or D's in a general letters and sciences program (he has not yet declared a major) has greatly discouraged him. Last quarter he was placed on academic probation and the thought of failing evoked a great sense of guilt and shame in him. While he had originally intended to become a social worker and had looked forward to his coursework, he now feels depressed, lonely, and alienated. He lives on the college campus. He believes that it was not so much his inability to do the work, but the meaninglessness of his courses, the materials in the texts, and the manner in which his courses were taught that contributed to the probation. Worse yet, he could not relate to the students in his dormitory or all the rules and regulations. He has not participated in many of the campus activities, and generally feels that it has not been a "winning experience." His family lives about a 2-hour drive away from his college campus. With the exception of his arm deformity, Luis is in good physical shape— he is not taking any medications, and has not had any serious health problems. His current part-time job is working at the circulation desk at a local library. At the beginning of this most recent semester, Luis is referred to you as a counselor to explore a career objective.

 ## Chapter 4 Case Study Questions

DIRECTIONS: With this information, please answer the following questions:

1. With the information provided, how would you structure the initial interview?

2. What particular issues should be addressed in this interview?

3. What information identified in Figure 4.1 could be used to guide interview exploration?

Understanding Selected Concepts in Vocational Assessment

Rehabilitation professionals have an excellent opportunity to perform vocational assessment when their clients are first seen in an intake interview. The previous chapter suggests structures for such an assessment. When the interview is used as an approach for obtaining facts relevant to rehabilitation planning, the outcome of other evaluation procedures can be carefully weighed against this newly gained information. Most clients involved in the rehabilitation process usually go through further assessment procedures. There are many reasons for this practice. Work samples can furnish backup information and a further understanding of the client already gained during the interview. When paper-and-pencil tests are selected appropriately, they often introduce a reliable, solid, and objective dimension into rehabilitation assessment. The paper-and-pencil approach has been used in rehabilitation to provide a sample of a person's intellectual functioning, developed abilities, and emotional behavior.

For many years, procedures for testing people with handicaps have left much to be desired (Parker & Schaller, 1996; Sherman & Robinson, 1982). Even when assessment measures are appropriately modified, the meaning of the scores is uncertain. Unfortunately, fully developed test modifications that are suitable for all individuals with handicaps do not currently exist. Also, there is little information about the way available tests compare for those who have handicaps and those who do not (Sherman & Robinson, 1982). Vocational evaluation for people with disabilities, women, and people from minority backgrounds has raised such questions as: What kind of norms should be used when testing persons with disabilities? For those with a severe disability, what types of assessment approaches are preferable? and Are evaluation measures that are developed on "normal populations" reliable and valid for individuals with disabilities (Parker & Schaller, 1996)?

Two important functions of tests are *selection* and *diagnosis*. This book focuses on the use of selected tests to explore and identify the client's independent living and work-related strengths and limitations. However, test results that reflect a person's disability do not provide an unbiased estimate of his or her potential. The issues of which tests and other evaluation approaches are appropriate for individuals with handicaps is a crucial one in rehabilitation assessment.

Paper-and-pencil tests are classified in many ways, including (a) individual or group, (b) verbal or nonverbal, (c) highly structured or unstructured, (d) closed choice or open-ended, (e) objective or subjective, and (f) machine-scored or scored by judgment. Psychometric tests may also vary a great deal in the degree of standardization quality and amount of interpretive information they furnish. Consequently, when using tests for vocational evaluation, the helping professional has to determine a test's appropriateness for particular clients. Certain standards for evaluating tests should be employed to choose the most appropriate and available measure. This chapter discusses these standards and other relevant issues, and explains the guidelines for interpreting test scores.

APPROPRIATE NORMS AND THE CRITERIA PROBLEM

A norm refers to the group of people on whom an assessment procedure has been standardized and from whom the scores on a particular test have been obtained to determine level performance. A test's normative group should be appropriate for the individual taking a test. In rehabilitation, many of the assessment procedures have not been standardized on a representative sample. This is true, for example, of most paper-and-pencil tests. Also, vocational evaluation involves prediction. A predictive assessment measure that cannot be used in exactly the same surroundings as the behavior that is to be predicted is definitely limited. For this reason, assessment procedures other than paper-and-pencil tests are frequently used in vocational evaluation. The best prediction of what persons will do in a given situation is usually what they did the last time in that situation. Consequently, the approaches of work samples or situational assessment (which are explained in a later chapter of this book) are frequently used for predictive purposes because they can tap into a person's previous experience.

Rehabilitation agencies have conducted a great deal of research and development on assessment procedures. However, norms are available on only some of the tests used by rehabilitation agencies, and rarely is there an interest in comparing test scores for those who have handicaps and those who do not (Sherman & Robinson, 1982).

Approximately 20 years ago, a practice that was adopted to make the results of selection tests minimally prejudicial was race norming, in which a client's test scores are compared only with those of his or hers own ethnic group. Race norming was used by the U.S. Federal Government, but because of the charge of reverse discrimination and because the Civil Rights Act of 1991 bans any form of "score adjustment" on the basis of race, color, religion, sex, or national origin, the use of separate subgroup norms for employment selection purposes is now illegal (Aiken, 1997). The issue of general versus special norms, as applied to the vocational evaluation of those with disabilities, is both confusing and controversial. On the one hand, general norms may discriminate unfairly against people with disabilities. The evaluator must consider the purpose of assessment—is it to compare an individual's performance with members of another group, or to estimate the person's future performance? Parker and Schaller (1996) believed that the major cause for the confusion is that "rehabilitation personnel frequently fail to make a conceptual separation between descriptions and predictions" (p. 144).

Because of these norm-referenced difficulties, many of the measures used in rehabilitation assessment should determine what a client can do, rather than how he or she stands in comparison to others. Initially, the rehabilitation professional needs to determine the skills necessary to accomplish satisfactorily tasks in an employment situation, sometimes consulting manuals that identify these demands. Then the assessment will provide an estimate of whether or not a client has the capability to perform, with training, the necessary skills.

In contrast to norm-referenced tests, some evaluation measures, particularly in the fields of rehabilitation assessment, are criterion-referenced. This approach is gaining widespread acceptance in the rehabilitation field, because this assessment method is more applicable to those with severe disabilities and can be used to determine if clients have learned employability and independent living skills. In rehabilitation practice, it has been discovered that the best prediction of a person's performance on a particular job is the person's actual performance on that job for an adequate period of time. In other words, the best predictor is the criterion behavior (Parker & Schaller, 1996).

Norm-referenced tests yield information about a test-taker's relative standing, while criterion-referenced measures yield information about a client's mastery of a particular skill. "Has this client mastered the skills necessary to be employable in a certain occupation?" is a type of question that a criterion-referenced test may seek to answer (Cohen, Swerdlik, & Phillips, 1996). Consequently, a client's performance is compared to a standard of mastery called a criterion. Criterion-referenced assessment "uses as its interpretive frame of reference a specified content domain rather than a specified population of persons" (Anastasi, 1988, p. 101). Examples of criterion-referenced measures include many behavior assessment tools, which may also use rating performance measures that target single or multiple skills. The criterion can be a specific behavior or behaviors, a test score, an amount of time, a rating, a psychiatric diagnosis, an index of absenteeism, and so on.

The criterion in criterion-referenced assessments usually derives from the values or standards of an individual or organization (Cohen et al., 1996). An agency determines, for example, a reasonable level of proficiency—regardless of how well other clients perform. Criterion-referenced interpretations provide information about what individuals with disabilities can do, whereas norm-referenced interpretations provide information that compares one person's performance to that of other people (Cohen et al., 1996). For a job-related criterion to be adequate, it should be quantitative, should parallel the actual job requirements, and should be measurable with some degree of consistency (Owings & Siefker, 1991).

The most basic score used in criterion-referenced assessment is pass–fail, or right–wrong, with single-skill scores ranging from completely correct to completely incorrect.

When multiple skill scores are used, such as scores resulting from multiple observations, then percentages and rates are used.

In vocational assessment a continued question for the evaluator is what qualifies as a "good" test or evaluation procedure. The criteria for a good test should include clear instructions for administration, scoring, and interpretation. A good evaluation approach measures what it purports to measure, is reliable, and has assessment results that are based on appropriate norms for the population being evaluated. The following sections on validity and reliability explain the issues that need to be addressed with these factors.

VALIDITY

Although Section 504 of the Rehabilitation Act of 1973 and the Americans with Disabilities Act of 1990 (ADA) specify many requirements, one in the ADA has important relevance for rehabilitation assessment: An organization covered by these regulations

> shall assure itself that tests are selected and administered so as to best ensure that the test results reflect the handicapped applicant's aptitude or achievement level or whatever other factor the test purports to measure, rather than reflecting the applicant's impaired sensory, manual, or speaking skills (except where those skills are the factors that the test purports to measure). (Sec 104.42 (b)37)

In other words, the concept of validity is important when considering the appropriateness of any use of a test. Validity provides an estimate of how well a test measures what it purports to measure, and this concept is central to rehabilitation legislation.

Rehabilitation professionals should always refer to the validity of a particular use of a test. It is the use and not the test itself that has validity (Cohen et al., 1996; Sherman & Robinson, 1982). Validity is not an either/or attribute of a use of a test; it exists in varying degrees in various situations. Conducting validity studies by no means ensures that a particular application of a test is appropriate (Sherman & Robinson, 1982). In fact, validation of tests for populations of people with a handicap has been rare. Few, if any, validation studies have given attention to the applicability of the test producer's validation to local conditions. Differential validation research on testing people with disabilities is virtually nonexistent in the private sector. Such studies are considered unfeasible because of the small numbers of employees with a handicap in similar jobs (Parker & Schaller, 1996; Sherman & Robinson, 1982). The ADA implies that a handicapping condition should have no effect whatsoever on test scores unless the test is explicitly designed to measure an ability directly related to the handicap. However, such an implication raises the question: Is a modified test or the test administration procedure sufficient to maintain the validity of the test content and the credibility of the testing medium? It may be too ideal to modify assessment measures to a degree such that they are unaffected by a client's handicap. Most test developers believe that this ideal is largely unattainable.

Predictive validity, however, offers the greatest promise for comparability of test results between the population of those who have a handicap and those who do not. It also gives an estimate of the strength of the association between test scores and a measure of performance on the criterion to be predicted (Sherman & Robinson, 1982). Consequently, it has been recommended that

> sponsors of large testing programs . . . modify tests to accommodate most kinds of sensory and motor handicaps and . . . conduct predictive validity studies in order to ascertain whether the modified tests have a predictive power near that of the standard test used with the general population. (p. 126)

It is believed that this is an achievable form of comparability, although empirical studies would have to be conducted in order to determine the actual feasibility of the approach (Sherman & Robinson, 1982). At the end of the research, it should be possible to determine whether modified and standard forms of a test actually have comparable predictive power.

The validity of a test may be evaluated by (a) scrutinizing its content, (b) relating scores obtained on the test to other test scores or other measures, and (c) performing a comprehensive analysis of "not only how scores on the test relate to other test scores and measures but also how they can be understood within some theoretical framework for understanding the construct the test was designed to measure" (Cohen et al., 1996, p. 175). These validity methods are called content, construct, and predictive or concurrent. Two other types of validity will also be explained, namely face and incremental validities.

Content Validity

Content validity refers to the representativeness of the test items in terms of assessing the behavior the test was designed to sample. One way to estimate the design sample is to determine carefully what items make up the domain or content of some specific behavior. Then, a sample of items are pooled together to represent different levels of the behavior. When the items are pooled together, it is thought that the resulting test will discriminate between individuals at different levels of mastery. A statistical procedure called *factor analysis* is sometimes used to assess content validity. This procedure groups test items together into different factors, suggesting that the items in a factor relate to some specific content or knowledge base. Content validity is most likely to be reported for achievement tests. Also, content validity for work evaluation procedures exists when the duties and tasks of the work sample or situational assessment are highly similar to those of the job itself.

Content validity is an important issue when considering test fairness. Although test fairness is not a fixed concept, and experts disagree on its meaning, it is particularly relevant for evaluators and employers when evaluation approaches are developed, and results are used for employment decisions. The ADA implies that when decisions are going to be made from test scores, the items on a particular test must be relevant to the specific job or jobs to which the applicant is applying. Employers must demonstrate that the skills measured by their selection tests and other hiring procedures are job related (Aiken, 1997).

Construct Validity

Construct validity is more theoretical than the other types of validity and refers to the degree to which a test measures any hypothetical construct. It is most likely to be used in measuring psychological traits and characteristics. For example, anger is a hypothetical construct that can exist in different forms. What anger is, as well as where and when it is likely to be experienced, is linked to psychological theory. In construct validity, it is suggested that something like anger exists; next, the anger is related to a theory concerning the phenomenon; and finally, a test, in measuring the construct of anger, attempts to predict the way anger differentiates people in terms of the construct. In vocational rehabilitation, a convenient starting place in determining construct validity of evaluation procedures is to examine the worker functions required in successful performance of the job. These functions are identified very clearly through job analysis techniques. Construct validation emphasizes the analysis of the job in terms of standard definitions of the constructs underlying successful performance of job duties and tasks. Examples of such constructs may be speed in performing the task, eye–hand coordination, and finger dexterity.

Predictive Validity

This refers to the relationship between a test and some criterion. It can be established by giving a test to a group of persons and then assessing the eventual outcomes for the group. Most commonly in determining predictive validity, a test is administered to a group of persons who are then placed into a training program or job. At some later time, data are collected on training or job success criteria, and these are correlated with the initial scores. These predictive validity procedures have an advantage in that they can show the capability of the evaluation device to differentiate between persons who are successful on the job and those who are not.

Face Validity

This is a subjective appraisal of what a test seems to measure. Face validity is a judgment based more on a test's measurement design than on a study of the test's actual content.

A test that measures anger should have items that look like they measure anger. Although face validity is a very crude technique, it is often necessary in order to ensure that a test is acceptable to potential users or test-takers. For example, if a test used to predict job performance has no obvious relationship to the job itself, rehabilitation professionals may be less likely to use it. However, face validity is not the same thing as content validity. Face validity concerns judgments about a test after it has been constructed; content validity implies that although the test is being constructed, the selected test items are a reflection of an adequate sampling of a defined domain of content that bears a relationship to the trait being measured. Face validity can establish "rapport" between the test-taker and the test administrator.

Incremental Validity

Many vocational evaluators are interested in using multiple predictors, because an additional predictor can explain something about the criterion measure not explained by predictors already in use. For example, a client's score on an aptitude test, such as the Bennett Mechanical Comprehension Test (Bennett, 1980), may be used as one indicator of training and future employment success. High scores on behavioral rating scales that have been validated may also predict training and employment success. An aptitude or work sample test may not be the most efficient way to predict successful training and employment productivity. An evaluator may find that another measure has good incremental validity because it reflects a different aspect of preparation for successful training outcomes. So, predictor measures are included only if they demonstrate that they can explain something about the criterion measure that was not already known from the other predictors (Cohen et al., 1996).

Issues pertaining to validity are particularly important to the rehabilitation professional when conducting vocational assessment. For example, if a written test is employed to make decisions about individuals or groups, all the available evidence should be studied before any attempt is made to interpret the scores. Also, a test that is going to be used for prediction or selection should be validated in the specific situation in which it is going to be used. Validity awareness further implies that the professional will be up-to-date, not only on new knowledge about assessment procedures, but also about the qualities or individual traits they measure.

Another issue with validity revolves around the term *validity coefficient*. This is a correlation between a test score and a criterion measure and is expressed by a number such as 0.51, 0.36, or 0.2. A measure may be used, for example, to select personnel for long-term training or to predict success in school. Anastasi (1988) explained that the validity coefficient "provides a single numerical index of test validity, and is commonly used in test manuals to report the validity of a test against each criterion for which data are available" (p. 163). However, validity coefficients may change over time because of changing selection standards. But the interpretation of a validity coefficient must take into account a number of concomitant circumstances (Anastasi, 1988). Although the correlation should be high enough to be statistically significant at some acceptable level, such as at the 0.01 or 0.05 level, the rehabilitation professional needs to evaluate the size of the correlation in light of the uses to be made of the test.

As an example of the use of the validity coefficient, Bolton (1979) reported that the validity coefficients for the Workshop Scale of Employability (with 500 clients of the Chicago Workshop) (Bolton, 1982) were 0.23, 0.23, and 0.26 for the three criteria of early placement, long-term placement, and maintenance. He continued to say that the corresponding validity coefficients for a sample of 100 clients of the Indianapolis Goodwill Workshop were 0.43, 0.43, and 0.31. Consequently, Bolton concluded correctly that placement in employment was clearly more predictable using the Workshop Scale in Indianapolis than in Chicago. The rehabilitation professional can then attempt to identify the factors that may have accounted for the difference, such as economic conditions or differences among the sample groups. But the question remains: "How good is a coefficient of 0.43?" (Bolton, 1979).

An answer may be obtained by asking, "What is the use of a particular measurement?" Is the measurement being used for prediction (i.e., employment), for selection of clients, or to support the validity of the instrument? Bolton (1979) believed, however, that a validity coefficient of 0.43 is about average, and seldom do coefficients exceed 0.60.

Validity concerns are also important when the rehabilitation professional refers a client to an evaluation resource or agency to determine vocational potential. Questions pertaining to validity include the following:

1. Does the vocational evaluation program have competently trained personnel?

2. Are there clearly specified objectives to the assessment program, and do they have the particular resources to accomplish the vocational evaluation?

3. Can my client, despite physical and emotional limitations, meet the demands of the particular vocational evaluation experience?

Thoughtful consideration of these questions can enhance the credibility of the assessment phase of the rehabilitation process.

RELIABILITY

Reliability refers to the dependability, consistency, and precision of an assessment procedure. A reliable procedure is one that produces similar results when repeated. An assessment task is reliable when clients who are involved in the evaluation process receive the same or similar score results if the evaluation measures are repeated.

Reliability is usually expressed by the coefficient r. It is a convenient statistical index for estimating indices of the relationship between distributions of test scores when a test (or some equivalent form) is administered to a single representative sample of subjects or clients on two or more occasions. The coefficient is expressed as a ratio, of which both numbers range from zero to one, and represents the degree to which a group's test scores fluctuate from test to retest. If test scores are reliable, the test–retest correlation coefficient should be high. For example, high scores on one occasion should be matched by high scores on a second, and low scores should relate to low scores. The following is an identification of some correlation coefficients:

0.80 to 1.00   Very high correlation
0.60 to 0.79   Substantial correlation
0.40 to 0.59   Moderate correlation
0.20 to 0.39   Little correlation
0.01 to 0.19   Practically no correlation

There are three traditional ways of estimating this coefficient:

1. *Test–retest.* The test or other assessment procedure is readministered to the same people after a 1- or 2-week interval. The scores on the first administration are correlated with the scores on the second administration, and a correlation coefficient is obtained.

2. *Alternate or parallel forms.* Although not employed as frequently as the test–retest method, the use of two or more parallel forms of the same assessment instrument can provide the best estimate of reliability. These parallel forms are administered to the same subjects within a 1- to 2-week interval.

3. *Split-half.* In this approach, the items within a written test, for example, are assigned arbitrarily to two forms. For example, even-numbered items may constitute one set and odd-numbered the other set. Yet, item pairs or test-halves must be equal in terms of difficulty and content, and individuals taking the particular measure must have the opportunity to complete the entire test. Then, each client receives two scores on the same instrument, and the two sets of scores are intercorrelated. Both halves, of course, are administered at the same time.

Unfortunately, the reliability data provided for most tests are incomplete (Aiken, 1997; Shertzer & Linden, 1979). Both the labor required and the cost involved prohibit the evaluation of the reliability of any measure for all people on whom the measure may be used. Rehabilitation professionals are then faced with the problem of searching among reliability data provided for a particular test or another appraisal measure in order to find the population that corresponds as closely as possible to the clients with whom they intend to work.

A question frequently raised is, "What constitutes practical, acceptable reliability?" The answer depends on the type of measurement instrument used (i.e., intelligence, personality, aptitude, or interest), the purpose for using the instrument, and the degree of accepted reliability. Different types of published tests show different ranges of reliability. Personality inventories, for example, tend to be less reliable than achievement tests. Importantly, the purpose of using a measurement instrument influences what is considered an acceptable level of reliability. If an instrument is used to make diagnostic decisions, such as the determination of the level of academic training at which the client should begin, then the test should have a reliability coefficient from 0.80 to 1.00.

Inherent in the reliability of assessment approaches, however, is the possibility of *error variance*. This can relate to random fluctuations in the behavior of the individual when responding to the measurement procedure, situational variables, or random flaws in the test itself (Shertzer & Linden, 1979). Client characteristics and behaviors that can influence reliability include fatigue, health, motivation, understanding the mechanism of testing, the ability to comprehend test instructions, overall level of ability, and emotional strains. Situational variables refer to external conditions of heat, light, ventilation; freedom from distractions; and clarity of instructions. Factors in the test itself that can influence reliability are the possible ambiguity of test items, length of the test, and level of difficulty. (The test may be so difficult for the less adept clients that their scores will be influenced unduly by guessing. Consequently, the reliability will be lowered.)

To enhance the reliability of the assessment situation, the rehabilitation professional should explore not only the clients' history in taking tests or other evaluation procedures, but also (a) their motivation for the vocational assessment process; (b) any emotional pressure they might be experiencing; (c) the possible effects of their disability on test-taking performance; and (d) the appropriateness of the difficulty level of assessment tasks in relation to the clients' current capabilities. Furthermore, the rehabilitation professional should be familiar with the environment in which the vocational assessment will take place. The situational variables mentioned previously can have a decided effect on a client's performance.

Reliability issues are also important when tests are considered for persons who have severe disabilities. Such factors as test instructions, item content and format, and methods for answering the test items are designed to make a particular test useful for a specific population. When a different population with different characteristics is introduced, the test procedures might have to be changed.

Enright, Conyers, & Szymanski (1996) identified the most common test modifications, such as administration in oral, large-print, or Braille format; individualized versus group administration; provision of extra time; use of an interpreter; use of word processors or nonwritten methods to record responses; and use of adjustable desks to accommodate wheelchairs.

Salvia and Ysseldyke (1995) conceptualized testing accommodations and adaptations in terms of presentation and response formats, as well as the setting and timing of the assessment measure. They suggest examples of accommodations or adaptations, such as in presentation using large-print editions of tests, oral reading of directions, and the use of magnifying equipment; and in the response format using a template typewriter or computer for responding and giving a response in sign language. The setting of a test could be modified to a small group or taking the test at home, and timing could be adapted to include more breaks during testing, if appropriate, or extending the testing sessions over several days.

Many of these accommodations were explained further in Chapter 2. Vocational evaluators should be aware, however, of the responsibilities for users of standardized tests (Cottone & Tarvydas, 1998). These standards state that evaluators should seek the expertise of professionals experienced with disability issues when considering test modification. This preparation is necessary because evaluators need to familiarize themselves with alternative test forms and special norms, and to report any modifications when drawing conclusions (Enright et al., 1996). Because modified tests raise several complex issues, clients with disabilities undergoing vocational assessment should learn as much as possible about the specific evaluation measures. It is important that these clients receive, as appropriately as possible, individualized guidance before taking any standardized test. When adapting or modifying tests or evaluation measures, the rehabilitation professional must be very careful, however, not to make changes that can alter the nature of the task.

Another area of test modification that must be carefully considered is individual or group administration.

Individual or Group Administration

Tests are often administered in group sessions, and many persons seem to perform better with this format. People with severe disabilities can also experience vocational evaluation with small groups, such as three or four persons. In this case, the test needs to be appropriate for each person in the group. A test should be individually administered when a client is extremely anxious or fearful of the testing situation or has a severe sensory impairment or motor disability that requires the adaptation of testing procedures. The reasons for individual test administration include the absence of a convenient and practical way to use a group administration; the desire not to interfere with others in a group taking a test; and further consideration for clients with a handicap, such as wanting to reduce their anxiety over the test (Sherman & Robinson, 1982). For example, the use of a Braille version of an assessment procedure that is used for blind clients should be individually administered.

When considering individual administration over group test-taking, the rehabilitation professional should be cautious of the interaction effect between himself or herself and the client. Such interaction might negatively influence the client's assessment experience. For example, the professional may be uncomfortable with a particular disability or inexperienced in the administration of a specific measure. These problems can cause him or her to become irritated or impatient, which, in turn, may deflate the test score of the disabled client.

There are instances, of course, in which a handicapping condition has almost no effect on test performance, and consequently, modifications are not needed. Furthermore, some modifications will have no effect on the test results. Yet, very severe disabling conditions can have a great impact on test performance, and their influence on test results can be considerable. Generally, when a disability imposes a language obstacle; interferes with the understanding of test items, problems, or materials; or prevents a person from making the responses required for indicating test answers (such as using a pencil or marking responses on answer sheets), then the evaluation measure falls considerably short of evaluating the factors it is intended to assess. Also, many people with a disability must take drugs that are antispasmodic, anxiety-reducing, or anticonvulsant. Many of these medications can easily lower the credibility of the assessment results. The rehabilitation professional should match the evaluation procedure to the particular limitations of the disability that affect assessment performance.

Consequently, when considering the use of different tests or evaluation procedures with persons with a disability, the rehabilitation practitioner should review the purpose, format, reading level, and length of a particular test. Also, the manual of instructions should be examined to determine whether it contains special information for persons with a disability. An affirmative answer to such questions as, "Has the assessment procedure been normed with a population of those with a disability?" and "Has it been used successfully with various disability groups?" can considerably enhance the value of assessment results.

As stated earlier in this chapter, the application of traditional assessment measures to those with severe disabilities presents problems because of technical limitations. As a result of evaluation, persons with disabilities seek advice regarding their future employment and career. To provide appropriate guidance in this important area, rehabilitation professionals should be aware that there are also cultural and gender considerations that influence the assessment process. Parker and Schaller (1996) explained that these factors include "performance motivation, response style, level of acculturation, inappropriate norms, and gender restrictiveness" (p. 135). Individuals from certain ethnic backgrounds, for example, may be uncomfortable with disclosing information. Performance on language-based measures, moreover, may be influenced by the level of acculturation of the test-taker. Also, the evaluator should ensure that the assessment process does not reinforce the existing segregation of men and women into traditional male and female occupations. To prevent many of these problems, the rehabilitation professional should explore with the test-taker—before beginning the actual assessment process—the person's level of acculturation and his or her past experience with testing. Such an exploration can alert the evaluator to specific, client needs and help the professional to become more sensitive to cultural characteristics (Parker & Schaller, 1996).

Interpreting Test Scores

When reading assessment reports from an evaluation resource or explaining test scores to a client, the rehabilitation professional should understand how to interpret various types of test scores. Raw scores derived from psychological tests and inventories are converted to some form of standard score that indicates a relative position in a distribution of scores obtained by the norm group. Norms are the bridge for converting raw scores into standard scores and percentiles. Test norms, usually found in the particular test manual, enable the rehabilitation practitioner to compare a client's performance to an appropriate reference group. Comparison must frequently be made to obtain specific information for predicting a client's performance level in various educational and vocational areas.

Some examples of scores that appear in client evaluation reports are as follows:

1. *Stanine scores*—Range from 1 to 9.

2. *T scores*—Transformed standard scores with a mean of 50 and a standard deviation (*SD*) of 10.

3. *Percentiles*—Not to be confused with percentage scores; express the proportion of the group that falls below the score obtained by the client. For example, a percentile rank of 55 means that 54 out of 100 of the scores in the normative sample were lower than the client's.

Figure 5.1 shows the relationships among different types of test scores in a normal distribution. It identifies, for example, that a *T* score of 60 is one *SD* unit above the mean, corresponds to a stanine score of 7, and is approximately equivalent to the 84th percentile. The figure is a useful guide when interpreting test scores, especially when explaining *T* scores and stanine scores in terms of the corresponding percentile score. Frequently, percentiles are more readily understood by clients.

It is important for the evaluator to be aware that any test or assessment modifications can affect the results, making the test interpretation problematic. Scores may reflect the effects of a modification. Certain types of modifications may actually alter the constructs the tests were developed to measure (Enright et al., 1996).

Critical Analysis of Assessment Approaches

Though it is possible for the rehabilitation professional to rely mainly on the opinions expressed in published reviews or manuals of a specific assessment approach, the evaluator should also conduct a personal review of the particular test or assessment approach to make a decision on its applicability to a designated client with a disability. The following criteria can provide some guidelines to the evaluator for making judgments on the useability of an assessment approach for those persons with a disability.

Critical Analysis of an Assessment Approach

1. Clarity of purpose and recommended use.

2. Dimensions that the assessment approach purports to measure.

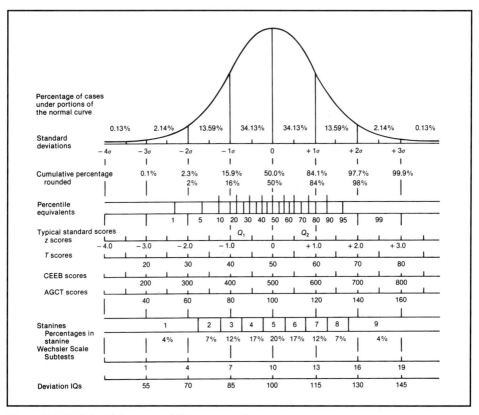

Figure 5.1. Relationships among different types of test scores.

3. Availability of particular test forms. If the forms are not essentially the same, major differences should be mentioned.

4. Clarity of administration (e.g., total time to complete the test). If parts of the test are timed separately, how many starting points are necessary? Do the directions appear easy, both for the administrator and the test taker?

5. Norm groups. How many subjects were involved? Are they representative and appropriate for your setting? Are there norms for each group with whom you might wish to compare a person's score?

6. Interpretation of scores. How are the scores expressed?

7. What criteria were used for item selection?

8. Item Analysis. Was an item analysis done to determine item discrimination and difficulty?

9. Method of validation. Validity as determined by the author and others.

10. Reliability. How was reliability determined? Is it adequate for using the instrument with confidence?

11. Test characteristics. In your opinion, what are the desirable and distinguishing characteristics of the tests?

12. Test problems. In your opinion, what are the problems you see in the test?

CHAPTER 5 CONCLUSION

When a client attempts to carry out a task during rehabilitation assessment, whether a paper-and-pencil test, work sample, or job tryout situation, his or her performance will be a complex function of several elements. These elements are the client's (a) capacity to carry out the task, (b) effort level, and (c) appropriate direction of efforts. With clients with a disability, the factor of capacity must be cautiously measured. This factor must take into account the issues of appropriate norms, the testing environment, and the possible mental and physical limitations of the client. Motivation and energy present particular concerns because there are no specialized techniques to measure them. A careful exploration of the client's capacity, motivation, and energy can lead to more accurate predictions in rehabilitation assessment.

Prediction is an integral part of rehabilitation evaluation. It involves finding out what the client can do. His or her capacities can be evaluated by many approaches, assuming that the rehabilitation professional is aware of validity and reliability issues. However, evaluating available drive and energy resources, as well as the appropriateness of the direction in which that energy is applied, calls for assessment strategies that go beyond psychometric measures. Among many options, situational assessment embraces a variety of evaluation paths and approaches. These assessment methods are explained in the following chapters.

 CASE STUDY: BEN

Ben plans on developing a situational assessment tool—more specifically, an observational measure to assess the behavioral characteristics of clients who are learning clerical skills in order to compete for entry-level positions that require basic office-related tasks. The men and women Ben is testing are between the ages of 26 and 38, are from different ethnic backgrounds, have been diagnosed with different mental illnesses, and are receiving some type of medication. Despite these limitations, the professional referring these individuals to the assessment centers believes that all of these clients are employable. They all have successful independent living skills, appropriate medication, and a high school diploma, and some have completed 2 years of college. There has not been a measure developed to assess whether clients such as these have the appropriate behaviors to work in an office setting.

 ## Chapter 5 Case Study Questions

DIRECTIONS: Considering the information provided on the critical analysis of an assessment approach, and the information explained in the chapter, please answer the following question:

> 1. What guidelines should Ben follow as he develops this observational measure?

Interest Assessment in Rehabilitation

In rehabilitation assessment, the exploration of a client's interests frequently becomes the beginning focus for both vocational evaluation and planning. An awareness of the client's interests is helpful in identifying and documenting a vocational goal and intermediate objectives to arrive at that goal. Interest exploration can provide a major focus for much of assessment. If understanding the client's interests is achieved during the initial interview, the rehabilitation professional can begin to delineate (a) the objectives of assessment; (b) the identification of needed services; and (c) the possibilities of appropriate outcomes for the client.

Interest exploration can also stimulate counseling by suggesting occupations that had not been previously considered by the client or rehabilitation professional. In other words, a comprehensive interest exploration for the client can increase considerably the person's employment options. In order to assist the professional in using interest assessment effectively, this chapter describes the types of client interests, the issues in interest exploration, and the measurement of interests. The chapter includes a specialized approach to interest assessment and discusses unique concerns in interpreting interest measures.

WHAT ARE THE CLIENT'S INTERESTS?

The term *interest* can be used to mean degree of interest, strength of motivation and drive, or need (Shertzer & Linden, 1979). Super (1949) identified three types of interests:

1. *Expressed interest.* The verbal statement of liking for any stimulus such as an object, activity, task, or occupation.

2. *Manifest interest.* The evidence of participation in an activity, occupation, or task that can be observed by others.

3. *Tested interest.* Interests measured by such objective approaches as free-association measures.

Salomone (1996) believed that "counselors may be inclined to rely more on the results of inventoried than on expressed or manifest interests" (p. 379). When predicting a future occupational choice, early research favors the verbal expression of interest or aspiration (Salomone, 1996). However, later research suggests that interest inventories are still the most sought-after and effective intervention strategies (Spokane, 1991). When assisting clients for interest assessment, perhaps rehabilitation professionals will need to explore the implications of clients' verbal statements of preference (expressed interests) and the results of both standardized and nonstandardized interest inventories.

Holland (1959) expanded the notion of interests when he stated that people project their views of themselves and the world of work onto occupational titles. He believed that interests reflect personality and that a career choice depends on a person's orientation to the environment. Holland identified six occupational environments: realistic, investigative, social, conventional, enterprising, and artistic. Each orientation expresses a somewhat distinctive lifestyle, which is characterized by an individual's preference for certain values, interests, interpersonal skills, and ways to deal with daily problems. A person's major lifestyle determines his or her main direction of occupational choice.

ISSUES IN INTEREST ASSESSMENT

Abilities Versus Interests

One of the most important generalizations in several decades of research is that interest assessment measures the direction rather than the strength of a person's interests. However, many persons show large discrepancies between interest and achievement. Interests and abilities are not highly correlated (Sundberg, 1977). A client may have a high degree of ability to do something but not be interested in it. Interests identify a domain of preference, and abilities point to the potential level of skill or attainment. Yet, abilities and interests interact. A person's interest in a certain occupational area can often motivate him or her to develop skills to become proficient in that line of work.

Vocational Aspiration Versus Realism

Frequently, the interests that are identified by paper-and-pencil inventories conflict with a client's verbalized interests, or clients express an interest in an area in which they have no measured aptitude or ability. It is not unusual for a client to "fix" on one vocational objective. This "locking in" might indicate parental, family, or other environmental influences. Various approaches can be used to resolve this discrepancy, including the identification and analysis of different levels of jobs in the client's interest area. In service-related occupations, for instance, there are differences both in the education and time of training required for the jobs of physician and policeman. Both occupations serve people and require a client's commitment to and interest in other persons. A description of the duties involved in the performance and training required in each employment area may assist clients in realigning their own career or job expectations.

Selection of Interest Measures

The "choice of interest" inventories should be based on the kind of information provided and not simply on availability, low cost, or time required for administration. Hood and Johnson (1997) offer many guidelines for the selection of the type of interest inventory—namely, whether the evaluator should choose a more lengthy measure, or whether the item content is the most appropriate for the client's expressed vocational goals. Several of these guidelines are the following:

1. The evaluator should determine how motivated the person with a disability is to participate in the assessment process. A clear understanding and acceptance of the purpose for testing, and an expression of an interest in the results beforehand, will facilitate an individual's motivation.

2. For clients who wish to make fine distinctions within a general occupational area—for example, inhalation therapist and physical therapist—many interest inventories are of limited value. Before a decision is made, interest inventories must be supplemented with other information about the person and the situation, such as abilities, values, previous work experiences, and job availability.

3. For those clients with significant emotional problems, interest inventories may not be the most appropriate measures. A reason for this is that these clients tend to make negative responses and endorse more passive interests than do people who are not emotionally disturbed. Before interest assessment can begin, the emotional issues should be addressed.

4. The evaluator should identify how long it has been since the client participated in formal interest assessment. For persons under age 20, interests are more likely to change, though adults who are experiencing an eventful life transition might begin to express a latent interest that has never been revealed by measurement. Hood and Johnson (1997) believe that evaluators should consider readministering an interest inventory if it has been longer than 6 months since the client last completed one.

Interest Inventories with Minority Clients

There are particular concerns to address when using interest measures with clients who have a disability and who represent an ethnic minority. The client's socialization and acculturation within a minority culture can affect career choices. The minority client may frequently embrace values that differ from those of the dominant culture. The family, for example, may be valued more highly than one's career. Asian American and Latino women may face pressures toward more traditionally feminine career directions. Because many persons from different, ethnic cultures may lack role models during the formative years of elementary and high school, interest assessment may not actually identify the range of possible career choices.

The usefulness of a particular inventory for a given minority population, consequently, must be questioned. Since a number of the most frequently used inventories organize interests around Holland's hexagonal model, the evaluator should explore whether the six-factor structure remains accurate and meaningful across cultures (Prince, Vemura, Chao, & Gonzales, 1992). Also, interest inventories that are normed on the dominant culture provoke necessary questions for helping professionals whose clients may not identify themselves with that dominant group. Prince et al. offered the following suggestions for using interest measures for those clients representing a minority culture:

A. If the client's primary language is not English, the evaluator should explore administering a version of the inventory that corresponds to the person's language.

B. The client's test-taking attitude and response style need to be explored. Clients from different minority backgrounds may have certain expectations in mind when responding to an inventory. A minority client with a disability, for example, may not wish to endorse interests that reflect a separation from one's parents.

C. When interpreting interest test results, the evaluator should be sensitive to the client's response, a response that may reflect cultural values and reinforce cultural stereotypes. It is also possible that the client may have a restricted range of interests. The helping professional, consequently, should encourage the client to broaden one's career considerations to read beyond those reflected by the measured interests.

Because of these multicultural issues that may inhibit a comprehensive exploration of the client's interests when using standardized inventories, it can be more appropriate to place more emphasis on the interview as an effective approach for the identification of interests. A thorough discussion of the client's likes and dislikes that follows the steps outlined later in this chapter (see section titled "A Specialized Approach to Interest Assessment") may elicit more useful and reliable information.

THE MEASUREMENT OF INTERESTS

Various approaches for measuring interest include self-estimation, interviews, checklists, questionnaires, and tests, known as inventories. Interest inventories were initially developed in the mid-1920s as "a facilitative response to an established premise which linked occupational interest with job satisfaction" (Phillips, 1978, p. 10). They were developed to assess individual areas of interest and compare subsequent subjective interest scores with the measured interest of successful professionals in a wide variety of occupations. Inventories have been used principally in vocational and education guidance (Shertzer & Linden, 1979). The inventory is the result of its interaction with the individual and cannot be considered separately in any way.

These measures attempt to quantify interests by providing a score to describe a client's feelings of like or dislike. They elaborate acceptance–rejection propositions. Individuals are asked to provide answers such as *most liked* and *least liked* to the content of items, which forces them to make a choice. Their choices are self-estimates of their feelings, emotions, and attitudes toward those items. Their responses yield scores of general interest from which, directly or by comparison, interest in particular occupations or fields of activity can be estimated. Shertzer and Linden (1979) believed that this approach assumes that each group of people "under investigation have a pattern of interest in common that is different from that of some other group" (p. 178).

If interest measures are used properly, they can be a helpful gauge for evaluating future job satisfaction. However, they should be used to complement other methods of assessment, and the test items should be carefully checked for age- and disability-related appropriateness. Interest evaluations may not be appropriate for every client (Phillips, 1978). A person who has incurred a disabling on-the-job injury may be quite satisfied with previous employment but seek another occupation in a similar interest area. This individual may not feel a need for occupational interest assessment.

When exploring a client's interest areas, the rehabilitation professional should associate this information with results from aptitude tests, a review of previous work experience, knowledge gained from the assessment interview, and medical reports. Harmony must be achieved between the person with a disability's interests and his or her capabilities. For example, if a client shows a dominant interest and willingness to work in data-related occupations, rather than people- or idea-related careers, then information is needed about the person's clerical skill; perceptual speed and accuracy; numerical computation; and, in many instances, spatial relations and eye, hand, and finger coordination abilities. In contrast, if interest evaluation results indicate a very strong preference for idea-related occupations, then information should be obtained about the individual with a disability's aptitudes in reading comprehension, language usage, math reasoning, and artistic and creative endeavors.

Interest inventories can be classified in a variety of ways, such as age or occupational level, or by type of item. Two types of interest scales predominate. One type measures the strength of a person's interests in broad fields of activity, such as outdoors, health-related activities, or technology. These scales are usually described as general or basic scales. They refer to one type of activity. The other type of scale assesses the similarity of a person's interest patterns to those of people in specific occupations. These scales are called occupational scales and are heterogeneous in terms of item content. Scales of this type are based on those items that differentiate between the interests of people in an occupation and people in general.

To facilitate interest exploration, the rehabilitation professional should be aware of the advantages of computer scoring. Interest measures, such as the *Strong Interest Inventory* (Strong, Hansen, & Campbell, 1994) and the *Career Assessment Inventory–Enhanced Version* (Johansson, 1986), have forms that can be completed, mailed to the nearest computer scoring service, and returned within 10 days. The computer processing provides client profiles that can be easily read and interpreted. They may include narrative-style interpretations, which individualize the interest scores and explain in detail the meaning, significance, and limitations of interest measurement (Phillips, 1978).

The following are some recommended interest measures that can be used to generate useful information in rehabilitation assessment. They are grouped into two categories: (a) inventories appropriate for clients with low reading skills and (b) measures for persons with a higher reading capability.

Tests Appropriate for Persons with Low Reading Skills

Wide Range Interest–Opinion Test (WRIOT)

According to the test manual, the WRIOT (Jastak & Jastak, 1987) was designed to measure "as many areas and levels of human activity as possible." The interest inventory contains items that represent jobs ranging from unskilled through the highest levels of technical, managerial, and professional training. It was also developed to measure interests that appeal to a wide variety of groups, from children to adults with disadvantages or mental retardation. The inventory contains 18 separate cluster descriptions of occupational areas (e.g., Art, Drama, Office Work, Personal Service, Physical Science, and Machine Operation) and seven work attitudes (e.g., Risk Ambition, Agreement, and Interest Spread).

The WRIOT contains 150 three-choice items, containing three clear black-and-white line illustrations of men and women of various racial groups engaged in different job activities. The drawings are contained in a spiral-bound 5½" by 8½" inch booklet. There is one item per page. Respondents use a separate answer sheet to select the job they would most like to do and the job they would least like to do.

There is no time limit; the average administration time is 50 to 60 minutes in groups of 30 to 40, and 40 minutes if administered individually. No reading is required for the test items. However, the client must be able to read *least* and *most*; the letters A, B, and C; and item numbers, all of which appear on the answer sheet and in the test booklet. Duplicate instructions are presented on a separate answer sheet, which is well designed and easy to use. If the test is administered individually, the professional records the response.

The manual contains special instructions for individual administration to "severely mentally or physically disabled persons." The client first identifies the best liked illustration by pointing to or naming it and then picks out the least liked illustration in the same way. The professional records each response on the answer sheet. No norms or special interpretation information are available for those with a handicap.

The WRIOT can be scored using computer software. The software runs on Apple II+ or Apple IIe computers. A software demo set is available to demonstrate how the WRIOT scoring software operates.

In its present form, this test is not recommended for persons who are blind, although the picture titles can be read to these individuals. Persons who are deaf should be able to take the WRIOT with little or no change in test materials, although the method of giving instructions would have to be changed.

The WRIOT is available from Wide Range, Inc., Wilmington, DE, 800-221-9728.

Geist Picture Interest Inventory–Revised

This measure (Geist, 1988) quantitatively assesses 11 male and 12 female general interest areas: persuasive, clerical, mechanical, musical, scientific, outdoor, literary, computational, artistic, social service, dramatic, and personnel service. The *Geist* can facilitate interest exploration with individuals with verbal disabilities. The test booklet contains 44 triads of drawings, representing major vocations and avocations, with 130 drawings in all. Only occupations that are recognizable in most parts of the United States are included.

With most clients, the *Geist* is self-administering. It can be used with individuals or groups and has no time limit. When a client has a severe reading disability, the directions and questions under the pictures are read aloud to the client, who circles the drawings of his or her choice. The test can be scored by the examiner, and the manual contains easily understood directions. The *Geist* also contains a motivation questionnaire for both males and females. This booklet includes the motivational analysis of occupational choices, which in turn suggests reasons or motivations behind each choice of drawings.

The *Geist Picture Interest Inventory–Revised* is available from Western Psychological Services, 12031 Wilshire Blvd., Los Angeles, CA, 90025, 800-222-2670.

Reading-Free Vocational Interest Inventory–Revised (R-FVII–Revised)

This measure, which was revised in 1988, is a nonreading vocational preference test for use with those 13 years and above who have mental retardation, a learning disability, or other disadvantage. The inventory consists of pictorial depictions of occupations in a forced choice format presented in 55 triads in a nonreusable booklet. All items in the measure depict the type of occupations in which clients who have mental retardation, a learning disability, or disadvantage have traditionally been productive and proficient (Becker, 1988). These occupations include automotive, building trades, clerical, animal care, food service, patient care, horticulture, housekeeping, personal service, laundry service, and materials handling. The R-FVII–Revised is suitable for both individual and group administration, and has no time limits (publisher's catalog indicates that the test takes about 20 minutes to administer). The inventory has been normed on a nation-wide basis to samples of males and females, grades 7 through 12, who are educable men-tally retarded (EMR), learning disabled (LD), and trainable mentally retarded (TMR). These sample groups generally consisted of approximately 1,000 individuals (Siefker, 1996).

Though the client must be able to visually perceive line drawings and mark responses with a paper and pencil, no reading is required. This inventory can be quite useful for a beginning interest exploration after a determination of employability has been made.

The R-FVII–Revised is available from the Psychological Corporation, 555 Academic Court, San Antonio, TX, 78204, 800-211-8378.

Tests More Appropriate for Those with Higher Reading Ability

Gordon Occupational Check List II (GOCL-II)

This interest inventory (Gordon, 1981) was designed for use with individuals who are not college-bound but who are ready to discuss vocational plans. As such, it is primar-ily a vocational counseling tool rather than a true interest survey. Scores are reported in sections titled Business, Outdoor, Arts, Technology, and Services, and the results are based on the frequency that individuals underline and circle activities they would like to do full-time and jobs they would especially like, respectively. This test enables the rehabilitation professional to obtain an overview of the client's areas of expressed inter-est as well as specific occupational preferences. The inventory consists of 240 activities that are performed in many different kinds of jobs.

The GOCL-II is administered in group or individual sessions and is hand-scored. It requires a sixth-grade reading level. The test is typically finished in 20 to 25 minutes. Although not suitable for persons who are blind, it can be taken by persons who are deaf and who have the requisite reading skills.

The *Gordon Occupational Check List II* is available from the Psychological Corpo-ration, 555 Academic Court, San Antonio, TX, 78204, 800-211-8378.

Strong Interest Inventory (SII)

The *Strong* (Strong, Hansen, & Campbell, 1994) is one of the oldest and most scien-tifically developed interest surveys. The inventory is easy to administer, requires at least a sixth-grade reading level, and requires a computer for scoring. Because the test authors have integrated Holland's (1959) theory of career development with the empirical approach traditionally used in scoring and interpreting the *Strong*, clients receive scores displayed on scales based on the Holland typology. The Holland theme scale contributes a conceptual framework within which to organize and interpret the data reported on the total *Strong* profile for both men and women.

There are 25 basic Occupational Scales in the *Strong*. Four new Personal Style scales have been added to the profile sheet of the 1984 edition, such as work style, learning environment, leadership style, and risk taking and adventure. This inventory produces scores on five sets of scales including the Administrative Indexes, General Occupational Theme Scales, Basic Interest Scales, Occupational Scales, and Personal Style Scales. In its current form, the *Strong* consists of 317 items and can be completed in 25 to 35 minutes (Hood & Johnson, 1997). This test is mainly applicable for use with those persons who are oriented toward professional, semiprofessional, or managerial occupations that attract college graduates. For others, the relevance of the instrument is questionable. Also, the interpretations of the *Strong* should be made only by persons who have had supervised experience in evaluating clients' objective interests.

The *Strong* is available from National Computer Systems, Inc., 4401 West 76th St., Minneapolis, MN, 55435, 612-830-7600 or 800-538-9547.

Kuder Occupational Interest Survey (Form DD)

In a forced choice, triad format, this inventory (Kuder, 1960) includes such occupational areas as outdoors, mechanical, computational, scientific, persuasive, artistic, literary, musical, social service, and clerical. Seven personal-oriented areas are also included: Group Activity, Stable Situations, Working with Ideas, Avoiding Conflict, Directing Others, Working Independently, and Acting Spontaneously. This measure employs a forced-choice, three-item response format. Clients select the item they prefer or would like most, and the one they least prefer.

The test is administered easily; its directions are explicit and may be understood readily. No time limit is specified, and most clients can complete the form in approximately 30 minutes. Scores are given on a profile covering 10 occupational areas. At least a sixth-grade reading level is required, and the inventory can be applicable for persons who are college-bound, or seek shorter training. The inventory can be used with deaf clients if their reading level is adequate. Because the test is not timed, it can be orally administered to clients who are blind.

The *Kuder Occupational Interest Survey (Form DD)* is available from Science Research Associates, Inc., 259 East Erie St., Chicago, IL, 60611, 312-984-7000.

The Self-Directed Search (SDS)

The result of more than 20 years of research by Holland (1959), the SDS (Holland, 1994) is a self-administered, self-scored, and self-interpreted vocational counseling tool. This measure has two main purposes: (a) to provide a vocational counseling experience for people who do not have access to professional counselors or who cannot afford their services and (b) to multiply the number of people a counselor can serve. Cutts (1977) explained that persons who have vocational questions such as, "What career shall I follow? Is my tentative choice reasonable?" or "What alternatives do I have in career choice?" and adults who are wondering about their current job status should be aided by this inventory.

The SDS is considered self-interpreting, but the manual states that the counselor is expected to aid in the interpretation. Assistance may be needed in explaining the five profiles in the assessment booklet. Each contains the estimate, on each of the five scales, of a person's resemblance to each of the six personality types (i.e., Realistic, Investigative, Artistic, Social, Enterprising, or Conventional). Each type was briefly described, as follows, by Hood and Johnson (1997).

> *Realistic*—People who enjoy or do well in technical, physical, mechanical, or outdoor activities.
>
> *Conventional*—People with interest or skills in keeping records, organizing data, attending to detail, or following through on others' instructions.
>
> *Enterprising*—People with interests or skills in business, management, sales, public speaking, or leading others.
>
> *Social*—People interested or skilled in working with or helping others (e.g., teaching, counseling, or nursing).
>
> *Artistic*—People who like or do well in music, art, writing, drama, or other creative activities.
>
> *Investigative*—People with scientific, mathematical, analytical, or scholarly interests or skills.

Cutts (1977) stated that because the order of the six types is always the same, the five profiles should have the same general shape. The professional should be aware that the implications of a well-defined, highly differentiated profile (showing high scores in some areas and low in others) versus a flat profile, which is undifferentiated, reflect client confusion and present a variety of client problems and counselor questions.

The SDS scales have a moderate degree of internal consistency. Samples of 2,000 to 6,000 first-year college students show a range from 0.67 to 0.94. Retest reliabilities show that the SDS summary codes have the highest degree of reliability as compared to the subscales that reflect a lower degree of reliability. Also, the item content and format reflect clear content validity. Items are stated in direct ways that require minimal interpretation and are related to the scale. Content is consistent with well-established vocational knowledge.

The SDS includes two booklets—an assessment booklet and an occupational classification booklet. To use this inventory, a client fills out the assessment booklet and obtains a three-letter occupational code. The code is then used to locate suitable occupations in the occupational classification booklet, "The Occupational Finder." Through a series of questions related to occupational daydreams, competencies, and preferences for activities and occupations, the assessment booklet provides an estimate of the client's interests in a number of occupational areas.

There is also a *Form E* of the SDS that was published in 1970 and is designed for students as young as the fourth grade, as well as for adults with limited reading skills. The directions use words that are known by 80% of fourth graders in the United States. The regular form of the test requires at least a sixth-grade reading level. Clients who have college or noncollege training in mind will find the SDS most useful. Clients can usually complete the SDS booklet in approximately 40 minutes.

The SDS can serve as a beginning measure for interest exploration, but it can be used periodically throughout a person's entire career. The SDS offers many alternative occupations.

The SDS is available from the Psychological Corporation, 555 Academic Court, San Antonio, TX, 78204, 800-211-8378.

Career Assessment Inventory–The Enhanced Version (CAI)

Developed to cover the vocational areas of occupations requiring less than a 4-year college degree, this inventory (Johansson, 1986) overlaps to some extent with the more "nonprofessional" occupations covered by the Kuder (1960) and Strong (Strong et al., 1994) tests (Johansson, 1976). The majority of items developed for the CAI were based on an understanding of job descriptions of various occupations and related activities detailed in the *Dictionary of Occupational Titles* (DOT) (U.S. Department of Labor, 1977) and the *Occupational Outlook Handbook* (U.S. Department of Labor, 1990). A determined effort was made to avoid items that would imply a career or interest that would be applicable more to one sex than the other. The professional reviews of the test items and the field-testing with sixth and eight graders provided the necessary data for the final wording of the CAI. The first 151 items are activity-type items, the next 43 relate to school subjects, and the remaining 101 include occupational titles.

Both versions of the CAI (i.e., regular and enhanced) are patterned after the *Strong Interest Inventory*. They both include the same types of scales: administrative indices, non-occupational scales, general theme scales, basic interest scales, and occupational scales. The CAI occupational scales have been coded according to Holland's classification system. The two systems produce similar results in most cases (Hood & Johnson, 1997).

The measure is written at a sixth-grade reading level and requires between 20 and 40 minutes to complete. The interpretive profile measures the client's interest on three separate scales:

> Scale 1—Gives a graphic representation of the way the client's individual orientation to work relates to six basic occupational themes: realistic, artistic, conventional, enterprising, social, and investigative.

Scale 2—Reveals the strength or weakness of the client's interest in approximately 23 academic areas such as mathematics, social science, and teaching.

Scale 3—Compares the client's interest with people already employed in 75 occupations on the CAI.

Reliability studies indicated that test and retest scores for the various samples showed very stable patterns for the groups. Also, the concurrent validity data presented for both the student samples and adult samples were of the same magnitude as data evidenced by similar scales on the *Strong Interest Inventory* (Strong et al., 1994) and the *Strong Vocational Interest Blanks* (Johansson, 1986).

There is an enhanced version of the CAI, written for the eighth-grade reading level, that focuses on careers requiring up to 4 years of college and includes many of the most rapidly growing professional occupations. This version consists of 370 items divided into three major categories, activities, school subjects, and occupations. Completion time is approximately 40 minutes. The scale scores provide information in such areas as the six general occupational themes and 25 basic interest scales, broken down into several specific areas of interest (i.e., animal service, mathematics, creative arts, community service, law and politics, and clerical service). A narrative report provides scale descriptions, score interpretations, and comparisons, and a profile report graphically presents scores on each scale.

This inventory is computer-scored, and the information obtained from the measure can be very useful to both the client and the professional for rehabilitation planning purposes. The CAI covers a wide range of occupations, and offers many suggestions for associations between the client's interest and particular occupations.

The CAI is available from National Computer Systems, Inc., P.O. Box 1416, Minneapolis, MN, 55440, 800-627-7271.

Interest Check List

Developed by the U.S. Department of Labor (1981), this inventory's primary purpose is to serve as an interviewing aid when the rehabilitation professional believes that further information on a client's interest is desired. There are 115 activities on the checklist, and they are divided into 23 job clusters. This inventory requires at least a sixth-grade reading level and 20 to 30 minutes to complete. The items and job categories were taken from the DOT and are related to occupations requiring limited post-secondary education. It can be hand-scored by the examiner, and the inventory is especially valuable in facilitating interest exploration with the client during the initial phase of the rehabilitation process.

Ohio Vocational Interest Survey–Second Edition (OVIS–II)

This measure was developed in 1981 to assist clients from Grade 7 through college, as well as adults with their vocational plans. This inventory has no time limit, though it usually requires about 45 minutes to administer. A microcomputer version for Apple II computers is also available. Hand-scorable documents are available, and machine scoring may be obtained through the Psychological Corporation. The OVIS–II is suitable for individual or group testing (Siefker, 1996).

This inventory has an acceptable reliability (from the .70s to the low .80s), and the norms were developed from a sample of occupations drawn from a pool of 2,700 occupations that represent 99% of the workforce. The appealing aspects of this measure include the wide range of persons for whom it is appropriate, the availability of both computer and hand scoring, and the test's similarity to the *Strong Interest Inventory* (Strong et al., 1994) and the *Career Assessment Inventory* (Johansson, 1986).

The test is available from the Psychological Corporation, 555 Academic Court, San Antonio, TX, 78204, 800-211-8378.

Career Decision-Making System Revised (CDM–R)

This inventory, developed by Harrington and O'Shea (1992), asks clients to rate themselves in terms of career fields, school subjects, school plans, job values, abilities, and interests. Each of the six Holland interest categories are represented by 20 of the 120 items. The measure has two levels (Grades 7 through 10 and high school students and adults), and clients score their own answer sheets by counting the number of responses in each category. The results are used to suggest career clusters that clients may wish to investigate (Hood & Johnson, 1997). The inventory promotes an exploration of values, abilities, interests, and training options.

The test is available from the American Guidance Service, 4201 Woodland Road, P.O. Box 99, Circle Pines, MN, 55014, 800-328-2560.

COUNSELING HELPS IN INTEREST EXPLORATION

Table 6.1 relates the usefulness of the different inventories that measure interests to varied levels of formal preparation required by occupations. Because interest exploration can facilitate vocational or life planning when it is begun early in the rehabilitation process, professionals find it helpful to structure this area of evaluation. The following guidelines are suggested when developing this assessment:

Interest Exploration with Clients Who Have at Least a Fifth-Grade Reading Ability

Step 1—To particularize interest, clients can take the *Interest Check List* or the *Ohio Vocational Interest Survey*.

Step 2—To particularize interest areas for occupations requiring preparation at least 3 years beyond high school, clients can take the SII (computer-scored), the SDS (hand-scored), or the CDM–R.

Or

To particularize interest areas for occupations requiring preparation not beyond high school or that require 2 years maximum training after high school, clients can take the CAI (computer-scored).

Interest Exploration with Clients Who Have Below a Fifth-Grade Reading Ability

Step 1—Interest Check List, but many of the items may have to be read aloud.

Step 2—Gordon Occupational Check List II (hand-scored), WRIOT (hand-scored), *Geist* (hand-scored), or R-FVII–Revised.

TABLE 6.1
Usefullness of Inventories for Occupational Preparation:
Formal Preparation Required by Occupation

Inventory	No high school degree	High school degree	2 years preparation beyond high school	3 or more years preparation beyond high school
Kuder (DD)	U	U	U	U
CAI	U	U	U	NU
WRIOT	U	U	LU	NU
Geist–R	U	U	LU	NU
Gordon Occupational Checklist (Gordon, 1981)	U	U	U	NU
SII	U	U	U	U
SDS	U	U	U	U
Interest Check List (U.S. Dept. of Labor, 1981)	U	U	U	NU
R-FVII–Rev.	U	U	LU	NU
OVIS–II	U	U	U	U
CDM–R	U	U	U	U

U = useful; LU = limited usefulness; NU = not useful.

Kuder (DD) = *Kuder Occupational Interest Survey (Form DD)*; CAI = *Career Assessment Inventory*; WRIOT = *Wide Range Interest–Opinion Test*; Geist–R = *Geist Picture Interest Inventory*; SII = *Strong Interest Inventory*; SDS = *Self-Directed Search*; R-FVII–Rev. = *Reading-Free Vocational Interest Inventory*; OVIS–II = *Ohio Vocational Interest Survey*; CDM–R = *Career Decision-Making System*.

Step 3—For all reading groups, identification of clients' interests are in Business sales and management (Enterprising); Business operations (Conventional); Technologies and trades (Realistic); Natural, social, and medical sciences (Investigative); Creative and applied arts (Artistic); or Social, health, and personal services (Social).

With a beginning knowledge of the client's interests in these job clusters (which relate to Holland's, 1959 typology), the rehabilitation professional can then consult resources that provide detailed descriptions of a wide variety of occupations. One volume that is particularly valuable is the *Guide to Occupational Exploration* (Harrington & O'Shea, 1984). The data in this publication are organized into 12 interest areas— 66 work groups and 348 subgroups. Each subgroup has its own six-digit unique code and title, taken from the DOT. Within each subgroup, related occupations are identified. For the 6 work groups, descriptions of kinds of job activities, work requirements, clues for relating individuals to the type of work, preparation for entry into jobs, and other pertinent items are included. One of the appendixes has information regarding how to organize career and occupational information resources. It contains techniques and procedures for cataloging and filing occupational information according to the structure in the *Guide to Occupational Exploration*.

When using the guide and when a client's assessment suggests interest in different work groups, each work group can be explored. This exploration determines whether the client still wants to consider each area and whether the training requirements are in harmony with the individual's capabilities. Subgroups that identify many occupations should be examined to assess whether one or more of them seems to suit the client's interests and qualifications better than the others.

When the exploration of all the relevant groups has been completed—with identification of possible occupations of particular interest—then the collected information is organized. This information can then be used, with other data and facts, for rehabilitation planning. The *Guide to Occupational Exploration* provides a convenient crossover from information about the person with a disability to potentially suitable fields of work or other areas of productivity.

A Specialized Approach to Interest Assessment

Within the past 15 years, more interest measures have been devised for nonprofessional occupations and for persons planning to enter the work force after high school. However, more effective assessment instruments for those who have physical and mental disabilities need to be designed. Other methods for interest exploration must also be used for those clients who have a very low reading ability or a very limited knowledge about jobs and activities. During the interview with a client, direct questions can be used to gain information about existing interest areas. This information may still be unreliable, superficial, and unrealistic. Such questions can elicit responses that are susceptible to a client's tendency to respond by giving socially approved answers. However, even apart from the difficulties of using direct questions, the interview can still be employed effectively to solicit information about a client's interests. Friel and Carkhuff (1974) devised a model to assist someone in identifying interests as well as expanding interest options. It involves understanding the client's total functioning in physical, emotional, and intellectual areas. This approach can be modified for use in an interview situation. It implies that the rehabilitation professional must become very active when assisting someone in exploring interest areas. The six steps to this approach are modified by the author for application to the interview.

Step 1. Assist the client in exploring interests by asking such questions as:

- From the jobs that you have had, what did you particularly like or dislike? For example, did you like working on your own, and was your supervisor was friendly to you?

- In these jobs, what did you feel you could do especially well?

- When you were in school, what subjects did you particularly like and dislike? Why?

- From the people that you know in your life, what jobs do they have that are of particular interest to you?

- When you watch television and see people doing various jobs, are there any that are of special interest to you?

- What do you enjoy doing in your spare time?

It is important for the rehabilitation professional to understand the reasons behind an identified interest. Is the interest caused by some external pressure (for example, what parents or friends told the client that he or she would like)? An added resource that can at least facilitate the client's exploration of interests is newspaper want ads, especially those in the Sunday edition. The professional can read these ads to the client and then encourage a response, or the client can carefully read them, check any openings that have an interest for him or her, and then discuss them with the rehabilitation professional.

Step 2. Assist the client in exploring his or her values by asking such questions as:

- When you were working, what do you feel was important to you?

- What is the reason that it was important to you? For example, was it important to work with your hands, or not to have close supervision, or you liked the particular job, or you knew it was something you could do well?

The goal in these questions is to develop an understanding of what a client means by a particular value.

Step 3. Categorize the information that has been generated about the client's values.

Friel and Carkhuff (1974) suggested organizing these values into the physical, emotional–interpersonal, and intellectual areas. For example:

Physical. Dressing well on the job, working in a comfortable office atmosphere

Emotional–interpersonal. Having job security, having people close by when working, interacting frequently with people

Intellectual. Liking the opportunity to make decisions

Step 4. Further categorize the information into:

People occupations. Includes the areas of service (nurse or social worker), education (teacher), business (salesperson), providing goods and services, and recreation (coach and artist)

Things occupations. Includes business (accountant or secretary), technology (providing mechanical services, e.g., mechanic or electronic technician), outdoors (forest ranger or landscaper), and science (developing research and methods, e.g., biologist)

Step 5. Now, help the client identify which of the interest categories best fits his or her values.

For example, if the client mentions that the most important work value to him or her is job security, then an interest area appropriate to that dominant value should be chosen. It could be helpful to the client to display his or her values in the physical, intellectual, and interest areas in one column and then match these values to the occupational information gathered under data and things. The specific occupations identified by the professional must be in harmony with the client's stated values. The more occupations that are suggested, the more extensive will be the client's own exploration.

Step 6. Finally, identify the educational and occupational requirements demanded of particular employment areas that are congruent with the client's values.

Some jobs require less than a high school diploma; others may require a high school diploma or its equivalent—namely, apprenticeship training after high school, 2 years of junior or community college, or 4 or more years of college. Clients should also decide how much education they want. The professional should find out the educational capability of the client from school records or previous paper-and-pencil testing. Of particular value during this interest exploration is the *Dictionary of Occupational Titles* (U.S.

Department of Labor, 1977). If the professional knows how to use this valuable resource, the number of occupational alternatives can be greatly expanded. Once a main interest area is identified and clients are aware that it is in harmony with their dominant values, then this book provides a large amount of information about the particular occupations relevant to this interest area.

Taking these six steps sequentially is often a lengthy exploration process, but it is a very legitimate use of the rehabilitation professional's time because it encourages the client's involvement in both interest exploration and rehabilitation programming. Most of the steps are designed to elicit the client's thoughts and feelings about past, present, and future career activities.

CHAPTER 6 CONCLUSION

When the client has completed the interest inventory, the evaluator should make sure that the client has answered a sufficient number of items. Also, providing the interest profile results to the client just before the interpretation session will assist this individual in understanding the information. This information may suggest what alternative courses of action are really feasible or satisfying for a client, and the effective use of the interview can further help to identify different paths to rehabilitation goals. But the questions remains: Which one of these possible alternatives does the client really wish to take or should take? This issue is discussed in the next chapter, "Interpreting Assessment Information."

 CASE STUDY: KENNETH

Kenneth, a 38-year-old married, former carpenter is referred to you as a post-traumatic brain injury case. Eighteen months prior to this referral he had been in a motorcycle accident and sustained head trauma (temporal–parietal skull fracture) and subsequent partial hearing loss. He is hesitant to use a hearing aid on that left side. During the initial session, Kenneth was seeking a "quick fix" for a number of residual effects of the accident, such as short-term memory loss, hearing loss, and back problems. He appears to be impatient with any delays in starting the assessment process. Neurological records indicate that he has limited cognitive impairment in the areas of abstract and numerical reasoning and comprehension, but the client states that he feels confident that these functions will gradually be fully restored. The evaluator wishes to begin the assessment process with interest exploration. The client has a high school diploma with additional courses in vocational schools to enhance his carpentry-related skills. Kenneth had been working for 12 years for a home building construction company, the last 4 years as a supervisor. But he firmly states that he would really like to enter another field because of his back and hearing diffi-culties, and "it is now time to do something else."

Chapter 6 Case Study Questions

DIRECTIONS: With the information from the case study, answer the following questions:

1. Identify your interest assessment approach, stating what approach you would pri-marily use to explore Kenneth's interests—the interview or paper-and-pencil measures?

2. Using the approach described in the last pages of this chapter, how would you help Kenneth to identify his main interests?

Intelligence Testing

An important area of rehabilitation assessment is the exploration of a client's capability to solve problems, adapt to new situations, and show competence when confronted with new learning demands. Competence itself is both ability-oriented, emphasizing positive coping skills, and situation-oriented, emphasizing a person's ability to function in environmental interactions (Sundberg, 1977). One of the approaches to measuring competence is the assessment of intelligence.

Intelligence tests represent a highly specialized field with a vast body of literature and research surrounding their use. Intelligent behavior is as much a function of drive and incentive as the more traditionally conceived components of intellectual ability, such as abstract and logical thinking, reasoning, judging, and retaining knowledge (Shertzer & Linden, 1979). Intelligence is not a single, unitary ability, but rather a composite of several functions. It is the global capacity of the individuals to act purposefully, think rationally, and deal effectively with the environment (Wechsler, 1981). Intelligence is a function of the total personality, and personality characteristics generally affect the direction and extent of the individuals' intellectual development. Affective life and cognitive life, although distinct, are inseparable (Shertzer & Linden, 1979).

No one has seen a thing called intelligence. Rather, intelligence is inferred from a sample of behaviors. These behaviors include discrimination, generalization, motor behavior, general information, vocabulary, induction, comprehension, detail recognition, analogies, abstract reasoning, and memory (Salvia & Ysseldyke, 1995). Intelligence can only denote practical problem-solving ability, verbal ability, and social competence, as well as the ability to adapt to life's changing demands (Tyler, 1984).

Precisely what intelligence tests measure has been the subject of dispute since their origin. Wechsler believed that they measure "the capacity of an individual to understand the world about him and his resourcefulness to cope with its challenges" (Shertzer & Linden, 1979, p. 123). However, no intelligence test available today measures innate ability (Shertzer & Linden, 1979; Tyler, 1984). Rather, such tests measure the extent to which an individual's innate potential has been modified or developed within his or her environment. Many factors other than intelligence (e.g., creativity, exploratory interests, economic supports, and environmental opportunities) may influence success in intelligence testing. Measured intelligence has been found to both reflect past schooling and predict future school success. The IQ score resulting from such tests could be viewed as "measured intelligence, not necessarily the adaptive intelligence used in everyday living" (Sundberg, 1977, p. 245). The concept of intelligence common to all intelligence tests, however, is the *ability to learn*.

Along with the ability to learn, another aspect of intelligence is *aptitude*. Although learning ability may be narrow or wide and specific or general in importance, intelligence is considered to have a wider scope. A reason for this is that intelligence includes a variety of closely related mental abilities that are most useful for predicting general achievement. Verbal and numerical abilities, which are essential in some degree to nearly all forms of achievement, have become the main ingredients of many intelligence tests. Verbal intelligence tests are most like achievement tests and, in that respect, are better suited for predictions of success at the next higher level of learning than for assessing the full range of trainability. Also, the great majority of intelligence tests include appraisal of the reasoning factor. These tests are especially useful for discerning the difference between past learning and present capacity. Intelligence testing, therefore, does not provide a comprehensive measure of all aspects of intelligence. Because the concept of intelligence is so complex, any test or assessment procedure attempting to measure all of its theoretical aspects would be too lengthy to be practical. What is measured is the client's performance on a series of tasks, and from this performance the amount of "intelligence" that a client possesses is inferred. Consequently, intelligence should be regarded as a descriptive, rather than explanatory, concept. It is an expression of an individual's ability at a given point in time in relation to age norms.

Because of the norm concept discussed in the previous chapter, the interpretation of intelligence test results in rehabilitation assessment must be done cautiously. Most intelligence tests do not include people with handicaps in their standardization sample. Unfortunately, IQ and intelligence have become so value-laden in society that persons are labeled on the basis of a small amount of evidence.

Is intelligence related to employment success? People tend, insofar as circumstances permit, to gravitate toward jobs in which they have the ability to compete successfully with others. In turn, having capabilities considerably in excess of those required by a job often causes dissatisfaction because of the lack of challenge and consequent loss of interest in the work. Correlation between intelligence test scores and job success may actually be an artifact, the product of their joint association with class status (McClelland, 1973). Although many employers select some employees who have gone to the "right" schools because they do better, intelligence does not necessarily make people proficient at their jobs. Tyler (1984) explains that "professional people average higher than skilled workers, skilled workers average higher than unskilled workers. But this might simply be a result of the fact that it takes more schooling to get into the higher level occupations, and IQ is correlated with school success" (p. 49). However, within any occupational group, the degree of success attained may depend largely on characteristics other than IQ.

Among college students, there is no consistent relationship between scholastic aptitude scores and actual accomplishments, whether in social leadership, the arts, science, music, writing, or speech and drama (McClelland, 1973). Likewise, in routine occupations that require speed and accuracy (whether clerical or semi-skilled factory jobs), intelligence measured by an alertness factor rather than standard time-powered test is more related to success in the learning period.

For the rehabilitation practitioner, it is important to remember that the reliability of most well-known intelligence tests is high (usually in the 0.80s or 0.90s), but even these figures allow for variation (Sundberg, 1977). Some people change markedly from time to time, especially if they have gone through periods of maladjustment. The IQ score obtained from an intelligence test does not represent a fixed characteristic of the individual. It should be interpreted as a particular score obtained on a particular test at a particular time. This is especially important for younger clients, for whom test–retest reliabilities are lower (Hood & Johnson, 1997). The attainment of physical growth does not mean that mental, emotional, and psychological growth have ended. For example, an adult at age 40 can learn new things almost as well as a 13-year-old. In fact, an adult who is motivated strongly enough to make up some slight loss in alertness and adaptability may learn better than a young person. The greatest difference in mental ability between younger and older persons may be in speed rather than accuracy or power (Shertzer & Linden, 1979).

It is important to remember both that intelligence tests are usually administered for the purpose of making a prediction about future academic performance, and that behaviors or attributes are being assessed by intelligence test items (Salvia & Ysseldyke, 1995). The rehabilitation professional must ask, "What is the relationship between the kind(s) of behavior sampled by the test and the kind(s) of behavior I am trying to predict? The closer the relationship, the better the prediction. In developing the validity of their mental ability tests, the authors usually correlated them with criteria such as the Stanford–Binet performances, grades, academic averages, or ratings of teachers and supervisors. Predictive validity coefficients usually fall in the 0.40 to 0.60 range, with grades as the criteria.

Because of the multitude of abilities and the complexity of mental activities, it is important not to base decisions for rehabilitation planning on any single measure of ability. Several different kinds of evaluation tasks, such as the interview or the job tryout, should be used. Sundberg (1977) believed that any one IQ should be treated as a range rather than as a single score, keeping in mind the reliability or accuracy of the instrument. Also, it is necessary to ask: How and where does my client want to use a certain capability? Many training environments, for example, do not demand a high level of abilities.

Intelligence is a complex concept. Vocational evaluators should give attention during assessment to the client's practical ability—namely, what does it take for a person with a disability to cope well with perhaps new environmental and personal situations? This could be referred to as *practical intelligence* or *experiential intelligence*—specifically, the ability to interpret information in a changing context or the ability to adapt to a changing environment (Tyler, 1984). Although an intelligence test does not give a comprehensive measure of all aspects of intelligence, it can still evaluate a person's general ability more quickly and economically than many other procedures. Also, its appraisal of ability is usually more accurate than subjective methods and can provide the professional with a beginning understanding of the client's ability to learn in a training situation.

FACTORS TO CONSIDER WHEN USING INTELLIGENCE TESTS

When considering the use of intelligence tests for people with disabilities, five factors should be kept in mind.

Factor 1

Who should administer and interpret these tests? Unless the rehabilitation professional has had specialized training, a psychologist or psychological examiner should give the measure and interpret the results. This is particularly true of four of the tests suggested in this chapter: the *Wechsler Adult Intelligence Scale–Third Edition* (WAIS–III) (Wechsler, 1997), the *Haptic Intelligence Scale for the Adult Blind* (Shurrager, 1961), the *Luria–Nebraska Neuropsychological Battery* (Golden, Purisch, & Hammeke, 1984) and the *Halstead–Reitan Neuropsychological Test Battery* (Reitan, 1974).

Yet the rehabilitation professional should still be familiar with these measures, specifically regarding their strengths and deficiencies, as well as the meaning of the test results. These scores frequently come from other sources, and the helping professional should understand their relevance to a particular client. This is especially true concerning the validity of scores with regard to the client's disability, socioeconomic state, and other variables in the testing process. Many intelligence measures, for example, rely heavily on the client's verbal ability, which is not a well-developed trait in many persons with disabilities.

The other measures suggested in this chapter can be administered and interpreted by rehabilitation professionals with a graduate degree or training in standardized instruments. The manuals of these tests contain clear instructions on administration and interpretation, and the tests themselves take a relatively short time for completion. Their results can be valuable in determining what occupations for training possibilities would not be appropriate for an individual as well as any intellectual strengths or competencies for eventual vocational programming.

Factor 2

Particular attention should be given to the selection of tests relevant to a specific disability. As Table 2.1 in this volume indicates, the WAIS–III is appropriate for all disabilities but has limited use with persons with visual and hearing impairments. The *Haptic Intelligence Scale for the Adult Blind* (Shurranger, 1981) is useful only for persons with a visual impairment (Cohen, Swerdlik, & Phillips, 1996). The *Peabody Picture Vocabulary Test–Third Edition* (PPVT–III) (Dunn & Dunn, 1997) is applicable for persons with mental retardation. The *Quick Test* (Ammons & Ammons, 1959) is a valuable instrument for identifying a general range of intelligence functioning, although it is not applicable for persons with a visual impairment. The *Shipley Institute of Living Scale* (Shipley, 1986) is more useful for clients who have at least some high school education. The *Slosson Intelligence Test–Revised* (SIT–R) (Slosson, Nicholson, & Hibpshman, 1990), and the *Raven's Progressive Matrices* (Raven, 1986) are appropriate for all handicaps, although they have limited use with persons with visual and hearing impairments (Siefker, 1996). The *Kaufman Brief Intelligence Test* (Kaufman & Kaufman, 1990) is applicable and very useful for several groups of persons with disabilities (Hood & Johnson, 1997).

An IQ test should be chosen according to the client's educational and life experiences as well as his or her disability-related limitations. Also, when administering an intelligence measure, the rehabilitation professional should consider how long it has been since the client took such a test. Records may state that many years have elapsed since the original identification of measured intelligence functioning. Though longitudinal research studies generally have suggested that above the age of 7, IQs tend to remain relatively stable over time (Cohen et al., 1996), mental growth can be a continuing and uneven process for many. The creative process, for example, can continue through adulthood and into old age. Another example occurs when deterioration of an individual's basic functioning is suspected because of the presence of head trauma or chronic disease. On the other hand, in some people, intellectual ability can continue to increase as one gets older. For all of these reasons, an update of the client's intelligence functioning should be considered.

Factor 3

When evaluating the vocational potential of persons with severe disabilities, many of the problems found in intelligence testing are magnified. If a physical disability limits a client's capacity to perform in the areas of social competence or psychomotor functioning, do the results of the test then reflect intelligence or simply the degree of physical impairment (Schlenoff, 1974)? Each disability has specific and characteristically limiting effects, and clients with a disability reflect adaptive and learning behavior aspects of intelligence differently. Consequently, it is necessary that the rehabilitation professional be aware of the problems and limitations that are characteristic of the client's disability. The initial interview can identify these concerns. Exploring the client's physical, social, educational, and occupational history can provide further information on the best possible ways to evaluate intelligence functioning.

When exploring intelligence levels with clients, it is often beneficial to administer at least two intelligence measures. This can provide more comprehensive information for rehabilitation planning. For individuals with severe disabilities, the assessment of intelligence is not really a process that is different in "kind" from traditional evaluation, but rather is different in "extent." At the same time, this testing process can be overwhelming to clients, particularly to those who are unaccustomed to testing. To alleviate client anxieties, time should be spent on explaining the goals of assessment and the purpose of each IQ test to be used. After the preparation, and when two or more IQ measures are to be used, the following sequence is recommended:

For clients whose records contain no recent information on intelligence functioning, and whose educational background and reading ability are apparently poor:

1. PPVT–III
   or
   Revised Beta Examination (Beta II)
   or
   Raven Progressive Matrices
   or
   SIT–R
   or
   Kaufman Brief Intelligence Test

Then:

2. WAIS–III

For clients who (a) have records containing no recent information on intelligence functioning, (b) have had no educational training in the past 5 years, (c) have records indicating some high school education:

1. any one of the measures identified previously in (1), but at least the *Revised Beta Examination* or *Kaufman Brief Intelligence Test*

Then:

2. WAIS–III

For rehabilitation professionals who want an update on intelligence functioning for a client who has graduated from high school when interview information suggests a well-developed reading ability or recent educational training:

1. *Shipley Institute of Living Scale*
   or
   Kaufman Brief Intelligence Test

Then:

2. WAIS–III

Factor 4

There are many influences on both the development of a person's IQ and the stability of an IQ score. Measured intellectual ability represents an interaction between innate ability and such environmental influences as family expectations and culture. Items on an intelligence test tend to reflect the culture of the society in which these tests are used. Culturally fair tests have been developed and tend to be nonverbal for the client, with directions that are simple, clear, and often administered orally by the evaluator. Culturally specific tests also have been developed for members of a particular group or subculture (Cohen et al., 1996).

Factor 5

Individual differences within disability groups must be carefully considered when identifying an appropriate intelligence test. Factor 2 explains the importance of selecting a test that is relevant to a specific disability. However, attention must be given to differences among individuals who have the same, identified disability. Visual and hearing impairments, for example, can be classified into different types, from someone who is totally blind or deaf to a person who can read ink print efficiently, although one may need larger type. Hearing-impaired individuals differ with respect to such variables as magnitude of hearing loss, age of loss onset, and consequential effects of the loss on language skills and social adjustment (Cohen et al.,1996). The verbal scale of the Wechsler intelligence tests has been frequently used in evaluating the intellectual functioning of people with blindness or visual impairments. The rehabilitation professional should be aware, however, of the issues of language development and socialization skills when selecting an appropriate intelligence measure.

VOCATIONAL IMPLICATIONS

With the exception of the WAIS–III, all of the IQ measures explained in this chapter can be administered by a rehabilitation professional who has had some training in assessment and has access to qualified supervisors. These tests also suggest a general estimate of intelligence competencies, although the WAIS–III provides more precise information. The tests further suggest levels of possible training, language development, and—with certain test results—levels of reasoning.

Among individuals with a severe disability, particular concerns arise with clients experiencing the trauma of head injury. Head injuries can produce a wide array of impairments, and the vocational evaluator is not concerned with differential diagnosis in the usual sense. What the evaluator needs is assessment feedback that identifies the full range of cognitive assets and deficits. A meaningful rehabilitation program can be formulated only through a complete identification of cognitive assets and deficits (Baxter, Cohen,

& Ylvisaker, 1985). Assessment results should indicate what clients know as well as what they do not know. It is most helpful to evaluate general intelligence with persons who have brain injury because this allows the professional to determine whether the client has access to previously acquired knowledge.

The vocabulary subtest of the WAIS–III is well-known as the best quick estimate of IQ. To interpret the results, however, the evaluator must have a general sense of the client's premorbid level of ability. Information regarding education and occupation is probably the best guide to assessing premorbid cognitive status. Also, because of the client's cognitive deficits, it is often necessary to have evaluation materials that require a variety of response modes and that have content presented in different formats (Baxter et al., 1985). Two widely used batteries to explore cognitive deficits for persons with cognitive deficits resulting from brain injury are the Luria–Nebraska Neuropsychological Battery and the Halstead–Reitan Neuropsychological Test Battery. Both instruments require specific skills in administration and interpretation that demand specialized preparation.

Luria–Nebraska Neuropsychological Battery (Golden, Purisch, & Hammeke, 1984)

Baxter et al. (1985) explained that the test items on the Luria–Nebraska are divided in such a way that composite scores can be obtained for each of 11 scales of functioning: Motor, Rhythm, Tactile, Visual, Receptive Language, Expressive Language, Writing, Reading, Arithmetic, Memory, and Intellectual Processes. Items within each scale are designed to measure, in both simple and complex forms, more than the particular ability suggested by the name of the scale. Items from each of the 11 regular scales are used to generate two additional sets of scales. The first of these scales provides a basis for inferring the lateralization and localization of cortical lesions, and the second provides specific information on such basic skills and abilities as visual acuity and naming, phonemic discrimination, simple tactile sensation, and 27 additional areas of cognitive function. Client scores are compared to a Critical Level, which is determined on the basis of age and education. The Luria–Nebraska batteries represent efforts to translate directly Luria's (1973) theories of brain–behavior relationships into a standardized test procedure.

Halstead–Reitan Neuropsychological Test Battery (Reitan, 1974)

Baxter et al. (1985) stated that these tests were devised by Ward Halstead (1947), and development has been continued by Ralph Reitan. In its current form, the battery consists of five tests (Category Test, Tactual Performance Test, Speech Sounds Perception Test, Finger Tapping Test, and Seashore Rhythm Test), which are supplemented by Reitan's inclusion of an aphasia examination, a sensory–perceptual examination, the Trail Making Test (parts A and B), and a measure of bilateral grip strength.

IQ CLASSIFICATION CHART

The following table, with information provided by Wechsler (1997), can be used when interpreting scores on intelligence tests:

IQ	Classification
130 and above	Very superior
120–129	Superior
110–119	High average
90–109	Average
80–89	Low average
70–79	Borderline
69 and below	Having mental retardation

The following section gives detailed information on the different measures of intelligence functioning that are useful when evaluating clients with a disability. These tests emphasize developed general ability (achievement) more than the raw aptitude for such development. Except for the WAIS–III, which identifies particular abilities, all the suggested tests provide a general estimate of intellectual functioning.

WAIS–III

The WAIS–III, which was revised in 1997 with expanded norms reflecting the ages and abilities of today's population, assesses general and specific intellectual abilities of people of ages 16 to 74. Wechsler (1997) believed that

> intelligence is a function of the personality as a whole and is responsive to other factors besides those included under the concept of cognitive abilities. Intelligence tests inevitably measure these factors as well. (p. 8)

The WAIS–III consists of 14 subtests, each of which is grouped under either the Verbal scale or the Performance scale. Eleven of the subtests remain from the previous edition and three new subtests have been added, namely Matrix Reasoning, Symbol Search, and Letter-Number Sequencing. Each scale explores particular dimensions of intelligence functioning, and the verbal and nonverbal group may be administered separately or together to yield, respectively, a Verbal, Performance, and Full-Scale IQ score. The administration of the current test has been changed so that Verbal and Performance tests are systematically alternated.

Although not normed with the population of those with a disability, the WAIS–III is perhaps the best general adult intelligence test available. Salvia and Ysseldyke (1995) noted that "the standardization of all the Wechsler tests closely approximates the highest level of standards associated by professional groups such as the American Psychological Association, and, each test has been thoroughly researched with respect to all facets of reliability and validity and in general has been found to be psychometrically sound" (p. 319). With a trained examiner and careful test preparation, this measure can provide very useful information in many areas of client functioning. The results allow the client to be compared to the normal population in "intelligence" areas. The different scales of the WAIS–III are as follows.

Verbal Scales

Vocabulary. Thirty-three words of increasing difficulty are presented both orally and visually. The subject is asked to define each word.

Similarities. Nineteen items (i.e., pairs of words) require the subject to say how two common objects or concepts are alike.

Arithmetic. Twenty problems are similar to those encountered in elementary-school arithmetic. Each problem is to be solved without the use of paper and pencil and is orally presented.

Digit Span. First task [Digits Forward] includes orally presented lists of two to nine digits that are to be repeated verbatim orally. In the second part [Digits Backward], the subject must repeat backwards lists of two to eight digits.

Information. Twenty-eight questions that are presented orally cover a wide variety of information (events, objects, places, and people) that adults in the American culture should presumably acquire. An effort was made to avoid specialized or academic knowledge.

Comprehension. Eighteen items require the subject to understand and articulate social rules and concepts or solutions to everyday problems.

Letter-Number Sequencing. [Supplementary Subtest] A series of orally presented letters and numbers that are presented in a mixed-up order. The examinee must reorder and repeat the list by saying the numbers first in ascending order and then the letters in alphabetical order.

Performance Scales

Picture Completion. Subtest includes a set of 25 color pictures of common objects and settings, each of which is missing an important part. Examinee must identify missing part by pointing or naming.

Digit Symbol-Coding. Examinee is presented with a series of numbers, each of which is paired with its own corresponding hieroglyphic-like symbol. Using a key, the examinee draws each symbol under its corresponding number.

Block Design. This test consists of increasingly complex designs made from two to nine cubes. Examinee must replicate two-dimensional geometric patterns using two-color cubes.

Matrix Reasoning. A traditional type of nonverbal task where the examinee looks at a picture of geometric shapes and either names or points to the correct answer from five response options.

Picture Arrangement. Subtest consists of 11 sets of cards containing pictures to be rearranged into a logical story sequence.

Symbol Search. [Supplementary Subtest] Subtest includes a series of paired groups, each pair consisting of a target group and a search group. The examinee indicates, by marking the appropriate box, whether either target symbol appears in the search group.

Object Assembly. [Optional Subtest] Puzzle pieces of common objects are assembled by the examinee to form a meaningful whole. The subtest contains five pictures to be assembled, including those of a man, profile of a face, and side view of an elephant, house, and butterfly.

Interpretive information of WAIS–III results is available from WAIS-Micro. There is also a Spanish version available, and the norms are based on a Puerto Rican population. Also, a WAIS–III expanded record form is a new addition to the Wechsler series, which greatly enhances the administration and scoring of the WAIS–III. This record form provides significantly more room to record responses and notes, useful scoring prompts, and new tables. The form also contains the design for Block Design and the figures for Object Assembly to facilitate scoring.

SLOSSON INTELLIGENCE TEST–R

The *Slosson Intelligence Test–R* (SIT–R) (Slosson et al., 1990) is an individually administered, oral test that can be used for initial screening purposes. The test is brief, and scoring is fairly objective. Because the test is oral, it can be used with individuals who are blind, have reading handicaps, have physical disabilities, cannot respond to paper-and-pencil tests, or cannot work effectively under the pressures of a time test (e.g., those who are on heavy medication or are "test anxious").

Siders and Wharton (1982) explained that when providing educational services to children with mild disabilities, the SIT–R as well as the PPVT–III may be used as a quick screening device. Also, if these tests do not rule out a disabling condition, such as mental retardation, they may be followed by a more in-depth exam.

As the manual states, the SIT–R has been restandardized and improved across many areas. It is still designed to be a quick and reliable index of verbal intelligence, and the following areas have been improved:

1. The distribution of items within the item classification system of the SIT–R is more even, and the SIT–R test items are referenced in contemporary language.

2. The standardization sample is significantly larger and reflects a stratification consistent with the modern-day U.S. census. Validity and reliability studies are more comprehensive.

3. The SIT-R permits answers in English or metric measures, where applicable.

4. The deviational Intelligence Quotient (IQ) is extended to a Total Standard Score (TSS).

Although no research is available on its use with adults with a disability, the SIT–R can be used as a screening instrument with a population of those with a disability. Siefker (1996) explained that though the SIT–R is a screening instrument that should not be used in final placement decisions, it can estimate the cognitive ability of a person who has a mental illness or mental disability. The examiner should give particular attention to the capability of the client to respond to the test items. The SIT–R can be administered in 10 to 30 minutes. Because of the brevity of the test, it should not relied on without other supporting information, particularly in situations in which important diagnostic decisions are required.

The SIT–R is available from Slosson Educational Publications, Inc., P.O. Box 280, East Aurora, NY, 14052, 800-828-4800.

PEABODY PICTURE VOCABULARY TEST–THIRD EDITION (PPVT–III)

The PPVT–III (Dunn & Dunn, 1997) is an untimed, individual intelligence test, orally administered in 11 to 12 minutes or less. Extensively revised, this test measures an individual's receptive (hearing) vocabulary for Standard American English. In addition, it provides a quick estimate of verbal ability or scholastic aptitude. Specifically, the PPVT–III can also be used for assessing the English vocabulary of non–English-speaking individuals and assessing adult verbal ability. Two parallel forms (IIIA and IIIB) can be used for testing and retesting. No reading is required by the client, and scoring is rapid and objective. Item responses are made by pointing. The total score can be converted to a percentile rank, mental age, or a standard deviation IQ score. No special training is required to administer, score, or interpret the PPVT–III.

The national norms of the PPVT–III have been extended to include ages 2-6 to 90+ years of age. This edition also was developed from adult norms obtained on 828 persons ages 19 to 40 selected to be nationally representative of geographical regions and major occupational groups (Anastasi, 1996; Siefker, 1996). No people with handicaps were included in the norm population. A technical supplement gives detailed standardization data.

The PPVT–III provides an estimate of the client's verbal intelligence and has been administered to groups who had reading or speech problems, had mental retardation, or were emotionally withdrawn. Because the manner of the client's response to stimulus vocabulary is to point in any fashion to one of four pictures that best fits the stimulus word, these tests also apply to rehabilitation clients who have multiple physical handicaps, but whose hearing and vision are intact. The test also has high interest value, and this can establish good rapport with the client. For its administration, the examiner presents a series of pictures to each client. There are four pictures to a page, and each is numbered. The examiner states a word describing one of the pictures and asks the client to point to or tell the number of the picture that the word describes.

The test is not useful in its present form for blind and deaf people, but can be useful for people with mental retardation, for whom no modifications in instructions or format are needed. The only possible problem is that the illustrations for about the first 50 items often use children. These may not be acceptable to the adult with mental retardation.

The PPVT–III is available from American Guidance Service, Circle Pines, MN, 800-328-2560.

REVISED BETA EXAMINATION– SECOND EDITION (BETA–II)

The BETA–II (Kellogg & Morton, 1978) is designed to serve as a measure of general intellectual ability of persons who are relatively illiterate or non–English-speaking. A nonverbal estimate of intelligence is given as a single IQ score. It is designed for individual or group administration. Including instruction, it can be administered in about 30 minutes. Subtests are timed from 1½ to 4 minutes. A Spanish translation of the directions for administration is also included in the manual.

The test contains six separately timed tests that measure different aspects of nonverbal ability:

1. *Mazes.* Marking the shortest distance through a maze without crossing any lines.
2. *Coding.* Matching figures with their corresponding numbers.
3. *Paper Form Boards.* Fitting figures together to form squares.
4. *Picture Completion.* Filling in the parts of pictures that have been omitted.
5. *Clerical Checking.* Marking pairs that are alike.
6. *Picture Absurdities.* Identifying drawings that are wrong or foolish.

No reading is required for this test; it is mainly designed for illiterate clients. All responses are recorded in a nonreusable booklet. The ability to hold a pencil, print numbers, and the dexterity to trace mazes are required for recording the responses. Each subtest includes several demonstration items and at least three practice items. The BETA–II includes several practice items for each subtest, along with instructions requesting that the examiner carefully check the client's performance on each item. Spanish language directions for administration are given at the back of the manual.

Thorndike and Hagen (1969) explained that although the test is claimed by some to be "culture fair," there is little evidence to support the claim. The BETA–II was standardized on a sample of 1,050 persons ranging in age from 16 to 64 years. A stratified sampling procedure was employed to ensure that the sample would closely resemble the U.S. population by age, sex, region of residence, race, and occupation (Kellogg & Morton, 1978).

For clients with severe visual limitations, this test is not usable in its present form. It can, however, be used effectively with clients who have mental retardation. The only problem that may arise is the abstractness of some of the items in several of the subtests. With modifications, the test can also be used with individuals who are deaf, because of visual content as well as the fact that the test can be individually administered. The problem is in giving the instructions, which could be signed or placed on cards for the client to read. The client who cannot understand signing and who cannot read could be administered the BETA–II if the examiner carefully goes over each practice exercise.

The *Revised BETA Examination* is available from the Psychological Corporation, 555 Academic Court, San Antonio, TX, 78204, 800-211-8378.

RAVEN PROGRESSIVE MATRICES

The *Raven Progressive Matrices* (Raven, 1986) are designed to measure general ability, especially the ability to perceive and use relationships between nonverbal materials. It taps such qualities of the intellect as spatial aptitude, inductive reasoning, and perceptual accuracy. The tasks or matrices consist of designs that are incomplete. The individual being tested chooses from several designs or patterns and selects the pattern that best completes the matrix.

The *Raven Progressive Matrices* are available at three levels and can be used with ages 5 or older. The test can be administered individually or in groups, and is hand-scored. It is easy to administer and relatively brief. Although not useful for individuals with visual impairment, the test is helpful with clients who have a physical handicap or emotional disturbance. There is no time limit to the test, and this is a favorable feature for many clients who have disabilities.

A literature review indicates no research on use or standardization of the *Raven Progressive Matrices* with the population of persons with disabilities. There are percentiles for children aged 5½ through 11½ years, percentiles for British school children, and means and standard deviations for several adult groups. This test should be used in conjunction with a vocabulary test, which will provide an index of the general information a client has acquired up to the present as well as his or her command of the English language.

The *Raven Progressive Matrices* are available from the Psychological Corporation, 555 Academic Court, San Antonio, TX, 78204, 800-211-8378.

QUICK TEST (QT)

The QT (Ammons & Ammons, 1962) is a carefully standardized, individual intelligence test in three forms and is based on perceptual–verbal performance. It takes 3 to 10 minutes to administer. Anyone who can see the drawings, hear or read the word items, and signal yes–no can receive this assessment instrument. The client is not required to read, write, or speak. With adequate administration, scoring is quick and objective. Item responses are easily scored during the administration of the test. Summary scores, mental ages, tentative IQs, and percentile ranks can be quickly computed or read from tables on the record form and in the manual. The examiner should be aware that the drawings are dated and that the standardization group, though controlled on an exact, simultaneous quota basis for age, sex, and educational level, is not representative of the diverse population currently in the United States.

This test is most helpful for gaining a general understanding of a client's perceptual–verbal functioning. The measure should be followed by a more comprehensive test, such as the WAIS–III, after an estimate of the client's functioning has been achieved, although many rehabilitation practitioners use the results of this test to move into an assessment exploration of aptitude and abilities functions.

The QT can be used with hearing impaired individuals, but it is not suitable for those who are blind. The test can also be used to build rapport in the testing situation, to test persons with a short attention span, and to estimate the intelligence of persons who have a severe physical handicap (for whom larger and more complicated tests may not be appropriate). Reported reliabilities of single forms of the QT have been high, with a range of 0.78 to 0.97. Validity studies were conducted during the development and standardization of the QT. These consisted mainly of comparisons of the QT with the *Full-Range Picture Vocabulary Test* (FRPV) (Ammons & Ammons, 1950), which has itself been found to give highly valid estimates of intelligence as indicated repeatedly by strong correlations with such tests as the *Stanford-Binet Intelligence Scale* (Thorndike, Hagen, & Sattler, 1986) and the various Wechslers. The QT is designed for quick, efficient estimations of general levels of intellectual ability when circumstances are less than optimum and time is limited.

The QT is available from Psychological Test Specialists, Box 9229, Missoula, MT, 59807, 406-728-1710.

SHIPLEY INSTITUTE OF LIVING SCALE

The *Shipley Institute of Living Scale* (Shipley, 1991) consists of a 40-item multiple choice Vocabulary subtest and a 20-item Abstract Thinking subtest. The *Shipley Institute of Living Scale* has the advantage of being a short, easily administered, and easily scored objective test, adaptable to group or individual testing and requiring little training for non-psychological personnel to administer, score, and interpret. The scale was devised to provide a quick, objective, self-administering measure of mental deterioration. It is based on the clinical, experimental observation that in mental deterioration, vocabulary level tends to be affected only slightly while the ability to see abstract relationships declines rapidly. These facts suggest using the differential between vocabulary and abstract thinking levels as a possible index of deterioration. Besides providing an estimate of mental deterioration, it is a good instrument for assessing whether clients have at least average intelligence before they begin training or employment. An option is available for computer administration, scoring, and interpretation.

The test cannot be used with persons who are visually impaired but is suitable for those with hearing deficits. As mentioned earlier in this chapter, the test is more applicable for those who have at least a sixth-grade reading level. However, the results have more use when the client has at least a 10th grade education.

Each subtest has a 10-minute time limit. Reliability coefficients are 0.87 for the Vocabulary test, 0.89 for the Abstract Thinking test, and 0.92 for the two combined. A revised manual for the *Shipley* was published in 1986, which improves the test's clinical utility by adding standard scores, updated norms, a new impairment index, and age-adjusted norms for estimating WAIS and WAIS–R IQs.

The *Shipley* is available from Western Psychological Services, 12031 Wilshire Blvd., Los Angeles, CA, 90025, 800-222-2670.

HAPTIC INTELLIGENCE SCALE FOR THE ADULT BLIND

A timed, individual test requiring 90 to 120 minutes, the *Haptic Intelligence Scale for the Adult Blind* (Shurrager, 1961) should be administered in two sessions because of its length. Cohen et al. (1996) explained that the "word 'haptic' refers to the sense of touch, and this scale exclusively employs the sense of touch in its administration; partially sighted examinees must wear a blindfold when taking this test, for viewing the test materials would invalidate the findings" (p. 610). The test explores how the client compensates for loss of sight and his or her flexibility in dealing with nonvisual materials. It consists of such subtests as Digit Symbol, Object Assembly, Block Design, and Object Completion—all of which were modified from the WAIS. Bead Arithmetic and the Pattern Board are two other subtests that have been added.

This test was developed as a nonverbal test to be used in conjunction with the Verbal scale of the WAIS (Anastasi, 1982). Both tests use a completely tactile approach and, if given to clients who are partially blind, require them to wear a blindfold. The standardization procedures closely follow those employed with the WAIS. Blind subjects tested in the standardization sample included a proportional number of non-Whites and were distributed over the major geographical regions of the country (Anastasi, 1982). Split-half reliability for the entire test was found to be 0.95.

The *Haptic Intelligence Scale* should be interpreted with caution. The client's degree of disability, age at loss of vision, special schools attended, knowledge of Braille, and use of an abacus should all be considered before administering this test. Some of its disadvantages are that it (a) is costly, (b) requires a lengthy administration time, and (c) requires the client to be readily available over a period of several days.

The *Haptic Intelligence Scale for the Adult Blind* is available from the Psychological Research Technology Center, Chicago, IL.

KAUFMAN BRIEF
INTELLIGENCE TEST (K–BIT)

An individually administered assessment of verbal and nonverbal intelligence of individuals ages 4 to 90, the K–BIT (Kaufman & Kaufman, 1990) is designed so that it can be administered by the evaluator in just 15 to 30 minutes. It is useful for (a) identifying individuals who may require further evaluation; (b) obtaining a quick estimate of the intellectual ability of adults in institutional settings, such as group homes, rehabilitation clinics, or mental health centers; (c) re-evaluating periodically the intellectual status of an adult who previously had been administered a thorough psychological battery; and (d) obtaining information useful for vocational and rehabilitation settings. The test provides three scores—verbal, nonverbal, and overall IQ composite.

The vocabulary or verbal subtest measures school-related skills and is divided into two parts—expressive vocabulary (45 items) and definitions (37 items). The nonverbal subtest measures nonverbal skills and the ability to solve new problems (48 matrices). All matrices involve pictures and abstract designs rather than words.

The K–BIT was normed on a national standardization sample that matched U.S. Census data and included over 2,000 individuals ages 4 to 90. Concurrent validity was established by analysis with the WAIS–R and the WISC–R. Concerning reliability, both test–retest and internal consistency studies showed 0.93 for the K–BIT composite, with equally strong reliability coefficients for the vocabulary and matrices subtests.

The K–BIT is available from American Guidance Service, 4201 Woodland Road, P.O. Box 99, Circle Pines, MN, 55014-1796, 800-328-2560.

CHAPTER 7 CONCLUSION

In rehabilitation, assessment of the client's competence in handling everyday situations can be most valuable. This information can help clients to appreciate their remaining capacities after a serious trauma has brought extensive physical limitations. Also, many clients may have no idea about their general range of intellectual functioning because they have received no feedback about this capacity for several years or even decades. An awareness of this information can be a stimulus to a more realistic, individually oriented rehabilitation plan. All the evaluation data should lead to effective, individualized rehabilitation programming.

While an assessment of intellectual functioning can be useful for the development of the client's rehabilitation plan—especially one that includes employment training—there are a number of difficulties revolving around the selection of IQ tests. Intelligence is an inferred construct and the evaluator should determine what behaviors are going to be assessed by the test items. Also, most group intelligence tests are often not standardized on representative populations, or they may be standardized on volunteer samples, which can introduce bias into the standardization. The choice of a test should depend on the training of the rehabilitation professional and the purpose for obtaining information in intelligence functioning.

The training of the rehabilitation professional is an essential consideration when administering many intelligence assessment measures. As noted earlier in this chapter (Factor 1), specific training is required for the administration of the WAIS–III, *Haptic Intelligence Scale*, the *Luria–Nebraska Neuropsychological Test Battery*, and the *Halstead–Reitan Neuropsychological Battery*. Educational institutions offer specialized courses in the theory and practice of these instruments. A rehabilitation psychologist or neuropsychologist who specifically works with populations who have incurred a significant cognitive or neurological deficit especially use these aforementioned tests. When vocational evaluation is conducted with those, for example, who are traumatically brain injured, it is important for the neuropsychologist to explain also the vocational implications of the test results. If a client's consciousness, perception, memory, learning, thinking, and reasoning have been weakened by the injury, as test results indicate, then what are the accompanying vocational restrictions? Head trauma can affect retentive memory, the understanding of meaning and relationships of words and sentences, attention to detail, ability to relate to people, and lucidity of expression. Each limitation can affect satisfactory job performance.

But assessment cannot end with an understanding of the client's intelligence potential. More information on other areas of client functioning, such as achievement, personality, and interest, is needed. The following chapters identify and describe these assessment tools.

 CASE STUDY: MR. L.

Mr. L., age 51, is a black male who injured his left leg in an industrial accident. He has a brace on this leg and walks with a cane. Before his accident, he was employed as a bricklayer for 26 years and has recently been told by his physician that, in the future, he will only be able to perform sedentary work. Prior work experience includes brief periods of employment as a pipelayer, a construction laborer, and a farm worker.

Mr. L. reports that he had to leave school in the third grade for economic reasons. Although he claims to enjoy reading history books, he states that one of his daughters has to help him interpret written material. He is married and has six children, is an active church member, and has social ties with his family and neighborhood companions.

During the initial interview, Mr. L. mentioned that he is very willing to learn a new trade. He was well-dressed for this session, and appeared enthusiastic for vocational evaluation.

Chapter 7 Case Study Questions

DIRECTIONS: Considering this information, please answer the following questions:

1. Because of the client's life history, what are some special concerns when selecting a measure of intelligence?

2. From the list of intelligence tests described in this chapter, which ones do you believe would be appropriate for this client?

Personality Assessment

8

O ne of the important goals in rehabilitation is to assist the client with a disability in achieving satisfaction in a job or similar productive outlet. This goal implies more than skill proficiency. Individual needs, motivation, ability to get along with others, and a capacity to cope with employment-related demands are all aspects of personal functioning that are of major importance for the client's suitable job adjustment and success. Moreover, many clients beginning the rehabilitation process bring with them continued problems of anxiety, difficulties in continuing with a job or training program, and behavioral patterns, such as overdependency and aggressiveness. All of these patterns are antithetical to appropriate placement in a job setting. All of these considerations emphasize the need for evaluation of personality functioning in rehabilitation.

In the early days of the rehabilitation movement, when services emphasized physical restoration, the assessment of personality was considered to be irrelevant for most clients. However, when vocational rehabilitation evolved and began to undertake work with clients who had mental retardation, severe disability, mental illness, alcoholism, and social disadvantages, many counselors resisted these populations, claiming that the client problems were too severe. When these persons were accepted for rehabilitation services, some counselors were determined to apply the same evaluation procedures that had succeeded with their previous clients. These approaches largely ignored the personality functioning of the people with a disability. When the proportion of failures grew and, out of necessity, the impact of personality functioning on job adjustment was explored, the practice of evaluating a client's personality characteristics gradually became more common in vocational rehabilitation. In fact, counselors learned that some personality traits may predispose the client to function well in some occupational areas and badly in others.

For those with disabilities, the relationship between personality and career development plays an important role in vocational evaluation approaches. An individual's personality affects career decision making, on-the-job performance, and occupational success, as well as dictating the relative strengths that influence job competencies and job satisfaction (Kjos, 1995). Effectiveness in assessment outcomes is enhanced by the evaluator's ability to identify personality styles and personality disorders that may inhibit or facilitate an individual's adjustment to a disability and achievement of appropriate, employment goals.

The purpose of personality assessment in rehabilitation is to identify personality strengths or deficits that influence job demands, including where and how the client can function effectively and what training may be needed to enhance behaviors demanded for suitable job adjustment (Maki, Pape, & Prout, 1979). In rehabilitation, the term *personality* refers to client information related to typical behaviors, rather than to intellectual attributes. Consequently, personality is defined as

> the system whereby the individual characteristically organizes and processes biophysical and environmental inputs to produce behavior in interactions with the larger surrounding systems. (Sundberg, 1977, p. 12)

In contrast to the traditional meaning that personality "connotes the superficial impression created by an individual's behavior" (Shertzer & Linden, 1979, p. 314), the term now further conveys the dynamic exchange between physiological status and environmental experience. Within the work environment, personality is directly related "to the degree to which it reflects work behaviors" (Maki et al., 1979, p. 120). Neff (1971) believed that work personality refers to the concrete set of interrelated motives, coping style, and defensive maneuvers with which an individual confronts the demands of work. Hershenson (1990) believed that work personality is composed of two elements: a person's self-concept as a worker and his or her motivation for work. This personality develops focally during the preschool years, primarily under the influence of the family.

For the rehabilitation worker, then, personality is a constellation of interests, needs, values, and behaviors that allows an individual to meet appropriate work rules in a particular job setting. In vocational evaluation, personality assessment should focus on behaviors necessary for employment or productive output. To provide some direction to the evaluation, the rehabilitation professional should explore the following questions:

1. Has the client shown emotional reactions toward the disability that may be obstacles to adequate vocational adjustment?

2. How is the client likely to respond in a high production or high stress type of job?

3. Will the client respond appropriately to supervision on the job?

4. On a job that brings close association or collaboration with other workers, can the client adjust to this demand? Can the client, for example, take criticism, get along with others, and when appropriate, be assertive?

5. How does the client understand the daily adjustmental implications of his or her disability?

6. Is the client able to work independently, control any tendency toward impulsiveness or continued anxiety, and take responsibility for job-related decisions?

In vocational rehabilitation, the traditional way to obtain an evaluation of personality functioning is to authorize a referral for a "psychological workup" from a psychologist or a psychiatrist. Vocational evaluators seeking to identify their clients' problem areas, to recognize their clients' domains of personality strengths, or to confirm their own hunches may use a battery of psychological tests. This combination of tests constitutes a "psychological workup" to supplement interview and other assessment tools that they have given. The report by the psychiatrist or psychologist usually consists of a brief description of the client, a sociopsychological history, and a clinical summary of the present condition. The result is a diagnosis. The report emphasizes the findings of testing and a summary of client behaviors. Unfortunately, these reports often contain information that is not vocationally relevant, or they do not provide an assessment of the client's residual emotional strengths that can be used in vocational training or employment. When reading these reports, the rehabilitation professional frequently has to translate the meaning of the described behaviors into vocationally relevant terms.

What is needed in vocational rehabilitation for an appropriate personality evaluation is the description of a client's behavior in observable, quantifiable, understandable, and functional terms (Field, 1979). Because a rehabilitation counselor is primarily responsible for planning and developing the client's rehabilitation process—which also implies collecting relevant and essential information needed for client planning—the counselor should be concerned about obtaining information on the client's personality or behavior functioning that is vocationally oriented. As client planning assumes that the counselor understands the particular behaviors needed to perform certain jobs adequately, so the assessment should focus on the behaviors that the client typically shows that are relevant to job situations.

Table 8.1 identifies personality traits that should be explored during the interview. The relationship of these characteristics to vocational functioning is also indicated. This table actually expands the model presented in Chapter 1 and explained in Table 1.1. It also includes personality factors that are found in the guidelines of client functioning discussed in Chapter 4.

In personality assessment, a definite personality pattern or cluster of behavioral problems is not associated with a particular disability. Problems associated with motivation or interpersonal relationships can be found with clients having orthopedic problems, visual impairments, or emotional difficulties. However, certain behavioral deficits, such as high distractibility or continued lack of sustained concentration, are very often identified among persons with neurologic illnesses or severe emotional problems. Also, medications that are used with certain conditions, particularly mental disorders, may cause passivity or related effects. All of these factors should be attended to by the rehabilitation professional, for they may influence the client's response to rehabilitation demands.

A client's work behavior, moreover, is a result of individual characteristics, such as interests, values, needs, motivation, self-concept, and previous experiences, as well as environmental characteristics such as the demands and support systems present in the

TABLE 8.1
Identification of Personality Traits

Personality traits	Personality measure	Vocational functioning problem areas
Mood and temperament (general appearance and behavior)	MMPI 16 PF CPI	Relationship to supervisors and other workers Frustration tolerance Adjustment to strains and pressures of work environment
Attitude Toward self Toward others (orientation toward other people)	PSI Tennessee Self-Concept CPI MBTI RSE	Sense of responsibility Successful job performance Cooperativeness On-the-job social skills Self-confidence in the work situation Follow instructions and practice work safety Self-presentation (dress, appearance, grooming, posture, method of talking to others)
Motivation Energy level Goal-directedness	EPPS 16 PF CPI	Seeks rehabilitation goals Energy on job Meets work demands, such as punctuality or continuing at task Work habits Response to pleasant or unpleasant tasks Acceptance of work role
Adjustment to disability Coping resources Capacity to face one's problems Strengths of client	PSI MMPI 16 PF CPI	Reality orientation—accepts limitations Dependent or independent role in work situation Coping mechanisms for dealing with stress on the job
Needs: Security Variety recognition Status responsbility Creativity Achievement independence	EPPS 16 PF	Change orientation Adaptability Ability to take risks with self
Values	MIQ WVI SWV	Clarify work or life goals Achievement orientation Work satisfaction

MMPI = Minnesota Multiphasic Personality Inventory; 16 PF = Sixteen Personality Factor Questionnaire; CPI = California Psychological Inventory; MBTI = Myers–Briggs Type Indicator; RSE = Rosenberg Self-Esteem Scale; EPPS = Edwards Personnel Preference Schedule; MIQ = Minnesota Importance Questionnaire; WVI = Work Values Inventory; SWV = Survey of Work Values.

environment. In their review of rehabilitation literature, Kaplan and Questad (1980) report that motivation, self-concept, and acceptance of and adjustment to disability are specific client characteristics that are critical for successful rehabilitation outcomes. Self-concept, particularly, is often a very useful predictor of rehabilitation success. Work behavior is a complex set of interactions between the client and his or her environment (Hursh & Kerns, 1988). Because of these interactions, personality assessment should identify factors that will facilitate adjustment between the client and the work environment. Two important characteristics that have often been overlooked in personality assessment are client needs and values. Both of these factors are identified in Chapter 1 as being integral to vocational functioning.

The major vocational needs of the "work personality," identified by Lofquist and Dawes (1969), are listed in Chapter 1 of this volume as part of the model of vocational functioning, and in Table 8.1. Lofquist and Dawes believed that an individual brings to a work opportunity certain work abilities and vocational needs. The job, in turn, has certain ability requirements and offers possibilities for workers to gain specific reinforcers. If the client is to achieve job satisfaction, then there should be congruence between vocational needs of an individual and the reinforcer systems of the job.

COLLECTING INFORMATION ON PERSONALITY FUNCTIONING

Table 8.1 specifically identifies both the personality traits that should be evaluated during vocational assessment and the suggested measures for exploring these traits. Besides these paper-and-pencil instruments, there are other methods of obtaining information on the adult client's personality traits, such as verbal, visual, and drawing methods. Verbal techniques include those approaches that involve both verbal stimuli and verbal responses. Projective questions (e.g., "If you could be anything you wanted to be, what would you be?"), sentence completion (*Rotter's Incomplete Sentence Blank–Second Edition* [RISB] in three forms—high school, college, and adult [Rotter, Lah, & Rafferty, 1992]), and story completion stories designed to investigate a client's attitudes and defense mechanisms, are all examples of verbal methods.

Visual techniques include visual stimuli that are presented to the client, who gives a verbal response. The Rorschach (1942) psychodiagnostic technique is a classic example of this approach. Ten bilaterally symmetrical inkblots, part in black and gray and part in color, are shown to examinees, who are then asked to tell what the blots remind them of. The *Thematic Apperception Test* (TAT–Z) (1976) is another example of this technique.

A number of drawing techniques have been used by professionals when exploring personality traits. Among them are the *Draw a Person: Screening Procedure for Emotional Disturbance* (DAP: SPED) (Naglieri, McNeish, & Bardos, 1991), the *Bender Visual Motor Gestalt Test* (Bender, 1962), and the *Kinetic Drawing System for Family and School* (Knoff & Prout, 1985). Many clients find that drawing is a more appropriate expression for their perceptions related to adjustment to a disability, as well as their reaction to the world around them. The way an individual approaches drawing often reflects how one approaches life situations. All of these techniques, however, require a great deal of education and training to administer and interpret correctly. Such training is usually not in the professional preparation of the rehabilitation worker—rather, psychologists are more specifically trained to administer these evaluation tools.

The most popular and widely used technique to assess personality is the personality questionnaire. It can be administered to individuals or to groups and usually is easily administered and scored. Questionnaires exist to measure all the different dimensions of personality—attitudes, adjustment, temperament, values, motivation, and anxiety.

Many personality inventories used currently require some training in their administration and interpretation, but do not have such intensive training demands as the projective measures. In the following pages, many personality measures are recommended for use in rehabilitation, some of which can be interpreted by the rehabilitation worker. When using these tests, evaluators must remember that test administration, scoring, interpretation, and reporting should be supervised by a person who meets the qualifications defined by state law and the American Psychological Association standards (Sax, 1981). Although the tests listed in this chapter were not developed primarily to predict behavior in work situations, the information they give—combined with an interpretation perspective that is job-focused—can be quite useful in rehabilitation.

Personality development, however, is not like cognitive development is such areas as verbal and numerical skills. A client can respond in very different ways in different contexts. Thus, as Anastasi (1982) stated,

> [the] same response to a given question on a personality inventory may have a different significance from one person to another. (p. 527)

In rehabilitation, the professional wants to know how an individual will respond within an independent living, training, or employment situation. Because of this need and the uncertain predictive validity of the personality measure for an individual, the personality test itself provides an estimate of the client's *current* emotional functioning. From interview information exploring the client's past behavior and current emotional functioning in areas other than vocational (e.g., family and social), the rehabilitation professional will be able to have some idea of personality-related problems in a training or work situation. For example, a 35-year-old man who was injured on the job now wants to return to work because he has completed physical rehabilitation treatment. A personality measure may suggest withdrawn or alienated behaviors, but work experience may have been highly productive. For accurate rehabilitation planning, other factors must be considered to develop appropriate goals. The client's current reaction to the disability, perception of work expectations, environmental influences, and opportunities for work adjustment should all be identified before predictions are made regarding the client's behavior in an employment setting.

PERSONALITY INVENTORIES

Minnesota Multiphasic Personality Inventory (MMPI–2)

The MMPI–2 (Hathaway & McKinley, 1990) is the most widely used personality inventory. Consisting of 567 affirmative statements, the test is designed for adults about age 16 and up and has been developed to assess major psychological characteristics that reflect an individual's social and personal maladjustment, including disabling psychological dysfunction. The inventory items range widely in content, and the measure provides scores on the 10 Clinical Scales that follow:

1. *Hypochondriasis (Hs)*. Thirty-three items derived from patients showing abnormal concern with bodily function.

2. *Depression (D)*. Sixty items derived from patients showing extreme pessimism, feelings of hopelessness, and slowing of thought and action.

3. *Conversion Hysteria (Hy)*. Sixty items from neurotic patients using physical or mental symptoms as a way of unconsciously avoiding difficult conflicts and responsibilities.

4. *Psychopathic Deviate (Pd)*. Fifty items from patients who show a repeated and flagrant disregard for social customs, an emotional shallowness, and an inability to learn from punishing experiences.

5. *Masculinity–Femininity (MF)*. Sixty items from patients showing homoeroticism and items differentiating between men and women.

6. *Paranoia (Pa)*. Forty items from patients showing abnormal suspiciousness and delusions of grandeur or persecution.

7. *Psychasthenia (Pt)*. Forty-eight items based on neurotic patients showing obsessions, compulsion, abnormal fears and guilt, and indecisiveness.

8. *Schizophrenia (Sc)*. Seventy-eight items from patients showing bizarre or unusual thoughts or behavior, and who are often withdrawn and experiencing delusions and hallucinations.

9. *Hypomania (Ma)*. Forty-six items from patients characterized by emotional excitement, overactivity, and flight of ideas.

10. *Social Introversion (O or Si)*. Seventy items developed from persons in the norm sample showing shyness, little interest in people, and insecurity.

The MMPI–2 has many supplementary scales, such as Anxiety, Repression, Ego Strength, MacAndrew Alcoholism–Revised, Back F, True Response Inconsistency, Overcontrolled Hostility, Dominance, Social Responsibility, College Maladjustment, Gender

Role–Masculine, Gender Role–Feminine, Post-Traumatic Stress Disorder–Keane, Post-Traumatic Stress Disorder–Schlenger, Shyness/Self-Consciousness, Social Avoidance, Alienation–Self and Others.

In addition, content scales newly developed for the MMPI–2 include Anxiety, Fears, Obsessiveness, Depression, Health Concerns, Bizarre Mentation, Anger, Cynicism, Antisocial Practices, Type A, Low Self-Esteem, Social Discomfort, Family Problems, Work Interference, and Negative Treatment Indicators.

According to the catalogue of the National Computer Systems (1989), the MMPI–2 contains many traditional features of the original test format that remain unchanged: the basic scale set, separate profile forms for male and female subjects, hand-scoring keys, and norms with and without K corrects.

Important refinements and modifications have been made in four areas: revised test booklet, restandardized national norms, uniform T scores, and new scales. The MMPI–2 test booklet contains 567 items. Some of these items are from the original MMPI. Many are new and were designed to augment test coverage. Items with sexist wording and outmoded content were modified. The 16 duplicate items were eliminated and items with "objectionable" content were excluded, thus slightly shortening five of the basic scales. The item order was changed, making it possible to score all of the basic scales from the first 370 items. Items 371 through 567 provide items for supplementary, content, and research measures.

The MMPI–2 norms are much more representative of the present population of the United States than were the original norms. The national reference group is also considerably larger than the original normative group. Experienced users of the MMPI will discover that T scores based on the new norms will not be as deviant as those based on the original norms.

The MMPI–2 incorporates representative samples of only two racial–ethnic minority groups (i.e., Black and American Indian). Examination of scores and MMPI–2 profiles indicates no substantial mean differences between these ethnic group samples and the general normative sample on the MMPI–2 validity and standard scales (Suzuki & Kugler, 1995).

Scores from the restandardization subjects on eight of the Basic Clinical scales (omitting scales 5 and 0) are uniform T scores. These scores were introduced because the traditional linear T scores are not strictly comparable from scale to scale due to differences in the distributions. The uniform T scores remove these differences and (unlike normalized T scores) preserve the general shape of the original T score distributions.

Many volumes have been written about the original inventory, and hundreds of additional scales have been developed beyond the basic scales described above. These scales also stimulated much research with varied types of clients. Moreover, the manual reports retest reliabilities on normal and abnormal adult samples from the 0.50s to the low 0.90s. Anastasi (1982) explained that certain scales (e.g., Depression) assess behavior that is variable over time, so as to render retest reliability inappropriate.

Anastasi (1982) stated that, in general, the greater the number and magnitude of deviant scores on the MMPI, the more likely it is that the individual has severe disturbance. Anastasi further believed that the principal applications of the MMPI are to be found in differential diagnosis. This inventory is essentially a clinical instrument, and its proper interpretation calls for considerable psychological sophistication. Although several computerized systems for completely automated profile interpretations have been developed, training is still necessary to interpret the results for clients. Many of these automated interpretations are largely descriptive summaries, whereas others provide highly interpretive statements.

The MMPI–2 is available in four administration formats: hardcover test booklet, softcover test booklet, audiocassette, and online MICROTEST assessment software. All formats consist of 567 true–false items written at the eighth-grade reading level. Both computer-scorable and hand-scorable answer sheets are available. Item order is the same for all formats. Basic Validity and Clinical scales can be obtained by scoring the first 370 items. A Hispanic version of the audiocassette and softcover test booklet is available.

Vocational Implications

Caution must be used in the choice of this instrument for certain clients. As a screening device, other measures described in this chapter might be more appropriate. For many emotionally disturbed individuals, for example, this inventory might simply be too long. Administration in two or three sessions might have to be considered. Also, for many clients who have no history of emotional disturbance and currently show good adjustment to their disability, differential diagnosis might not be necessary. However, when a client is suspected to have strong emotional undercurrents caused by adaptive problems, the MMPI–2 can provide some useful information. For example, with the client who reports continued back pain, the MMPI–2 can suggest emotional factors that should be considered when developing rehabilitation plans. Many of the clients described in Chapter 3 may be using their pain as a source of secondary gain or a reason for their ambivalence. Furthermore, this measure can suggest a level of a person's depression, thus identifying the professional adjustment problems for different types of occupational situations. However, unless a rehabilitation professional has special training, another qualified person should interpret the results for the MMPI–2. When using computer-generated reports on the MMPI–2, the professional should be cautious that such data may not be able to integrate all the relevant cultural information.

The MMPI–2 is available from National Computer Systems, P.O. Box 1416, Minneapolis, MN, 55440, 800-627-7271.

Edwards Personnel Preference Schedule (EPPS)

The EPPS (Edwards, 1959) was designed to be an instrument for research and counseling and to provide a quick and convenient measure of a number of relatively independent *normal* personality variables. Percentile scores are given for 15 personality variables: achievement, deference, order, exhibition, autonomy, affiliation, intraception, succorance, dominance, abasement, nurturance, change, endurance, heterosexuality, and aggression.

The EPPS consists of 225 items, each having two short statements. Clients choose the statement that best describes them. Items have been carefully selected to minimize the influence of social desirability. A separate answer sheet is used. This untimed group or individually administered test takes between 40 and 55 minutes to complete.

In considering the EPPS for persons with handicaps, no reading level is given in the manual. However, because the test is designed for college students and adults, the reading level is fairly high. In its present form, this test is not usable for individuals with visual impairments, nor is it usable for those who are deaf or have mental retardation, unless the person has a high level of reading comprehension.

To be noted with the EPPS is that ipsative scores are used—namely, the frame of reference is the individual, rather than a normative sample. In other words, the strength of each need is seen in relation to the strength of the client's other needs.

Retest reliabilities of the 15 scales reported in the manual range from 0.74 to 0.88 (Anastasi, 1982). Published validation studies have yielded conflicting and inconclusive results, and Anastasi believed that the measure is in need of revision to eliminate certain technical weaknesses, particularly with regard to item form and score interpretation. However, the inventory is still rather widely used in rehabilitation facilities, and when the rehabilitation worker understands the meaning of the different needs explained in the manual, he or she can then interpret the profile, which is developed from the client's responses.

Vocational Implications

Many of the EPPS scales can provide insights on the client's unique personal attitudes and needs. Both are as much a part of a person's vocational and training choices as they are of his or her friendships and love affairs. The Change, Endurance, and Order scales can suggest adaptability patterns in a work situation as well as the client's work flexibility and change orientation.

The EPPS is available from the Psychological Corporation, 555 Academic Court, San Antonio, TX, 78204, 800-211-8378.

The Myers–Briggs Type Indicator (MBTI)

The MBTI (Myers & Briggs, 1988) was developed by Isabel Briggs Myers and her mother, Katharine Briggs, who, in the 1920s, developed a system of psychological types by conceptualizing her observations and readings (Hood & Johnson, 1997). The measure is based on Jung's concepts of perception and judgment. Each of the several forms of the MBTI are scored on eight scales (four pairs) yielding four bipolar dimensions. These dimensions are:

1. *Extroversion (E) Versus Introversion (I)*. This dimension reflects the perceptual orientation of the individual. Extroverts prefer to direct their energy to the outer world of

people and things; introverts look inward to their internal and subjective reactions to their environment.

2. *Sensing (S) Versus Intuition (N)*. People with a sensing preference rely on that which can be perceived and are considered to be oriented toward that which is real (Pittenger, 1993); Intuitive people rely primarily on indirect perception, incorporating ideas or associations that are related to perceptions coming from the outside (Hood & Johnson, 1997).

3. *Thinking (T) Versus Feeling (F)*. A thinking orientation shows a preference for drawing conclusions using an objective, impersonal, logical approach. A feeling individual will indicate a preference to make decisions that are based on subjective processes that include emotional reactions to events.

4. *Judgment (J) Versus Perception (P)*. The judgmental person uses a combination of thinking and feelings when making decisions; the perceptive person often delays judgments as long as possible, preferring to collect information through either a sensing or intuitive process.

A person's MBTI personality type is summarized in four letters; this combination indicates the direction of the person's preference on each of the four dimensions. All possible combinations of the four paired scales result in 16 different personality types. An ESTJ, for example, prefers to organize projects, operations, and people, and then act to get things done. This person takes an objective approach to problem solving and uses thinking capabilities to organize life and work, and usually has little patience with confusion and inefficiency.

Although an individual's type is supposed to remain relatively constant over a lifetime, Cummings (1995) believed that norms on several MBTI dimensions change substantially between adolescence and childhood, as well as during the adult years. Pittenger (1993) explained that a factor analysis of the MBTI has not produced convincing results, and the factors found in the statistical analysis were inconsistent with the MBTI theory. He also believes there is no evidence to show a positive relation between MBTI type and success within an occupation.

The MBTI is appealing to many evaluators because it has no good or bad scores and it has no good or bad combinations of types. All type combinations can be viewed as having strengths. Each preference includes some positive characteristics, though each also has its problems and blind spots (Hood & Johnson, 1997). It does bring an added dimension to vocational assessment, and it should be used along with interest inventories and other psychological test results.

Vocational Implications

Because one of the most important motivations for a suitable occupational adjustment is a desire for work that is intrinsically interesting and satisfying, and that will permit use of preferred functions and attitudes, one's MBTI type can suggest a match between the individual and a particular job. There is no perfect match between type preferences and work tasks, but good occupational choices can prevent major mismatches.

According to type theory, a mismatch causes fatigue and discouragement. Tasks that call on preferred and developed processes require less effort for better performance and can give more satisfaction. The MBTI manual provides extensive information on examples of frequent occupational choices made by each type.

The MBTI is available from Consulting Psychologists Press, Inc., 577 College Ave., Palo Alto, CA, 94306, 800-624-1765.

Sixteen Personality Factor Questionnaire (16 PF), Form E

Form E is the new "low literate" form of the *16 PF* (Cattell, 1986) and, as in other forms of the *16 PF*, the manual states that it is designed to "make available . . . information about an individual's standing on the majority of primary personality factors" (p. 4). Final scores are given on 16 bipolar primary factors:

A: Warmth
B: Reasoning
C: Emotional Stability
E: Dominance
F: Liveliness
G: Rule-Consciousness
H: Social Boldness
I: Sensitivity
L: Vigilance
M: Abstractedness
N: Privateness
O: Apprehension
Q_1: Openness to Change
Q_2: Self-Reliance
Q_3: Perfectionism
Q_4: Tension

Scores are reported in standard 10 scores (stanines).

Form E uses forced-choice items such as: "Would you rather play baseball or go fishing?" The person selects the activity, feeling, preference, and so on, that he or she would rather do or be. A few questions, however, require a reasoned, factual answer: "After 2, 3, 4, 5, does 6 come next or does 7 come next?" The *16 PF* manual contains no information on the average time needed to complete *Form E*. The 128-item test is not timed.

When considering this test for persons with disabilities, the publisher estimates that *Form E* requires between a third- and sixth-grade reading level. Answers are always recorded on a separate answer sheet, which can be either hand- or machine-scored.

Although no information is specifically given, *Form I* is designed for "personality evaluation for vocational and general guidance of culturally disadvantaged and intellectually limited persons." In its present form, it is not applicable to clients who are blind. Because of its low reading level, *Form E* should be usable with people with hearing impairments who read fairly well. Also, a rehabilitation professional who understands basic personality concepts can, after reading the manual carefully, interpret the 16 PF profile to the client. Sufficient information on the profile is provided to do this appropriately.

Vocational Implications

Many of the 16 personality factors can be applied to the client's rehabilitation planning. Factor C (affected by feelings or emotionally stable), Factor E (assertive or conforming), Factor F (liveliness), and Factor Q_2 (self-sufficient or group dependent) are particularly relevant to adjustment issues in a training or occupational situation. Furthermore, they can indicate a pattern of adjustment to disability itself, which is a critical variable in successful rehabilitation. Factor H (venturesome or shy) suggests a client's change orientation or work flexibility. Also, persons with disabilities who score low on Factor C (affected by feelings or emotionally stable) tend to be low in frustration tolerance for unsatisfactory work conditions, easily annoyed, and perhaps evading necessary job demands. Moreover, many of the factors in this measure can alert the rehabilitation professional to such client characteristics as low energy for work demands (Factor G); overly pessimistic about possibilities for job adjustment (Factor F); or continued difficulty in getting along with others, working with people, and accepting supervision (Factor L).

The 16 PF, Form E, is available from the Psychological Corporation, 555 Academic Court, San Antonio, TX, 78204, 800-211-8378.

California Psychological Inventory–1987 Revision (CPI)

The CPI (Gough, 1987) is a multipurpose questionnaire designed to assess normal personality characteristics important in everyday life. It can be used to assist clients in making vocational plans and when supplementing other clinical tests. It can also be used to understand client maladjustments and to evaluate such specific problems as social immaturity and vulnerability to physical illness. The CPI can be given under normal conditions to individuals aged 14 through adult, and includes such basic scales as (a) interpersonal style and manner of dealing with others (dominance, capacity for status, sociability, social presence, self-acceptance, independence, and empathy); (b) cognitive and intellectual functioning (achievement via conformance, achievement via independence, and intellectual efficiency); (c) thinking and behavior (psychological mindedness, flexibility, and femininity/masculinity); (d) internalization and endorsement of normative convention (responsibility, socialization, self-control, good impression, communality, tolerance, well-being); (e) special scales and indices (managerial potential, work orientation, leadership potential index, social maturity index, and creative potential index). The CPI includes the following features: (a) its 462 items are printed in a reusable text booklet, (b) it can be taken under normal conditions in 45 minutes to 1 hour, and (c) its manual contains extensive reliability and validity information.

Vocational Implications

Many of the CPI factors can be applied more specifically to vocational assessment purposes, such as flexibility, responsibility, socialization, tolerance, well-being, work orientation, and social maturity index. These work readiness factors can be identified during rehabilitation planning. This measure, however, is not applicable to individuals with mental retardation disabilities.

The CPI is available from the Psychological Corporation, 555 Academic Court, San Antonio, TX, 78204, 800-211-8378.

The Psychological Screening Inventory (PSI)

The PSI (Lanyon, 1978) was developed to meet the need for a brief mental health screening device for situations in which time and professional manpower may be at a premium. It is intended only as a screening device, to be used in identifying persons who might profit by receiving more intensive attention. There are five scales of the PSI: Alienation (AL), Social Nonconformity (SN), Discomfort (DI), Expression (EX), and Defensiveness (DE). The combination of these scales is designed to assess the degree of defensiveness characterizing the test-taker's responses.

The PSI consists of 130 personal statements or items to be answered *true* or *false*. It is printed on the front and back of a single 8½" × 11" sheet. Items are at a fifth- to sixth-grade level, and the test can normally be completed in 15 minutes. It can be administered either in group or individual settings, both with a minimum of instructions. In its present form, the test is not usable for persons with visual impairments. However, if a person who is deaf has at least a fifth-grade reading comprehension level, it can be applicable.

Vocational Implications

The PSI can be particularly useful in rehabilitation, because it can provide a beginning awareness of how a client is coping with a disability. The scales of alienation, discomfort, and expression are especially valuable for this purpose. For example, the Discomfort scale was designed to assess the personality dimension of anxiety or perceived maladjustment. Persons who score highly on this dimension tend to complain of varied somatic symptoms and admit to many psychological discomforts and difficulties. When a rehabilitation professional wants to understand how the client's handling of pain is associated with a disability, this scale provides some suggestions that can be further explored in counseling. An accompanying high score on the Alienation scale may indicate that because of disability, the client is withdrawing from family and social involvements. Consequently, high Discomfort and Alienation scores for a client with a disability can suggest difficulties in adjustment to the strains and pressures of a work environment or many of the demands of competitive work (e.g., getting along with coworkers or maintaining an adequate production rate).

The PSI is available from the Sigma Assessment Systems, P.O. Box 610984, 1110 Military Street, Port Huron, MI, 48061, 800-265-1285.

Tennessee Self-Concept Scale

The *Tennessee Self-Concept Scale* (TSCS) (Fitts, 1988) was designed to be used with both healthy and maladjusted people. Atkins, Lynch, and Pullo (1982) explained that self-concept involves the dynamic interaction of the client's beliefs, needs, body image, sexual identity, values, and expectations. Many of these factors can be explored when interviewing persons with disabilities, but understanding such a client's self-concept is a critical element for understanding his or her psychological makeup. The *Tennessee Self-Concept Scale* explores many dimensions of self-concept, such as family self, physical self, moral self, and identity.

The scale consists of 90 items, equally divided for positive and negative responses. It is self-administering and requires no instructions beyond those on the inside cover of the test booklet. The answer sheet is arranged so that the subjects respond to every other item and then repeat the procedure to complete the sheet. The Counseling Form answer sheet is easy to interpret because the score sheet can be presented directly to the client for interpretation and discussion. However, the manual should be read before any interpretation is given to the client. A trained rehabilitation professional should be able to understand the concepts explained in the manual.

This scale has particular use for rehabilitation professionals because it can provide information and suggestions on the sources of the client's self-esteem and pattern of adjustment to disability. No reading level is indicated in the test manual. A review of the items indicates that at least a sixth-grade reading level is necessary. In its present form, the test is not usable for persons with severe visual impairments and is applicable to persons who are deaf, only if their reading comprehension is at this sixth-grade level. It is important to understand, however, that the normative group for the development of the varied scales did not include the population of those with disabilities. This should be explained to the client.

Vocational Implications

Self-concept is an important concept in rehabilitation planning, for it influences the client's motivation and is linked to self-confidence in work situations. Also, the Physical Self, Personal Self, and Social Self scales can indicate clients' attitudes toward their own disability. A high score on Family Self scale may suggest a coping resource for the client. When the scales (with the exception of the Physical Self scale) reveal high scores, it may indicate to the rehabilitation professional that the client has many perceived strengths for adjusting to work situations. These can be explored during counseling with the client.

The *Tennessee Self-Concept Scale* is available from Western Psychological Services, 12031 Wilshire Blvd., Los Angeles, CA, 90025-1251, 800-222-2670.

Rosenberg Self-Esteem Scale (RSE)

The RSE (Rosenberg, 1979) is a 10-item scale with one dimension that was originally designed to measure the self-esteem of high school students. However, since its development, the scale has been used with a number of other groups, including adults working in a variety of occupations. One of the RSE's greatest strengths is the amount of research that has been conducted with a wide range of groups on this scale over the years. This research has demonstrated the concurrent, predictive, and construct validity of the RSE. As a screening device for clients with a physical or mental disability, it can serve a useful purpose.

With the different inventories that explore the varied dimensions of personality functioning, one area that is also important for personality assessment is value's evaluation. An understanding of a client's values will not only highlight the individual's uniqueness, but also strongly suggest an added factor that can contribute to job satisfaction. A synonym for the word *value* is *worth*, and when we speak of a client's values, the evaluator is talking about whatever the individual prizes or believes is important (Cohen, Swerdlik, & Phillips, 1996).

The RSE is available from the Department of Sociology, University of Maryland, College Park, MD 20742.

IDENTIFYING A CLIENT'S VALUES

Although understanding a client's values may be a lifelong process, there are ways to help a person identify work-related values. Such values include advancement, achievement, altruism, competition, fairness, friendships at work, health, income, independence, interesting work, variety, location of work, people contact, physical appearance, security, work environment, and perhaps predictable work. The evaluator might perceive that many of these values are actually client needs. Lock (1988) affirms that values are related to needs, but they are not the same as needs. "Technically," he states, "a need is a lack of something desirable . . . values are internal in nature" (p. 237).

There are several ways to identify client values, including both informal and formal approaches.

Informal Approach

Similar to the material discussed in the chapter on interest assessment (Chapter 6), the evaluator may ask the client such questions as:

- Would you work if you didn't have to? Why or why not?
- In what kinds of work situations would you work harder than you ordinarily do?
- In what kinds of work situations would be you be willing to work for less than normal pay?
- Name some people whose work you really admire. Why do you admire the kinds of work they do?

Simon, Howe, and Kirschenbaum (1972) suggest a sentence completion activity, using sentences such as:

- What I want most in life is . . .
- I do best when . . .
- I think my parents would like me to . . .
- People who know me well think I am . . .
- I am concerned most about . . .

The evaluator can generate a list of the values that are important to the client. Pierce, Cohen, Anthony, and Cohen (1978) explained that a simple step is to begin by reviewing with the client his or her educational and work experience, along with any information gained from interest exploration. Particular emphasis should be placed on the client's likes and dislikes. The evaluator may have to explore the client's values with a list of values that past experience has shown are important in selecting a job. Traditional job value categories are physical, emotional–interpersonal, and intellectual, and each category includes many of the work values identified earlier. Physical values include personal appearance, physical working conditions, physical activities, and salary and benefits. Emotional–interpersonal value categories include job security; emotional–interpersonal working conditions (structure, pressure, amount of supervision, amount of isolation); and emotional–interpersonal activities (amount of interaction with people, what one does with the people; e.g., help, persuade). Intellectual value categories include the chance for advancement, supply and demand, and such intellectual activities as planning, decision making, computation, and writing (Pierce et al., 1978).

Formal Approach

Measures to identify work values are available, four of which are briefly explained below.

Work Value Inventory (WVI)

The WVI (Super, 1970) is designed for clients who are Grade 7 through adult. It takes 15 minutes to administer. It has 15 values relating to such factors as creativity, intellectual stimulation, economic return, security, prestige, and altruism. The test manual contains normative data based on a national sample of close to 10,000 students in grades 7 through 12. Test–retest reliability estimates obtained from the WVI based on a 2-week interval were found to range from .74 to .88 with a median reliability coefficient of .83.

Survey of Work Values (SWV)

The SWV (Wollack, Goodale, Wijting, & Smith, 1976) was designed for those in the range of late adolescent to adult. The test measures intrinsic (work-related values) and extrinsic (reward-related values) aspects of the Protestant work ethic. It includes 54 items and the six scales (9 items per scale) that follow: social status of job, activity preference, upward striving, attitude toward earnings, pride in work, and job involvement.

Hall Occupational Orientation Inventory

This inventory (Hall, 1976) is published by the Scholastic Testing Service. It has three levels—Grades 3 through 7, high school and college, and adults with handicaps. This measure is based on Maslow's personality need theory and the *Dictionary of Occupational Titles* (U.S. Department of Labor, 1991). It yields the following scale scores: Creativity, Independence, Risk, Information, Knowledge, Belongingness, Security, Aspiration, Esteem, Self-Actualization, Personal Satisfaction, Routine-Dependence, Data Orientation, Thing Orientation, People Orientation, Location Concern, Aptitude Concern, Monetary Concern, Physical Abilities Concern, Environment Concern, Coworker Concern, Qualifications Concern, Time Concern, and Defensiveness.

Minnesota Importance Questionnaire (MIQ)

The MIQ (Rounds, Henly, Dawis, Lofquist, & Weiss, 1981) is a measure of vocational needs and values. It asks individuals to evaluate 20 different work needs or values in terms of their importance in an ideal job. The 20 needs derive from studies of job satisfaction based on the theory of work adjustment developed by Dawis and Lofquist (1984). The 20 needs have been reduced to six broad factors called values (Achievement, Comfort, Status, Altruism, Safety, Autonomy) by means of factor analysis. Though two forms of the MIQ exist, most people prefer the simplified version, which usually takes about 20 minutes to complete. Computer scoring is available through the publisher (University of Minnesota, Minneapolis, MN) (Hood & Johnson, 1997).

Other Personality Tests

Although most of the preceding measures have been the object of extensive validity and reliability studies, there are other personality tests that, though not the focus of continued research, can be quite useful to the rehabilitation practitioner as a quick screening instrument. These measures identify factors that are important when determining job readiness, and the information produced from the tests may alert the evaluator to the client's need for a further referral for possible extensive counseling. The following tests are suggested as quick screening instruments for rehabilitation professionals. All four of these measures are available in a volume titled *The Mind Test* (Aero & Weiner, 1981):

1. Self-Acceptance Scale. Developed by Emanuel Berger, this 36-item scale focuses on self-esteem and self-acceptance. Berger listed nine characteristics of the self-accepting person, such as "has faith in one's capacity to cope with life." The measure is self-scoring, and adequate information is provided with the test for interpreting scores.

2. Physical Anxiety Questionnaire. Developed by Lawrence R. Good and Chester C. Parker, this measure was designed to identify the degree to which a person is worrying about physical problems. The questionnaire contains statements about worries, not about actual physical problems. It is self-scoring and information is provided for interpretation.

3. Beck Depression Inventory. From his extensive research and clinical experiences, Beck has developed a test of 21 items, each of which has a label that represents a symptom of depression. An important part of the test score interpretation is an examination of those symptoms for which a client scored the highest. Beck's research has established the relationship between each symptom and one's overall level of depression.

4. Zung Self-Rating Depression Scale. Zung's 21-item scale provides a general awareness of the level and pervasiveness of depression feelings. The scale can easily be completed by the person involved and serves as a measure of how the person was feeling at that particular time.

Evaluating Personality Measures

Because there are countless inventories, techniques, and related approaches available to the rehabilitation professional, there are some useful guidelines to follow when selecting a particular measure.

1. What is the purpose of the personality test? What is it designed to do?

2. Is it to be used to measure traits, types, states, or some combination thereof?

3. Is it to be used to measure the relative strength of various traits? If so, which traits are to be measured?

4. What kinds of items does the test contain? Did the test authors rely on a particular theory of personality when devising these items?

5. Does the test have a reported validity and reliability?

6. Is (Are) the reported standardization sample(s) appropriate for the group that is being evaluated? Also, does the test content appropriately avoid discriminating against racial and ethnic minorities?

SELECTED ISSUES
IN PERSONALITY ASSESSMENT

Cautions

Responses to a personality inventory make up clients' attempts to describe—for themselves and specific others, such as the rehabilitation professional—the way they see themselves in terms of the behaviors described in each inventory item. Such inventories provide a picture of the extent to which clients are able to face themselves or are willing to have others see them as they think they are. Personality inventories probe into feelings and attitudes that many people normally conceal and regard as private. It is the rehabilitation professional's responsibility, consequently, to create conditions that assist the client in generating information that is useful for self-understanding and self-acceptance.

There are many ways in which clients avoid this self-revelation. They may fake information during evaluation to avoid threatening feedback. When responding to personality inventories, they may offer a positive response regardless of which questions are asked. Or, they may simply attempt to manipulate or convince the rehabilitation professional that they must enter a certain occupation. An additional difficulty is the forced choice technique used in constructing the varied items. Clients are asked to pick one or two items most descriptive of themselves. However, not all possible combinations of stimuli are presented, and a given item may consist of two alternatives of equal social desirability. A situation is created in which the person may have no logical basis for making a choice (Shertzer & Linden, 1979).

Although all of these difficulties cannot be eliminated, they may be reduced by the professional's careful structuring of the assessment situation. Another way rehabilitation professionals can avoid difficulty is to thoroughly prepare clients for the different paper-and-pencil tests given in rehabilitation assessment. To help the client feel more comfortable when performing a personality inventory, the rehabilitation professional can explain the purpose of the particular test, respond to the client's possible anxiety, stress the importance of obtaining an accurate picture of the client for effective rehabilitation planning, and emphasize the necessity of confidence in the assessment results.

The counselor should also be aware, when working with clients from different minority groups, that these individuals may not be accustomed to talking personality inventories as they are presented in current assessment practices. Issues of motivation, test practice, and lack of understanding regarding the purposes of testing may influence the accuracy of test results. When using personality measures with clients representing diverse, ethnic backgrounds, cultural equivalence becomes important. In other words, does the personality construct being measured have equivalent or similar psychological meaning within and across different cultural groups? Inaccurate conclusions may be based on differences in construct meaning or even language bias (Suzuki & Kugler, 1995).

The fakeability aspect when taking a personality inventory should be always considered by the evaluator, especially in personality assessment. Many test items can be, for some clients, quite threatening, and the person with a disability will attempt to look good and respond untruthfully on selected items. To minimize this problem, the professional may explain that in a personality measure, test-takers are describing themselves, and untrue statements can inhibit appropriate rehabilitation planning. Confidentiality of the results can also be stressed.

Uses for What Groups?

When personality assessment is performed with a client, certain tests described in this chapter may be more useful than others. The main purpose of these measures is to screen the client or gain more supportive information for the professional's perceptions acquired during the interview. With these goals in mind, the following approaches are recommended:

Screening or Supportive Information

Step 1. PSI
Step 2. RSE
Step 3. CPI
Step 4. *Tennessee Self-Concept Scale* or MBTI

An understanding of the client's self-concept is helpful when evaluating attitudes toward self and motivation for rehabilitation. Also, the results of the PSI suggest the ways in which the client is reacting behaviorally to the disability. For example, is the client showing much discomfort and feeling greatly alienated from others?

Client's Understanding of Needs and Personality Factors

Step 1. EPPS or MIQ or WVI
Step 2. *16 PF, Form E* or CPI or MBTI

To be useful for rehabilitation planning, the results of these inventories must be interpreted in the perspective of rehabilitation needs and goals. For example, if a client shows high achievement, affiliation, and endurance scores on the EPPS, then this information can suggest some client motivational factors that can be considered when developing rehabilitation plans. If further information obtained from the 16 PF indicates high scores on assertiveness, conscientiousness, practicality, and controlled personality factors, then this personality style of the client in a work or independent living situation might be explored. In other words, the results of the two measures can be interpreted together, and such interpretation enables the client to gain added self-insight into rehabilitation strengths and weaknesses.

Differential Diagnosis

Step 1. MMPI, when appropriate
Step 2. *Tennessee Self-Concept Scale*

Other Approaches

Information about behavior functioning, for example, can also be obtained by placing the client into a real or simulated, but controlled setting for the purpose of a behavioral observation of the work personality. This is called situational evaluation. Behavior rating scales, such as those described in Chapter 12, can be used to collect this information.

CHAPTER 8 CONCLUSION

Personality assessment is one of the most important areas of client self-knowledge. The measures described in this chapter have all been used by the author. Other inventories could be suggested, but these measures have proven particularly helpful and are, therefore, recommended. Although tests cannot always accurately describe a client's basic underlying motivations, they do provide a sample of behavior. Such indications can facilitate personal insight (Biggs & Keller, 1982). For many clients, the evaluation process in rehabilitation is not really an end in itself, but can be the first step toward achieving self-awareness. Rehabilitation plans that evolve from vocational assessment build on this self-understanding. Clients who are aware of their own strengths and weaknesses—and who realize that some deficits may have to be modified before training or job placement occurs—often become more involved in the formulation of rehabilitation plans.

In rehabilitation, effective personality assessment begins with the rehabilitation professional's own awareness of the close relationship between behavioral traits and job-related or other productivity-related adjustment. This awareness enables the rehabilitation professional to make referrals to psychological consultants for personality information on the client that will be more specific and relevant to rehabilitation needs. Also, in understanding both the relationship between work and personality and the fundamental ingredients of personality assessment, the rehabilitation professional can generate referral questions or utilize appropriate evaluation measures that will provide more useful information for rehabilitation planning.

 ## CASE STUDY: LIONEL

Lionel, a 31-year-old African American male, has been experiencing epileptic seizures resulting from a closed head injury he incurred when he was 29. At that time he suffered a severe concussion, and, after having surgery, Lionel began to have seizures approximately three times a week. He takes appropriate medication that has reduced both the intensity and frequency of the attacks. However, Lionel still has a severe seizure once a week. He has lived at home with his parents for his entire life, and prior to his accident maintained a part-time semi-skilled job. He still has several friends and a girlfriend with whom he maintains contact. Recreational activities include watching TV and dancing. Since the accident trauma, his parents describe problems associated with memory, organizational abilities, and motivation. Now Lionel would like to explore employment options and presents himself for evaluation.

 # Chapter 8 Case Study Questions

DIRECTIONS: With this information, please answer the following questions:

1. What further information do you need—especially from the initial client interview—that could be important for planning a personality assessment approach?

2. What personality measures would you suggest for the purpose of exploring Lionel's personality characteristics and disability circumstances that could have an effect on his vocational rehabilitation?

Understanding Achievement and Aptitude Assessment

9

One of the objectives of vocational assessment is to help clients understand their strengths and weaknesses in relation to the world of work, while at the same time recognize the usual demands flowing from most employment opportunities. These demands include reading, writing, perceptual abilities, and the capability to understand and follow directions. Whether or not a client possesses such skills or has the capability to acquire them is determined through two traditional approaches—achievement tests and aptitude tests.

Achievement tests are designed to provide an evaluation of the specific information that individuals have learned from their education and experience. For example, these tests can be used for the following reasons: to explore the material that a client has or has not learned since leaving school or other formal training and to assess competencies needed for many occupational opportunities. From this information, a client can begin to explore both appropriate occupational choices and the amount of training that might be needed to enter a particular field. Also, the two achievement areas that a rehabilitation worker should especially consider are the client's verbal and numerical skills. Verbal achievement is demonstrated in reading and spelling. In numerical achievement, such factors as counting, reading number symbols, and performing written computations are necessary for efficiency in related jobs.

Aptitude tests, however, attempt to identify an ability or characteristic, mental or physical, native or acquired, that is believed or known to indicate a client's capacity or potential for learning a particular skill or knowledge. As achievement tests attempt to measure the outcome of specific training, education, and experience, so aptitude tests focus on performance capabilities that have been developed without conscious effort. Anastasi (1982) believed that achievement tests measure the outcomes of standardized school experiences, such as courses in mathematics or social studies, while aptitude tests measure the cumulative influence of a multiplicity of daily experiences. Also, aptitude tests can be used to determine the extent to which clients will profit from training.

Although aptitude cannot be directly measured, it can be inferred from the client's performance on an evaluation instrument. Frequently, multiple aptitudes are required for successful performance in a particular vocational area, and the matching of an individual's aptitudes with the abilities needed for the vocational area is an indicator for potential or possible success in this area. With the information gained from aptitude assessment, the professional has a better opportunity to assist clients who are trying to choose among training or occupation possibilities.

The reliabilities for aptitude and achievement tests tend to cluster in the high 0.80s and low 0.90s. The validity of these tests is also relatively high. For clerical, service, trade, craft, and industrial occupations, the client's potential for successful training at different levels can be predicted rather well by tests. Examples of tests that can measure successfully this potential are tests of intellectual abilities, spatial and mechanical abilities, and perceptual accuracy. However, prediction of job proficiency for these occupational groups is much more tenuous. For example, a client may take a mechanical aptitude test and score at the 75th percentile. If the group that was used to standardize the scores of this test, called the norm group, was made of successful auto mechanics, it might be predicted that this client would also be successful as an auto mechanic. This kind of prediction does still involve a subjective judgment, however, because there is no conclusive research evidence that a score at the 75th percentile ensures a high probability of success in auto mechanics. Norms are not foolproof predictive devices. Although aptitude and achievement tests can indicate whether a client has the potential or capacity to meet the training or occupational demands, these tests do not necessarily predict success.

Unfortunately, norms for these tests often are inappropriate for comparison purposes when used with individuals with a handicap, and this caveat should be considered when interpreting results. Norms can be useful, however, if certain minimum acceptable performance levels are established for various training opportunities or placements into local workshop situations. Many achievement tests, consequently, are based on standards or criteria that have been developed by an organization or a relevant group for a level of performance. Such measures assess what a person can do; they do not provide interpretations regarding one client's success as compared to another client. This chapter identifies both achievement and aptitude tests that use either norm-referenced or criterion-referenced interpretation. Following each test description is a brief section on the vocational implications of the particular measure for rehabilitation planning purposes. Before an explanation of these measures, however, learning styles and their implication for vocational rehabilitation are discussed.

Each client develops a unique learning style. This learning style affects the client's capacity to acquire, during training, employment-related information and skills. Individuals learn in various ways, and traditional or standardized approaches may not be consistent with a client's ability to learn. Learning styles that conflict with the way subject matter is presented during training can severely inhibit vocational and educational progress. Evaluating a client's learning style preference can help him or her adapt to training and employment demands.

The majority of learning style assessment tools described in the literature are standardized approaches. Whether a client learns best through the written or spoken word;

through charts, pictures, or demonstration; or by the experience of actually doing a task, learning generally combines these learning styles. Assessment approaches should identify an individual's preferred style. Preferred learning style is a variable that depends on the nature of the material to be learned and the personality of the learner. An evaluation of an individual's learning style, consequently, may encompass personality measures and task analyses. The interview can initially be used to explore the client's learning preference. The rehabilitation professional can ask such questions as:

1. What has been your most enjoyable learning experience?

2. Can you remember the best way that you have learned school subjects or job tasks?

3. When learning to do some of your favorite spare time activities, what kind of learning style (e.g., the spoken word, seeing things through pictures, or actually performing the activity) has been most successful?

Kolb (1976) developed the *Learning Style Inventory* to measure differences in learning styles along the two basic dimensions of abstract–concrete and active–reflective. Test results yield an identification of four statistically prevalent, dominant learning style users: (a) *Convergers* (use abstract conceptualization and active experimentation, strength lies in the practical application of ideas); (b) *Divergers* (use concrete experience and reflective observation, strength lies in imaginative ability); (c) *Assimilators* (use abstract conceptualization and reflective observation, strength lies in inductive reasoning); and (d) *Accommodators* (use concrete experience and active experimentation, strength lies in doing things and becoming involved in new experiences [Kolb & Goldman, 1973]).

Another measure, the *Learning Capacities Approach*, was originally developed in 1973 by Herbert and Rusalem and became the basis for learning capacities assessment in Ohio. The purpose of the instrument is to evaluate the learning style preference and functional limitations of clients with disabilities, and to identify specific strategies that will assist in their vocational or educational success. It is based on four fundamental methods of instruction: visual, auditory, kinesthetic, and in vivo demonstration. The *Learning Capacities Approach* is a more nontraditional approach to explore learning preferences because it fits the assessment to the needs of the client. The screening battery consists of approximately 30 to 35 tasks, none of which are scored or timed. If an instructional approach does not appear to be understood by the client, another approach is attempted often until the client is able to complete the task. Visual perceptual skills, auditory tasks, and motor and cognitive perception make up the assessment areas. To administer the screening, however, a 4 to 6 week training program must be completed. The ability to administer, observe, and interpret the information requires extensive understanding and practice. Further information about the instrument can be obtained from either the Jewish Vocational Service, Cincinnati, Ohio, or the Upjohn Health Programs, Toledo, Ohio.

ACHIEVEMENT TESTS

Wide Range Achievement Test–Third Edition (WRAT–3)

The WRAT–3 (Wilkinson, 1993) is one of the most frequently used achievement tests. It is primarily an individually administered test, but the sections on spelling and arithmetic can be given in a small group. Unlike previous versions, the 1993 edition has two equivalent alternate test forms. The two test forms (called *Blue* and *Tan*) can be used for pre- and posttesting or combined for more comprehensive test results (Siefker, 1996). This latest edition of the WRAT has returned to a single-level format for use with all individuals ages 5 to 75.

The WRAT–3 is a brief measure that can provide a rough indication of a client's academic achievement; it also can serve as an adjunct to intelligence and behavior adjustment tests administered by rehabilitation professionals. The achievement factors measured by the test include (a) reading—the ability to recognize and name letters and pronounce words; (b) spelling—copying marks resembling letters, writing the person's name, and writing single words to dictation; and (c) arithmetic—counting, reading number symbols, solving oral problems, and performing written computations.

The WRAT–3 yields raw scores, grade equivalents, standard scores, and percentile ranks. The total test time is 15 to 30 minutes, depending on age. Scoring by hand takes less than 5 minutes. A large-print edition is also available, as well as monographs from the Jastak Assessment Systems on validity issues. The normative sample consisted of 4,433 individuals ages 5 years to 74 years, 11 months who were matched for gender, ethnicity, regional residence, and socioeconomic level to 1990 U.S. Census data. Normative data are given on 23 age groups for reading, spelling, and arithmetic for both forms of the test and the two forms combined. Reliability coefficients, as listed in the manual, were generally in the 0.80s and 0.90s.

For many years, the WRAT has found widespread use in rehabilitation facilities. The findings of Moore, Gartin, and Carmack (1981) supported the validity of using the WRAT to assess achievement among such workshop populations of clients 16 years and older who have vocational handicaps that limit their employment opportunities. These populations included those with developmental disabilities, emotional disturbance, and physical handicaps. The directions for administration are clear in the manual, but the test is not appropriate for clients with visual impairments. Also, the emphasis on hearing the examiner and the necessity of having to pronounce words correctly on certain parts of the test place clients with a hearing impairment at a disadvantage. The WRAT–3, however, is particularly helpful in assessing academic achievement when the client has not had recent educational experience and the rehabilitation professional wants to determine basic reading and arithmetic capabilities for possible training. The items in each part of the test are arranged in order of difficulty. For clients with mental retardation or others for whom many items may be too difficult, an oral section with easier questions is provided with each test.

Vocational Implications

The WRAT–3 explores an adequate level of basic educational skills and development and provides suggestions for the level of possible training. However, the functional application of the scores is not always evident. The importance of functional and criterion measurement is more critical for individuals with lower achievement.

The WRAT–3 is available from Wide Range, Inc., Wilmington, Delaware, 800-221-9728.

Adult Basic Learning Examination, Second Edition (ABLE)

The major purposes of the ABLE (Karlsen & Gardner, 1986) are to determine the general educational level of adults who have not completed a formal eighth-grade education, diagnose individual strengths, and assist in the development of educational plans. According to the publisher, the second edition of the ABLE is the only adult achievement test designed specifically for adults. The test was written for adults and standardized with adults, reflecting current philosophies regarding adult education. The ABLE provides scores in five areas: vocabulary, reading, spelling, computation, and problem solving (math). This paper-and-pencil test contains three levels: Level I—Grades 1 through 4; Level II—Grades 5 through 8; and Level III—Grades 9 through 12. Each level has two alternate forms. There are five subtests at each level: Vocabulary, Reading, Spelling, Arithmetic, and Computation and Problem Solving. Each test consists of multiple-choice items, as well as items requiring the writing out of the word that is the answer to an arithmetic problem.

The ABLE was designed to be adult-oriented in content, and was specifically designed for use in connection with adult education classes or job-training programs (Anastasi, 1982). Vocabulary, reading, spelling, and arithmetic are related to the everyday life of adults. The test is administered in group form and can be hand- or machine-scored. Machine scoring is somewhat impractical because all math problems must first be hand-tallied before machine scoring. Total testing time for Levels I and II is about 2½ hours; Level III takes about 3 hours.

Anastasi (1982) indicated that split-half and Kuder-Richardson reliabilities of each test in the ABLE range from 0.80 to 0.96. Correlations between corresponding tests of the ABLE and the *Stanford Achievement Test* (Psychological Corporation, 1988) in the elementary and high school samples range from the 0.60s to the 0.80s.

When a rapid estimate of an adult's level of learning is needed or when testing time is limited, the ABLE screening battery is a useful alternative to the full ABLE battery. It can be administered in about an hour, yet it provides a reliable measure of an adult's functional reading and mathematics ability. A new edition of the ABLE, for use with individuals whose primary language is Spanish, includes measures of reading and mathematics.

Regarding the use of the test for persons with handicaps, the reading level for each of the three tests gets progressively more difficult. There is no information on individuals with disabilities in the test manual. For persons with severe visual or hearing impairments, the test is not usable in its present form. However, it can be used without modifications for clients with mental retardation. The parts of the ABLE that are administered orally can be used with persons who are blind if responses are recorded using a Braille answer sheet; typewriter; or, in the case of individual administration, given aloud for the test administrator to record. The major problem with the test is the arithmetic parts; although some of the arithmetic problems could be presented orally, many problems require computation using paper and pencil. For individuals who are deaf, major modifications are needed in the orally administered parts. The items read by the examiner could be printed together with multiple-choice answers found in the test booklets. Clients who are unusually proficient in signing or lipreading can have the test administered to them by these methods. Although no modifications are necessary, individual administration may be considered for clients with mental retardation. Extra practice items may also be necessary.

Vocational Implications

The ABLE explores an adequate level of basic educational skills and current levels of reasoning, mathematics, and reading development and assists in the determination of basic job-getting behaviors, such as completing the interview form.

The ABLE is available from the Harcourt Brace Educational Measurement, 800-228-0752.

Peabody Individual Achievement Test–Revised (PIAT–R)

The purpose of the PIAT–R (Markwardt, 1989) is to provide a wide-range screening measure of achievement in the areas of mathematics, reading, spelling, and general information. The test yields six final scores: mathematics, reading recognition, reading comprehension, spelling, general information, and a total score. The PIAT–R is individually administered, and none of the six subtests are timed. All items are presented orally, and the examinee responds by selecting the appropriate number or illustration from four alternatives. The items are contained in two booklets. Results are given in grade scores, percentile ranks, age scores, and standard scores. The length of the test varies with the individual. The manual states, however, that this untimed test usually requires between 30 and 40 minutes to administer and score. A written language composite may be obtained by combining scores on the spelling and written expression subtests.

The PIAT–R is a thorough update of the original 1970 PIAT. In addition to new items, new artwork, redesigned test materials, and new norms, a written expression subtest is offered for screening written language skills.

Additional features in the revised edition include an audiocassette tape that may be used by examiners as a guide to the accepted pronunciation for words used in the Reading, Recognition, and Spelling subtests. The test's norms have been updated and represent a national standardization that employed the most recent Bureau of Census projections of the U.S. school population at the time of publication.

No information is given in the test manual on persons with disabilities. The test is not useful in its present form for individuals who have severe visual or hearing impairment; however, for persons with mental retardation, it is very useful in its present form. The usefulness of this test for persons who are blind depends on the extent of the visual disability. The high-contrast black-and-white drawings may be perceived accurately enough to permit the use of the test with clients who are partially blind. Such clients should try a few practice items in each section to determine if they can accurately perceive them. Those who cannot should not be given the PIAT–R.

The emphasis on hearing the examiner and the necessity of having to pronounce words correctly on certain parts of the test place persons with deafness at a severe disadvantage on the PIAT–R. However, the visual content of the test has much to offer this group. The questions can be signed or printed on separate cards and presented one at a time. The person who is hearing impaired and who does not speak very well can easily point to the correct answer or respond by signing.

No modification of this test is necessary for persons with mental retardation. However, it is helpful for the rehabilitation worker to know that the Mathematics subtest requires the client to know numbers and some symbols, and that Reading Recognition requires examinees to know letters, identify words, and read and pronounce words aloud. In the Reading Comprehensive subtest, the client reads a sentence silently and then matches it with the appropriate illustration.

Vocational Implications

The PIAT–R explores an adequate level of basic educational skills, provides the client with a pool of learned skills that can be drawn on and used, and suggests educational skill readiness for training.

The PIAT–R is available from the American Guidance Service, 4201 Woodland Road, P.O. Box 99, Circle Pines, MN, 55014, 800-328-2560.

APTITUDE TESTS

General Aptitude Test Battery (GATB)

The GATB (U.S. Department of Labor, 1970) is a group test designed for use in the vocational and occupational counseling program of the United States Training and Employment Service and is provided for use through local state employment services. The traditional procedure for testing students with the GATB is through referral to local state employment service. However, several agencies have entered into a cooperative agreement with their state employment service for use of the GATB by the agency staff.

This battery is administered to applicants who have not yet chosen a field of work or who are uncertain as to the appropriateness of their choice. Among the groups usually tested are (a) high school graduates with no specialized training, (b) young people who are uncertain about their abilities, (c) experienced workers who want to or must change their field of work, (d) applicants who have not discovered their aptitudes through training or experience, (e) applicants suspected of having untapped abilities, and (f) those with a number of interests who have difficulty choosing among a number of seemingly suitable fields. In other words, a counselor suggests the GATB for all applicants for whom vocational choice is involved, if the counselor feels that further exploration of aptitudes will assist clients in making vocational decisions. There are nine aptitudes measured by the GATB (U.S. Department of Labor, 1982).

1. *General Learning Ability (G).* Ability to "catch on" or understand instructions and underlying principles; ability to reason and make judgments. These abilities closely relate to doing well in school.

2. *Verbal (V).* Ability to understand meaning of words and ideas associated with them and to use them effectively; ability to comprehend language, understand relationships between words, understand meanings of whole sentences and paragraphs; and ability to present information or ideas clearly.

▶ *Examples in Work Situations.* Reading comprehension required to master books used in work process; presentation of understanding of oral or written instructions or specifications; mastery of technical terminology.

3. *Numerical (N).* Ability to perform arithmetic operations quickly and accurately.

▶ *Examples in Work Situations.* Situations in which change is made, time or production records kept, geometric patterns laid out, things weighed, accurate measurements made, or numerical entries made or checked.

4. *Spatial (S).* Ability to comprehend forms in space and understand relationships of solid objects to a plane; ability to "visualize" objects of two or three dimensions; and ability to think visually of geometric forms.

▶ *Examples in Work Situations.* Blueprint reading; activities such as laying out, positioning, and aligning objects; observation of object movements, such as vehicles in traffic or machines in operation; comprehension of the way object movements affect their spatial position; achievement of balanced design; and understanding and anticipation of the effects of stress in structural situations.

5. *Form Perception (P).* Ability to perceive pertinent detail in objects, in pictorial or graphic material; ability to make visual comparisons and discriminations and see slight differences in shapes and shadings of figures.

▶ *Examples in Work Situations.* Inspection of surfaces for consistency in coloring, scratches, flaws, grain, and texture; observation of lint, dust, and so on, on surfaces; determination of whether patterns match or are correct; and recognition of small parts.

6. *Clerical Perceptions (Q).* Ability to perceive pertinent detail in verbal or tabular material; ability to observe differences in copy, to proofread words and numbers, and to avoid perceptual errors in arithmetic computation.

▶ *Examples in Work Situations.* Reading of work orders, specifications, dials, gauges, and measuring devices (in trade and craft jobs); proofreading of words and numbers from the standpoint of perceiving individual characters.

7. *Motor Coordination (K).* Ability to coordinate eyes and hands or fingers rapidly and accurately in making precise movements with speed; ability to make a movement response accurately and quickly.

▶ *Examples in Work Situations.* Guiding of objects into position or assembly of parts.

8. *Finger Dexterity (F).* Ability to move the fingers and manipulate small objects with the fingers rapidly and accurately.

▶ *Examples in Work Situations.* Handling of bolts and screws; manipulation of small tools or machine controls; playing of musical instruments; and fine adjustment and alignment of instruments and machines.

9. *Manual Dexterity (M).* Ability to move the hands easily and skillfully; ability to work with the hands in placing and turning motions.

▶ *Examples in Work Situations.* Hand and wrist movements to place and turn in pushing and pulling activities.

Hood and Johnson (1997) explain that cut-off scores have been established for aptitudes that are important for success in various occupations, and these cut-off scores have been used to determine occupational ability patterns (OAPs) for different work groups. All of the occupations in the *Dictionary of Occupational Titles* (DOT) have been classified into 66 work groups, most of which are represented by OAPs. Also, the GATB predicts occupational performance more effectively than other ability measures for both minority and majority group members (Bolton, 1994). A Spanish language version (BGPA) is also available.

Certain limitations of the GATB should be noted. Anastasi (1982) explained that all the tests have significant time requirements, the coverage of aptitudes is somewhat limited, a comprehension test is not included, and tests of reasoning and inventiveness are not well represented. Anastasi believed that a more comprehensive investigation with a large sample and a wider variety of tests would provide more solid and useful information.

The test manual for the GATB, however, provides extensive standards on the occupational requirements of jobs. The evidence for many of the jobs on which the determination of minimum scores and the assignments of jobs to patterns are based is rather limited; however, the information can still be quite helpful for the rehabilitation worker. Also, the GATB data available in the records at the U.S. Employment Service represent one of the major pools of data on the relation of test-to-job success (Anastasi, 1982). Importantly, it has been more thoroughly studied than any other occupational ability test (Hood & Johnson, 1997).

Vocational Implications

The GATB (a) explores the client's current level of reasoning, mathematics, and language development; (b) provides the client with a pool of learned skills that can be drawn on and used for skill transfer following onset of disability; and (c) suggests marketable job skills and necessary job-getting behaviors (e.g., completing the interview form). When appropriate, the GATB can assist clients in developing more realistic job expectations, and can suggest a level of possible training and training capabilities. The ability to read standard print and use paper and pencil to mark answers is necessary, as well as the ability to use one's hands to manipulate pegs, small rivets, and washers. All of the subtests do not have to be administered for the test to be valid (Siefker, 1996).

The GATB can be obtained from the U.S. Employment Service.

Non-Reading Aptitude Test Battery (NATB)

The NATB (U.S. Department of Labor, 1971) is an adaptation of the GATB for nonreaders. Many of the mechanics and principles of use and interpretation are the same for the two test batteries. Both batteries, for example, have the same norms; both use the same occupational aptitude pattern format; and both use the same technique for matching the client's aptitude scores with occupational aptitude requirements. The NATB is not a nonverbal test, but a nonreading test. The NATB measures the same nine aptitudes as the GATB but adds the following 10 subtests:

1. *Picture–Word Matching test*. Examiner reads stimulus word and client chooses which of the five pictures offered best associates with examiner's word.
2. *Oral Vocabulary*. Examinee decides whether two words read by examiner are the same, opposite, or different.
3. *Coin Matching*. Examinee decides whether two groups of coins have the same value.
4. *Design Completion*. Examinee completes 29 matrices.
5. *Tool Matching*. Examinee indicates which of four black-and-white drawings of tools matches the stimulus drawing.

6. *Three-Dimensional Space*. Examinee is presented with a stimulus picture of sheet metal with lines indicating where it is to be bent or rolled, then chooses a picture that represents what the metal will look like after it has been reshaped.

7. *Form Matching*. Examinee matches two identical line drawings.

8. *Coin Series*. Examinee performs mental manipulations of coins as required.

9. *Name Comparison*. Examinee decides whether two sets of names are the same or different.

10. *Mark Making, Placing, Turning, Assembling, and Disassembling*. Examinee performs these subtests taken from sections of the GATB other than those listed earlier.

The most important distinction between the two batteries is that the GATB is designed for use with a literate population and the NATB is designed for individuals with limited reading skills. The GATB Screening Exercises are used to determine which of the two batteries a client will take. The NATB makes it possible to test the vocational abilities of individuals with few or no reading skills, and to interpret these scores over a wide range of occupations.

The NATB was originally introduced on a trial basis, and although it has been subject to continuing research and revision, many believe that the NATB has proved disappointing (Anastasi, 1982). Apparently, it has not correlated highly enough with the GATB to permit equivalent interpretations of scores. Starting in the 1990s, alternative procedures for assessing this group have begun to be explored, especially for those who are educationally disadvantaged.

Vocational Implications

The NATB explores a level of possible training and the current levels of reasoning, mathematics, and language development.

The NATB is available from the U.S. Government Printing Office.

Differential Aptitude Test (DAT), Fifth Edition, Form C

The fifth edition of the DAT (Bennett, Seashore, & Wesman, 1982) features two levels that collectively measure aptitudes of students in Grades 7 through 12, as well as adults. Level 1 is designed primarily for students in grades 7 through 9; Level 2 is designed primarily for students in Grades 10 through 12. Both levels can be used with adults. Separate norms are given for males and females, and the rationale for separate norms to reduce sex bias is carefully explained to clients. The test items and the directions, as well as the student report, have been carefully edited with the needs of non–college-bound students in mind, such as those in various adult basic education and vocational technical school programs (Siefker, 1996). Reading is called for only when it is a part of the ability being measured.

The tests can be administered in groups and can be hand- or machine-scored. The term *differential* implies not only that the test measures different aptitudes, but also that differences in score levels within one person's profile are likely to be significant and interpretable. The DAT consists of the following tests: Verbal Reasoning, Numerical Reasoning, Abstract Reasoning, Perceptual Speed and Accuracy, Mechanical Reasoning, Space Relations, Spelling, and Language Usage. A computerized adaptive edition is also available, which is an integrated battery of eight aptitude tests that provide assistance in educational and vocational guidance. The computer software tailors the test to the client's ability level, and this test is administered and scored by the computer. The DAT adaptive software will work on all Apple IIc and IIe computers. It will also work on Apple II+, Franklin Ace 1000, and Laser 128 computers with at least 64 K memory. The IBM version runs on the IBM PC, XT, AT PS/2, and compatibles.

Mastie (1976) and Siefker (1996) believe that the DAT offers a psychometrically sound and logistically convenient source of information for young people, particularly for the educational and vocational decision-making process. The DAT has been validated extensively against various criteria such as school grades, related tests, and previous editions of the DAT, but validity studies have not been made using job or training success as criteria (Siefker, 1996).

If the complete battery is given, test administration requires slightly over 3 hours. Also, Omizo (1980) believed from the research findings that several of the variables tested by the DAT series are valid predictors of performance in engineering, mathematics, and science courses. Moreover, reliability coefficients are high and permit interpretation of interest differences with considerable confidence (Anastasi, 1982). The manual provides both percentile and stanine norms.

There is no information in the manual on the use of the DAT with the population of persons with disabilities. For educationally deprived individuals, the use of this test for an initial exploration of aptitude is really not appropriate. More basic measures should be used. The DAT is not applicable for persons with visual impairments. The tests, however, do provide valuable information for those clients with disabilities, who have at least a 10th-grade education and who are interested in occupations demanding technical skills—for example, in science and math areas. Also, for those who have completed high school and are not going to college but are planning an occupational career in technical fields, the DAT can be most useful for assessment purposes.

Vocational Implications

Because of their level of difficulty, these tests can assist clients in (a) developing more realistic occupational and training goals; (b) exploring their pool of learned skills that can be drawn upon and used for possible skill transfer following disability onset; (c) finding suggestions for marketable job skills; and (d) exploring their current level of reasoning, mathematics and language development. Many DAT tests, such as Abstract Reasoning, Numerical Ability, Mechanical Reasoning, and Space Relations, can also be used to explore client capabilities in electronics-related occupations (e.g., computer technology and television repair).

The DAT is available from the Psychological Corporation, 555 Academic Court, San Antonio, TX, 78204, 800-211-8378.

The World of Work Inventory (WOWI)

The *World of Work Inventory* (WOWI) (Ripley, Hudson, & Neidert, 1992) is a comprehensive, multidimensional career assessment instrument developed to help individuals better understand themselves in relation to the total world of work. It consists of three distinct scales: Career Interests Activities, Job Satisfaction Indicators, and Vocational Training Potentials. Appropriate job recommendations are selected from the 12,000 possible occupations listed in the DOT. The WOWI was normed on a national sample of over 90,000.

This inventory is available in a modified version, which is written at the fifth-grade level and designed specifically for remedial readers and those with hearing impairments. A Spanish version of the WOWI is also available. Test results are available in two forms: The Profile Report and the Narrative Interpretation. In the 6 to 8 page narrative report, information is structured in three areas: (a) *Vocational training potentials*, which includes verbal and numerical school achievement and four measures for aptitude for learning—abstraction, spatial—form, mechanical—electrical, and clerical; (b) *Job satisfaction indicators*, which include such traits as versatile, adaptable to repetitive work, adaptable to performing under specific instructions, dominant, gregarious, influencing, self-controlled, valuative, objective, subjective, and rigorous; and (c) *Career interest activities*, which should only be used as a broad guide for career exploration. The report then recommends jobs based on scores on all three sections of the test.

Vocational Implications

The comprehensive nature of this instrument identifies a wide-range of factors needed to explore employment potential and provides useful information for vocational planning.

The *World of Work Inventory* is available from World of Work, Inc., 64 E. Broadway Rd., Tempe, AZ 85282, 602-966-5100.

Bennett Mechanical Comprehension Test (BMCT)

The BMCT (Bennett, 1968) was designed to explore one's aptitude for understanding mechanical principles involved in a range of practical situations (Aiken, 1997). There is one final score in percentile form for mechanical comprehension. The test is group-administered with each examinee receiving a test booklet and separate answer sheet.

Most of the 68 items contain two illustrations and a written question about each illustration dealing with mechanical principles or general physical concepts. Examinees have three choices for each answer.

Anastasi (1982) explained that the Bennett is a widely used test and is suitable for such groups as high school students, industrial and mechanical job applicants, and candidates for engineering programs. The manual provides percentile norms for several groups, including educational levels, specialized training, or prospective job categories. Odd–even reliability coefficients of each form have been reported from 0.81 to 0.93. A fourth-grade reading level is necessary, and visual acuity to read standard print and see the details in the illustrations is required. For clients with limited reading skills, Forms S and T may be administered with tape-recorded instructions and questions. Spanish versions are also available for both regular and oral administration. Form T is the Mechanical Reasoning Test of the DAT.

The test can be completely administered in 40 minutes, including directions and questions. The test itself has a 30-minute time limit. When considering the test for persons with handicaps, the manual states that the test falls within the "fairly easy level of popular magazines." In the manual, no information on persons with disabilities is given. Although not usable in its present form for persons with blindness, this test should be appropriate for clients who are hearing impaired and who can read instructions. Also, the instructions are easy for persons with mental retardation to comprehend, but the concepts evaluated by the test may be too difficult for many of them to grasp. If the rehabilitation worker is planning to give the test to these clients, then individual administration and sufficient practice during the first two trials should be carefully followed.

Vocational Implications

The BMCT explores training capabilities in mechanical fields and is also recommended as an initial measure for clients who wish to pursue occupations in one of many technical areas (e.g., computer technology or electronics repair fields).

The BMCT is available from the Psychological Corporation, 555 Academic Court, San Antonio, TX, 78204, 800-211-8378.

Minnesota Paper Form Board–Revised (MPFB–R)

The MPFB–R helps the client explore aspects of mechanical ability that require the capacity to visualize and manipulate objects in space. The administration time is 20 minutes, and though a speed test, it is suitable for group or individual test administration concerning vocational implications. The test is suitable for nonreaders and non–English-speaking populations. It was normed on those in grades 10 through 12, as well as on industrial applicants and employed workers (Siefker, 1996). This measure is a useful complement to the BMCT.

This test is available from the Psychological Corporation, 555 Academic Court, San Antonio, TX, 78204, 800-211-8378.

Career Ability Placement Survey (CAPS)

The CAPS (Knapp & Knapp, 1994) contains eight subtests: mechanical reasoning, spatial relations, verbal reasoning, numerical ability, language usage, word knowledge, perceptual speed and accuracy, and manual speed and dexterity. All of these subtests were designed to measure abilities focusing on entry requirements for the majority of jobs in each of 14 occupational clusters. Each subtest is printed on a separate form, and the individually or group-administered battery can be completed in approximately 50 minutes or less. Each subtest has a time limit of 5 minutes. Clients can score their own tests and convert their raw scores to stanines on a profile sheet in 30 minutes. Mail-in machine scoring is available and software for on-site scoring can be purchased from the test publisher. This battery of tests is appropriate for persons who at least have a junior high school education and have the ability to read standard print and to use paper-and-pencil method of marking answers.

The CAPS is available from the EdITS/Educational and Industrial Testing Service, P.O. Box 7234, San Diego, CA, 92107, 619-222-1666.

Minnesota Clerical Test

The *Minnesota Clerical Test* (Andrew, Patterson, & Longstaff, 1961) was designed both to aid in the selection of clerical employees and to advise individuals interested in clerical training. The specific trait measured by the test is the client's ability to notice, within a specified time period, the differences between two items. The test consists of two parts: Number Checking and Name Scoring. Each part contains 200 items, with 100 identical and 100 dissimilar pairs. The client is to identify and check the identical pairs. No special training is needed to administer and score this test, and the test is hand-scored. Although not suitable for clients who have a visual impairment, this test can be adapted for individuals who have a hearing impairment.

Percentile norms have been reported in the manual for several large samples of clerical applicants and employed clerical workers, as well as for boys and girls in 8th through 12th grades. Moderately high correlations have been found between scores on this test and rating by office supervisors and commercial teachers, and with performance records in clerical courses (Anastasi, 1982). Note that the test measures only one aspect of clerical work.

Vocational Implications

This test suggests specific capacities in the clerical area (a good beginning test for many clients whose stated occupational interest is clerical work).

The *Minnesota Clerical Test* is available from the Psychological Corporation, 555 Academic Court, San Antonio, TX, 78204, 800-211-8378.

Hand–Tool Dexterity Test

Because the *Hand–Tool Dexterity Test* (Bennett, 1981) measures gross motor dexterity and uses hand tools to measure manipulative skill and the ability to use common hand tools, it is a good complement to the *Crawford Small Parts Dexterity Test*. The test uses an upright wooden frame clamped to a table or work bench in front of the client. The person must remove the nuts, bolts, and washers from the left side and mount them on the right side using wrenches and a screwdriver. Since there are three different sizes of nuts and bolts, separate tools are required for each. The *Hand–Tool Dexterity Test* is timed, and most individuals can complete it within 5 to 20 minutes. Percentile norms are based on the completion time and are given for such groups as maintenance mechanics, technical trainees, physically injured workers, special education students, vocational training students, and trainees with mental or emotional disabilities (Siefker, 1996).

Vocational Implications

Though the test requires the ability to comprehend verbal directions, follow physical demonstrations, and use both upper extremities, it does not work well for people who have visual deficits. It can be used successfully for clients who would like industrially related employment. Workers who have been industrially injured or who have emotional or mental disabilities can find this instrument to be quite useful.

This test is available from the Psychological Corporation, 555 Academic Court, San Antonio, TX, 78204, 800-211-8378.

Purdue Pegboard

According to Aiken (1997), the *Purdue Pegboard* (Tiffin, 1948) consists of five tasks for measuring manual dexterity and fine finger dexterity. There are five separate final scores, given in percentile form: right hand, left hand, both hands, right plus left plus both hands, and assembly.

The *Pegboard* includes pins, collars, and washers, which are located in four cups at the top of the board. Each subtest involves a separate task. For example, the right-hand test involves placing pins into holes on the board for a 30-second period. The left-hand test involves the same process but with the opposite hand, whereas the both-hands measure involves placing pins as fast as possible into holes with both hands. The right plus left plus both hands score is obtained by adding the above three scores together. The assembly task consists of assembling pins, collars, and washers on the board for a time period of 1 minute. This test should not take more than 10 to 15 minutes to administer and score.

When considering this test for clients who have a handicap, note that no reading is required. Although there is no information regarding persons with disabilities in the manual, the client who has a hearing impairment can be given this test with no problem; however, the directions and timing of the test may need to be adjusted. The *Purdue Pegboard* can also be used with clients who have mental retardation.

Vocational Implications

This test is found in many rehabilitation agencies, explores a client's finger and hand dexterity, and helps a client to identify many of the physical capabilities needed for some basic tasks in industrial or clerical occupations.

The *Purdue Pegboard* is available from the Science Research Associates, Inc., 259 East Erie St., Chicago, IL, 60611, 312-984-7000.

Other Measures

Significantly, achievement tests can also occasionally be developed by rehabilitation workers to quickly evaluate a client's daily living and employment-related skills. Although such tests are of the "homemade" variety, they can be more criterion-referenced, containing test items that are closely associated with the client's daily life demands. These tests have not been standardized, but can still provide much useful information for rehabilitation planning purposes.

SUMMARY OF ACHIEVEMENT AND APTITUDE ASSESSMENT

When working with different clients in rehabilitation, the following batteries of achievement and aptitude tests are suggested. It is assumed that the GATB will be administered when resources are available.

Clients Who Have No Recent Educational Experience and Little Formal Education

Step 1. WRAT–R or ABLE

Step 2. BMCT, *Minnesota Clerical Test*, or MPFB AND CAPS

Step 3. *Purdue Pegboard* or *Crawford Small Parts Dexterity Test* AND *Hand–Tool Dexterity Test*

Step 4. DAT series, if appropriate for rehabilitation planning purposes

Clients Who Have No Recent Educational Experience But Are High School Graduates

Step 1. ABLE or PIAT–R

Step 2. DAT series

Step 3. *Purdue Pegboard* or *Crawford Small Parts Dexterity Test* AND/OR *Hand–Tool Dexterity Test*

Both achievement and aptitude assessments are needed approaches to help the client achieve a better knowledge of work-related strengths and weaknesses. Fortunately, many standardized tests are available to provide an evaluation of achievement- and aptitude-related skills. If the rehabilitation worker uses these measures according to their specific directions, he or she will gain information about the client that is invaluable for rehabilitation planning.

 CASE STUDY: BILL

Bill has repeatedly made requests to see a counselor. He would like to return to work, but feels he needs some help from a professional counselor.

Bill was a sturdy, industrious, and dependable employee of the Southeastern Electric Company who had specific responsibility for several repair crews. There is evidence that he was regarded highly by his employers. According to his wife, Bill had always been vigorously healthy until, at age 42, he suffered a severe cerebrovascular accident. He was hospitalized for 5 months, beginning in July 1987, under the medical supervision of a general practitioner engaged by his employer. Damage resulting from the stroke is right hemiplegia and occasional grand mal seizures, occurring about once a week. During his hospital stay, speech and physical rehabilitation potentials were evaluated and therapy engaged. There was some response to these efforts, and now he has good use of his left side and some mobility in his right hand and right leg—although he must use a cane when walking and walks very slowly. He is unable to do any prolonged standing. There is only a slight, detectable slurring in his speech, but the speech therapist claims that this may improve.

Inquiry was made about Bill's interests and personality before the cerebral accident. His wife described him as a man who needed at all times to be going somewhere and doing something. His preferred diversions were hunting and fishing, which he liked to share with his two sons, ages 19 and 14. Bill also has one daughter, age 11. Before his illness, he had consumed at least a six-pack of beer on Saturdays and Sundays. When intoxicated, he sometimes became quite verbally abusive to his family. Bill has no intellectual interests and reads very little, with the exception of the local newspapers and manuals related to his work. He graduated from high school, but has received no formal education since then. His social activity typically has been restricted to family get-togethers. Apparently, he was keenly conscientious about his work, rarely missing time because of illness.

He also used to take much satisfaction in participating with repair crew members in some of the dangerous activities required. Bill was described by his wife as a stern, demanding husband and parent, who expected instant response to his demands.

Bill has worked for Southeastern Electric for the past 10 years. Before his employment he was an electronic technologist for a small company for 5 years. Upon leaving high school, he joined the Army for 5 years, where he was a medical corpsman and achieved the rank of sergeant.

 ## Chapter 9 Case Study Questions

DIRECTIONS: From the information presented in this chapter, please answer the following questions:

1. What aptitude tests do you believe would be appropriate for this client?

2. What difficulties do you identify with Bill that would create obstacles for him when taking any achievement or aptitude tests?

Work Samples and Transferable Skills Assessment

WORK SAMPLES: AN ASSESSMENT TOOL

Since 1970, the availability of work sample systems have been a significant part of the vocational assessment process. Although many practical tasks and activities are employed by vocational evaluators to explore a client's capabilities, the most highly structured technique that provides an exploratory vehicle is the work sample. It can provide a most productive approach to evaluation, especially for those clients with a severe disability. A work sample is defined as:

> A well-defined work activity involving tasks, materials, and tools that are identical or similar to those in an actual job or cluster of jobs. Work samples are used to assess a person's vocational aptitude(s), work characteristics, and/or vocational interests. (Dowd, 1993)

This chapter contains explanations, discussions, and suggestions regarding the following topics: different work samples, validity and standardization issues associated with work samples, the work sample evaluation process, advantages and disadvantages in using this form of vocational evaluation, the development of in-house work samples, questions that the rehabilitation worker can ask when selecting a commercial system of work samples, guidelines for the effective use of a work sample, and an overview of selected commercial work sample systems. When vocational evaluators wish to explore the vocational potential of individuals who have severe disabilities—especially those who have average to above average mental abilities—they usually use traditional psychometric tests, functional assessment, or assessment techniques that measure traits defined by the Department of Labor that can match jobs of varying skill levels (Peterson, 1984). However, other evaluation approaches need to be identified, especially because technology is continually opening doors to a variety of fields for people with severe disabilities. There has been an increase in technical and professional jobs, and traditional approaches do not respond to the emerging needs of the client population of individuals with severe disabilities.

There are several types of work samples. Some are either replicated directly—in their entirety—from specific jobs in industry and include the equipment, tasks, raw materials, supplies, and procedures found in the industry setting. Other samples replicate a segment of the essential work factors and tasks, materials, equipment, and supplies that may simulate one or more jobs to be performed in the community (Hursh & Kerns, 1988). Other types of samples include single-trait or cluster-trait samples. The former evaluates a single-worker trait or characteristic that may have relevance to a specific job or many jobs; the latter sample is designed to assess a group of worker traits, and contains a number of traits inherent in a job or variety of jobs. The differences among these several types of samples are matters of emphasis: All disclose specific abilities either by observation or by measurement, and in every case the results of a series of individual work samples are combined to form a profile of client potential.

Validity, Norming, and Standardization Issues

Work samples are usually found in controlled settings such as the rehabilitation center or laboratory. Nevertheless, there has been quite a bit of discussion regarding the validity, soundness, and appropriateness of the standards provided with work samples. These statistical elements, however, are much more difficult to provide in the case of the work sample than in the case of most psychological tests. The Vocational Evaluation and Work Adjustment Association (VEWAA) requirement explains that work samples shall be representative of realistic, competitive worker skills (VEWAA, 1975). To achieve this goal, a content validity approach is recommended, and the approach incorporates the techniques of (a) approval by a panel of experts, (b) job analysis, and (c) task analysis. Useful references to facilitate this development of validity are the *Dictionary of Occupational Titles* (DOT) (U.S. Department of Labor, 1977) and the *Handbook for Analyzing Jobs* (U.S. Department of Labor, 1972). The criteria employed in validity development can include the similarity of activities, the similarity of proportional distribution of activity, and the similarity of criteria performance.

Work samples should also be standardized in terms of materials, layout, instructions, and scoring. The best approach for achieving this goal of standardization is to prepare an examiner's manual. Standardized administration procedures become quite difficult without a manual offering uniform procedures for administration, use, and interpretation. The criteria employed in a manual's development should include (a) relationship to the DOT; (b) explanation of the work sample's purpose; (c) a complete list of all materials, tools, and parts needed for the sample; (d) detailed instructions for the client, including instructions for timing, evaluation of errors, and scoring; (e) instructions for the interpretation of scores; and (f) preparation and layout directions.

The above information is absolutely necessary, because if industrial norms (or any norms) are provided with the sample, any change in layout, materials, or any component of the sample's original design will invalidate these norms. Norms should be based on administration of the sample in the exact manner designated by the instructions. Also, inadequate norms—especially ones that lack checks on institutional norms by use of the work sample with an industrial population—may give very misleading results. When industrial norms are not used, there is no real assurance that performance on the work sample is predictive of employability in a competitive job. When using industrial norms, one must present this information in a manner that is relevant to the vocational opportunities in the local labor market area. It would serve no purpose for work sample evaluations to recommend areas of training or placement that are nonexistent in the local economy.

When attempting to obtain competitive norms for work samples, McCray (1979a) described three basic methods. First, workers from industry can be administered the work sample, and their performance can be used as a basis for establishing a norm group. Second, where industry has already developed production standards for a specific job, a job sample may be developed and the existing standards directly applied to the assessment tool. Third, industrial engineering techniques such as time study or predetermined motion time systems may be used to analyze a work sample and develop production standards for this work sample. For example, a methods–time measurement (MTM) procedure can be used to analyze any manual operation by studying the basic motions required to perform this operation. The MTM procedure also assigns to each motion a predetermined time standard that is determined by the nature of the motion and the conditions under which it was made (Dowd, 1993). This method can be quite helpful for evaluating performance, especially when a detailed job analysis is conducted and the evolution can identify aspects of a task that may be particularly demanding for those with a severe disability. Work samples, moreover, are usually criterion-referenced assessments, as opposed to norm-referenced assessments. Work samples are designed around a specific task or series of tasks. The steps of the task are determined ahead of time, and the client is then asked to complete the task while someone else observes and notes the completion of the task. The task analysis provides the criteria in a criteria-referenced test (Wheeler, 1996).

The rehabilitation professional must be aware, however, that performance on the work sample does not necessarily reflect or predict performance in competitive environments. The work sample is a simulation of work tasks and is not intended to contain the range of social and physical demands of real work (Hursh & Kerns, 1988).

Traditionally, work samples have been used with populations for which valid measurement with paper-and-pencil tests is unobtainable. These groups may be low in verbal skills, unable to read, or unable to relate to standard testing situations for any number of reasons. Work samples, consequently, are an evaluative technique, and are not designed to produce a significant change in the individual being assessed. However, in rehabilitation facilities the client's performance, behavior, and interest are significant factors in vocational assessment. The main body of the work sample research has been in terms of performance norms. The rehabilitation professional often has to rely on subjective judgments for behavior and interest appraisal when standardized behavior checklists and interest measurements are not available. Many work samples, however, allow the opportunity to observe behavior in a relatively controlled setting and can reveal aspects of the client's personality, interests, and attitudes toward a job. Work samples can promote interest exploration and generate exploration of problem-solving and decision-making abilities in a more realistic, hands-on vocational situation.

The Work Sample Evaluation Process

The work sample evaluation process can be understood by describing the following steps:

1. While the client does the work sample, the evaluator observes him or her and records observations on

    A. explicit behavior factors

    B. performance factors related to the demands of the task, such as aptitudes and skills

    C. possible learning style and preferences, as the client should adequately learn all aspects of what is to be done before he or she is required to perform the task

    D. possible indications of interest through observing the client's behavior during task performance

    E. possible job-related needs and potential job modifications for the client

2. Upon completion of the sample, a score is determined regarding how well the client has performed relative to others who have taken the sample.

3. A summary of the results of all the actual work samples performed that day should be conducted. This summary is accomplished in terms of the client's behaviors, interests, and performance.

4. After the completion of all the work samples, the daily observations are summarized and a meeting with the client is arranged. The following topics are discussed:

    A. The client's reactions to the work sample process, and the work samples the client especially liked or disliked

    B. The client's estimate of one's own behavior and performance, and then the client's actual behavior and performance

    C. The client's reaction to this information

5. The evaluator will then write a report and include information on indications of interest, learning preferences, possible vocational aptitudes and skills, and qualities and behaviors that appear to be characteristic of an individual at work.

Advantages and Disadvantages

When using work samples to obtain a comprehensive assessment, work samples have many advantages. They can reduce the cultural, educational, and language barriers of one's vocational potential. Work samples emphasize psychomotor ability and skills rather than verbal ability. As clients realize that they are working on practical tasks, they may accept the assessment activity as being significant to their vocational planning. Work samples may be as close to the reality of work as can be obtained within the rehabilitation facility. Also, performance of concrete tasks provides direct and immediate information to the evaluator and, in turn, immediate feedback to the individual about his or her performance (Hursh & Kerns, 1988).

There are disadvantages, however, to using work samples. Although work samples may be an improvement over traditional psychological tests, they are still viewed by many examinees as yet another test; this perception can be quite anxiety-provoking for individuals with disabilities. Also, a person's abilities—at a given moment of time within a contrived, time-pressured situation—do not necessarily indicate his or her success level within a more normal situation. The lack of standardization of most work samples, moreover, may result in very dissimilar results when they are used by different evaluators. Inconsistent administration and scoring reduce reliability. Work samples may also fail to distinguish between aptitude and achievement. For the evaluator, there is a great responsibility to interpret results in the light of how much related experience the client has had. Further, work samples tend to emphasize quality and quantity of production rather than personality factors. Often, it is not feasible to develop work samples for the many different types of jobs in the labor market, and little comparison can be drawn between the environment in industry and the work sample method. Also, because work technological change is so rapid, there is a risk of developing a good appraisal instrument for jobs that no longer exist.

An additional caution when using work samples was explained by Walk (1985). In a work sample system, the tasks are constructed to determine the client's skills in a given area. Failure to complete a task successfully usually indicates limited or no ability in the area tested. However, this may not be the case with individuals with a disability. Failure to successfully complete a task could mean, instead, that certain characteristics of the task itself, coupled with the disability, interact, leading to failure. As Walk (1985) stated, "A reviewer must be careful to distinguish the two" (p. 29).

In-House Work Samples

Because of the severity of the client's disability, and the changing nature of jobs due to economic and technological factors, commercial work samples do not always provide the functional information that is needed for rehabilitation planning. Also, the commercial work samples may not relate to the jobs available to the client in the local labor market. When there are gaps in information provided by commercial systems, in-house work samples may be developed to complement selected commercial work sample systems.

The development and use of in-house work samples is based on a job analysis and identification of important dimensions for a job or cluster of jobs (Peterson, 1984). Local job analyses may be performed to determine job tasks, physical demands, and potential job modifications, and published job analyses such as those published in the DOT may also be used. The individual developing the work sample must get to know the labor market, vocabulary, tools of the industry, and positive characteristics of workers. Contacts may have to be made within the local business or industry. The job analysis should include the identification of worker function information and worker trait characteristics. Other steps in work sample development include (a) identifying worker characteristics and assessment needs, as well as the accommodations that need to be made to maximize client performance; (b) standardizing work sample activities (such as the identification of the equipment, tools, and materials to be used), the instruction and administration format, and the measurement, scoring, and interpretation procedures; (c) developing norming procedures that include gathering normative data; and (d) establishing reliability and validity procedures (Hursh & Kerns, 1988).

Questions To Be Asked When Selecting a Work Sample System

Although in-house work samples may be a response to the local labor market, many commercial systems are available that have been standardized and that can be of great assistance to the rehabilitation worker who is exploring vocational potential. An evaluator can be easily confused, however, about which system or systems will best satisfy one's assessment needs. The following questions can be asked by the evaluator and are developed from suggestions provided by Brolin (1973) and Hursh & Kerns (1988):

1. What type of classification system is used by the commercial work samples—trait factor or job cluster?

2. Does the manual provide normative information (such as data on the normative population sample) and reliability and validity information?

3. If one were to use the particular system, what are the initial costs, equipment maintenance and replacement costs, necessary computer time allotments and printouts, space requirements? What is the evaluator–evaluee ratio?

4. Are the behavioral, performance, and physical capacity measures clearly identified?

5. Are appropriate forms available for recording and reporting observations and recommendations?

6. Does the system provide a practice orientation period?

7. Does the system penalize the client for low verbal skills or low academic achievement?

8. Is it necessary to buy the whole package, or can one or more components be purchased?

9. What is the length of time required for the average client to take the work samples in the system?

No one system can provide appropriate opportunities for all clients and all vocational rehabilitation facilities. As Hursh and Kerns (1988) stated,

> In another sense, any one or two of the systems can be both individualized and at the same time broad enough to meet these varied needs. The primary key to this individualized versus comprehensive coverage question is the vocational evaluator. This person's competencies and ability to establish rapport, and individualize the work samples, will determine the system's effective usefulness. (p. 151)

Guidelines to the Effective Use of Work Samples

For work samples to be used optimally in the rehabilitation facility, specific guidelines should be followed.

1. *A manual on the particular work sample system should be used, because it can offer uniform procedures for administration, use, and interpretation.* The evaluator can also explain when the information is available, the relationship of the particular work sample(s) to available jobs, and training opportunities.

2. *Instructions should be given to a client prior to beginning a work sample.* These instructions (a) orient the client to the usefulness of the work sample, (b) inform the client about what to do and exactly how to do it, and (c) aid in the assessment of the client's ability to learn to do the task if he or she does not perform adequately following the standardized instructions. If the client cannot perform the task from these standardized instructions, then a determination will have to be made on what type(s) of instruction will facilitate the client's understanding of the task to be performed in the work sample. But this explanation of the instructions can provide valuable information on the client's learning preference. The client should thoroughly understand what one is going to do and how to do it. This understanding involves learning the instruction, and this learning is different from the actual performance of the work sample (McCray, 1979). There are many different ways to provide instructions to clients, and it is necessary that the instructional format used be compatible with the client's learning capabilities.

3. *Once the client has demonstrated his or her ability to perform the work sample, then performance is measured.* If possible, an evaluation should be conducted of the whole

person, because an understanding of the client's skills and interests may not be enough for successful work adjustment and job progress. Behaviors that are crucial to acquiring and holding a job in industry include the ability to follow directions, use tools, understand work method, exercise an attention span, have physical stamina, and accept criticism. However, because the environment of the rehabilitation facility does differ from an actual work setting, the behaviors of the client during the evaluation process may not accurately reflect eventual job-related behaviors.

When using work samples, the evaluator should attempt to individualize these measures for each client. Work samples, for example, do not have to be used in the same sequence with all clients. It should be further recognized that work samples are not likely to be used as a pass–fail mechanism. Performance on a work sample fits somewhere on a continuum between total inability to do the task and the industrial standard. Recommendations for each client relate to where one's performance falls on that continuum.

Overview of Selected Commercial Work Sample Systems

Table 10.1 shows a selection of commercial work sample systems, including source, description, training required, and cost.

Transferable Skills Assessment

One of the practical ways to explore the client's abilities in relation to employability goals is transferable skills assessment. Skill analysis has a long and diverse history, and its development has been facilitated by business and industry. The concept of transferable skills analysis was popularized by the book *What Color is Your Parachute?* (Bolles, 1980), which prompted counselors to look for similarities among skills rather than differences. This form of assessment has received increased attention from evaluators because employers are looking for people with particular competencies, and not necessarily with special interests. Clients also want job situations in which they use the skills that are important to them. If individuals with disabilities are to become more marketable in the competitive job environment, then they should be clear about their skills. People are hired based on their qualifications—a mix of experience, skills, knowledge, attitudes, and abilities—and how well their qualifications match what is needed on the job.

A skill is simply an ability to do something. It may be a natural ability or one acquired through training or education. Skills have been classified into the following categories:

1. *Adaptive skills,* which are self-management skills and personality orientations an individual brings to the job. Examples of such skills include attention to details,

(text continues on page 201)

TABLE 10.1
Selected Work Sample Systems

Sample System	Developer	Description	Training
JEVS Work Samples	Vocational Research Institute 1528 Walnut St, Suite 1502, Philadelphia, PA 19102 1-800-VRI-JEVS or (215) 875-7387	Provides 28 work samples for special needs populations; administered over 5- to 7-day period; normative data on over 1,100 individuals; simultaneous assessment of 15 persons possible with standard hardware; supplemental hardware available	Required and included along with follow-up consultation in cost of training; training available in Philadelphia, Atlanta, and the West Coast
VIEWS (Vocational Information and Evaluation Samples)	Same as above	Provides 16 work samples designed and normed for trainable people who have mental retardation; incorporates individualized training to a level of compentency before assessment of performance; an industrial team standard (MODAPTS) provided for each work sample to compare client productivity with average practiced professional; the expanded system includes component hardware for four additional work samples.	Training and consultation included in cost of system (in use throughout United States, Canada, Japan, Mexico, and Israel); training available in Philadelphia, Atlanta, and the West Coast
VITAS (Vocational Interest, Temperament and Aptitude System)	Same as above	Provides 22 work samples for disadvantaged persons, educable people who have mental retardation, learning disability; takes 2½ days to administer; assessment of 10 clients per week possible with standard hardware, up to 30 with supplementary hardware; expanded system includes component hardware for eight additional work samples.	Training included in cost; available in Philadelphia, Atlanta, and the West Coast

(continues)

TABLE 10.1 (*continued*)

Sample System	Developer	Description	Training
McCarron-Dial Evaluation System (MDS)	McCarron-Dial System P.O. Box 45628 Dallas, TX 75245 (214) 247-5945	Consists of eight separate instruments that assess five neuropsychologic factors: verbal, cognitive, sensory, motor, emotional, and integration coping (adaptive behavior); provides predictive information regarding work potential and suggests rehabilitation strategies for disabilities related to central nervous system damage	Training of 3 days required at Dallas and selected sites
Hester Evaluation System (HES)	Evaluation Systems, Inc. P.O. Box 10741 Chicago, IL 60610	Computer-based method of assessing vocational potential; consists of 20 to 27 tests measuring abilities in various fields; printout of job titles from DOT furnished; takes 5 hours to administer, 12 persons at a time	
Talent Assessment Programs (TAP)	Talent Assessment, Inc. P.O. Box 5087 Jacksonville, FL 32207	Provides 10 tests of perception and dexterity to measure gross and fine manual dexterity, visual and tactile discrimination, and retention of details; ages above 14 and all mental levels except "trainable"; measures attributes common to hundreds of work areas (not specific jobs); can be administered in 2½ hours; profile sheet gives Talent Quotient; norms provided	Training required and available at the purchaser's site in 1½ days

TABLE 10.1 *(continued)*

Sample System	Developer	Description	Training
Singer Vocational Evaluation	Singer Education Division/ Career Systems 80 Commerce Dr. Rochester, NY 14623	Series of over 20 job samples for those with or without handicaps or disadvantages; each sample fitted into a carrel (work station) using an audiovisual approach complete with specific equipment, tools, and supplies for completing a series of work tasks; assesses full range of a person's abilities, aptitudes, interests, and tolerances for specific job areas related to DOT and OE career clusters	Recommended but not required
MICRO-TOWER	MICRO-TOWER Institutional Services, ICD Rehabilitation and Research Center 340 East 24th St. New York, NY 10010	Provides 13 work samples for persons who are educable and have retardation through those in the normal range, adolescents, and adults; takes 3 to 5 days to complete; instructors presented on cassette tape with opportunity for questions and supplemental instructions; administered to 5 to 10 people at a time; each work sample divided into a learning, practice period; group discussion conducted at end of each day; profile of scores in five aptitude areas provided; verbal, numerical, motor, spatial, and clerical perception; norms provided; testing of jobs from DOT given	Not required, but available at ICD (Institute for Crippled and Disabled) or at purchaser's agency at their cost

(continues)

TABLE 10.1 *(continued)*

Sample System	Developer	Description	Training
Valpar	Valpar International Corporation P.O. Box 5767 Tucson, AZ 85703	System 2000 is a modular software system for assessment, DOT access, work hardening, work sample scoring, and database applications. The software is supplied on 3½" floppy disks.	Contact Valpar
Wide Range Employment Sample Test (WREST)	Guidance Association of Delaware	Contains 10 individual work samples; approximate time of administration for one client is 90 minutes; task instructions are oral and demonstrated; readily adaptable for use with deaf clients; samples are related to work stations commonly used in sheltered workshops.	None required

cooperation, concentration, empathy, enthusiasm, punctuality, reliability, spontaneity, and tolerance.

2. *Functional skills*, which are generic behaviors related to people, data, and things that are brought into play in a work environment. Examples of such skills include the following:

Data	People	Things
Synthesizing	Mentoring	Precision Working
Analyzing	Negotiating	Manipulating
Computing	Supervising	Operating
Compiling	Consulting	Controlling
Copying	Persuading	Handling

3. *Specific content skills*, which are competencies that enable an individual to perform a specific job according to the expectations of an employer. These are skills related to a given discipline, such as a mechanic knowing the parts of an engine or a physical therapist understanding the different components of the human body.

Another way to think about job-related skills is to organize them by Holland (1977) types, such as:

Realistic: assembling, physical activities, outdoor activities, building, and operating tools or machinery

Artistic: formulating ideas, inventing, designing, composing or playing music, and expressing feelings and thoughts

Enterprising: managing money and developing a budget, seeing a problem and acting to solve it, organizing people, making decisions, taking risks, and selling and persuading

Investigative: calculating, researching, analyzing, diagnosing, experimenting, and observing

Social: helping, listening, motivating, counseling, consulting, working on a team

Conventional: keeping records, comparing, attending to details, classifying, organizing things

Skills, of course, can be acquired, and the required skills for any career field can be determined. Most skills are developed from education, but the level of a client's educational attainment does not usually identify the specific skills attained. A person with an undergraduate degree in history, for example, may convey a vast array of achievable skills, but the major itself does not denote necessarily the level of skill attainment. Skills, moreover, can also be derived from work and leisure experiences. What is important for the evaluator is to assist clients to identify their skills for general self-assessment. There are usually two ways to conduct this identification. One is to provide clients with an already designed checklist; another is a more informal approach that follows a step-by-step procedure.

Checklists

A variety of checklists have been developed, called inventories, many of which are found in career development and counseling texts. Examples of such checklists follow.

A. Bolles' (1980) *What Color is Your Parachute?* contains an inventory that is quite useful in assessment situations when exploring transferable skills.

B. *Transferable Skills Inventory* (1983), developed by the Job Search People (720 N. Park Street, Indianapolis, Indiana 46202), is an inventory that contains three columns: "Educ," for all skills that were acquired through education or vocational training; "Life," for all skills acquired elsewhere, such as paid employment, volunteer activities, and general experience; and "Next Job," for those skills the client believes will be needed to reach a selected job objective.

C. A Skills Inventory, an adaptation of a skills inventory created by Bolles (1989), was developed by Robert Lock (1992) and follows the Holland typology of Realistic, Investigative, Artistic, Social, Enterprising, and Conventional. A workbook of student activities titled "Taking Charge of Your Career Direction" that contains the inventory also has useful information on adaptive, functional, and specific content skills that the client can identify while taking the inventory.

Step-by-Step Procedure

Whereas an established checklist can provide insightful information into an identification of transferable skills, a more informal method can be quite useful for assisting clients during a self-assessment for future career options. The following is a suggested, sequential approach:

1. The evaluator asks the client to discuss, describe, or explain his or her work and leisure experiences. A review of these experiences will reveal a pattern of skills that may have been used repeatedly. This description can be facilitated by the following questions:

- What were the skills that were most important to perform in your different jobs?
- What was the happiest role occupied during work or leisure activities?
- What skills and abilities did you need for this kind of work?

If each work and leisure activity is discussed in detail, then a pattern of skills will emerge. The more details that are gathered from memory and from the remembrance of other people's positive responses, the more skills will be identified with confidence.

A question that emerges from this identification is the following: Could any of these skills be used in another setting?

2. Once the in-depth work history is completed, the evaluator can then develop a transferable skills and abilities profile (Saxon & Spitznagel, 1995) that is structured in the following manner:

Job (from work history) _____

Skills and Abilities _____

    1.

    2.

    3.

    4.

    5.

Job (from work history) _____

Skills and Abilities _____

    1.

    2.

    3.

    4.

    5.

3. The evaluator determines client's current interest pattern (see Chapter 13), identifying the client's stated and measured interests.

4. The counselor finds the *Guide to Occupational Exploration* (GOE) (JIST, 1998) work group that is appropriate for the client's job history and skills and abilities from the profile developed in Step 2. The work group presents the skills and abilities that may be needed for jobs that relate to the client's interest pattern and the pattern of skills and abilities that make up the client's profile. Within the GOE, all jobs are divided into 66 work groups.

5. In completing Step 4, the evaluator must consider the client's disabling condition in relation to his or her residual vocational functioning capacity. Skills and abilities that have been deleted or limited by the disabling condition must be reflected in the client's transferable skills and abilities profile (Saxon & Spitznagel, 1995).

6. The counselor needs to check the local labor market. The jobs that are identified as job matches from previous activities are only "suggestions" and should be evaluated by common sense and good judgment. These job suggestions should be compared to jobs that actually exist in the local or regional labor market.

This six-step process, in summary, includes an analysis of a client's previous work history and leisure activities, the demand characteristics of jobs within that work history, and the current level of functioning (which may have been affected by illness or injury). With the reduction in job functioning because of disability-related factors, this process requires that additional or alternate job titles be identified. These jobs need to be consistent with the worker's level of functioning, while taking into account previous work skills and leisure activities.

An assumption for the completion of either a structured transferable skills inventory, or the six-step approach, is that clients possess the self-confidence to identify skills accumulated throughout their employment history. Clients may doubt their abilities or may be skeptical about possessing any skills. However, many clients realize that they have many more skills than they had previously acknowledged. The issue of self-confidence, consequently, may need attention before the exploration of transferable skills can proceed.

 ## CASE STUDY: RICARDO

Ricardo was a computer programmer who was laid off because of downsizing within his company, and 2 weeks later was involved in an accidental shooting incident while hunting with friends. The accident resulted in psychomotor seizures. Ricardo has been working with a neurologist to achieve seizure control, and though his condition has stabilized, he has a seizure without warning about every 6 weeks. Ever since his accident occurred 18 months ago, Ricardo has been looking for work in the computer field, but has been unsuccessful. He presents himself now to an evaluation center, referred to this agency by his vocational rehabilitation counselor, and states that he "really is no longer interested in the computer field," but is interested more in woodworking, especially hand-crafted furniture. He states that recent interest test results from *The Self-Directed Search* (Holland, 1985), which was given by the counselor, corroborate this interest.

 ## Chapter 10 Case Study Questions

DIRECTIONS: With this information, please respond to the following questions:

1. How would you proceed with a transferable skills assessment for Ricardo?
2. Outline the assessment steps eventually leading to skill identification.

Computer-Assisted Vocational Assessment

USE OF COMPUTERS IN VOCATIONAL ASSESSMENT

Although computers have been part of the American scene since the late 1950s, their use in vocational rehabilitation for a wide range of work demands is fairly recent. The greatest stimulus to the growth of computer-assisted assessment has been the development of the desktop microcomputer, which has upheld the promise of in-office, computerized test administration combined with quick and accurate test data interpretation (Cohen, Swerdlik, & Phillips, 1996). Rehabilitation professionals were first introduced to computers as a means to score psychological test instruments used in the counseling process (Golter & Golter, 1986). Computers also have been used to assist the person with a disability in taking psychometric tests—for example, through voice-operated response units (Growick, 1983).

Although the emergence of computerized assessment has not been without controversy, advocates of computer use see computerized testing, scoring, and interpretation as being more reliable, cost effective, and sophisticated. It also allows for more complex handling of variables and the production of highly sophisticated reports from a statistical standpoint (Brown, 1991). Computerized assessment facilitates the economy of professional time, with usually a negligible time lag between the administration of a test and its scoring and interpretation. A computer also has a capacity to combine data according to a rule that is more accurate than the capacities of humans. In addition, computers provide the potential for systematically gathering and accessing extensive normative databases that transcend the capacities of human test interpreters (Cohen et al., 1996).

Today's computer systems are now being used in a variety of rehabilitation settings for different agency needs (Perlman & Austin, 1984). Analyzing data has historically been the most common application of computer technology. The use of computers in state rehabilitation agencies, for example, revolves around statistical and financial reporting related to client services. Other uses relate to personnel, in-service training, program planning, program evaluation, assessment and eligibility determination, and job matching (Edwards, 1989).

Vocational evaluation is a complex process that draws on many theoretical perspectives. Because it is typically performed within a work evaluation facility, vocational evaluation represents a merging of the traditions of standardized testing and on-the-job evaluation (Chan & Questad, 1981). Assessment and evaluation processes appear to be likely areas in which microcomputers are useful. Computers traditionally have been used for test scoring and interpretation. Automated scoring of standardized tests; structured interviews; and assessment components of computer-assisted career guidance, vocational evaluation, and job-matching systems have become popular because of the speed and computational accuracy of the computer (Burkhead & Sampson, 1985).

This chapter identifies the varied components of a computer assessment system, explains the considerations for making decisions about computer use during the vocational evaluation, identifies selected computer-assisted career information and guidance systems, and discusses several problems of computer use.

Components of a Computer Assessment System

Golter and Golter (1986) explained that counselor applications are of two types: client assessment and job matching. They state that

> client assessment is mainly oriented to computerized psychological testing for determining vocational interests, attitudes, and personalities. Such information can be scored quickly by computer and a profile of test results generated for use in the counseling process. Computer systems also can be used to administer tests, including voice operated response units that record oral responses for persons with impaired hand function or limited writing skills. (p. 160)

Maze (1984) identifies three areas of computer systems that have application to vocational assessment:

1. *Self-Assessment Components.* As stated earlier, computers provide an effective medium for administering and scoring evaluative instruments. Assessment instruments can be scored instantaneously, and the results can be explained to the client without delay. Subjective exercises can also be administered by the computer, with prompts and extra assistance for those who have difficulty understanding the instruction. As Maze (1984) states:

> Clients' responses can then be compiled and printed out by the computer in a format that facilitates self-understanding. Any self-assessment topic can be computerized, including aptitude, abilities, skills, interests, work preferences, values, and personality types. (p. 159)

2. *Occupational Selection.* To bring more reality into the client's vocational evaluation, computers are able to sort occupational titles and select appropriate vocational

categories to offer to a client. Maze (1984) believes that, in general, computers are more accurate than counselors, as they can retain hundreds of titles and accurate details about each occupation simultaneously in their memories. They also sort objectively by applying only the screening criteria programmed into them for the sorting process, without regard to sex, race, or socioeconomic status. In other words, computers open up career options and are able to present a wide selection of relevant titles. In fact, many assessment components offer occupational titles as part of their results. However, the two components can be separate, as when an instrument produces personality types or goal statements that are later translated into occupations, or they can be combined as they are in many computerized interest inventories (Maze, 1984).

3. *Informational Components.* Computers are excellent information retrieval devices. A computer can score the information, retrieve parts of the information simultaneously, and provide a printed copy for the client. Computerized information can include facts about educational programs, industries, occupations, financial aid, job openings, and bibliographic materials.

Although the use of the term *computer-assisted assessment* always implies that the evaluator is somehow being assisted by a computer, it does not necessarily imply that the evaluator is being assisted directly by a computer or even using a computer to enter data. There are examples of assessment instruments that are designed for computer scoring, yet computer-assisted assessment increasingly means computerized test administration. The degree of interaction between the evaluator and the client depends on how interactive the computer has been programmed to be (Cohen et al., 1996).

Computerized career information systems provide a wide array of information regarding employment and specific jobs. These systems are online databases in which comprehensive information regarding various occupations is provided. This information can include detailed descriptions of the occupation, educational requirements for entry into the occupation, and extensive information regarding the day-to-day activities of persons engaged in the occupation (Brown, 1991).

Emerging from computer-assisted, self-assessment activities are different types of scoring reports. These reports represent computer output options, and can include (a) *simple scoring reports*, which provide test scores, either listed or drawn on a profile; (b) *extended scoring reports*, which provide key statistical information about the results, as well as the relationships between the various subtests or scales. This scoring is very useful for intelligence, ability, and vocational interest tests; and (c) *interpretive reports*, which provide a written interpretation of test findings. The report can give both descriptive and screening information.

Decisions To Make About Computer Use

After determining which components a computerized assessment system contains, the quality of each system should be evaluated. Maze (1984) offers a checklist for developing guidelines for computer use in career guidance, and I have adopted this checklist for use in vocational evaluation. The following questions are to be asked by the rehabilitation professional when attempting to choose among different systems and components for use in vocational evaluation.

1. What do you perceive are the essential elements in the vocational assessment process? What role is the system intended to play in this process?

2. Which assessment instruments does the system offer? Can these instruments be taken either online (at the computer) or off-line (on paper with entry of scores into the computer)?

3. What are the outcomes the system intends to achieve, and what population is it intended to serve?

4. Is the assessment material presented in an interesting and lively manner? How often will it be in need of updating?

5. Is the assessment material relevant to your client population, and is the assessment material developed at an appropriate reading level? Is normative information provided on the assessment system?

6. Are the assessment and job-matching components effective in selecting relevant occupations or educational programs?

7. Are there aids to self-assessment that help the client answer questions accurately?

8. Do the assessment modules make full use of the interactive capabilities of the computer?

9. Is the interpretation accurate, usable, and understandable?

10. Is the occupational and educational information localized to your region or state? Is it possible to add data?

11. What philosophy is used in interpreting the data?

12. How is the system intended to be used? How easy is the program to use? To what extent is the program interactive? Does the system allow individuals to change or rethink answers? Are corrections allowed for simple mistakes? How much time does the average user need? How many sessions do most users need to complete a useful assessment?

13. Is the system adaptable to the complex evaluation needs of your clients?

14. Does the manual explain the objectives and logical structure for each assessment component?

15. To what extent have the software packages been tested by a variety of users?

16. Are there assessment exercises available for special populations?

17. Does the system actually keep the data as up-to-date as it claims, and are the updates produced on a dependable schedule?

18. Is information provided in the user manual on such issues as concurrent and predictive validity? Has this information been well researched?

19. Does the user manual provide information on whether criterion groups are used to determine the ratings of skills and values of occupational groups?

20. Is knowledge provided about computerized estimates of skills, interests, or values and their reliability over time?

21. Does the system provide a way to determine whether an individual is faking answers or responses?

22. What are the professional credentials of the system developers?

23. Does the system run on machines already available on site?

24. Is the system supported by a reputable, stable organization?

25. What is the cost of the system compared to the competition?

Computer Programs for Vocational Assessment

With an identification of these questions, selected computer-assisted assessment systems are now presented. This list is not exhaustive, and the systems that are discussed are those that I have used frequently in assessment work with clients.

Valpar 2000

Valpar 2000 (Valpar International Corporation, 1991) is a highly integrated, modular family of software products for assessment, work hardening, work sample scoring, and database applications. Of particular interest to the rehabilitation professional conducting evaluation is the computerized assessment (COMPASS) package of Valpar 2000, which assesses individuals from middle school students to adults who are making career choices for placement into jobs or training programs. It is a criteria-referenced assessment instrument that uses adaptive testing techniques and measures a person's knowledge, skills, interests, and abilities as they relate to jobs and training programs, using the very developed rating system of the *Revised Handbook for Analyzing Jobs* and the *Dictionary of Occupational Titles* (DOT), both developed by the U.S. Department of Labor.

This instrument provides 13 computer-based subtests plus three short work samples and a paper-and-pencil survey. The work sample component of COMPASS includes a block assembly, a wiring box, and a selection of tools and parts. They are used primarily to assess manual dexterity, motor coordination, and finger dexterity. All results are gathered directly by the computer and scored automatically. The system is designed to be administered by one evaluator to an individual or small group, and requires 60 to 90 minutes. The reports include a DOT profile and a time-on-task section. The evaluator is also able to modify information to identify additional jobs for consideration. These capabilities make the Valpar 2000 an interactional tool for the client. The system requires IBM PC/AT/XT/PS2 or 100% compatible clone, hard drive, color monitor, printer, and 640K memory. With this product there are two content domains of interest: (a) the system of work-related factors of the Department of Labor as described in its *Revised Handbook for Analyzing Jobs* (1972), and (b) scholastic verbal and math content. Scores for COMPASS subtests are automatically converted into scores that are called collectively the Worker Qualifications Profile, which reflects levels of various demonstrated work-related abilities. The measure is also applicable to those with hearing impairments, because visual feedback is given in response to each test answer.

This system is available from Valpar International Corporation, P.O. Box 5767, Tucson, AZ, 85703, (602) 293-1510, or, 800-528-7070.

The APTICOM Aptitude Test Battery

The *APTICOM Aptitude Test Battery* (Vocational Research Institute, 1989), a portable computerized desktop testing console, was designed to measure vocational aptitudes studied by the U.S. Department of Labor. This government agency is exploring how performance on measures of these aptitudes is related to job performance. The *APTICOM Aptitude Test Battery* includes 11 separate tests that are all administered on a wedge-shaped computerized testing console that automatically determines the test being administered, times the test, shuts down at the end of the standardized testing period, and scores results. Each test is preceded by a practice phase during which the client must demonstrate a functional understanding of test demands. In the overall battery, only 2 of 11 tests require the ability to read test items, and all 11 tests are administered with standardized oral instruction. Total administration time ranges between 70 and 90 minutes (Harris, 1982). The vehicle for relating *APTICOM* aptitude scores to jobs involves linkage with the Occupational Aptitude Pattern (OAP) structure based on the *General Aptitude Test Battery* (GATB). When the *APTICOM* testing console is connected to a computer printer, a printout is generated that lists the client's 11 raw and corresponding standardized test scores, 10 aptitude scores (computed by *APTICOM*) via the combination of appropriately weighted test scores, and all of the OAPs and work groups for which critical normative cutoffs have been attained (Harris, 1982).

A new *APTICOM* A5 has been developed, which allows for customized reports and selection of norm populations ranging from ninth grade to the adult employed. This new system also allows for downloading client data to a personal computer disk. All existing *APTICOM*s are upgradable to A5 specifications.

The *APTICOM* also provides an inventory of occupational interests in 12 areas—artistic, scientific, plants/animals, protective, mechanical, industrial, business detail, selling, accommodating, humanitarian, lead/influence, and physical performing. This interest inventory is yoked to *APTICOM*'s aptitude component to supply clients and rehabilitation workers with an efficient means of starting the process of occupational exploration with accurate information refined down to the *Guide to Occupational Exploration* (GOE) (Harrington & O'Shea, 1984) work group level.

Talent Assessment Program (TAP)

The TAP (Talent Assessment, Inc., 1985) measures functional aptitudes and relates them to specific types of work. It has a series of 10 hands-on assessment tests using real work materials in which aptitudes for visualization and retention, discrimination, and dexterity are determined. The test results are correlated both to the DOT and to the workers groups of the GOE. Norms are nondiscriminatory and apply to all population groups. To eliminate discrimination risks with nonreaders who are blind, as well as with individuals with learning disabilities, reading is not required and verbal instructions are normally used. Written instructions are provided for hearing impaired persons. The tests can be used as an initial screening device in conjunction with other work evaluation assessment programs.

The *Instant Report Instant Summary System* (IRIS), a five-disk scoring, placement search, and report-writing program, is available as part of the TAP system. The scoring disk scores and profiles the TAP results, provides a summary of strength areas, and relates those strengths to jobs. The job search disks look for jobs in the general market, in those areas specified appropriate for handicapped individuals, or in specific local job markets.

System of Interactive Guidance and Information Program (SIGI)

Developed by the Educational Testing Service (1980) of Princeton, NJ, the SIGI provides interactive assistance in career decision making. It was designed to serve primarily students in, or about to enter, 2-year and 4-year colleges. The six interrelated subsystems are the heart of the SIGI system, and they provide a system of value clarification and disseminate occupational and educational information. Each of these subsystems offers a critical question and helps the student answer it through a series of statements and questions. The questions and answers form the distinctive steps in decision making that a client would also follow in future decisions. The subsystems are as follows:

1. *Values*. Examines 10 occupational values and weighs importance of each one. The values are income, independence, interest field, variety, security, leisure, leadership, helping others, prestige, and early entry.

2. *Locate*. Assigns specifications to five values at a time and gets lists of occupations that meet specifications. The client is provided with exercises devised to explore the consequences of the value choices.

3. *Compare*. Asks pointed questions and gets specific information about occupations of interest. Such questions include occupational description, education and training requirements, income based on national averages, personal satisfaction, conditions of work, and opportunities and outlook.

4. *Prediction*. Finds out probabilities of getting various marks in key courses of preparatory programs for occupations. The predictions are based on local data that may include test scores, self-estimates, and other local predictors.

5. *Planning*. Gets displays of programs for entering each occupation.

6. *Strategy*. Evaluates occupations in terms of rewards they offer and risks of trying to enter them.

The database from which the information is taken in the various steps is continually updated and reviewed. Regional differences are considered in the review process. The SIGI was developed to supplement and complement the work of the rehabilitation professional. The flexibility of the SIGI in adapting to local resources is an attractive part of the system.

The DISCOVER Program

This program was developed by the American College Testing Program (1989) to assist counselors in providing career guidance to students in grades 7 through 12. The system contains 20 modules, each of which is completed during one class period, although the student has the option to spend more time on any one module. A college/adult version has also been developed.

The system consists of modules such as (a) entry, (b) clarifying values, (c) values and occupations, (d) effective decision making, (e) decision making in careers, (f) organization of occupational world, (g) browsing occupations, (h) reviewing interests and strengths, (i) making a list of occupations to explore, (j) getting information about occupations, (k) narrowing a list of occupations, and (l) exploring specific career plans. These modules can be grouped into four components: (a) self-assessment (Self-Information), (b) identification of occupational alternatives (Strategies for Identifying Occupations), (c) reviewing occupational information (Occupational Information), and (d) identification of educational alternatives (Searches for Educational Institutions).

Realistic Assessment of Vocational Experiences (RAVE)

The RAVE program (American College Testing Program, 1993) is a computerized tool for identifying appropriate occupations for clients. This system performs a transferable skills analysis if a client's work history is provided. The RAVE needs two types of information about the client's past work experiences: a DOT number and approximate length of time spent at the job. The RAVE uses these occupations to find the skills the client used and then lists them in the first section of a report.

The RAVE also includes an eliminators section. Occupations for which the client is not qualified are eliminated based on client responses. This section includes such areas as academic, physical, stress-related, and work environment demands. A third section, "Descriptions," focuses on data, people, things, educational and vocational skills, aptitudes, temperaments, industries, work fields, and GOE interest areas. The RAVE calculates a value for each item in this section based on the client's work history. The report that the client receives, consequently, includes a summary of the skills used in past jobs, a client profile, a list of 60 occupations that could possibly be entered without retraining, a list of 60 occupations that match the client's profile if retraining is available, and a detailed description (called a view) of the 10 highest-scoring occupations.

There are customization capabilities available for the RAVE, which allows the system to adapt to local labor market information, add local employers, and customize the realistic occupations database. It also enables the evaluator to demonstrate graphically to clients how retraining or disabilities can change earning capacity and employment opportunities. Another important feature of the system is that it uses a unique process to identify potential jobs that would otherwise be eliminated. This search scans the 2,500 occupations that are most prevalent in the U.S., in addition to those in which clients are most likely to find openings.

The RAVE is available from the American College Testing, 230 Schilling Circle, #350, Hunt Valley, MD, 21031, 800-645-1992

Vocational Transit (Vocational Research Institute, 1992)

Vocational Transit was developed to measure four U.S. Department of Labor aptitudes: Form Perception, Motor Coordination, Finger Dexterity, and Manual Dexterity. *Vocational Transit* uses computer technology to measure these aptitudes through the use of computer-controlled testing modules. All tests are individually administered and then computer scored and interpreted. The results are included in a standardized report that contains specific testing behaviors as well as the client's aptitude scores and aptitude ratings on the four aptitudes.

The system is designed to assess vocational capabilities for persons with moderate or severe mental retardation, and it is also useful for persons with traumatic brain injury. The entire database of jobs was selected to meet the lowest levels of reasoning, mathematics, and language, as well as jobs requiring a 30-day–or–less training period. Eight hundred jobs met this criteria, which became the database for the system. Like most other assessment approaches, *Vocational Transit* is more effective when combined with additional behavior observations and other methods of assessment.

This system is available from Vocational Research Institute, 1528 Walnut St., Suite 1502, Philadelphia, PA, 19102, 800-VRI-JEVS.

Other Computer-Assisted Systems

Other computer-assisted assessment systems are available that can be useful to the reha-bilitation professional. Some of these systems are the following.

Career Information System (CIS). This system evaluates the client's temperaments, abil-ities, and other work-related variables, and relates them to appropriate occupations. It also provides occupational and educational information. The CIS has been expanded to include job and work-site modifications as a part of the occupational database. The system facilitates this client understanding because, with these modifications, clients might be able to complete predisability work tasks (Sampson, McMahon, & Burkhead, 1985).

Computer Assessment Program (CAP). This system interprets assessment data from the *McCarron-Dial System* (MDS) (McCarron & Dial, 1986) and generates a consultation report useful in the development of evaluation plans.

All of these computer-assisted systems focus on client assessment and a structured search for occupational and educational information, with a special emphasis on the availability of local and state data. Some of the systems place less emphasis on local and state data than other guidance assessment systems. However, all of the systems explained in this chapter were developed to help individuals understand themselves, the world of work, and the process of career decision making.

As Sampson et al. (1985) explained, however, rehabilitation-specific computer systems tend to

(1) stress the assessment of past work history, abilities, and transferable work skills;

(2) involve the counselor as the direct user of the computer system, thus placing the rehabilitation professional in the role of intermediary between the client and the computer; and

(3) use the U.S. Department of Labor's data as the principal source of occupational infor-mation. (p. 249)

Disadvantages of Computer-Assisted Programs

Although the use of computer-assisted systems may help the rehabilitation professional during the assessment process, there are several problems associated with using com-puters. They are as follows:

1. Most systems for job matching and vocational evaluation require a professional who is trained in computers to operate the system for the client. Such a requirement may limit the potential effectiveness of the system, because many clients are restricted

in their ability to articulate appropriate data for input into the computer. Another limitation can occur when rehabilitation professionals lack the ability to receive such information accurately (Sampson et al., 1985).

2. Some designers of computer applications in rehabilitation may inadvertently limit the range of occupations considered by a client on the basis of disability type. A database, for example, may only identify selected jobs obtained by persons with disabilities, and then this data can be used as the main ingredient of a job-matching component.

3. There is a continued concern that many computer assessment systems have not been developed sufficiently to permit adequate decision making regarding future behavior.

4. From the perspective of the client, especially someone who is not experienced in computers, a computer-administered test may be in itself an intimidating experience. Persons with disabilities who have developed various test-taking strategies that have been successful in the past, such as reviewing test materials or skipping around to answer only questions they are certain of first, may not be able to use these strategies during a computerized test administration (Cohen et al., 1996).

5. For tests that were originally developed for paper-and-pencil administration and now have been developed for computerized administration, there is the question of equivalence. There have been relatively few studies to test the equivalence factor, but findings have ranged from major differences as a function of format to relatively moderate ones. Some differences emerge as a function of the format of test administration. If the rehabilitation professional doubts the equivalency of a particular mode of test administration, the questionable test administration method should not be used (Cohen et al., 1996). However, not all computer-administered evaluation tests have a paper-and-pencil predecessor.

The appropriate application of computer-assisted evaluation measures depends, consequently, on the judgment and professional experience of the rehabilitation professional. Computer-derived information does not consider how jobs may be modified (as is required under the ADA of 1990) or how assistive technology may be applied to promote greater accessibility to jobs. The evaluator becomes an important component by taking job information and identifying how modifications may be made. Although no governmental regulation exists for these products—and opinion is divided as to whether such regulation should be introduced—the evaluator should be discriminating as to which products are appropriate for clients with disabilities. The validity of the program, as well as test security considerations, need to be ascertained carefully. Gati (1994) recommends that professionals can contribute to the effective use of computer-assisted programs by (a) constructively criticizing available systems; (b) participating in the selection of the systems to be used by their clients; (c) designing diagnostic prescreening procedures regarding who should be encouraged to use the available programs, when they should be used, and which systems are appropriate; and (d) discussing with the client, integrating, and interpreting the information received from the computer systems. All of these steps make the process more meaningful to the individual.

CHAPTER 11 CONCLUSION

Although the cost of computer-assisted systems is still relatively high, the computer can be used with a wide variety of clients seeking vocational assessment, and the assessment information can be updated quickly and easily. The development of different adaptive devices provides a more comprehensive assessment opportunity for individuals with severe disabilities than has been available in the past. Rehabilitation professionals need to become knowledgeable about computer technology, the importance of keeping information updated, and the modification of programs when necessary.

 CASE STUDY: COMPUTERS

You have been asked to develop a computer laboratory for vocational assessment at your agency. This rehabilitation facility primarily serves the needs of adults, ages 21 to 35, who have been industrially injured and who now have varied physical disabilities. Vocational evaluation must take place within 3 days, and the unemployment rate is high in the immediate job area. The educational backgrounds of the adults are varied, ranging from clients who left high school in the 10th grade to those who completed 2 years of college. Referral sources have stated to the agency that any vocational assessment report developed by the facility must also contain an extended list of possible training and employment options.

 Chapter 11 Case Study Questions

DIRECTIONS: From the information provided in this chapter, please answer the following questions:

1. Identify the questions you would ask to determine the most appropriate computer system.

2. Are any systems explained in the chapter that you believe would be appropriate for your rehabilitation facility?

Assessment with an Environmental Focus

T o achieve an accurate measure of the potential of the client's independent living or employment future, it is often necessary for the rehabilitation professional to explore environmental influences that have a possible impact on client functioning. One of the most important influences is the client's family, and increased attention has been given in the literature and in professional practice to the impact of the family system on the achievement of rehabilitation goals (Power, Dell Orto, & Gibbons, 1988; Sutton, 1985). Another area of influence is the identified work environment in which a client may pursue supported employment. Both of these areas are explored in this chapter as sources of diagnostic understanding.

VOCATIONAL ASSESSMENT OPPORTUNITIES IN THE SUPPORTED WORK MODEL

The traditional vocational rehabilitation model consists of first evaluating and then training the client prior to job placement. In contrast, a supported employment model was introduced in the early 1980s that proposes that the client be placed on the job and then receive specific training by a professional staff person on site. The Rehabilitation Act Amendments of 1986 (P.L. 99-506) defined supported employment as

> competitive work in integrated settings for individuals with severe handicaps for whom competitive employment has not traditionally occurred, or for whom competitive employment has been interrupted or intermittent as a result of severe disability, and who, because of their handicap, need on-going support services to perform such work. Such a definition includes transitional employment for individuals with chronic mental illness. (p. 1811)

The author expresses his gratitude to Mrs. Roberta G. Cohen and Mrs. Uma Krishnaswami for their review and comments on the supported employment section of this chapter.

Forms of Supported Employment

The basic nature of supported employment is (a) intensive, initial training of persons with severe vocational handicaps in natural work environments; (b) continuing intervention (support) often provided by a job coach or employment training specialist to help the person sustain acceptable work performance and maintain employment; (c) work in individual jobs, small groups, or mobile work crews; and (d) social integration at the work site with nondisabled individuals who are not paid caregivers. The job coaches or employment specialists perform such direct services as job analysis, matching of clients to the job, on-the-job training, advocacy with employers, and perhaps transportation and housing assistance (Rehabilitation Brief, 1987).

One asset of supported employment is the variety of forms it can take. Such models strive to offer immediate opportunities for work and preparation rather than emphasizing readiness and preparation (Rogan & Hagner, 1990). These models include (a) the *individual placement approach*, in which individuals are placed in regular community jobs and support is provided at the work site as needed; (b) the *enclave approach*, which consists of a small group (commonly eight individuals) trained and supervised together in the midst of an ordinary mainstream work environment; (c) the *mobile crew approach*, in which a singular purpose business is established by a service provider, such as janitorial and grounds-keeping services, and the crews of about five work under an individual supervisor; and (d) the *bench-work approach*, which offers more individualized, supervisory attention than the other approaches and frequently addresses behavioral problems that exceed a mobile crew's ability to respond. In most of these approaches, support for the client is continuous and long-term.

The typical supported work model is, therefore, industrially integrated. The industry or employer is described as the host industry, and clients with disabilities may be placed in on-the-job training either individually or in groups. Supported work approaches have also been run as satellites of community rehabilitation facilities or as alternatives replacing community workshops altogether. Programs are usually designed to take account of varying circumstances, including such matters as local industry and available funding. Some programs are purely transitional and others provide long-term (lifetime, if necessary) support to the client worker.

Although the overall concern of a counselor in supported employment is advocacy for integration, both the demand and the opportunity also are present for many counselors to conduct or supervise a vocational evaluation while the client is engaged in training. In supported employment, the counselor, as an advocate, is involved in service coordination and individualization, and attempts to ensure that quality services are being provided (Rehabilitation Research and Training Center Brief, 1988). With these responsibilities, opportunities exist in each supported employment approach for an effective vocational assessment.

Traditional Assessment

Traditional evaluation practices are generally used in supported employment programs. Aptitude batteries, work samples, and behavioral inventories have dominated in the general vocational evaluation of persons with severe disabilities (Menchetti & Uduari-Solner, 1990). However, problems related to reliability and validity demand that the process of assessment be reconceptualized for supported employment. An individual's performance, for example, is likely to change significantly as a result of exposure, training, and practice; an instrument may not include all of the necessary skills, domains, or variables to measure accurately what the instrument intends to measure (Menchetti & Udüari-Solner, 1990). The vocational evaluation process, moreover, has traditionally been conceptualized as more of a linear process that identifies interest, abilities, and aptitudes at one point in time and assumes that the individual with a severe disability will not change. What is needed for assessment practices is a cyclic evaluation approach that allows for client change in behavior, gradual restoration of residual functions, and emerging interests resulting from a post-traumatic experience. A cyclic approach allows for periodic evaluations as the client changes during the long period of adjusting to a severe disability.

Traditional assessment of individuals with severe handicaps in vocational rehabilitation has been based on the belief that measures of existing aptitudes, interests, and traits can be used to predict subsequent learning, performance, and adjustment at a job. Historically, evaluation has been concerned with what a client can do, rather than what is required for eventual, successful work adjustment (Irvin & Halpern, 1979). Traditional vocational evaluations typically occur in artificial, simulated environments such as evaluation centers. The reliability and validity data regarding many traditional assessment tools are either absent or deficient, and the settings in which evaluations are conducted have usually been closely associated with sheltered work facilities (Rogan & Hagner, 1990).

However, for many individuals with a severe disability entering the vocational rehabilitation system who do not have marketable skill levels at the time of their assessment, the predictive model of vocational assessment is discriminatory at best and all-too-often exclusionary. The predictive model is also based on norm-referenced measures that yield information about an individual's standing relative to other persons. Traditional measures of assessment have been found to be poor predictors of vocational adjustment and learning ability in the supported work model. Aptitudes, interests, abilities, and other so-called traits are not static, but are influenced by situational variables surrounding a person's learning experiences (Mischel, 1968). Psychometric tests have focused on measuring and reflecting between-individual differences (Schalock & Karan, 1979).

In summary, the limitations in traditional assessment approaches for individuals with a severe disability include "(a) the skills and abilities (e.g., reading, abstract language facility, auditory comprehension) that are irrelevant to the construct being predicted (e.g., work performance), (b) instructions and items that often require reading and comprehension levels that exceed the client's abilities, and (c) tests and work evaluation systems that frequently possess inadequate reliability and validity for people with severe disabilities" (Parker, Szymanski, & Hanley-Maxwell, 1989, p. 27). For individuals with a severe disability, consequently, assessment concerns should focus on domain-referenced measures, which emphasize not only individual growth but also an individual's status relative to a domain (content area) of information or skills, such as the domain of successful employment (Frey, 1984).

As Rogan and Hagner (1990) stated, "the most fair, reliable, and useful way to evaluate an individual with severe disabilities is within the actual work setting using materials that are naturally present" (p. 64). In other words, criterion-referenced assessment is more appropriate when the evaluator is exploring whether the person with a severe disability can meet the requirements of a job. Criterion standards may include performance times, acceptable rate of learning ability, and skills needed to meet job demands. Criterion-based assessment allows for more flexibility when determining client employability.

Consequently, assessment procedures, including norm-referenced evaluation measures, work samples, and tools based on psychological measurement, are seen as obstacles to competitive employment by proponents of supported employment (Rusch, Mithauge, & Flexer, 1986). Because assessment services must be considered among the most critical of all vocational rehabilitation services provided to adults with disabilities, rehabilitation service providers should seriously consider any and all assessment alternatives that can supplement present practices. Menchetti, Rusch, and Owens (1983) identified an alternative that consists of (a) the measurement of adaptive behavior, (b) the use of socially valid measures of work behavior, and (c) a "process assessment" in the content of skill training.

To provide for a more useful vocational evaluation approach for supported employment than traditional aptitude batteries, work samples, and behavior checklists, Menchetti and Uduari-Solner (1990) suggested an ecological model that consists of measurement, analysis, and decision making. In this model, measurement focuses on several variables, including the abilities of the individual, the requirements of the job, and the ecology of the workplace (physical aspects of the work environment, social and relationship dimensions of the site, and organizational factors, such as the degree of work pressure). The analysis dimension in the model consists of determining the type and level of support required to successfully maintain persons with a disability in employment. In the third component of the model, decision making, the goal is not to make eligibility screening decisions but rather to accept the individual for employment with or without support (Menchetti & Uduari-Solner, 1990). Each component represents a distinct area of assessment, and emphasis is on the reciprocal interactions or transactions that occur between an individual and the environment.

The use of the client's training opportunities during supported employment, as well as the development of skills in performing a job, also creates alternative resources to traditional evaluation approaches. Assessment procedures conducted in an environment in which there is a close and interactive relationship between evaluation and training provide the person with a severe handicap a greater opportunity to succeed within the vocational rehabilitation system. Guidubaldi, Perry, and Walker (1989) believed that "the on-the-job evaluation meets the demand of supported employment leaders who want to replace psychological testing with community-referenced assessment procedures" (p. 163).

On-Site Assessment

Using actual employers and their places of business as job sites for purposes of evaluation, though a relatively untried approach, can provide a real and concrete experience for the client and a realistic basis for assessment. Such assessment is based on the assumption that vocational rehabilitation incorporates a learning potential format, as well as includes a training process concerned with assisting clients to develop their work strengths and to remediate work deficits in an employment environment. On the actual job site, assessment and training can be viewed as interdependent parts of the evaluation process. The job site, where the client can experience job changes, production demands, and a hierarchy of supervision, can also provide for a functional appraisal of behavioral dynamics on the job by both the rehabilitation worker and the job supervisor.

Using supported employment sites for vocational evaluation requires, therefore, an ecological approach in which both clients and prospective work environments are assessed. As Parker et al. (1989) explained, "the term 'ecological' when used to describe a framework for assessment and intervention, reflects an underlying assumption that individuals interact with their environments and that both change as a result of the interaction" (p. 29). A client's ability to learn from an optimal training experience is ascertained in a format that includes opportunities for clients to learn and practice what they are expected to perform (Irvin & Halpern, 1979). Individual assessment information gathered from a wide range of services is coupled with a job analysis of various possible jobs and a behavioral analysis of specific client setting characteristics. In other words, an individual's abilities are identified and a match is then attempted between a client's abilities and the specific skills allegedly required on particular jobs. "The subsequent remediation provided is designed to alleviate or ameliorate any existing basic ability deficits" (Schalock & Karan, 1979, p. 39). The focus of vocational assessment in supported employment then shifts from a prediction orientation—a psychometric approach—to an ability training orientation that fosters the remediation of skill deficiencies and the development of skills needed to sustain employment (Schalock & Karan, 1979). This evaluation emphasizes the importance of direct assessment of actual skills and behaviors over a period of time and in the actual work environment (Halpern & Fuhrer, 1984). Such a shift in perspective underscores the fact that vocational assessment is not merely an event yielding data but a highly dynamic process charged with meaning for both evaluator and client.

Goals for a Supported Employment Assessment

The goals for an assessment approach within supported employment emphasize that assessment is an ongoing process. As the demands and requirements of a job can change, so clients can change as they learn new adjustment behaviors or acquire new, physical, and restorative functions. These goals are as follows:

1. The identification of the client's employment goals and vocational interests or preferences. However, some clients, by virtue of their need for supported employment, may have difficulty articulating appropriate goals.

2. The identification of the client's entering behaviors in relation to those required by the existing job.

3. The identification of the resources, such as people, places, things, and activities that a client needs to be successful in the work environment, given his or her present skill level or projected skill level (Cohen & Anthony, 1984). This may also include an estimate of the quantity and quality of remedial resources that are needed to facilitate the acquisition of necessary work behavior by the client, as well as an appraisal of job modification or restructuring and assistive devices that enable the client to maximize productivity. An understanding of resources also includes an assessment of the ongoing need for support that may increase independent productivity and how this information integrates into a work or rehabilitation plan.

4. The appraisal of the client's work performance, especially those problem behaviors or skill deficits that impede job adjustment and productivity. This appraisal should also focus on (a) specific work adjustment behaviors (e.g., arriving on time; dressing appropriately for the specific work environment; observing safety rules; returning from breaks or lunch on time; caring for tools, equipment, and the work area; working independently as appropriate to the client's limitations and the job demands); (b) interpersonal skills; (c) productivity behavior (Does the client demonstrate the emotional and physical tolerance to work steadily and consistently through the work period? Is the client able to adjust to work demands that may vary throughout a work period?); and (d) occupational job skills (Does the client demonstrate such job skills as being able to use the equipment, tools, or materials, and can the client perform services that the job requires?) (Hursh & Kerns, 1988).

5. The formulation from the assessment information learned during the client's job training of a rehabilitation remedial program that proceeds on a step-by-step basis toward specified behavioral objectives derived from the actual job demands.

6. An exploration of the client's satisfaction with a particular job in supported employment.

7. The identification of such social factors as the attitudes of co-workers, the extent of supervisory support or encouragement, the degree of work stress or pressure, an understanding of the physical setting that specifically includes lighting, temperature, task variety, and an awareness of the financial rewards and the ability and train-

ing requirements. Transportation resources to and from the work-site should also be considered.

For the rehabilitation worker who endorses these goals, the evaluation derives meaning both from the belief that jobs and supports be structured around individuals rather than individuals being placed into existing programs or slots (Rogan & Hagner, 1990), and from the specific behavioral objectives to be achieved. Jobs are viewed as complex sets of specific behaviors that should be broken down into sequential component parts (Schalock & Karan, 1979). To achieve the assessment goals, the evaluation process should be kept simple so that the client, the supervisor, and the evaluator can easily understand and quickly communicate to each other what is of diagnostic significance. Also, the evaluation can frequently be individually tailored to fit the specific characteristics of the setting and the target behaviors.

The Assessment Process

There are six steps in this assessment process, and each step is now explained. The steps imply that the rehabilitation worker has already developed many job leads and has identified a number of sites that have been or can be used in supported employment.

This identification does not preclude the possibility for developing other job opportunities. Although many practitioners prefer to identify the employment resource after the client's initial interview, in harmony with the "fit the job to the client's needs" principle, already having resources available when talking with the client often facilitates the individual's own work motivation. Such a belief does not mean that clients will only be placed stereotypically in certain job opportunities. Stereotyping is always a danger when helping those with severe disabilities find productive employment. Even so, when balancing the realities of available supported employment sites with job resources to be developed, I have leaned toward the direction of having resources available when initially discussing supported employment with the client.

A specialized approach to a client's interest exploration is suggested as follows. It involves six steps, does not rely on the use of standardized tests, and can be a part of the client's interview.

First Step

An understanding of the client who is a candidate for supported employment should be a priority. The identification of the client's interests is a beginning task in the assessment process because it helps the rehabilitation worker—once he or she understands the client's main occupational interests—to specify the job environments in which training and work adjustment can be pursued. Note that many clients who are candidates for supported employment may be very limited in their repertoire of experience due to physical or mental conditions. The job site itself may have to be the resource for interest assessment if no interests or very few are elicited from clients. Because of these client limitations, the rehabilitation worker may not have the opportunity to develop an initial match between interest and the job site.

Further tasks within this step focus on collecting information related to work readiness, as discussed in Chapter 1, as well as exploring what kinds of jobs would be satisfactory to an individual. Many of the questions suggested in the psychological, physical, occupational, and socio-environmental areas can be either used or adapted for the initial interview. During the initial interview, the rehabilitation worker can also determine whether the client recognizes that there are quality standards for work performance and can accept them as reasonable demands on him or her (Krantz, 1971).

An additional area to be explored within this step emphasizes the identification of the way the client learns. The rehabilitation professional may have access to the client's records, which explain the client's learning style. In other words, it is important to determine whether the client acquires information primarily by reading, by demonstration, or by hearing. Each client has a learning-style preference, and the identification of this preference can strongly facilitate adequate work adjustment. The learning capacities approach (Rusalem & Malikin, 1976) is an individualized program that assesses clients' learning styles through a nonstandardized screening battery, determines their learning strengths, and generates a specific learning prescription for the client.

Though a structured interview can be a valuable source of self-report, office interviews offer a restricted sample of behavior and not all clients can respond to the verbal interview formats that require sophisticated communication and introspection skills (Rogan & Hagner, 1990). Other ways to learn the previously stated information and such additional areas as the client's social skills and interpersonal behaviors, transportation skills, functional academics, and job expectations are to visit with the client at home, to talk with family members or school personnel, or to review information from secondary sources such as past Individualized Education Plan (IEP) goals or personal files (Rogan & Hagner, 1990).

Second Step

A job analysis of an existing supported work environment should have been performed, or one should be conducted regarding a possible employment site. This analysis is similar to the one explained later in Chapter 14. Additional information of the guidelines described in Chapter 14 should include perceived attitudes of employer and coworkers toward the client with a disability, the communication required on the job, the behavior acceptance range, the attention to job perseverance demanded, job safety, the sequencing of job duties, the daily changes in routine, any reinforcement available during job performance, and time requirements (e.g., requiring the client to identify breaks and meals, as well as tell time to the hour or minute). Further areas requiring understanding are the social interaction and the social climate of the workplace. A great deal of informal interaction occurs within any work setting, and a considerable amount of support is available within work environments that can be used for workers with severe disabilities (Rogan & Hagner, 1990). This second step also involves the identification of discrepancies between job or task performance and individual abilities or characteristics. These discrepancies may relate to architectural accessibility, acceptability of appearance or general behavior, and prerequisite credentials (Parker et al., 1989). There also may be discrepancies that relate to specific work skills and abilities, individual response to natural cues, required task-related social behaviors, and task sequence.

Third Step

The rehabilitation worker needs to identify the resources and activities that are available to clients and that can assist individuals in achieving success in the work setting. Such resources are, for example, the client's family, neighbors, relatives, or community programs that provide ongoing support to clients. An approach to understanding family dynamics is suggested in the second section of this chapter. Also, such community programs as group counseling are more educational in nature, and help clients address certain skill deficits, learn about suggestions on how to remediate them, and build on existing strengths. As suggested in the previous step, this information may have to be collected apart from the structured interview, and the client's significant others may be excellent resources.

Following this interpretation, the rehabilitation worker can develop an individual training plan. These individual training plans may include the following types of modifications: *individual modifications*, such as a change in appearance or learning compensatory skills; *general job modifications*, such as job restructuring or the addition of job-coach support; and *specific task modifications*, such as cue highlighting or mediation checklists or picture prompts (Parker et al., 1989).

Fourth Step

While the client is engaged in supported employment, an assessment can be conducted by either the rehabilitation worker or the client's supervisor. The ideal person, when possible, is the client's supervisor, because the use of this "natural support" might serve to validate an assessment conducted by the rehabilitation professional. The assessment is usually a behavior analysis, an evaluation that uses systematic behavior observations to identify how adjustment behaviors, interpersonal skills, and production performance interact with the social, technical, and production demands of the work environments (Hursh & Kerns, 1988). Rating scales and checklists are very useful in this assessment, and they are most helpful if they are similar to those measures used in business and industry. These scales are also useful in planning future training or employment with clients, and they can facilitate communication between the professional and the client. A variety of vocational behavior checklists and rating scales have emerged that contain, for example, social–interpersonal skill items expressed in terms of observable behavior.

Several of the more recently developed checklists also include some specification of conditions under which relevant behavior is to occur (Foss, Bullis, & Vilhauer, 1984). Although these checklists are not sufficiently specific about the particular situations in which a relevant behavior is to occur, one instrument, the *Test of Interpersonal Competence for Employment* (TICE) (Foss, Cheney, & Bullis, 1983), has been developed that calls for the detailed analysis of criterion behaviors and problems in the context in which they occur. (Further information on this instrument can be obtained by contacting the University of Oregon's Rehabilitation Research and Training Center in Mental Retardation.)

However, because of the specificity of client behavior, and frequently the uniqueness of supported employment sites, composing one's own evaluation form can be the most feasible way to collect necessary information. Checklists frequently are developed with employer input, because in-house points of view can often be more realistic regarding behavioral performance goals for clients on the job. Suggestions for items or information on such a form include the following:

1. The client arrives and leaves on time.

2. The client maintains regular attendance.

3. The client takes meals and breaks appropriately.

4. The client maintains an appearance appropriate to the work site.

5. The client communicates adequately with other employees.

6. The client can work independently.

7. The client can maintain attention to task.

8. The client can perform independent sequencing of job duties.

9. The client shows initiative in the work station.

10. The client is able to adapt to change in supervision or coworkers.

11. The client is aware of time demands during work performance.

12. The client is able to handle criticism and stress.

13. The client is aware of rules and safety precautions.

14. The client can follow supervisor instructions.

15. The client is able to request assistance.

16. The client can work without being distracted by other people.

17. The client can work without stopping until the designated break time.

18. To maintain adequate work performance the client needs specific prompts.

19. The client does not show bizarre or irritating behavior.

20. The client works more efficiently at specific times of the work day.

21. The client responds negatively to such factors in the work environment as noise and movement.

When using a checklist, the evaluator should link behaviors to work performance conditions, such as identifying when and where the behavior occurred, how often the behavior occurred, the duration of the behavior, the frequency of the behavior, and who was involved. Also, the observed behavior should relate to the performance criterion established. For example, is it performed 50% of the time and is it appropriate to industry standards (Hursh & Kerns, 1988)? However, the rating scale method of assessment has some serious flaws. Reliability is often a problem, item scoring is subjective, and the measures that result from ratings are typically limited to descriptions of the conditions under which a person functions, rather than providing clear prescriptions for remediation of specific target behaviors (Irvin & Halpern, 1979).

Fifth Step

During training and working in supported employment, behavioral deficits that need remediation should be identified. A behavior-oriented approach can be used for possible improvement, and might follow guidelines such as:

1. Determine the problem or unusual behavior.

2. Take a baseline of how many times the individual exhibits the inappropriate behavior within a time period.

3. Identify a reinforcer.

4. Set an initial goal of behavior occurrence.

5. Determine a reinforcement schedule.

Sixth Step

Soon after the beginning of supported employment, and periodically thereafter, an assessment should be made of the client's job satisfaction. The traditional service structure within vocational rehabilitation has been designed around the client who will succeed at and keep for life the first job obtained (Rogan & Hagner, 1990). However, the client may wish, like others employed in the work sector, to change jobs numerous times.

Although most people with no disabilities identify closely with their jobs, it is less clear how those with severe disabilities who have never experienced the "world of work" and who may have led lives cut off from the mainstream of society view their working experience. Individuals whose vocational training has not gone beyond sheltered situations, and whose previous experience may have included long periods of institu-tionalization or "training" in day activity programs, may see a workshop or other segre-gated facility as the most desirable, and most satisfying, alternative (Moseley, 1988).

One approach to exploring job satisfaction is to ask questions such as:

1. How do you feel at the end of a working day?

2. Does your job underuse or overstrain your abilities?

3. Do you daydream about having a different job?

4. Do you feel unappreciated at work?

5. What do you most dislike and like about your job?

6. Would you be happy to do the same job if it paid less?

7. If you were not working at your job, which would you miss most—the money, the work itself, the company of your coworkers?

8. When Monday morning comes, do you feel hesitant to go back to work?

To provide additional assessment information, as well as to supplement Steps 3 and 4, the evaluator can consider using the *Work Environment Scale*, developed by Moos (1986). This scale was designed to measure the social climate of work milieus by assess-ing the 10 dimensions of involvement, peer cohesion, supervisor support, autonomy, task orientation, work pressure, clarity, control, innovation, and physical comfort. The mea-sure has been normed on a sample of over 3,000 employees in a variety of work groups. The manual provides information that this scale has acceptable test–retest reliability and internal consistency coefficients (Menchetti & Uduari-Solner, 1990).

Evaluating Progress

While the client is engaged in supported employment, evaluative feedback can be given to assist the client in assessing his or her own progress. The assessment within supported employment requires that the client and the rehabilitation worker under-stand both the present skill functioning of the client and the level of skill functioning needed to adjust to the demands of the work environment (Cohen & Anthony, 1984). This assessment is not something done to clients; rather, it is performed with clients. If clients are to remain motivated during the entire period of supported employment, and if appropriate vocational planning is to be accomplished, then client input is important. During the initial interview, as well as during the supported employment, clients should begin to understand what is necessary to reach appropriate work goals. Because of this feedback, many clients can be given the opportunity to make decisions relevant to future directions of training and work. During the initial interview, every attempt should be made by the rehabilitation service worker to solicit information from clients on work preferences and perceived capabilities and limitations. This information may help the worker determine the complexity level of tasks in the supported work assignment.

In addition to client feedback and involvement in the evaluation process, another issue to consider is who obtains the assessment. Ideally, the job coach trained in evaluation skills, including observation skills, is the person who handles the evaluation. However, because of time demands and a caseload that requires that different clients be on varied supported employment sites (e.g., custodial, office clerical, or food preparation), this rehabilitation worker may not have the time to perform an effective evaluation. A supervisor may have to assume this responsibility, but he or she may also have to be trained in what to look for and how to complete the necessary forms. Both training and objectivity are necessary when completing a rating scale or interpreting the behavioral data associated with this assessment. The perceptions of the evaluation can be selective and somewhat prone to error (Cohen, 1988). Consequently, someone is needed who has realistic expectations for the client's work potential, especially when the client has a severe disability. If supervisors are familiar with the application of appropriate job behaviors, and can relate effectively to the client, then these persons may become useful partners to the job coach. In deference to the supervisor's own job demands, however, the evaluation should not be time-consuming or complicated.

Another issue concerns the scheduling of the assessment within supported employment demands. Because this evaluation information is usually collected using observation techniques, observations should be accomplished in short periods of time during the client's work day, and the information recorded, if possible, at each day's conclusion. This recording of information is particularly necessary for critical behaviors that need immediate attention.

Conclusion—Using a Supported Work Model

Evaluation, training, and job performance are factors that go together when assessment information is needed for individuals with a severe disability. The content areas for evaluation suggested in this chapter provide a structure to the assessment process. Though there are disadvantages of conducting vocational evaluation within supported employment (e.g., the work offered at the job site may be too simple, too difficult, or not congruent with the client's interests), and inaccurate conclusions about the client's work behavior may be drawn (Pruitt, 1986; Sax & Pell, 1985), the employment opportunity may be the most appropriate way to learn about the productivity of persons with a severe disability. It is important to remember that assessment conducted within supported employment is not an end in itself; it is a springboard for future training or continued employment.

CASE STUDY: BERT

Bert, age 19, has just completed a special education program in a local high school, and is anxious to seek employment on a regular basis. His high school counselor has referred him to the state vocational rehabilitation office. The state does not provide any school-to-work transition programs, and Bert has achieved a special education certificate. In high school, he learned basic, academic skills and, through a vocational education program, acquired some fundamental work behaviors (i.e., punctuality, steady work performance, and behavior controls when working with others). Bert's parents are reluctant to encourage him to find a competitive job, because they feel the work pressure may cause behavior problems that would result in Bert getting fired. Bert has a *Wechsler Adult Intelligence Scale–Revised* (WAIS–R) (Wechsler, 1981) full-scale IQ of 78, lives at home, and enjoys watching TV and talking with friends as hobbies.

 Chapter 12 Case Study Questions (Set 1)

DIRECTIONS: Considering this information and the assessment goals identified in this chapter, please answer the following questions:

> 1. How would you structure the first interview with this client?
>
> 2. What difficulties do you foresee? What would be your plan to alleviate them?

ASSESSMENT OF FAMILY DYNAMICS

Family involvement in the rehabilitation process has become a topic of importance in recent years (Bray, 1980; Cohen, 1982; Power et al., 1988; Sutton, 1985). Disability is actually a family affair, and the client's performance in vocational rehabilitation is a function of both the person and the family environment. Progress toward rehabilitation goals cannot be achieved without considering and evaluating the family influences that can facilitate this progress.

An appraisal of what it is in family life that influences the family member who has a disability can become the basis for the development of appropriate intervention strategies. Without an understanding of the family situation, intervention approaches often go awry (Power et al., 1988). When contact with the family is possible, an identification is needed of the family factors that may disrupt the client's rehabilitation. Unfortunately, however, rehabilitation professionals have been reluctant to have any

involvement with families, and their role and functions with the family in the rehabilitation process are issues that are seldom addressed in the literature (Power & Dell Orto, 1986).

One of the main reasons for the uncertainty harbored by rehabilitation profession-
als over any possible interaction with the family is their understanding that attention to the client's family is not encouraged by most state and private vocational rehabilitation agencies. However, such contact really requires only a small, additional expenditure of time and money for a potentially great return. For many rehabilitation professionals, the time for assessment purposes with the family can frequently be accomplished during office visits with the client. A family meeting may be initiated during the beginning interview, when both eligibility for vocational rehabilitation and extent of services are being determined. Such a meeting can be particularly beneficial when the rehabilitation helper has doubts about the client's sincerity to pursue the rehabilitation process, or perceives that there may be factors within the client's home environment that are detri-
mental to the achievement of rehabilitation goals.

For these and other reasons, such as when the client states that the family is seeking information on the vocational rehabilitation process, or mentions that family members are seeking information on resources that will assist them in their adjustment efforts, the helper realizes that contact with the family would serve a most beneficial purpose, and a meeting is discussed. When clients are living with their family or the family is easily accessible, the client's permission can be obtained to bring the family members to the next agency visit. All the family members or significant others with whom the client lives should be invited, when possible, to this agency meeting. Each person can have an influence on the client's vocational rehabilitation. The focus of assistance is still primarily on the client, and the purpose of the initial family visit is both to help the client and to identify the persons who can facilitate or hinder the rehabilitation process.

Any family assessment is usually conducted within a brief time framework. Today, in many rehabilitation agencies the rapid flow of clients through these systems usually necessitates short-term attention. Because families can often be seen only briefly, assistance to family members must be carefully designed to make effective use of this lim-
ited assessment opportunity.

Because of the briefness of the helper's opportunity to meet with families, assessment information may need to be obtained at only one meeting. To facilitate the fam-
ily's verbal expression of important information, the helper needs to exercise such basic communication skills as (a) attentiveness, (b) a nonjudgmental attitude, (c) using understandable words when talking with family members, (d) using verbal reinforcers such as "I see" or "Yes," (e) reflecting back and clarifying the family's statements, and (f) phrasing interpretations tentatively to elicit genuine feedback from family members (Okun, 1987). The helper should not assume anything, and should ask only what he or she believes the family member can answer so that the person feels competent and productive. Also, the helper should ask questions that family members can handle emotionally at the time (Satir, 1967). In other words, the helper must create a setting

during a family meeting in which people can, perhaps for the first time, risk sharing their emotions and seek information about their concerns.

Areas of Family Dynamics To Explore

There are basically eight areas of family dynamics that need to be explored if an appropriate evaluation is to be made on the family's role during the vocational rehabilitation process.

1. *What has the family done so far to respond to the disability or illness?* The helper can ascertain whether family members have encouraged the client to participate in the process of vocational rehabilitation. Further, he or she can determine whether the family has made plans for dealing with problems associated with the disability (e.g., identifying other financial resources when family income has been reduced or shifting home responsibilities so that a family member may obtain at least a part-time job to alleviate economic hardship). Exploring with families these concerns can be difficult for evaluators, and the following questions are suggested:

- Can you describe your family life since the occurrence of the disability or illness?

- What are the differences in your family life since the beginning of the disability or illness?

- What are your feelings about having your husband or wife at home?

2. *What information does the family have about the disability or illness condition?* The counselor can also explore whether family members are aware of what the client can still do in the home, what community resources may be used for respite care, whether various work options are still available to the client, and what are the different phases of the rehabilitation process. Information about the disability may already have been given by health professionals. However, family members, because of their anxieties, tend not to process information very well during their conferences with the physician (Polinko, 1985).

3. *What is the unique composition of the family and what are the strengths and pitfalls inherent in that structure that would influence the client's rehabilitation?* To identify the presence of family dynamics that may promote the client's vocational rehabilitation, the counselor can be aware, during the visit, of several indicators: warm and trusting attitudes shown in familial interactions; open and mutual respect demonstrated toward each family member; honest dialogue between family members about any adjustmental concerns, and assumption of personal responsibility, when appropriate, for the client's treatment and rehabilitation needs. Included in this exploration is an identification of who is the family spokesperson and who are the principal caregivers for the client (Doherty & Baird, 1983).

On the other hand, the meeting might reveal confusion and disagreement about events affecting family life, conflicts over the performance of family responsibilities, or family communication that reveals distorted or unrealistic views of family members toward one another. Family members may also be angry because the presence of the disability has interfered with their lifestyle, privacy, vacations, future plans, or amount of time spent together. Much of the anger may have existed prior to the onset of disability, and the disability itself may only have exacerbated longstanding family feelings. The anger may take the form of neglecting the treatment and vocational needs of the client or excluding the person with a disability from family activities.

4. *What is the perceived threat to family functioning because of the disability?* This is an important area to explore in any family assessment, because all families are especially vulnerable to unwelcomed stress and prolonged anxiety after the occurrence of a disability or illness. For example, if a disability causes unemployment of the principal family wage earner, how does the family make up for this deficit? This is just one of the many issues that emerge with a disability in a family. In other words, how does family life change because of the disability? An awareness of what happens to a family in a disability situation can make a difference in whether family members can be used for the eventual rehabilitation of the person with a disability.

5. *What are the resources available to the family?* These resources include both those available from within the family and those external to the family members. They include financial resources; the availability and willingness of extended family members; and the presence of community support systems such as respite care, child day care, or programs for the elderly. The availability of these resources can make a difference in the family's adjustment to a trauma. Family members frequently state that the main reason they have adapted to a disability, and then have become a source of help to the ill family member, is that support external to the family itself is available.

6. *What secondary gain issues interrupt the rehabilitation process?* Examples of such issues are financial disincentives to the continuation of employment, or family influences that actually oppose work activities. Exploring these issues with families may be difficult, but during evaluation they should be explored. The following questions can be helpful:

- Has life in your family been better for you since the occurrence of your injury?
- What kind of financial benefits are you receiving now?
- What do you believe your family's reaction is to the fact that you are not working?
- Does your family expect you to return to work?

7. *Are family beliefs about the maintenance of role responsibilities in the home and in the world of work acting as deciding factors for employment re-entry?* Families that communicate attitudes of essential worth to the client help to stabilize the self-concept, foster a positive attitude toward the future, and facilitate maintenance of rehabilitation gains. During assessment, these issues can be explored with clients by asking questions such as:

- Do you still perform your customary duties around the home? Do you still participate with your family in social activities?

- Could you please describe what happened in your family life yesterday?

- What kinds of things does your family expect you to do, especially around the house?

8. *What are family needs as the client begins the rehabilitation process?* An awareness of these needs provides relevant suggestions on how rehabilitation professionals can assist the family during this time of client transition. These include the need (a) to receive concrete services (e.g., available community resources, financial information); (b) to be listened to and understood as a concerned person who is attempting to cope with a disability; (c) to process information already communicated by health professionals; (d) to care for himself or herself; (e) to recognize potential problems that may develop from the client's involvement in the rehabilitation process (e.g., transportation, negative attitudes from peers or employers); and (f) to learn information about the rehabilitation process as it applies to the family member with a disability.

During the initial phase of the rehabilitation process, many families are reluctant to voice their needs in the above areas, and these needs may have to be anticipated. The recognition of family concerns by professionals can help considerably in a family's adjustment efforts and in their assistance in promoting rehabilitation goals for the client. The client's involvement in vocational rehabilitation is a critical time for most families, and the rehabilitation professional can facilitate the family's cooperative efforts by asking them certain questions. For example, a professional can ask the following questions:

- How do you feel about your family member beginning vocational rehabilitation ? Do you foresee any problems?

- What is family life going to be like, now that your family member is starting vocational rehabilitation?

- What services do you believe you need now to help your family assist your family member during his or her involvement in the rehabilitation process?

Conclusion—Family Dynamics

Although family visits by the rehabilitation professional employed in a vocational setting are usually brief, the meeting can be quite productive for identifying family strengths or negative influences that can make a difference in the achievement of rehabilitation goals. Depending on disability circumstances and the opportunities for family contact, a family evaluation will vary in extensiveness and subject matter. Family needs also change as the client continues in the rehabilitation process. However, the assessment areas identified in this chapter can provide guidelines to help the family become a useful partner to both the helping professional and the client.

 ## CASE STUDY: MALCOM

Malcom is 45 years old and presently living with his wife of 24 years and two of their four children in their own home in the suburbs of the Greater Boston area. Malcom is of slight build and medium height, and he and his wife have two other children who are married and live in neighboring communities. Malcom's parents are deceased.

Malcolm graduated from high school, and then obtained employment as a clerk in an auto parts store. However, because he needed a better paying job, he left this position after 7 years and became a route salesman for a retail dairy product. He held this job for 8 years. During this employment, he took the firefighter's exam. When he was finally appointed to the fire department of a large, neighboring city of Boston, he left his employment as a salesman. Malcolm started his work as a firefighter in 1983 and rose to the rank of lieutenant just 2 years before his heart attack in January, 1995. He has not been employed since that trauma, and states that he liked his job with the fire department very much, but is unable to return to it because of its physical demands.

At the present time, Malcolm claims that he is fully recovered from his attack and is seeking employment. He reports that he has sent out 76 resumes, but has only heard from 15 companies and has yet to be hired. He states, "I don't get discouraged." He went to the State Rehabilitation Commission, at which the counselor remarked in Malcom's report: "pleasant, somewhat withdrawn, but anxious to talk about his medical history and his desire for employment . . . very distractible and appears to have poor planning skills and a lack of attention to immediate tasks." After stating to his counselor that a "heart attack hangs over you like a scepter," Malcom went into detail about the circumstances relevant to his heart attack. He was given an intelligence test by the counselor, and it indicated that Malcom is in the superior range of intellectual functioning.

Apart from looking for a job, Malcom has remained during the past 12 months mainly at home, where he follows carefully a daily lifestyle of exercise prescribed by the doctor. He also helps around the house and works in the garden. Periodically he and his wife go out for dinner, but they seldom entertain at home. His wife works during the day, and the two teenage children are in school. Malcom's hobbies evolve around the family. Occasionally he visits his brother who lives about 100 miles away, and talks with him about the heart attack, because the brother had a similar trauma 5 years ago. Malcom is worried about being treated as a disabled, handicapped person. Malcom had no history of heart disease, though he has had an ulcer for many years. Financially, he is receiving compensation of $900 a month, and during the last 6 months he has completed a business management certificate program at a vocational technical college.

Chapter 12 Case Study Questions (Set 2)

DIRECTIONS: Please respond to the following questions:

1. Identify the family dynamics that could impede Malcom's return to any type of employment.

2. What is the threat to family functioning because of Malcom's disability?

3. Identify the family resources that could facilitate Malcom's return to any type of employment.

Interpreting Assessment Information

One of the most important aspects of vocational assessment is the way the rehabilitation professional communicates to the client the information gained from the evaluation. This communication involves interpreting test data in an understandable way, helping clients to make decisions about their future plans, and perhaps alleviating some difficulties that might be obstacles to effective rehabilitation planning (such as unrealistic vocational aspirations or poor motivations for training). Especially for clients with disabilities, reporting assessment data may be crucial to making a decision regarding which course will lead to possible employment. For the professional, this interpretation session demands skills in integrating assessment data about the abilities, education, and motivation of individuals with what is known about the nature of various occupations (Shertzer & Linden, 1979).

Because rehabilitation assessment should be part of the continued counseling process with the client reaching productive goals, the time of reporting evaluation information requires particular counseling skills. Also, the rehabilitation professional often has to interpret test information gained from nonvocational sources (such as a psychiatrist or psychologist) into vocational terms. This vocational translation necessitates a knowledge of customary instruments used by such sources and even special training in order to make the test results meaningful to the client. Some of the principles underlying this training are explained in this chapter. This chapter also identifies the general principles involved in interpreting and communicating assessment information to the client, explains the types of interpretation, discusses the actual situation of communicating evaluative information to clients, indicates the special problems that often occur in the interpretative session, and offers some responses to these questions. The role of the rehabilitation professional in developing resources for occupational information is also discussed. Selected occupational literature is identified, along with ways to generate knowledge about the local world of work.

TYPES OF INTERPRETATION

Goldman (1971) identified four kinds of interpretation—descriptive, genetic, predictive, and evaluative—all of which fit within the structure of rehabilitation assessment.

Descriptive

This interpretation asks such questions as: What kind of person is this client? What are his or her hobbies, vocational interests, particular capabilities, and personal strengths? What does the evaluation reveal about this client, especially when the person is compared to other people on specific test scores (such as aptitude functioning)? Does the client do better in one area than another?

Genetic

In this aspect of interpretation, various reasons are explored as to why or how the client is functioning in a certain manner. For example, if the client has a work history in outdoor activities, but interest testing reveals that he or she actually has little interest in this area, then the reasons for this discrepancy could be explored. Low aptitude scores can also be discussed. Particular obstacles, either from the client's environment (i.e., family) or from within the client (i.e., attitude or emotional disposition), can be identified. Such obstacles might represent reasons why the client is against a particular vocational direction, especially when evaluation strongly suggests an exploration of the latter area.

Predictive

There are many factors that constitute the client's vocational or training success. Prediction should be done cautiously during the reporting of evaluation data because of such realities as motivation, the client's own adjustment to disability, and environmental forces influencing the client as he or she moves from medical treatment or inactivity to more active involvement in the rehabilitation process. If interpreted properly, most evaluation information suggests reasons why a certain vocational direction is feasible for the client. Soliciting clients' feedback during interpretation can also facilitate their awareness of what is needed for an effective adjustment to training or to employment.

Evaluative

In this area of interpretation, the emphasis is more on such objective considerations as specific behavioral and ability-related job demands, what the *Dictionary of Occupational Titles* (DOT) (U.S. Department of Labor, 1991) says about job qualifications, and what occupations are particularly in demand in the client's geographical area. The results from the assessment are then compared or matched to this objective information. From this comparison, the professional can begin to determine what occupation or level of training would be more feasible to enter and how long a course of vocational training should be pursued. This area of interpretation, however, necessitates value judgments by the rehabilitation professional, which in turn generate recommendations for the client.

In reporting evaluation information, all of these varied kinds of interpretation are used. When considering the interpretation of assessment results, the validities of evaluation measures must be carefully identified. If an instrument has a low predictive ability and has been used in evaluation, then this should be discussed when communicating the results to the client. As explained in Chapter 5, the validity issue is a continuing problem when using traditional assessment tools with individuals who have a disability. The population of those with a disability probably was not included in the norm group, and although the measure may be strong in content validity (which has reasonably good descriptive use during the interpretation session), it should not be used for prediction.

GENERAL PRINCIPLES OF INTERPRETATION

Many guidelines make the interpretation session an effective experience for both the rehabilitation worker and the client. It is important for the evaluator to remember that test scores identify how well individuals perform at the time of testing, not why they perform as they do. The cause of a person's test performance may emerge from an exploration of the client's learning history, an understanding of the environment in which the individual developed, the events or influences that the individual encountered, and the person's response to these influences (Anastasi, 1992).

Principle 1

The rehabilitation worker should communicate evaluation information at the level of the client's understanding. Ideally, at this time in the evaluation process, the professional has some knowledge of the client's mental abilities as well as the deficits that may limit the client's capability of understanding important assessment facts. People who have chronic anxiety or who have been showing continued resistance to exploring new alternatives for life planning often have a difficult time endorsing assessment feedback. In these instances, the client's point of view, attitudes, or goals can be used as a point of reference or departure. When preparing for the interpretive session, the professional can then identify information that may be favorable or unfavorable to the client's point of reference. Once this "for-and-against" evidence has been summarized, an explanation can be offered as to why the client should shift goals or consider a certain direction for rehabilitation planning. In other words, the inventory or test results that are the most positive, and perhaps most consistent with the client's self-image and the easiest to understand, should be first explained. The interpretation process should begin with a focus on what is personally meaningful to the client.

Principle 2

The recommendations that are offered in this reporting of the information session should be made in terms of alternatives so that the client can then make a choice. It is the client who basically interprets the test information (Biggs & Keller, 1982), but it is the professional who must understand the different options that are available to the client. Knowing how to use the DOT is an invaluable asset in assessment. This resource identifies the many occupational choices available in the labor market and gives the requirements for each job. The discussion of alternatives or the exploration of different job options feasible for the client reflects the professional's experience in handling job-related information and knowing the different opportunities that may exist within the client's community.

Principle 3

The client should participate as much as possible in this interpretive session. Promoting client involvement ensures that the client will appropriately evaluate the test results (Biggs & Keller, 1982). This participation implies the encouragement of the feedback, reactions to the information, and exploration of client questions. Although it might be easier for the rehabilitation professional simply to present the test results or other related information to the client without soliciting any feedback and then make recommendations without much time allowed to deal with the client's response, this approach will usually not be facilitative for realistic rehabilitation planning. If clients participate in gaining an understanding of assessment results, they will then be likely to introduce new information about themselves from other sources and to produce new insights regarding the significance of all the information (Goldman, 1971). The more clients contribute to the results provided by the assessment measures and the more the rehabilitation professional is "client-centered" (putting stress on the client's feelings about the assessment data), the more accepting clients will be of the conclusions and their implications regarding future activities. Importantly, a client who is involved in reporting evaluation information stands a better chance of remembering accurately what is communicated. The evaluator's avoidance of jargon and technical terms can facilitate this involvement.

Principle 4

It is not the test information itself, but the rehabilitation professional's and client's perceptions of these results that are important. One of the emphases in reporting evaluation results should be on the attitudes and readiness of clients to use the particular kind of information being given in this session. For this reason, the professional should also be aware of clients' views toward themselves as clients and toward the rehabilitation process, their expectations about the assessment process itself, and the feasibility of future job-related productivity. Some clients, for example, may see no need to learn more about themselves or to explore options that are even marginally different from their present lifestyle. The client also may still be attempting to adjust emotionally to the disability. Consequently, the client who perceives that there is little hope for a satisfying life may have quite a low self-concept. The client's perception of test scores is often associated with his or her self-view. Clients have great difficulty accepting information that conflicts with their self-concepts. It is the professional's responsibility to facilitate the kind of interaction that leads the client to a more accurate perception of assessment data.

Principle 5

During this information-imparting session, the professional should avoid persuasive methods that might convey brusqueness or aggressiveness. The evaluation data should speak for itself and be the motivational tool for rehabilitation planning—not the professional's personality alone. Of course, the professional provides suggestions, options, attractive choices, and reasonable alternatives. However, it is the client who makes the final decision about whether to act on such recommendations. One of the goals of this session is not to force the professional's interpretation of assessment data upon clients, but rather to allow clients to relate this new information to their view of previous experiences and rehabilitation expectations. It is helpful if the evaluation information is presented to the client as objectively as possible. A statement such as, "Eight out of 10 clients with scores like yours have a good chance of succeeding in this electronics program" is preferable to one that begins, "You should . . . ," "I believe . . . ," or "If these were my scores, I would . . ."

Principle 6

The professional should be as familiar as possible with the different tests, measures, or approaches used during the client's evaluation. Such questions as, "How well and what does this instrument measure?" and, "What do the scores mean?" should be answered before the interpretation session with the client. This information can be obtained from the test manual or, when testing was done by another source such as a psychologist, this information should be received from that person. Moreover, rehabilitation professionals can learn a great deal about a particular paper-and-pencil test by taking the same tests that are used with their clients in vocational assessment.

Associated with this principle is the belief that clients should understand which test is being interpreted and what it measures.

Principle 7

The client should not be confronted with unsuspected, negative information. For example, the professional may say, "On the one hand, your scores in the mechanical aptitude suggest that you would have a difficult time succeeding in training in that area. But on the other hand, your clerical aptitude is very high and merits serious attention for future planning."

All in all, these principles emphasize that the interpretation session is both a teaching and counseling opportunity for the rehabilitation professional; for the client, it is primarily a learning situation. During the session, clients have the chance to explore alternatives, to discuss their own views about the meaning of the evaluation results, and to gain added self-understanding that might be needed for subsequent life-planning decisions. Importantly, however, the professional also has the opportunity to learn more about the client. The extent of this learning depends on how the evaluation information has been communicated, how the goals of the evaluation process have been formulated earlier with the client, and how clients themselves respond to the learning of this newly discovered information.

Principle 8

Information on test results should be presented, not only in the context of what is already known about the client, but also with a holistic viewpoint. Interview data and information gathered from school records, previous employment experience, and earlier test results can provide a background upon which to understand existing evaluation results. A comparison of past and recently acquired information may identify areas of client growth or regression. Because disability trauma represents a major transition of life functioning for most clients, an understanding of pre-onset emotional, physical, and cognitive-related strengths can establish a direction for the interpretation session.

THE ACTUAL
INTERPRETATION SESSION

The interpretation meeting with the client should be structured so that the rehabilitation professional has a clear idea of what is to be accomplished. For example, if the goal is to formulate rehabilitation plans for the client, this aim becomes a perspective for the organization of evaluation results. When structuring this session, attention should be given to (a) emphasizing capabilities that can be used in vocational planning; (b) the order in which assessment data will be discussed; (c) how the professional will deal with negative information generated by the evaluation; and (d) what particular data will be used for vocational planning. Also, information should not be forced upon the client, but related to his or her previous experiences. Assessment results should be presented in such a way that clients are encouraged to follow an appropriate rehabilitation direction. All of this demands preparation; when this planning is done, the reporting of evaluation becomes much more effective.

The interpretation session can be "structured" into four phases.

First Phase (Introduction)

At the beginning of the session, the professional should help the client feel at ease and receptive toward assessment information. Reviewing the goals of evaluation and soliciting responses from the client on how he or she felt about the evaluation can help reduce feelings of anxiety. Clients are usually anxious because of the evaluative and judgmental aspects of assessment. For example, they may fear that tests will be bearers of bad news. Clients may also perceive that the results may change their expectations about a definite area of training. Providing them with the opportunity to talk about these concerns may give the professional some ideas about how to present the evaluation results. When the professional provides the chance for clients to express their thoughts and uses an active listening style to show that he or she is genuinely interested in what is being said, then the clients' cooperation in acting upon assessment information is frequently promoted. Clients may have many concerns about the evaluation information. Asking them about how they felt during the time that the tests were administered achieves an understanding of attitudinal factors that may have influenced them during the assessment procedures (Miller, 1982).

Second Phase

When the professional believes that the client is receptive to listening to the evaluation results, the original purposes of the rehabilitation assessment and what tests or measures were used should then be discussed. Interest tests should be identified first, because their information usually is less threatening to the client and can establish a direction for the feedback of the other evaluation data in the personality, aptitude, and intelligence areas. It is also important to review the particular assessment tools used in all the evaluation areas, discussing why they were selected and what they measure. Furthermore, concepts such as norms, percentiles, percentile ranks, and stanines may need to be thoroughly explained (Miller, 1982).

Third Phase

After reviewing all the measures used for a particular client's evaluation, the professional can explain the results of each assessment area, beginning with interest inventories. The client is usually shown the interest profile and told about the information it presents, and then particular results are identified. In this phase of test reporting, statistical data or test-score numbers must be translated for the client. Percentiles probably are the safest and most informative numbers to use, provided their two essential characteristics are made clear: (a) that they refer not to the percentage of questions answered correctly but to the percentage of people whose performances the client has equaled or surpassed and (b) specifically, who are the people to whom the client is being compared.

The second point, a definite description of the comparison or norm group, is particularly important in making the meaning of test results clear. The reporting of numbers should be minimized when communicating test results and, if used, should only be done incidentally. One suggestion for a response is, "Your results are similar to those people who . . ."

After imparting the interest information, the client should be asked about his or her own relevant feelings or reflections. Two questions that solicit client responses are, "Do you feel these results present an accurate picture of you?" and "Is this information a surprise to you?" The client should be able to understand the assessment results and talk about what they mean to him or her.

When the interest results are given, then achievement and ability or work results can be reported. Frequently, the interest results are encouraging to the client and set the stage for a very productive reporting session. Any negative data should be communicated carefully. In reporting these results, the professional should emphasize the information that identifies the client's vocational strengths and the patterns of strengths and weaknesses interpreted in terms of the client's educational and work history. It is important to present this information objectively, using norm comparisons when they are available. Attention should also be given to the consistency of the results with the client's past and present level of functioning. Also, two questions need to be answered in light of the achievement and ability results: (a) Do the results suggest that the client could handle the work or training required at other, higher levels? and (b) What does this information mean in terms of an occupational choice?

Because assessment reporting has already identified general areas of interest, it is most helpful now if the professional suggests particular interest areas, respective occupations, and the physical, emotional, and intellectual qualifications for each area. In this regard, the DOT is a valuable resource. Before the interpretation session, the professional can examine the client's assessment results and use the DOT to consider different occupations and their qualifications that are appropriate to these results. (This resource is further described in the last section of this chapter.)

After these results have been explained and the information has been related to the client's past experience, statements about vocational goals, prior interest exploration, and overall feedback should again be solicited from the client. It is necessary for the client to understand the results as they relate to future rehabilitation planning. Encouraging the exploration of feelings and perceptions regarding this data should further facilitate this comprehension.

Following this interaction, the intelligence test results can be communicated if these measures have been used in assessment. The rehabilitation professional should be cautious about giving the client a definite IQ score. When clients receive all the evaluation results, they tend to remember just their IQ score, which distorts its meaning for rehabilitation planning. Also, the score can vary to a small degree, depending on both testing conditions and the client's current level of functioning. Rather than report the IQ number, a range (such as "Average," "Bright Normal," or "Superior") can be given.

Personality assessment then follows, and frequently this part of the interpretation session is very threatening to clients. To alleviate some of the client's anxiety, the purpose of each test and what it measures can be explained. Furthermore, the professional should avoid terminology that has unfavorable emotional connotations, such as "neurosis" or "emotional instability." The particular test results can also be related to occupational goals or job requirements. Often, these personality measures reveal negative information about the client that may have the client's troubled past as its source. The professional should decide whether these data have any relevant bearing on current rehabilitation planning. For example, test results or evaluations may reveal that the client has certain phobias or experiences severe anxiety, both of which may affect work adjustment. Therefore, the professional may recommend therapy before any training is pursued. In this area of interpretation, it is particularly important for the professional to identify personality strengths that relate strongly to work functioning. Limitations that might affect employment must also be presented, but these are more readily acknowledged when viewed through the perception of some strong personality assets.

Fourth Phase (Conclusion)

When terminating the reporting of assessment information, the rehabilitation professional should keep in mind the results that are important for rehabilitation planning. This information should again be identified in summary fashion, and then rehabilitation directions for training or employment can be suggested. Clients should be asked to provide some feedback on what they have learned from the evaluation and what results they consider to be the most important. They should leave the interpretation session with an understanding of themselves that raises hope and strong expectations for their future. This often demands that rehabilitation professionals frequently repeat in the interpretation session those results that show capabilities for employment; however, it is time well spent. The results often become motivational factors for later rehabilitation involvement. The professional should remember that the interpretation of test results usually leads to the development of rehabilitation plans. Any planning should involve the client, and options need to be explored with the client. Table 13.1 shows a summary of an actual interpretation session.

SPECIAL CONCERNS IN INTERPRETATION

Different problems often arise during the interpretation session. Problems that are not handled promptly can eliminate the effectiveness of this important part of assessment. Three concerns frequently occur when the professional provides feedback on evaluation results.

TABLE 13.1
Summary of Actual Interpretation Session

Phase	Tasks
First phase (Introduction)	1. Know about measures that need to be interpreted to the client. 2. Establish a relationship. 3. Review goals of evaluation for the client.
Second phase	1. Give the client an opportunity to talk about the assessment experience. 2. Summarize in a general manner the overall results of evaluation, emphasizing positive test results. 3. Solicit feedback from the client.
Third phase	1. Interpret carefully each evaluation measure—Interest, Aptitude/Ability, Intelligence, and Personality. Use such guidelines as norms, percentiles, and so on. 2. Solicit feedback about the client's feelings concerning the results. 3. Deal with such problems as contradictory test scores, reluctance, and unrealistic vocational aspirations. 4. Suggest particular interest areas; respective occupations; and qualifications for each in the physical, emotional, and intellectual areas.
Fourth phase (Conclusion)	1. Summarize results for the client and discuss how this information can relate to rehabilitation planning. 2. Ask the client for further feedback, especially about what has been learned from the evaluation experience. 3. Develop rehabilitation plans.

Contradictory Test Scores

Occasionally, two evaluation measures may give two different scores on the same factor or individual trait. How can those differences be reconciled? For example, can the discrepancy between the results of two interest inventories be resolved when one of them shows a high score in business-related activities, and the other a low score? In responding to these differences, three basic viewpoints can be considered, as identified by Goldman (1971).

Differences Among the Tests Themselves

There may be differences in the types of items found on paper-and-pencil tests (e.g., free choice versus forced choice). The latter might be more irritating because of the necessity of making choices, even when the client feels no preference for use of the alternative choices. Often, the norm groups used in developing normative data for the tests are quite different from one another in both age and intelligence levels. The characteristics that each test measures might also be quite different. The *Quick-Test* (Ammons & Ammons, 1959), for example, measures school ability and then provides an IQ score; the *Shipley Institute of Living Scale* (Shipley, 1986), however, includes both Verbal and Abstract reasoning and then gives an IQ score. The same client taking both tests may score lower on the *Shipley* test because of less developed abstract reasoning ability.

Differences Within the Individual

On two occasions during rehabilitation assessment, a client may function physically and psychologically in different ways. Fatigue; the presence of mental distractions; situational anxiety; acute, temporary stress; and motivation can all be sources for the difference in scores on two measures evaluating the same area. When the professional notes this difference, he or she should explore with the client reasons for the discrepancy.

Differences in Test Administration and Scoring

Occasionally, the conditions in the testing room or environment (e.g., temperature that is too hot or cold) represent inhibiting factors to test performance. Sometimes, the test administrator may increase anxiety among the clients. Many professionals induce tension because of the way they present themselves, whereas others try to relax clients before a testing experience. These realities may contribute to a difference in the way a client handles test items. Consequently, on two occasions, scores on the same measure may differ. Again, the professional should ask the client for reasons why the scores are different, especially when there is little difference between the tests themselves.

Reluctance To Believe Test Scores or Follow the Professional's Recommendations

During the interpretation session, the client may seem unwilling to believe the assessment results or reluctant to act on this information. This problem needs attention because one of the goals of this session is to use assessment data to help clients become motivated enough to pursue appropriate rehabilitation goals. The first step in alleviating this concern is to identify the source of the reluctance. The client's responses can be influenced by hostility toward the professional as an authority figure, assessment information that apparently goes against the client's perceived self-concept, or the client's predetermined resolve to follow a course of action, regardless of the evaluation results. Also, because of past failure experiences, the client may lack the flexibility to take risks or attempt new ventures suggested by evaluation results and rehabilitation planning. Change is viewed as very threatening, and there is a marked hesitancy to try new directions. Whatever the reason, the source of the client's reluctance should be explored and identified.

During this exploration, empathy with the client should be established. When the client is aware that the rehabilitation professional is an active listener who also expresses warmth, sincerity, and genuine interest, usually there will be more willingness to reveal obstacles that may deter rehabilitation. Empathy can convey client acceptance and facilitate professional trust.

Once the source of the reluctance is identified, the professional can begin to deal with the problem. The training and occupational alternatives suggested by evaluation information often have to be made attractive to the client. Any suggested course of action must be perceived by the client as personally rewarding. Providing emotional support for those clients who hesitate to take a risk, while at the same time emphasizing the assets revealed by the evaluation, may generate movement toward rehabilitation goals. Frequently, when clients enhance their confidence in themselves and in their professionals, they are motivated to overcome apparent obstacles to vocational planning. For example, a client's family can influence his or her reluctance; many clients are afraid to counter the expectations of family members. It takes a considerable amount of courage for the client to tell the family that he or she is going to follow a certain direction in rehabilitation, even when the family does not endorse the choice. When the client believes that a certain course of action is the most appropriate, trusts the rehabilitation professional, and feels that this training or the next step in the rehabilitation process will eventually bring personal satisfaction, then he or she may follow this direction over the family's wishes.

Unrealistic Vocational Aspirations

Although this difficulty is discussed briefly in a previous chapter, it often arises again during the interpretation session. Because of the client's insufficient awareness of his or her abilities, limited exposure to the working world, and fear of certain training areas that lead to employment, the client's own perception of the best rehabilitation goals may be very different from what the evaluation information suggests. When this problem inhibits appropriate rehabilitation planning, the professional must explore carefully with the clients their educational and work history, level of skill proficiency suggested by the evaluation results, and feasible training or employment possibilities. After the identification of the client's work-related qualifications, various employment alternatives can be presented, based on emotional, physical, and intellectual qualifications. The DOT provides information on job requirements and working conditions. The professional should also know about salary and promotional possibilities. If this information is given in relationship to the client's training and job capabilities, emphasizing as many employment alternatives as possible, the client will at least have a considerable amount of useful information to make a choice.

It is the client's responsibility to make the decision about which vocational direction should be pursued. When the rehabilitation professional is patient, identifies the sources of the client's unrealistic vocational goals, and attempts to make rehabilitation alternatives as appealing as possible, there is a greater possibility that the client will consider carefully the professional's recommendations. Many times, it is also helpful for clients to talk to someone in a field toward which they may be unrealistically aspiring. This reality exposure helps clients to confront personal options and obtain some concrete information on their feasibility. Often, these encounters help to break down clients' resistance and allow them to acknowledge the impracticality of an initial vocational choice. Moreover, workers can also recommend that the client meet people in those occupations or training opportunities that are more in harmony with his or her evaluation results.

Issues with the Minority Client

Explaining test results to those with a disability and who represent a specific ethnic background that is not in a dominant culture necessitates distinct interpretation approaches. It is particularly important to prepare carefully the interpretation session and to know the tests that have been used. Because of the standardization process for a specific test, the measure might be biased against an ethnic group. Because evaluation might be viewed as another failure experience for certain minority clients, the helping professional should take steps to ensure that the assessment process can especially promote the individual's self-esteem and self-awareness. The value of this feedback session can be enhanced by exploring early in the evaluation process the client's world-view and perception of the testing situation, identifying clearly the person's reactions to the assessment information that is being presented, and reviewing the contextual influences that influence test-taking performance. These influences include family expectations, cultural attitudes regarding rehabilitation service providers, and educational and work backgrounds. The interpretation session should provide an opportunity for dialogue, an occasion to increase client clarity and confidence, assistance in long-term perspectives, and enhancement of the decision-making process that follows the learning of assessment results. All of these goals cannot be accomplished without an understanding of the client's learning style, perceptions of successful evaluation outcomes, and mind-set about the assessment process itself.

Professional's Role in Developing Occupational Information

A knowledge of occupational resources and local opportunities for employment considerably enhances the credibility of the interpretation of test results to clients. Goldman (1972) suggested that if counselors, for example, continue to use tests, they must collect information about local experiences. This makes interpretive statements more meaningful and brings a perspective for understanding assessment results. Using varied occupational information resources can provide a more realistic picture of evaluation results, which adds more credibility to rehabilitation planning. During the interpretive session, it is also important to increase the client's options for training or employment. A knowledge of occupational resources facilitates the exploration of alternatives.

To aid in the development of one's understanding of occupational information, selected occupational literature is described, and approaches are identified for generating information on the local world of work.

Occupational Literature

Dictionary of Occupational Titles (DOT)

This version of the DOT was published by the U.S. Department of Labor in 1991. Originally published in 1939, the DOT was brought up-to-date by a second edition in 1949. The book was totally revised in 1965, to include a new coding system and additional comprehensive information provided in its structure. The fourth edition was published in 1977. A revision of the fourth edition was released in 1991. This revision consists of two volumes including 12,741 occupation descriptions, of which approximately one fifth are new or revised. The 1991 revision also incorporates codes and information from the *Guide for Occupational Exploration* (GOE) (JIST, 1998a) and *Selected Characteristics of Occupations Defined in the Dictionary of Occupational Titles* (U.S. Department of Labor, 1997). There are three basic parts of a DOT definition—namely, code number, occupational title, and registry designation. A definition is a brief description of the job as it most commonly occurs. The DOT code number assigned to each defined occupation consists of nine digits divided into three sections, with three digits in each part. Isaacson and Brown (1997) explained that "the parts have a particular purpose and provide specific information about the occupation. In the first two parts, each digit supplies certain information" (p. 116).

Figure 13.1 explains the DOT code, and Figure 13.2 illustrates a DOT definition. There are nine occupational categories: (a) professional, technical, and managerial occupations; (b) clerical and sales occupations; (c) service occupations; (d) agricultural, fishery, forestry, and related occupations; (e) processing occupations; (f) machine trades occupations; (g) bench-work occupations; (h) structural work occupations; and (i) miscellaneous occupations.

Readers should be aware that the Department of Labor has initiated an effort to replace the DOT with the *Occupational Information Network* or ONET (JIST, 1998b). In developing this network there are three objectives: (1) provide a common language that can be used to describe workers and the jobs they perform; (2) develop a database about jobs that is relational in nature; and (3) provide users who access the system with information about skills transferability as well as the ability to estimate the time it will take to retrain for related jobs (Isaacson & Brown, 1997).

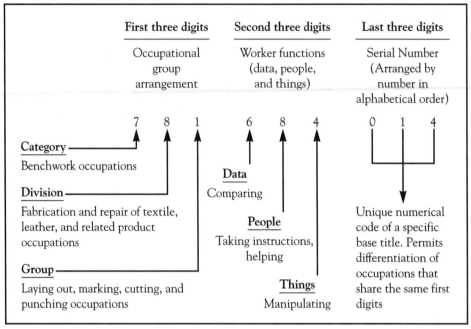

Figure 13.1. Parts of the DOT code.

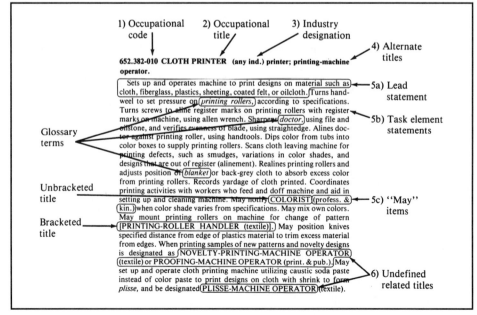

Figure 13.2. Parts of a DOT definition.

Complete Guide for Occupational Exploration

This excellent resource for evaluators who are preparing an interpretation session provides an easy-to-use method of identifying general clusters of occupations and specific job titles. There are 12 major interest areas, which include Artistic, Scientific, Plants and Animals, and Mechanical. Each of these are broken down into more specific subgroups of related jobs. The 12 major interest areas and 66 work groups provide general information on the occupations within each group, including skills required, type of work, education required, and other details. This volume includes all of the new and revised job titles listed in the 1991 edition of the DOT.

The *Complete Guide for Occupational Exploration* (JIST, 1993) greatly facilitates the exploration of career and employment alternatives based on general interests, previous experience, training, and other factors. This book uses standard cross-referencing systems that allow the evaluator to obtain more information on career areas or specific job titles. It can be an important tool for the evaluator who is interpreting assessment results and needs readily understandable information about work and careers with which they can match evaluation results. The *Complete Guide for Occupational Exploration* can be obtained from: JIST Works, Inc., 720 North Park Avenue, Indianapolis, IN, 46202-34431, 317-264-3720.

Also available is the *Enhanced Guide for Occupational Exploration*, Second Edition (Maze & Mayall, 1995). In this new edition, more job descriptions comprising 95% of the workforce have been added, and 793 new job descriptions and revised data for all coded information have been included. Obsolete jobs and those employing few people were eliminated in this enhanced edition to make room for new jobs, high-tech jobs, and jobs employing large numbers of people.

Two other resources can be quite useful for the interpretation session: the *Occupational Outlook Handbook* (U.S. Department of Labor, 1990) covers about 185 occupations and includes data on job outlook; and the *Occupational Outlook Quarterly*, published by the Bureau of Labor Statistics (1998), provides updated information related to the *Handbook* and other relevant outlook data.

Approaches for Generating Information on Local Working Opportunities

The rehabilitation professional should be familiar with the varied resources that provide information on job opportunities. Some resources are:

1. Private and independent schools

2. Apprenticeships (the best source of information is the regional representative for apprenticeships in the client's area)

3. Professional and trade associations and labor unions

4. State and private employment agencies

5. Local newspapers

6. The chamber of commerce

When seeking information about possible employment opportunities, following certain guidelines provides the most useful facts. In 1980, the National Vocational Guidance Association published guidelines (Fredrickson, 1982); those relevant to rehabilitation assessment are as follows:

1. Duties and nature of work

2. Work setting and conditions

3. Personal qualifications

4. Social and psychological factors

5. Preparation required

6. Special requirements

7. Methods of entering

8. Earnings and other benefits

9. Usual advancement possibilities

CHAPTER 13 CONCLUSION

A central aim of rehabilitation assessment is to identify the client's vocational assets and capabilities. Counselors can follow recommendations, such as the tentative recommendations provided in this book, for developing rehabilitation plans. The communication of the evaluation results is a necessary step, which includes both the identification of assets and the formulation of appropriate plans. The manner in which the rehabilitation professional handles the interpretive session often determines whether the client will achieve rehabilitation goals.

 CASE STUDY: LUDMILLA

Ludmilla, age 38, was employed for several years as a program consultant for a large urban bank. There, she collaborated with economists on the preparation of guidelines for company mergers. Prior to her immigration to the United States from Russia, she achieved in her native country the equivalent of a master's degree in economics. She also had been employed as an international program manager, an international symposia secretary, and a project coordinator before she came to the United States and worked for 6 years as a program consultant for a New York City bank. Ludmilla then had a nervous breakdown and was institutionalized for 18 months. Now, 12 months after leaving the hospital, she presents herself for vocational assessment and career exploration. As a result of her medication and regular outpatient therapy, Ludmilla believes that her condition has stabilized. However, she has no interest in returning to her previous occupation and would like to enter another career field.

Ludmilla is not married, attends church services regularly, and lives with her mother in an upper–middle-class neighborhood. Prior to her hospitalization, Ludmilla was both a docent at an art museum and an active member of a Russian cultural group. Ludmilla has been accepted for rehabilitation and will spend 3 days at a vocational assessment center. As an evaluator, you are to meet with Ludmilla and explain the following results of testing:

1. *Quick-Test*[1]—109 IQ score

2. *Shipley Institute of Living Scale*[2]—128 IQ score

3. *Wide Range Achievement Test–Third Edition* (WRAT–3)[3]—Arithmetic = 12th+ grade level; Reading = 10th grade level; Spelling = 10th grade level

4. *Myers-Briggs Type Indicator* (MBTI)[4]—INTJ

5. *Self-Directed Search*[5]—AIC

6. *Minnesota Importance Questionnaire*[6]—High Priority Values: safety, status, and comfort

7. *Strong Interest Inventory*[7]—C Theme = very high; R Theme = very high; I Theme = high

A situational assessment of 2 days indicated that Ludmilla was cooperative and friendly with co-workers and particularly liked packaging artistic materials. Assessment report indicated that Ludmilla easily understood directions but became bored after 2 days of packaging.

---

[1] Ammons & Ammons, 1962.

[2] Shipley, 1959.

[3] Wilkinson, 1993.

[4] Myers & Briggs, 1988.

[5] Holland, 1985.

[6] Vocational Psychology Research, 1981.

[7] Strong, Hansen, & Campbell, 1994.

Chapter 13 Case Study Questions

DIRECTIONS: With this brief information, please answer the following questions:

1. What do you foresee as problems in communicating the assessment results to this client?

2. Are there any discrepancies in the test results?

3. How would you proceed in communicating the assessment results to Ludmilla? Also, how would you help this client develop realistic rehabilitation plans?

The Rehabilitation Professional as a Consumer

The previous chapters in this volume emphasize the idea that the rehabilitation professional is the main person to conduct the vocational assessment. Apart from the initial interview, however, evaluation services are often performed by another agency or professional. Chapter 8 on personality assessment discusses some reasons for using other resources, such as the lack of training in the administration of certain psychological tests, interpretation of these tests, or the agency's decision that the evaluation of personality functioning be conducted by an identified "expert" in that field. An agency's policy may be that all clients must receive a comprehensive evaluation at a specific assessment center. Because of the in-depth assessment opportunities available at an evaluation center, including the specialized training of personnel, services for clients with particular problems may have to be purchased at this resource. When an evaluation is conducted by another agency, the referring rehabilitation professional is a "purchaser" of services. This chapter discusses the many issues and questions that arise in these circumstances and suggests guidelines that can assist rehabilitation professionals in making good decisions when purchasing services.

ISSUES TO CONSIDER WHEN PURCHASING SERVICES

Reason and Time to Evaluate

As the first chapter in this book indicates, clients who present themselves for rehabilitation services bring different goals, varied emotional reactions to their disability experience, and assorted personal needs. After a client is determined eligible for receiving services from a particular agency, then the rehabilitation professional judges what kinds

The author wishes to acknowledge Mr. Joe Shulpulski, a vocational evaluator in Maryland, for his many ideas shared in conversation, which have resulted in the development of the material in the first part of this chapter.

of evaluation would develop an appropriate rehabilitation plan. A physical examination, possibly a psychiatric exam for understanding mental health status, and vocational evaluation are usually the necessary components of this overall evaluation.

The professional should substantiate any beginning hunches about the emotional, physical, and intellectual levels of the client's capabilities. He or she should also update any information in the client's record that indicates levels of functioning. Either need can serve as a rationale for vocational evaluation. From the time of the initial interview, the professional gains an estimate of what the client seeks from rehabilitation services. The goals of an independent living opportunity, immediate job, or the need to receive appropriate training all influence what kind of vocational assessment should be pursued.

A good time to use evaluation resources is when realistic information is needed to support a beginning awareness of a client's abilities or when the professional believes that a standardized, sophisticated assessment can help determine a client's complex functioning. Such resources, however, should not be used to keep the client busy for a period of time or, worse, to supply all the answers for the professional who has no idea of what the client can or wants to do. Many clients are also referred for evaluation as a matter of routine, even when the evidence of the client's potential is already available and there is no need to further substantiate these data. In these situations, clients often feel that their pursuit of their own perceived rehabilitation goals is being unnecessarily delayed. Because of all these concerns, the initial meeting with the client should ascertain just what the client's goals are and how vocational evaluation can fit into the development of rehabilitation plans.

Timing is also important when referring the client for vocational evaluation services. Timing refers to determining when assessment should be conducted after a disability-inducing trauma, during hospitalization, or after long-term institutionalization. For most clients, the psychological adjustment to their mental and physical limitations may take weeks, months, or even longer. Some persons never really adapt to disability-related limitations and prefer a lifestyle that expresses overdependence or a decided reluctance to become work-productive. Whatever the length of time, a period of psychological adjustment is to be expected. As clients go through this process of emotional adaptation, feelings of anxiety, depression (with its concomitant anger, confusion, and uncertainty about the future), and helplessness may dominate. When the professional perceives that these feelings are a strong influence, a formal, planned evaluation should be delayed. The presence of these emotions at the time of assessment can affect the reliability of the evaluation results.

Many rehabilitation professionals argue that assessment should not be delayed because the process itself may reduce these emotional feelings and thus facilitate the client's progress toward rehabilitation goals. These professionals believe that imparting assessment results that emphasize the client's residual strengths may alleviate their perceptions of helplessness. However, most persons with a disability do need some emotional adaptation to the disability before formal assessment begins. Even so, clients who request rehabilitation services for themselves or who are eager to be employed again suggest a more positive attitude and psychological readiness that is conducive to involvement in vocational assessment.

Formulating Specific Questions

After a client receives vocational evaluation services from another agency, the assessment results are reported to the referring source. This report is crucial to the rehabilitation professional, who is responsible for the case management of the client's rehabilitation, because it should contain information that can be directly used for rehabilitation planning. Nevertheless, this report often conveys testing results and recommendations in impractical language or jargon. Therefore, at the time of referral, questions should be directed to the evaluation source that, in turn, will generate responses feasible for the development of rehabilitation goals. It is assumed that vocational evaluation explores the client's level of intelligence, achievement, and personality functioning, as well as his or her interest areas. Many tests that are traditionally used for intelligence and personality assessment, such as the *Wechsler Adult Intelligence Scale–Revised* (WAIS–R) (Wechsler, 1981) and the *Thematic Apperception Test* (Murray, 1943), can also provide information about the client's vocational functioning. When these measures are used, a rehabilitation perspective offered by the referring source is needed. This direction is developed by the rehabilitation professional's questions suggested at the time of initial referral. The following are some questions that, when asked by the referring source, help to explore the client's job readiness:

1. Is the client aware of activities and situations that tend to aggravate the disability or impair his or her general health?

2. What aspects of the client's emotional functioning may be viewed as obstacles to appropriate job adjustment?

3. What does the particular assessment measure indicate about client emotional strengths and achievement areas that can facilitate his or her adjustment to a work environment?

4. What is the relationship between the identified client interest areas and the client's capabilities as indicated by the vocational evaluation?

Of course, there are other questions that can also solicit information about the client's more specific interest areas and behaviors. For example, are the client's behaviors appropriate for usual job demands such as punctuality, attention to a task, and following directions? Significantly, the usefulness of the report from an evaluation agency or professional is largely determined by the type of questions asked.

Job Analysis

Many appropriate questions to be asked by a rehabilitation professional can emerge after this professional has done an analysis of available jobs in the community. Though many job analyses are performed after the reporting of test results, yet before the planning stage of the rehabilitation process, an understanding of the demands that come with the jobs that are available can provide a necessary structure to the assessment process itself. Job analysis can generate ideas about whether a client can adapt to training or job requirements and can further pinpoint the behavioral tasks and work-related capabilities that are necessary to do a job effectively. In other words, job analysis can be a prerequisite for the development of a variety of services and procedures related to vocational rehabilitation.

Job analysis is the identification of worker activities and skills required to complete a set of associated actions or operations that make up a job. It is different than job restructuring, which is the act of assembling identified worker activities from one set of jobs in order to build a different set of jobs, for the purpose of accomplishing the same product or output. Job analysis can be used, consequently, to accomplish the following goals:

A. To improve safety through the disclosure of job hazards

B. To identify requirements of jobs that may be modified to meet the needs of persons with handicapping conditions

C. To explore the transferability of skills

D. To restructure jobs to better use available workers

E. To identify essential and marginal functions of a job, such important skills and abilities, temperaments, stress factors, supervisory characteristics, and accessibility issues (e.g., slickness of floor, wheelchair accessibility of bathroom and cafeteria, height of telephones), all of which can be considered when planning necessary job modifications as required by the Americans with Disabilities Act of 1990 for a qualified job applicant.

Job Analysis Procedure

Preceding the process of job analysis are two recommended steps that provide a foundation for the analysis:

Step 1

Identify the particular available jobs in the community. The state employment office, the chamber of commerce, and local civic organizations are a few resources for job openings. If available, placement personnel are also a valuable source of information. Whatever the job leads, the range of jobs found in various industries should be known.

Step 2

Identify the two categories of job analysis elements that are required for the analysis of any job. These categories are:

A. *Work performed*, including (1) worker functions; (2) work fields (specific methods characteristic of machines, tools, equipment, or work aids, such as drafting, riveting, sawing, installing, and repairing); (3) machines, tools, equipment, and work aids; and (4) materials, products, subject matter, and services

B. *Worker traits*, including training time, aptitudes, temperaments, interests, and physical demands and environmental conditions.

This two-step analysis is a logical process to obtain information about the major tasks, setting, and worker qualifications of a specific job. The following outline describes one way to perform a job analysis. I have found it very useful in my vocational rehabilitation practice.

1. Job name or title. In describing a job, particular attention should be given to what differentiates this job from others. Although several titles may be used for a particular job, distinctive tasks must be emphasized. For example, a clerical job may involve taking dictation, typing, photocopying, and filing. These functions may be given titles. It is important to consider precisely which functions any given job demands.

2. Tasks the worker performs. Counselors and clients must be aware of the skills involved in doing the job. These individuals may consider the following questions:

A. What three or four work activities are really necessary to accomplish the purpose of the job?

B. What is the relationship between tasks, and is there a special sequence that the tasks must follow?

C. Do the tasks necessitate sitting, standing, crawling, walking, climbing, running, stooping, kneeling, lifting, carrying, pushing, pulling, fingering, talking, seeing, listening, feeling, or cooperating? To what degree does the job require muscular discrimination, depth of vision, color perception, the understanding of oral and written instructions, arithmetical computation, oral expression, intelligence, and the ability to work with people? All of these characteristics may be rated according to how important they are to the job. Note that the characteristics required to perform the job, not the characteristics of the present worker on the job, are rated.

D. What are the personality characteristics that are required or suggested in order to perform the job successfully?

E. To do this job, is previous training or experience required? If so, how much, and is vocational, technical, or on-the-job training required?

F. What level of required training and mental capabilities is necessary for performing the job adequately? For example, how complex is the job, and how much is required in terms of responsibility for the work of others, equipment, materials, and safety? Also, to what degree are initiative, adaptability, mental alertness, and judgment required?

G. What specific knowledge is required for this job? This may include knowledge of machines, processes, materials, techniques, or policy and government regulations.

3. *Methods required for the worker to perform job tasks.* What tools, materials, and equipment are used? What are the methods and processes used?

4. *Physical setting of the job.* This includes the pay scale, the hours and shifts, and the standards for productive output. How would one describe the physical conditions of the job setting—hot, cold, damp, inside, outside, underground, wet, humid, dry, air-conditioned, dirty, greasy, or noisy? Does the job environment have vibrations, hazards, odors, high places, sudden temperature changes, toxic conditions, solitary conditions, or crowded conditions?

Once information needed to perform a job analysis is understood, the worker must collect this information. The professional can use the *Dictionary of Occupational Titles* (DOT) (U.S. Department of Labor, 1991), which contains an abundance of facts about thousands of jobs. However, not all work converts to a DOT classification; an available job in the community can be a combination of two or more jobs in the DOT. Also, when the DOT identifies the physical demands of a job, it is assumed that a person possesses the physical capabilities in an amount equal to that job. Without job restructuring or bioengineering, many people with handicaps are eliminated from such jobs.

There are other approaches to the development of a job analysis. A questionnaire can use the format suggested in the above four steps. People working in varied occupations who are most familiar with a particular job can then complete the questionnaire. Although a large amount of information can be obtained rapidly, the success of this method depends on the client's ability to provide accurate and easy-to-classify answers. Another method is to use an interview format to question employers about the duties and tasks of their jobs. Although this can be quite time-consuming, it gives the rehabilitation professional the opportunity to collect all the desired facts about a particular job. Also, employees can be observed performing their respective jobs at a work station. If this method is used, the information should be carefully recorded on a job observation form. This form can follow the guidelines of a job analysis.

Because the success of a job analysis is affected by the reliability of the information collected, a combination of methods can be used to obtain job information. Whatever the approach, however, job analysis itself is a valuable skill for the rehabilitation professional. It can help to identify the types of jobs that are physically, emotionally, and intellectually appropriate for clients who have a disability. Such identification can establish a perspective for the client's vocational evaluation.

What Is the Best Type of Evaluation for the Client?

As discussed earlier in this book, there are many clients for whom the traditional measures of vocational assessment are not appropriate. For many clients with severe disabilities, for example, standard aptitude tests emphasize verbal directions, providing little information that can be translated into suitable plans for education and training. Rehabilitation professionals, therefore, must look elsewhere for assessment resources for this population. The professional should appraise carefully the available evaluation resources and determine which resources will provide the most usable information for rehabilitation purposes. For example, a rehabilitation counselor whose caseload is mainly with clients who are blind should use only those assessment resources that have valid and reliable measures for this client population. Types of assessment other than traditional paper-and-pencil tests often have to be used. Work sample evaluation for certain clients can be a valuable source of diagnostic data, while a situational assessment may have a more far-reaching applicability than standard measures for individuals with severe disabilities.

Work Samples

One of the resources available for assessment purposes comes in the form of the many commercial work sample systems. A work sample itself is a simulated task or work activity of an actual industrial operation. *Actual* work samples are taken directly from business or industry and reproduce the processes actually conducted there; *simulated* work samples are developed by evaluators to simulate jobs. The difference between the two is only a matter of emphasis; both identify either by observation or by measurement specific abilities. The results of a series of individual work samples are usually combined to develop a profile of client potential.

There are many advantages to using work samples, including (a) the approximation to real-life jobs; (b) the opportunity to assess many personal characteristics in a controlled setting; (c) the appropriateness to the evaluation of groups of people with a disability, such as those who have brain damage, deafness, blindness, or any combination of these; and (d) the realization that, during the assessment process, clients can perceive themselves as being involved in a work task rather than feeling as though they are taking a test. However, there are some disadvantages to using this method. In its current form, work sample evaluation for persons with severe mental retardation is still considered to be an unsatisfactory source of diagnostic data. The verbal nature of the instructions usually requires a higher language capability than these individuals commonly display. Also, a lack of standardization of work samples often exists; there is still no assurance that performance on the work samples always predicts performance in actual jobs. In addition, commercial work samples are expensive and need periodic revision so they do not become obsolete.

Even with these limitations, work samples can be very valuable in the assessment of many persons with handicaps. To use work samples, the rehabilitation professional must identify the resources in the client's community and what kind of work samples are being used in that agency. The rehabilitation professional should also determine whether the evaluations relate the client's performance on the work samples to the real world of work and, as a result of this type of evaluation, whether the client better understands the demands and expectations of a specific job or group of occupations.

Table 10.1 of this volume describes commercial work sample systems that are frequently used by different rehabilitation agencies. There is no intent to endorse any one commercial system, but this list can be helpful in identifying what particular system may be especially useful for a client.

Situational Assessment

When traditional tests for vocational assessment do not provide relevant information for rehabilitation planning with clients with severe disabilities, the possibilities of a situational assessment should be carefully explored. After the initial interview, the professional should have a beginning idea of what kind of vocational assessment to pursue. Also, when assessment questions are formulated, the approaches to evaluation and the places to obtain reliable and valid information can be identified more easily.

Situational assessment is essentially the observation of people in work situations. It involves a practice of observing, evaluating, and reporting over a period of time. During this assessment, a client's behavior and work performance while working in a job situation with other employees is observed. This type of evaluation also helps the client learn the role of a worker, allows the evaluator to assess many more work behaviors than can be explored with either standardized vocational testing or work sample approaches, and minimizes the typical test-situation anxiety.

For situational assessment to be effective, an appropriate site should be used, adequate supervision provided, and a means used to gather information that, in turn, can be translated into rehabilitation planning. Because the observational approach is the basis of situational assessment, these observations must be carefully planned and scheduled, and well-designed rating and observation forms should be used. This demands that the rehabilitation professional understand the work evaluation opportunities in respective agencies, the experience and educational background of the staff, and what kind of ratings are used to record the situational assessment information.

Preparing the Client

Once the decision is made to obtain a certain type of vocational evaluation and the facility or agency to conduct this assessment is selected, the client must be carefully prepared. This is the one area often neglected during the entire rehabilitation process. Assumptions are often made that either the assessment source will perform this task or that clients do not need any preparation apart from the name and address of the evaluation facility and the types of tests or assessment procedures that will be used. However, the worker can facilitate the reliability of the entire assessment experience by explaining the purpose of evaluation and the ways the results can aid the client in achieving realistic rehabilitation goals.

Imparting information and responding to the client's own questions and related concerns should be the focus of this preparation. Professionals should discuss with their clients the purpose of assessment, its part in the rehabilitation process, and the ways evaluation information can help to identify the client's strengths and indicate obstacles to reaching rehabilitation goals. Procedures that will be used in the assessment can be explained, after which advice can be given to the client about what is the best way to prepare mentally and physically for the evaluation. For example, getting a good night's sleep the night before and eating a good breakfast can contribute to a better performance during the evaluation. Additional knowledge that should be communicated includes the starting time, the amount of time the assessment usually takes, and the transportation directions to the facility. Finally, the professional should mention that he or she will receive a report from the evaluation resource and will discuss it with the client. This can often alleviate client concerns about learning the assessment results. If it is the policy of the particular agency or other evaluation resource to carefully explain test results to the client, then this practice should be mentioned.

It is further suggested that the professional be alert to any signs of client hesitancy or ambiguity about being involved in evaluation. The possible source of this resistance should be identified. For example, many clients know from past experience that they test poorly. The thought of another possible failure experience arouses tremendous anxiety. Information about vocational evaluation opportunities, how the assessment results will be used, and the relationships between assessment and the world of work can all reduce some of this fear. When the client is told that the actual purpose of vocational evaluation is to identify strengths or capabilities that can be used for potentially satisfying, work-related goals, some of the threatening aspects of an upcoming assessment experience are minimized. Clients may still remain anxious, but at least they realize that the professional is supportive and understand why the evaluation is going to be conducted.

Evaluating the Report

Following the vocational evaluation, a report of the results is sent to the referring professional. When the report is received, the following questions should be considered:

1. Did the report answer specific questions?

2. Was the evaluation directed to areas that were needed for rehabilitation planning?

3. Are there unresolved discrepancies among the reported test evaluation results?

4. Does the report integrate all the information into a picture of the client that shows vocational capabilities, behaviors, and limitations that are usable for appropriate vocational planning?

5. What are the recommendations for the client? Are they too broad or too specific? Are options given? Are the recommendations consistent with the test results? Are they realistic?

Of course, if the professional has serious concerns about the report, the evaluation resource should be contacted. Problems can be reduced if the professional initially communicates his or her own expectations about the kind of information that should be obtained from the assessment.

All of the preceding questions represent issues that are to be explored when the professional purchases evaluation services. Acting as a skilled consumer can be just as important as being a well-trained vocational evaluator. After the rehabilitation professional evaluates the report received from the assessment resource, then a further exploration is often conducted with the client in order to determine areas of job feasibility.

CHAPTER 14 CONCLUSION

As a consumer, the rehabilitation professional has the continued opportunity to make choices about the types of services that can be provided for clients. Although the assessment needs of clients differ, the range of available evaluation services should critically be explored to plan how these needs will be identified and then met. As a knowledgeable consumer, the professional must identify assessment resources that provide the best chance for generating relevant information for rehabilitation planning. Conducting a relevant assessment for clients, especially these who have a severe disability, has been a rehabilitation problem for a long time. This problem can be minimized as rehabilitation professionals not only assume the role of an enlightened consumer as part of their responsibility, but also provide choices for clients that reflect this understanding.

 CASE STUDY: ROSANNA

As a rehabilitation counselor, you have interviewed Rosanna, age 26, who, 2 years previous to your introduction to her, was in a serious car accident and experienced amnesia and mild brain damage. After 1 year, she returned to her previous job as an accountant but couldn't keep up. Rosanna felt that she had fallen far behind the ever-increasing technology in her field and thought she could never catch up. Most of her memory functions have returned, but she claims that she finds it difficult to handle work pressure and becomes easily irritated with co-workers. Now Rosanna has no idea what she wants to do. She lives in a large, urban city, has no health problems other than her now minor cognitive problems that would affect more the technical demands of advanced computer work. Rosanna has been married 3 years to a successful stockbroker; they have no children. She has thought about going back to school, but really would like another job.

Chapter 14 Case Study Questions

DIRECTIONS: With this information, please answer the following questions:

1. What agencies in your community that offer vocational evaluation services would be appropriate for Rosanna's assessment, and what criteria would you use for this determination?

2. What specific question would you ask personnel at this resource to obtain suitable information for rehabilitation planning?

3. When talking with Rosanna before the vocational evaluation, you learn from her that she may be interested in employment as a buyer for a large retail store chain. How would you obtain a job analysis of these particular jobs?

4. How would you prepare Rosanna for the vocational evaluation experience?

Assessment of Industrially Injured Workers

A staggering amount of time and money is spent each year attending to the needs of industrially injured workers. Since 1978, insurance companies have spent billions of dollars on employee benefits for disability insurance. Such benefits include medical and surgical expenses that include the following: costs incurred as a result of on-the-job injuries, reimbursement for miles traveled to obtain services, payment of two thirds of injured workers' average gross weekly pay, stipulated dollar amounts awarded to those who have lost the function of a body portion, and compensation for the pursuit of a vocational rehabilitation program for workers who are unable to return to their usual employment. These awards and compensation coverages, however, vary widely from state to state.

In response to the growing incidence of workers who sustain catastrophic injuries, private rehabilitation firms were developed to assist clients with rehabilitation goals. Working closely with insurance companies who provide compensation coverage, these private resources employ personnel to evaluate the rehabilitation potential of their clients; provide counseling for disability-related, adjustmental concerns; and, when possible, generate job placement opportunities.

Vocational rehabilitation in the private, profit-making sector usually involves many types of clients: (a) the client who returns to his or her former employer in the same or a modified position; (b) the person with a disability who would like the same job, but with a different employer, or a different job entirely; (c) the client who wishes to be retrained for new employment; and (d) the client who needs independent living. The range of disabilities seen in the private sector mainly includes orthopedic problems, and back injury is the most prevalent disability. There are frequently other difficulties associated with the disability. Workman (1983) indicated that the industrially injured worker may have other problems, such as secondary gains, conflicting party involvement, and lack of financial incentives. Also, clients sometimes have hidden disabilities that were undiagnosed prior to the injury, such as learning disabilities, emotional problems, and substance abuse. These conditions can affect performance in vocational training and may influence a choice of an occupational career. The combination of the pre-existing condition and the current injury often produces magnified effects. Further, many industrially injured persons receive tax-free compensation, and these payments diminish the incentives to participate in a vocational rehabilitation program.

Clients are most often referred from insurance companies, attorneys' litigation is frequently involved, and these clients are usually unemployed as a direct result of the disability. Further, injured clients more often have substantial work history and acceptable work habits, but usually experience pain that may develop into a chronic pain syndrome (Stewart & Vander Kolk, 1989). From their experience, Stewart and Vander Kolk reported that persons with an injury need relatively timely, fast-paced, intensive, and comprehensive rehabilitation services.

The vocational rehabilitation process pursued in this sector of human service is based on models developed by the federal–state rehabilitation system. Restoration of loss (physical, financial, emotional, etc.) is the main purpose of both the insurance system and insurance rehabilitation. However, the rehabilitation professional in private practice generates services "from specific referral instructions that may not be necessarily related to the total rehabilitation needs of the injured person" (Workman, 1983, p. 306). Many services require extensive evaluation and then training in job-seeking skills. Another alternative is for assessment to be conducted only as part of a professional's preparation for trial testimony, during which no other services are provided. Job placement is a central goal for most efforts in the private, profit-making sector. Sanchez (1981), in defining vocational rehabilitation for the California worker's compensation system, stated that it is "the process of restoring the injured worker to the competitive labor market at a wage level as close as practical to his/her pre-injury level as soon as possible" (p. 131).

Within the private sector vocational rehabilitation process, there is an emphasis on job analysis, labor market surveys, physician visits, attorney contacts, and job placement (Workman, 1983). However, the steps that the client may take to reach rehabilitation goals (Workman, 1983) are similar to those traditionally used by public agency programs. They include the following:

1. Vocational rehabilitation evaluation

   Initial interview

   Qualified injured worker assessment

   Job analysis

   Information analysis (medical, personal, social, work history, vocational testing and work evaluation, and labor market analysis)

2. Development of vocational objectives

3. Development of rehabilitation plan

4. Plan implementation

5. Job placement and follow-up

6. Case closure

The key ingredient in this entire process is an expeditious, appropriate evaluation of the injured worker's life situation, behavioral characteristics, and residual physical and intellectual capabilities. Although the ingredients of this assessment do not significantly differ in type from the evaluations previously discussed in this book, there may be differences of perspective and time. The injured worker may be receiving benefits or be involved in litigation; or, family influences may be acting as obstacles to rehabilitation goals, and the many years spent in a particular job may be viewed as the culmination of employment efforts. A paramount consideration when developing assessment approaches for those who are industrially injured is the speed of service. A speedy return to work has always been considered a major factor in judging the success of insurance rehabilitation, and a major reason to provide vocational rehabilitation services is to save on benefits paid for wage loss by returning the injured worker to work quickly (Siefker, 1992). On the other hand, systems are not in place in public sector rehabilitation to speed up the process, because this sector of vocational rehabilitation attempts to carefully maximize the client's potential.

Early identification of an injured worker in need of rehabilitation services, and consequently, the provision of appropriate services in a timely manner, are essential. The sooner services begin, the sooner the individual will return to employment. Importantly, the need for a determination of the vocational potential of an injured worker who has lost his or her wage-earning capacity should be addressed prior to a ruling of the nature and extent of the disability. There are many factors other than the specific medical disability that affect an injured worker's successful return to employment. Many of these factors are discussed in this chapter, with particular attention given to assessment issues related to the development of different vocational objectives, an interpretation of the medical report, the client's emotional reaction to disability, the family's response to the client's disabling condition, and the professional's preparation for court testimony.

To provide a context for understanding these factors and the demands of the evaluation process in the private sector, Siefker (1992) identified the following considerations for the vocational evaluation:

1. Become medically familiar with the types of disabilities that are common in insurance rehabilitation.

2. Obtain complete information regarding the rules and regulations governing the system or jurisdiction in which one is working, and become familiar with insurance and insurance terminology.

3. Recognize time and financial guidelines that are available. An evaluation program with individuals who already have a work history may have to be completed in a day or two.

4. Think in terms of returning the worker to the job or employer he or she had at the time of the injury.

5. Be familiar with the emotional aspects of loss, because many injured workers go through the grieving process for an extended period of time.

6. Recommendations should be phrased in terms of what they will cost in both time and money. Dollar savings to the insurance company and cost effectiveness are essential ingredients for vocational planning with injured workers.

ASSESSMENT ISSUES RELATED TO THE DEVELOPMENT OF VOCATIONAL OBJECTIVES

The rehabilitation professional must determine whether the industrially injured worker is prepared to reenter the work situation or is even motivated enough to consider such possibilities, and if so, then what training or similar preparation is needed to facilitate this return. A down-to-earth assessment should be made of the factors that affect employability. The interview is the beginning medium through which this evaluation is conducted. It can help determine the vocational objectives that are feasible for the client, and is the most critical point in the rehabilitation professional's involvement with the injured worker. This interview must be as comprehensive as possible in order to ultimately save time in the rehabilitation process. Chapter 4 of this book discusses the use of the interview for assessment purposes. It identifies the many areas that need to be explored. With industrially injured clients, however, there are further considerations and modifications of the interview structure suggested in that chapter. The following is a recommended format for this interview that can generate information for rehabilitation planning purposes.

Pre-Interview Period

Before meeting with the client, all relevant case materials, such as medical reports and work history, should be reviewed. If there are any missing data, topics requiring additional exploration or validation should be identified. During the interview, such topics should be stressed. For example, if the client's records contain very little information about prior work history, this area should be carefully explored. The evaluator should make a list of questions to ask the client to clarify any confusing, incomplete, or contradictory information (Olson, 1992).

Beginning the Interview

The client's perception of himself or herself as a worker is particularly relevant to employability concerns. To assist clients in evaluating feelings about themselves, it is helpful to encourage the clients to talk about the accident, its emotional impact, and the needs that accompany some clients' belief that they cannot return to their previous job. Early in the interview situation, clients should also discuss their life situation since the accident, as well as their own employment expectations. It is most helpful if the injured worker also can identify any compensatory work-related skills and realizations that he or she gained from the previous work experience. Included in this discussion may be topics such as:

1. What was the most satisfying experience in the client's previous job?
2. What is he or she looking for in a job?
3. What are the present limitations to continuing work?

Conducting the Interview

With the development of information on the client's current living situation and an awareness of the client's feelings and attitudes about working again, additional factors must be explored for rehabilitation planning. The following outline highlights these important areas and suggests questions to solicit the respective information:

1. Vocational goal

    a. What kind of a job would the client like to have?

    b. What are the client's preferences for certain types of work activities, such as clerical, outdoor, or service occupations?

    c. What specialized vocational skill training does the client possess, and does he or she have the interest and physical capability to pursue these skills?

    d. What are the areas of physical and mental difficulty that may prevent the client from achieving a vocational goal?

    e. Is there any relationship between the client's education and career possibilities?

2. Client significant factors

    a. What are the current legal involvements, and should vocational training or employment be delayed until these are resolved?

    b. What are the client's transportation needs?

    c. Are there any problems in using community resources?

    d. If necessary, can the client relocate?

    e. What is the attitude of the client's family toward reemployment, and what influences on rehabilitation does the family bring?

    f. Most recent and past vocational history

g. The injured worker's social environment, family peers, and friends. How do these people influence the client, self-perception, and actions taken toward adjustment?

h. What specific activities or environments aggravate the disabling condition?

i. Are there unique or particular financial needs that resulted from the accident and the disability? Are current benefits adequate to meet financial obligations?

j. What is the injured worker's perspective on the physical restrictions received as a result of the injury?

3. Occupational job significant factors

a. What credentials (e.g., education, training, memberships, licenses, and certificates) does the client have for further employment?

b. In previous employment, was the client able to do the job productively, efficiently, and accurately?

c. What are the client's learning capabilities and speed of learning?

d. Has the client been a dependable worker, and is he or she capable now of meeting attendance, promptness, and speed of production demands?

e. In previous employment, was the client able to get along with co-workers and supervisors? Will the client's current emotional reaction to his or her disability be an obstacle to adjusting well to others in a work environment?

4. Getting a job

a. Will the client be able to get a job, or must he or she be helped?

b. Is the client able to prepare a personal information package for prospective employers?

c. Does the client have the initiative to contact employers as well as make telephone inquiries and applications?

d. Can the client participate appropriately in a job interview?

Such questions may not be generated from the interview itself. Even so, the interview should be able to provide some initial suggestions for the most feasible vocational objective. With an objective in mind, the rehabilitation professional in the private-for-profit sector can then plan, when necessary, a more detailed or formalized exploration of the injured worker's interests, aptitudes, and current labor market opportunities. To assist in planning this assessment, one can adhere to the following guidelines for the different possible vocational objectives:

1. Modified job

a. The onset of a disability represents a discontinuity in what was previously a fairly constant self-concept and environmental interaction (Weinstein, 1983). The client's emotional reaction to the disability event should be evaluated (approaches to this assessment are provided in this chapter). Often, temperaments must be reexplored to evaluate ongoing applicability to the modified occupational environment. This adjustment includes the abilities to handle job pressure, interact appropriately with fellow workers, and meet new job demands willingly.

    b. A job analysis should be conducted and then appropriate modifications made according to the willingness of the employer, the nature of the work environment, and the availability of technology to make the modifications.

2. Other work with same employer

    a. An essential evaluation for this objective is an analysis of transferable skills. Although the client may have a defined physical impairment that prevents return to the same job, many skills and aptitudes remain entirely unaffected. These residual capabilities can be quantified and recombined to meet the requirements of a different job (Weinstein, 1983). Field and Sink (1980), in their development of an evaluation approach titled "Vocational Diagnosis and Assessment of Residual Employability," highlighted five methods of skill identification and skill transference, which enable the professional to quantify the client's residual, occupation-related assets:

Measurement by valid tests
Measurement by job history
Measurement by worker's expressed preference
Measurement by medical report
A combination of the above

Assessment by valid tests, job history, and expressed preference (determination of vocational interest) are discussed in other chapters of this book, and the medical report is explained later in this chapter. In addition, specific worker traits associated with past occupations should be identified. Sink and Field (1981) developed a manual method of compiling this data, in which the professional collects and summarizes the job demand characteristics of the individual's work experience, using the trait-factor profiles of the *Dictionary of Occupational Titles* (DOT) (U.S. Department of Labor, 1991). Once a composite profile is produced, it is altered to reflect the client's current, post-injury, functional capacities (Weinstein, 1983). The profile is stated in the language of jobs and is consistent with traits that were characteristic of the individual prior to the injury.

    b. After the skill identification, a job analysis of opportunities still available with the previous employer should be made.

    c. Evaluation of the client's emotional adjustment to the disability should also be conducted.

3. Direct job placement

    a. An assessment of residual and transferable skills.

    b. An evaluation of the client's emotional adjustment to disability.

    c. An analysis of jobs currently available in the labor market.

    d. An analysis of the client's job-getting and job-keeping behaviors, especially the manner in which the person with a disability may present himself or herself in a job interview situation.

4. On-the-job training or formal training. The same assessment should be conducted as with direct job placement.

5. Self-employment. The same assessment as direct job placement can be given, with particular emphasis both on the client's capabilities to meet the distinctive demands of self-employment (e.g., independence, knowledge of business management) and the feasibility of the environment in which the client intends to establish a business.

Earlier chapters in this book provide more detailed information on the varied assessment approaches, each of which can be used for different occupational objectives. Testing, for example, can help to identify whether a worker still possesses the abilities to perform the job he or she had at the time of the injury, as well as to be useful in identifying options for job modification. But tests that are specifically designed for people with disabilities (i.e., those with a developmental disability, blindness, deafness, etc.) are very infrequently used in working with this population (Olson, 1992). Because time is a critical factor in worker's compensation rehabilitation, tests should be chosen that are quick to administer and score. The evaluator may have to conduct vocational assessment in 1 to 2 days. In order for a credible evaluation to be achieved, the client may have selective homework tasks that focus on self-assessment. Moreover, it is important to choose tests that will stand up to legal scrutiny. Attorneys are becoming more sophisticated in their knowledge of standardized tests "and are starting to challenge test results with more incisive cross-examination questions" (Olson, p. 102).

Olson (1992) explained that most worker's compensation systems require that claimants meet certain criteria to be eligible for vocational rehabilitation services. The criteria include that, as a result of the injury, (a) clients cannot return to the job or employer they had at the time of injury, and (b) clients must be able to benefit from vocational rehabilitation. Determination of eligibility is usually based on a job analysis of the job the client had at the time of the injury, as well as a transferable skills analysis. As stated in an earlier chapter, an appropriate transferable analysis requires as a first step a complete work and educational skills history.

With many clients, the previous employer may have to be contacted because he or she can give valuable information about the client's work capabilities. Much of this exploration can be done while the client is still involved in litigation or compensation settlements. The injured worker may delay any decision about rehabilitation planning until some decision is reached. However, vocational exploration should still be pursued, if for no other reason than to help the client realize that he or she possesses work-related capabilities. This awareness can become a beginning motivating factor for one's return to employment.

THE MEDICAL REPORT

The appropriate use of medical information is invaluable to vocational evaluation and planning. Medical professionals are responsible for evaluating the physical limitations an injury may present. Often, direct contact with the professionals who have or are providing medical treatment to the client who is injured is critical in determining specific injury-related limitations. When the rehabilitation professional has carefully reviewed the client's medical report, any residual capacities should be identified so that possible transferable skills can be evaluated. The following outline shows the specific areas that should be covered in this report:

1. Functional limitations

   a. What work activities are possible?

   b. What is client's tolerance for work activity?

   c. What are the client's concerns about the limitations he or she may experience at work?

   d. What is client's current level of performance in strength, climbing, stooping, reaching, talking, and seeing?

   e. What client abilities can be developed, perhaps with the use of devices, to compensate for the disability? Has there been substantial deterioration in all possible physical areas that could have been used for work?

   f. Does the client have secondary or multiple disabilities with which to cope?

   g. What is client's current level of response to work location, cold, heat, humidity, noise, hazards, and atmospheric conditions?

2. Diagnosis. Readiness for work activities

3. Prognosis

   a. Will the condition worsen or improve?

   b. Is the condition chronic or temporary?

4. Medication

   a. Is the medication taken regularly, and can the client function independently of it?

   b. What are the effects of medication on working? For example, does it cause drowsiness or lethargy?

Understanding the client's medical report can be the first step in formulating realistic rehabilitation plans. Through this awareness, the rehabilitation professional can further comprehend whether (a) the current disability status precludes employment; (b) the client is unable to work full-time because of a mental or physical condition; or (c) the person can work full-time but must have a sedentary job with low stress and close supervision. This report may also indicate whether the client is limited to occupations requiring light physical activity but is still able to work full-time, or whether the client is minimally restricted in terms of the type of work that he or she can do.

In many instances, however, rehabilitation professionals may have specific questions, which may have to be given directly to the physician. Medical report forms are not designed to cover completely every specific situation. It often helps if the examining physician's attention is directed to the things for which specific kinds of information are needed.

CLIENT'S EMOTIONAL
RESPONSE TO DISABILITY

Workers with a disability vary in their abilities to deal with occupational and possible social losses caused by job-related injuries. The time required for medical treatment, the stress of rehabilitation, the lack of mobility, and concern with changing personal appearance, may precipitate a number of crises for the injured worker (Versluys, 1980). The client may not be motivated to reach and maintain projected functional levels of performance. Instead, a life of social isolation and dependency on others may be preferred to one in which all the person's energies are exhausted in the attempt to reach a maximum level of occupational and family productivity.

Weinstein (1978) identified a "disability process," illustrating the idea that the work-related disability results from a complex process rather than a discrete accident or illness. The accident is preceded by the development of tension and stress, which leads to feelings of inadequacy and depression. Weinstein believed that the initiation of the accident process is a matter of personality style that makes the worker unusually sensitive to perceptions of increased expectations and reduced support and approval. Consequently, the worker experiences increased subjective distress and harbors an attitude that makes it difficult to ask for help. When an accident occurs, the worker perceives that his or her distress and possible resulting impaired performance is caused by an externally generated event (i.e., something that could happen to anyone). Thus, as Weinstein explained, the accident transforms an "unacceptable disability" into an acceptable one. The disability even becomes a way of life, facilitated by the worker's continued personality characteristics, and perhaps reinforced by the social and financial responses to the initial disability.

This reaction to an industrial injury becomes, of course, a deterrent to the achievement of rehabilitation goals and, with varied emotional responses to the accident trauma, needs to be identified. When a person sustains a disability, the usual result is a change in self-concept, which is the result of an altered body image. This body image can profoundly affect the client's readiness for work (Forrest, 1963). The injury may be a devastating experience for the client. Not only may his or her self-concept change, but also the person's method of relating to others may be drastically altered (Forrest, 1963). Feelings of inadequacy and self-depreciation may dominate the client's outlook. The areas of human activity that usually receive the impact of these feelings are work and productivity.

Following the occurrence of the injury—and the accompanying emotional shock that the person's occupational and perhaps family and social life has been severely disrupted—is the lingering thought, "Although this has happened, I will soon have a full restoration of my physical capacities. I will be able to do all that I used to do." The worker denies the implications of the injury for employment and physical functioning. At this particular time, the person needs a helping professional who may allow temporary harboring of this denial while at the same time assisting the client in realizing slowly that there may be some permanent limitations.

An understanding of the emotions that the injured worker is experiencing can help considerably when one considers the possibilities of the client's return to work. The emotional reaction of the injured worker usually takes the following sequence:

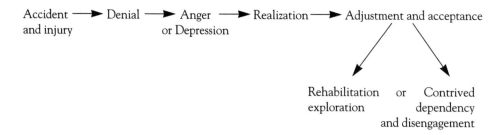

As the reality of the injury situation becomes more apparent, the client usually becomes angry about the perceived occupational and related economic losses. Depression may begin, dominated by feelings of, "What's the use . . . Is there going to be any opportunity for me?" Clients may also start to isolate themselves from former friends or accustomed social opportunities. At the same time, however, they become acquainted with possible compensation benefits or the reassurance that economic deficits can be lessened with the help of other family members. Rehabilitation intervention should certainly have begun by this time, offering the person with a disability a variety of productive options and attractive alternatives to a possible life of dependency. In other words, appropriate information needs to be communicated.

As clients gradually realize that their disabilities may be permanent, they begin to acknowledge their limitations and the necessity to explore other work opportunities. The client's depression may continue as his or her thought processes contain more reality-based information. Support, reassurance that rehabilitation can lead to renewed feelings of productivity, and an identification of one's residual strengths are particularly needed at this time. Otherwise, the client may feel that dependency and the economic reliance only on compensation benefits may be a more satisfying way of life.

From this stage of acknowledgment, the person with a disability begins to adjust to the disability. This adjustment can take the form of positive expressions, including rehabilitation exploration or disengagement from any rehabilitation opportunities. There are many reasons why these persons make such a choice: the person's satisfaction with work, the presence or absence of therapeutic intervention, the life (developmental) stage of the person, the individual's reaction to previous crises, the personality makeup of the individual before the disability, and the person's philosophy of life. When the rehabilitation professional observes that an especially negative reaction to the incident is occurring, these factors should be carefully explored. Also, it should be determined whether the client is using symptoms for secondary gain. If the person is actually getting more reinforcement or benefits from being disabled than nondisabled, it will be very difficult to motivate the client for rehabilitation purposes.

Assessing all of these emotional factors and identifying the degree to which the client is coping with the disability can generate invaluable information for the determination of work readiness. Just as emotional reactions differ, coping styles vary as well. Clients have several choices: they can minimize the disability through selective inattention, ignoring, denial, or rationalizing the significance of the injury; they can make attempts to "master" or "control" the implications of the disability by identifying other compensating abilities and using their energy for productive purposes; or they can simply give up and lead a life of inactivity and passivity. An awareness of the injured person's coping style can often influence the direction of rehabilitation intervention.

Atkins, Lynch, and Pullo (1982) discussed another adjustmental process that particularly applies to the injured worker. The basic components of the model are the following:

1. **Coping**

   What is the emotional effect of the disability? Does it include depression, anger, denial, uncertainty, or confusion?

   Has the client had the chance to mourn the loss implied in the disabling condition?

   Has the client begun to enlarge his or her scope of values?

2. **Focus**

   Is the client concentrating on his or her assets and capabilities or only on disabilities and limitations?

   Does the client extend his or her limitations beyond that which the disability actually dictates?

   Are client limitations underestimated?

3. Blame

Where is the responsibility placed for the causation of the disabling condition—on the client, others, or toward the isolated situation itself? (The last direction of blame is the most conducive to the adjustment process; Wright, 1960).

4. Societal influence

What factors outside the individual influence him or her and affect adjustment?

What is the perception of an individual with a disability of the nondisabled environment—family, social relationships, and co-workers?

Is the individual withdrawing from society or attempting to be accepted by family and friends?

Is the person attempting to normalize his or her disability-related limitations and recognize his or her self-worth despite negative attitudes from others?

The tools and process of evaluation with injured workers demand, consequently, a knowledge of the worker's compensation system, an ability to select appropriately different approaches to determine both eligibility for vocational rehabilitation services and capability to return to work, an awareness of psychosocial factors influencing the client's rehabilitation, and an understanding of the medical limitations caused by the injury. A great deal of the focus in assessment with the injured worker is also on readiness, a readiness for employability. Determination of readiness includes a knowledge of such issues as incentives, disincentives, legal involvement, financial factors, medical support, family involvement, and the Americans with Disabilities Act of 1990 (ADA) legislation with regard to evaluation of need for accommodations, definition of disability, and eligibility requirements under each area of legislation.

PREPARATION FOR COURT TESTIMONY

Since the 1970s, increased demands have been made on rehabilitation professionals to present quantifiable evidence for insurance companies, attorneys, claims agents, physicians, and social security hearings (Godley, 1978). Professionals in the private-for-profit sector of rehabilitation who serve those with industrial injuries are more inclined to solicit legal advice than other rehabilitation professionals; therefore, they may find themselves making court appearances quite frequently. When providing these services for clients, the rehabilitation professional confronts a new variety of responsibilities. These responsibilities require the professional be well prepared to give court testimony about the client, as well as to have a well-developed knowledge of vocational evaluation. In the eyes of the court, the professional is an expert and will have to answer in an objective and unbiased manner a wide range of questions concerning the occupational possibilities of the client.

Expert witness work involves the use of a vocational rehabilitation professional to assess an individual "who has experienced an injury to determine the effects of the injury on the person's ability to work and earn money" (Choppa & Shafer, 1992, p. 135). Forensic rehabilitation involves the use of assessment for Social Security Disability Insurance (SSDI) determination, worker compensation employability determination, long-term disability determination, and personal injuries and capability to return to work. Personal injuries may include auto and other types of accidents, professional malpractice, product liability, and injuries resulting from a crime.

To perform successfully expert witness work, the evaluator should have an in-depth knowledge of the labor market and training facilities, an ability to perform accurate job analyses, good knowledge of community resources, an understanding of how medical aspects of disabilities affect employment, and comprehensive knowledge of how the legal system works (Owings, 1992). This work focuses on determining whether wage earning capacity has been lost, the extent of the loss, and how much it will cost to eliminate or minimize that loss. The eventual outcome of expert witness work is usually an oral or written presentation of information gathered (Choppa & Shafer, 1992).

In conducting forensic rehabilitation, there may be the temptation to take sides because the evaluator is retained either by the defense or the plaintiff. However, the evaluator should be careful to avoid favoring the viewpoint of either the defense or the plaintiff. The value of an expert's testimony is severely compromised if it can be demonstrated that the expert witness favors the side that has hired him or her. Objectivity should be maintained, and the evaluator needs to provide realistic information that is not edited to fit the viewpoint of either the defense or the plaintiff. Ethical guidelines, consequently, must be followed closely. Accepted codes of ethics and professional standards are established by many rehabilitation-related organizations, including the National Rehabilitation Association, the Vocational Evaluation and Work Adjustment Association, and state licensing boards (Choppa & Shafer, 1992).

Sink and King (1978) identified the many questions that may be asked of rehabilitation professionals when testifying on behalf of their clients. The questions themselves suggest the type of preparation required in order to make an adequate court presentation. Godley (1978) suggested that such questions could be prepared and reviewed by the professional and attorney before the court appearance. The following outline can be followed by the professional when preparing court testimony, and contains information originally stated by Sink and King:

1. The rehabilitation professional (vocational expert)

   a. Do you have a knowledge of physical and mental disabilities and their relationship to employment potential, as well as of jobs and their requirements common to the labor market? How did you obtain this information?

   b. Have you had experience in job analysis, and can you give examples of local industries in which you have observed and analyzed jobs?

c. Have you talked to your client's employer? Would this employer hire the client?

d. If a job is possible with the employer, what would be the salary level, career ladder sequence, and length of time between steps? What would be the anticipated income in 1 year? In 5 years?

2. The client

a. Describe the details of your client's previous employment, including work performed; tools used; supervision given and received; communication skills required; temperaments, interests, physical demands, and intelligence needed for the job; typical salaries for such jobs; working hours and days; mode of transportation to and from work; and use of arms, hands, fingers, legs, back, and so on.

b. Define for the court the occupational significance of both physical and mental conditions as defined by the physician. Please also define the client's daily (social, avocational, recreational) activities, including work around the house and care for or play with children or grandchildren, and whether or not the client drives, attends religious services, or goes shopping?

c. Describe for the court the occupationally significant characteristics of the jobs the client has held and the relationship of the client's physical (or mental) conditions to these jobs.

d. Are there any jobs in the labor market that may be done by the client without additional training, or are there jobs in which the client could be employed with additional training or education? If so, what are they and where are they located?

e. If training or education is needed, is the client qualified for acceptance into training or educational programs? What kind of training or education is required, how long is it, what is the cost, and what are the qualifications for training?

f. What are the client's perceptions of going back to work, not working, the physical limitations as stated by the physician, and being trained or educated for another job?

g. If the client has had a vocational evaluation, describe the types of psychological tests or work samples administered during the assessment process. What are they supposed to evaluate, what are they supposed to measure, and what is their validity? To what kinds of skills or jobs do the work samples relate? If you did not administer the tests or work samples, what are the qualifications of those persons who did so?

Sink and King (1978) explained that the questions should be answered in terms of magnitude, frequency, and duration. To obtain the information requested by many of the questions, the client may be observed or questioned. The DOT should be used for classification of job title, worker trait group arrangements, physical demands, working conditions, general educational development, specific vocational preparation, aptitudes, interests, and temperaments. The rehabilitation professional should also have a job market survey that applies to the client's living area.

CHAPTER 15 CONCLUSION

Among many rehabilitation concerns about the injured worker, the problem of motivation is often dominant. If the worker has been employed for many years, but now is being influenced by compensation benefits and family pressures to not return to a job, rehabilitation will be more difficult. This motivation variable is a distinctive focus in evaluation efforts with industrially injured clients. If the client possesses all the necessary prerequisites and is ready for immediate placement, the rehabilitation process will run more smoothly. If the disabled person is not ready, then attention must be given to all the issues that relate to the client working again. Skill development, resolution of emotional feelings, and cooperation from the family should all be attended to if the worker is to achieve rehabilitation goals. The evaluation period becomes, consequently, not only a time for the identification of job readiness factors, but also an opportunity for the rehabilitation professional to counsel the injured worker and help him or her begin to understand new options for productivity.

For effective evaluation, the rehabilitation professional must know the local job community and understand the dynamics of job analysis. Many injured workers have well-developed employment skills. From an awareness of the varied job requirements, the rehabilitation professional can suggest appropriate job modifications. Through these changes, the client's compensatory skills can find a new opportunity for usefulness.

 CASE STUDY: ANGELICA

Angelica is a 31-year-old, single, African American woman. Prior to her on-the-job injury, she was an assistant curator at an art gallery located in a large Eastern city. She graduated with a Bachelor's degree in art history from a state university, and prior to her present employment held several jobs in the areas of sales and retail.

While preparing for a recent exhibition, a large, framed painting fell unexpectedly on her left shoulder, causing injuries to the neck, shoulder, and left arm. Angelica was immediately hospitalized for several days, and following a period of physical rehabilitation, returned to her home with the realization that she could not perform many of her previous duties in the art gallery. She has limited motion in her left arm, has difficulty turning her neck, and is unable to lift more than a few pounds of weight. She also has recurrent pain emanating from her left side, which is managed by medication, but is a continued worry for her.

Since the accident, Angelica has been receiving worker's compensation benefits. Though sufficient to meet her daily needs, Angelica has begun to realize that she may have to look either for another occupational career or to be retrained in the field of art. The insurance company would like her to return to her former job, though Angelica believes that it could be mentally too painful for her, and she also feels angry at another employee whom she believes was careless and contributed to the accident. This belief, however, cannot be proved.

Angelica's parents are both retired after many years as college teachers, and live in the same city as their only daughter. While working as an assistant art curator, Angelica was involved in a local political organization, enjoyed sewing, and volunteered as a tutor for elementary school children in the inner-city, assisting them with their reading and art classes.

 # Chapter 15 Case Study Questions

DIRECTIONS: With this information, please answer the following questions:

1. What guidelines or structure would you establish for the initial interview with Angelica to generate information for vocational planning?

2. What are the issues that must considered if the insurance company wishes to settle Angelica's personal injury claims out of court and make a final compensative payment for injuries incurred?

3. If Angelica decides to sue the art gallery for injury compensation, what information as a vocational evaluator should you gather in order to prepare for court testimony?

Rehabilitation Planning ⟨16⟩

During the entire assessment process, much information is generated about client functioning. At the beginning of vocational evaluation, the rehabilitation professional usually has either a goal or a perspective for collecting this information. An objective might be to identify client assets needed for employment or training that will lead to a job. Other possible goals are independent living, the identification of transferable skills for eventual return to a job, or the determination of eligibility for rehabilitation services. When employment or independent goals are being considered, the client should participate in planning immediately following rehabilitation assessment. This planning is an end product of assessment and an essential step for the client to reach appropriate rehabilitation goals.

Many models for the vocational planning process have been developed in the last 10 years. Roessler and Rubin (1982) discussed some different approaches. For example, Dolliver and Nelson (1975) formulated a three-part counseling approach: occupational information, values clarification, and decision making. To reach meaningful vocational alternatives, the client integrates information regarding work with personal values. Then, a feasible goal is selected, and a sequential plan of action is developed.

Carkhuff (1971) built vocational planning around the terms *exploration, understanding,* and *action.* The client explores the relationship of vocational objectives to his or her personal capabilities, interests, and situation and then attempts to understand the way these different factors influence vocational potential. This personalized understanding then helps the client to develop the steps of the rehabilitation plan (Roessler & Rubin, 1982). MacKay (1975) initiated a two-stage plan, of which the stages are model identification and integration. In identification, the importance of exploration of self and world is stressed. Hopefully, the client can then identify personal strengths and weaknesses affecting the vocational plan. During the integration phase, the "professional assists the client in understanding the personal relevance of the discoveries that have been made during the identification phase" (Roessler & Rubin, 1982, p. 122).

With all of these models, there seems to be a basic process, which was conceptualized by Roessler and Rubin (1982) as *analysis* and *action.* The analysis phase focuses on occupational information and client feelings. The action phase consists of the appraisal of client strengths and weaknesses, a statement of goals and problems, a survey of possible resources and services, and a sequence for expected completion of the program (Leung, 1974).

This chapter develops and explains a rehabilitation planning model that has been used in professional practice. As a background to this presentation, the components necessary for effective planning are discussed. This chapter's case study illustrates the steps in vocational planning.

WHAT IS NECESSARY FOR EFFECTIVE PLANNING?

During the interpretation of test or assessment results, the ideas and information that are generated (ideally by both the professional and the client) represent different directions or ways to reach satisfying rehabilitation goals. To perform adequate and meaningful planning necessitates both knowledge and skills on the part of the professional regarding client involvement; the job market, training, and requirements; and the acquisition of specific competencies.

Involvement of the Client

One of the underlying principles in this book is that input or client participation should be solicited at the very beginning of the assessment process. Earlier chapters identify various ways to accomplish this involvement, including the careful explanation of varied, possible rehabilitation goals; the identification of client assets; and the opportunity to explore different options or alternatives for satisfaction in rehabilitation. All of these methods stimulate client participation in the assessment process. Such participation is an instrumental activity that promotes client decision making, responsibility, problem solving, and self-direction.

Client involvement is essential during the interpretation session of evaluation results; it can provoke further input into the planning phase of vocational evaluation. Moreover, if there has been client involvement during assessment, such areas as client needs and values also will be identified. An analysis of these areas is crucial for appropriate rehabilitation planning, and most of this information from clients with a disability has to be generated from client discussions rather than psychometric measures.

When clients participate in the vocational planning process, many potential problems relevant to reaching rehabilitation goals may be anticipated. Roessler and Rubin (1982) also identified other important results such as: (a) being aware of potential vocational objectives; (b) being able to evaluate these objectives for personal relevance, desirability, and practicality; (c) understanding what counseling, restoration, and training steps need to be taken to reach the intermediate objectives and vocational goal; and (d) assisting in the development of a concrete, step-by-step rehabilitation plan. In all stages of rehabilitation, the professional and client must work together (insofar as this is functionally possible for the client) in the development of rehabilitation plans. This involvement has been a longstanding objective of evaluation and was reinforced by the Rehabilitation Act Amendments of 1992 (Bongiorno, 1993). If this participation is not enthusiastically promoted, a wide gap may develop between client expectations and the professional's perception of realistic opportunities available to the client.

Knowledge of the Job Market, Training, and Requirements

Throughout the rehabilitation assessment process, the professional must consider viable alternatives for employment, training, and independent living. Evaluation is conducted within the context of goals (vocational or independent living). This focus implies that the professional knows occupational information, availability of jobs in the client's geographical area, and the varied opportunities for training. These issues are discussed in the chapter on test interpretation (Chapter 13).

Rehabilitation planning demands an extensive awareness of occupational resources, such as the *Dictionary of Occupational Titles* (DOT) (U.S. Department of Labor, 1991), the *Occupational Outlook Handbook* (U.S. Department of Labor, 1990), and assorted publications that identify job requirements and employment conditions and help the professional to place the results of assessment into a realistic perspective. This perspective enables the rehabilitation professional to generate alternatives or options relevant to training and eventual employment. Roessler (1982) believed that

> knowledge of work routines, requisites, and rewards has a direct effect on the individual's preferences, values, and self-concept regarding different types of work. (p. 172)

Acquisition of Specific Competencies

For effective vocational planning, the rehabilitation professional should possess certain skills. Roessler (1982) identified two of them:

1. *An understanding of the problems that impair client efforts to obtain work.* These problems can pertain to work experience, job availability, or the disability itself.
2. *A knowledge of the world of work.* To select a vocational objective, clients also need to understand job requirements and local employment conditions. To gain this understanding usually implies that the professional possesses this information and is able to communicate it effectively.

Added to these skills or competencies is the ability of the counselor to organize assessment information and formulate and implement a decision-making approach. In the next section of this chapter, a model suggests a structure for organizing evaluation data. Regarding decision making, many models that have been developed are applicable for the decision-making process in vocational planning (see Clarke, Gelatt, & Levine, 1965; Harrington, 1997; Herr & Cramer, 1979; Pierce, Cohen, Anthony, & Cohen, 1978). These approaches generally follow the format of (a) defining the problem, (b) generating alternatives, (c) gathering information, (d) processing information, (e) making plans and selecting goals, and (f) implementing and evaluating plans. Implied in these systems is a value system that permits decisions to be made among preferences and expectancies for action within a climate of uncertainty (Herr & Cramer, 1979). Of course, an effective decision-making approach also necessitates accurate and complete information about occupational resources, the results of the client's evaluation, and the client's needs and values.

A PLANNING MODEL

The planning model in Figure 16.1 provides a structure for organizing assessment information. It incorporates areas of exploration that are discussed in both Chapters 1 and 4. The planning process is conceptualized in stages, and each stage must be completed before moving to the next one.

 CASE STUDY: GARY

Gary, age 34, is an unemployed airplane mechanic who, 14 months before his first interview with the rehabilitation professional, incurred a serious injury while working. According to accident reports, the client was apparently doing some maintenance work on a 747 when a fellow employee accidentally hit the ladder he was using. Gary lost his balance and fell to the ground, breaking both ankles and severely injuring his back. There were also severe bruises and contusions, and Gary was hospitalized for 6 months, particularly to stabilize back problems caused by the accident. The recent doctor's report indicated that Gary is unable to stand for any prolonged period of time and cannot perform the physical demands of climbing, stooping, and bending that were required in his job. In the initial interview, the client explains that he has almost constant back pain, realizes that physical limitations will keep him from returning to his employment, and feels that he is learning to live with this pain. Gary states that he is coming to see you to explore employment alternatives. He has contacted his former employer and union officials, and they all have encouraged Gary to pursue rehabilitation opportunities.

The client is a high school graduate who maintained a B average in college preparatory subjects. He received particularly good grades in math and science-related subjects.

(text continues on page 295)

Step 1: Collecting and Organizing Evaluation Information

A. Sources of Assessment Data
1. The interview
2. Psychometric or standardized tests
3. Work samples
4. Situational assessment
5. Medical records, psychologists' reports, and so forth

Relevant Results
for Vocational
or Independent
Living Goals

B. Client Areas of Functioning
1. Physical characteristics
a. General appearance   _____
b. Health status   _____
c. Motor coordination   _____
d. Physical limitations   _____
e. Energy level   _____
2. Intellectual characteristics   _____
a. Educational experience   _____
b. Abilities and aptitudes   _____
c. Work experience and specific skills including   _____
acquired and developed work habits   _____
d. Disability-related knowledge (understanding   _____
assets and disability limitations in relation   _____
to work)   _____
e. Cognitive-related limitations (attention span,   _____
memory)   _____
3. Emotional characteristics   _____
a. Mood and temperament   _____
b. Identified needs   _____
c. Motivation   _____
d. Adjustment to disability   _____
e. Coping resources   _____
4. Interests related to employment   _____
5. Values (Friel & Carkhuff, 1974)   _____
a. Physical (activity, comfort, salary, cleanliness,   _____
money, location, temperature, work with hands)   _____
b. Intellectual (specialization, learning, planning,   _____
creativity, structure, preparation time, chance   _____
for advancement)   _____

Figure 16.1. Planning model for organizing assessment information.

c. Emotional–interpersonal (challenge, teamwork, _____
commitment, stability, job security, helping _____
people, independence, unpressured situation, _____
structure) _____
6. Environmental factors _____
a. Family situation and attitude toward _____
rehabilitation _____
b. Available financial resources _____
c. Employer concerns and interests _____
d. Incentives and disincentives _____
e. Characteristics of the recreational and com- _____
munity environment (i.e., attitudes toward _____
disability, accessibility and potential for _____
architectural modifications) _____
7. Special considerations _____
a. Medications as they would affect job performance _____
b. Needed aids (transportation, prosthetic devices) _____
c. Job modifications required _____

Step 2: Focusing the Evaluation Results

A. Client Interest(s)   Areas of Competence

_____   _____
_____   _____
_____   _____
_____   _____
_____   _____

Values   Limitations

_____   _____
_____   _____
_____   _____
_____   _____

B. Priorities of   Areas of Competence
    Occupational Interest(s)   Related to Interest(s)

_____   _____
_____   _____
_____   _____
_____   _____

Figure 16.1. (continued)

Prioritized Values
Related to Interest(s)

Limitations Related
to Interest(s)

_____   _____
_____   _____
_____   _____
_____   _____
_____   _____

C. Occupational Information Related to Interests

1. Available jobs and career opportunities

_____
_____
_____
_____

2. Occupational and entry-level requirements

_____
_____
_____
_____

3. Training needed and training opportunities

_____
_____
_____
_____

**Step 3: Selection of Rehabilitation, Occupational,
or Training Independent Living Goal**

A. Examine again values and competencies in relation to two identified interests. Consider environmental factors and client limitations in order to achieve rehabilitation goals.

B. Examine specifically occupational requirements and job availability in relation to each of the two prioritized interest areas and client competencies and limitations.

C. Select Goals: _____

Step 4: Formulation of Rehabilitation Plan

A. Major Goal: _____

Figure 16.1. *(continued)*

B. Subgoals
(steps needed to achieve
major goal)   1. _____

Date of implementation   _____

Date of completion   _____

Resource   _____

Monitor   _____

                                     2. _____

Date of implementation   _____

Date of completion   _____

Resource   _____

Monitor   _____

                                     3. _____

Date of implementation   _____

Date of completion   _____

Resource   _____

Monitor   _____

                                     4. _____

Date of implementation   _____

Date of completion   _____

Resource   _____

Monitor   _____

                                     5. _____

Date of implementation   _____

Date of completion   _____

Resource   _____

Monitor   _____

                                     6. _____

Date of implementation   _____

Date of completion   _____

Resource   _____

Monitor   _____

Figure 16.1. (*continued*)

Although accepted at a nearby state university, Gary decided to enlist in the Air Force because he wanted to marry his high school sweetheart and "for a young person, the service is a better place to be when you are married." He remained in the military for 9 years and achieved the rank of E-6, staff sergeant. His military specialty was airplane maintenance and mechanics. During the interview, Gary explained that his military record was excellent, but that he decided to leave because of relocation demands and the time he had to spend away from his family on the weekends. Upon discharge, he immediately obtained a job with a major airline company and worked with them for 7 years until the accident.

Gary has been married for 16 years and has three children—ages 14, 12, and 5. During the interview, he explains that his family life is extremely important to him and states: "My wife and I are very close." The family members regularly take camping trips together, are active members in a local church, and participate in many school functions. Gary further states that for the past 4 years, his wife has been working as an executive secretary because "we wanted more money for some extras in our life, and she wanted really to get out of the house." Gary also claims that his family is very supportive of rehabilitation efforts because "they want me to do something worthwhile with my life."

During this first interview, the client explains that he has had few hobbies, although he likes to read and use his video camera for taking pictures at athletic events. Apart from training associated with his job, he has not taken any formal, post–high-school courses. Gary also mentions that he is receiving worker's compensation payments, which are "quite adequate for us to live on, especially with my wife working." Yet, he explains that he is bored just sitting around the house, and "perhaps there is some training I can take that will put me back in the work force."

Having gathered this information from the interview, including knowledge about the client's emotional reaction to his disability and his values as they relate to work, the rehabilitation professional then proceeded with an assessment. The assessment results can be found in Figure 16.2.

CHAPTER 16 CONCLUSION

During rehabilitation planning, the professional uses many types of skills—communicative, diagnostic, occupational information, and perhaps placement. An important goal in the development of many plans, however, is not simply job placement, but career development (Vandergoot, Swirsky, & Rice, 1982) as well. During the planning session, the client should learn the many possible options that are available, considering his or her competencies and values. As assessment helps a client identify the strengths and assets that apply to the world of employment or independent living, so planning shows the client how these capabilities relate to different rehabilitation options. Rehabilitation planning is actually similar (although perhaps on a smaller scale) to career preparation, whereby plans are made and implemented to equip the client with specific,

(text continues on page 301)

Step 1: Collecting and Organizing Evaluation Information

A. Sources of Assessment Data
   1. The interview
   2. Psychometric or standardized tests
      a. *Quick-Test*
      b. *Shipley Institute of Living Scale*
      c. WRAT–3
      d. *Differential Aptitude Tests–Fifth Edition* (DAT)
      e. Kuder Preference–Form D
      f. *Strong Interest Inventory*
      g. PSI
      h. *Edwards Personnel Preference Survey* (EPPS)
      i. MMPI
   3. Medical records

	Relevant Results for Vocational Goals
B. Client Areas of Functioning	
1. Physical characteristics (interview discussion and medical report)	
a. General appearance	Well-groomed; dresses appropriately and neatly; maintains eye contact; appears assertive of manner
b. Health status	Apart from residuals of back injury, good
c. Motor coordination	Eye–hand coordination above average
d. Physical limitations	Reaching, bending, stooping, climbing
e. Energy level	Client is concerned about pain; has to sit often during the day, but claims he has much energy.
2. Intellectual characteristics	
a. Educational experience	High school graduate, B average; specialized training in airplane mechanics
b. Abilities and aptitudes (WRAT–3, *Quick-Test*, *Shipley Institute of Living Scale*, DAT)	Grade 12 functioning in reading and math; 90th percentile in space relations and mechanical ability; IQ functioning in the bright-to-normal range

Figure 16.2. Rehabilitation planning for Gary.

c. Work experience and specific skills, including acquired and developed work habits (interview discussion)	15 years airplane mechanic; mechanical comprehension high; technical knowledge above average; understands and has followed basic work habits; good work record
d. Disability-related knowledge (interview discussion)	Understands limitations; takes medication regularly; not involved in any activities that would aggravate back condition; regularly attends physical therapy sessions
e. Cognitive-related limitations	Pain occasionally affects client's attention while reading and watching TV; belief that pain will get better; memory functioning seems good for immediate, recent, and remote recall

3. Emotional characteristics

a. Mood and temperament (interview discussion)	Friendly, outgoing, but claims frustration tolerance has been lowered since the accident; describes himself as someone who is usually patient with others; claims he is also ambitious and was interested in reaching seniority or administrative positions within the union; also feels he likes structure and methodical work
b. Identified needs (interview discussion and EPPS)	Job and financial security, recognition; claims does not need that much variety in work; needs good working conditions and advancement opportunities EPPS: Achievement—80th percentile, Affiliation—85th percentile, Change—20th percentile
c. Motivation (interview discussion)	Claims he is ready to explore rehabilitation, training, or employment-related goals
d. Adjustment to disability (interview discussion, MMPI, PSI)	Believes that he is very angry because someone was responsible for the accident, but tries to suppress the anger; otherwise, feels that he is coping, but appears to have a "sense of isolation" and privately

Figure 16.2. (*continued*)

	grieves over not being able to return to his former job; very concerned about allowing his emotions to be visible to others; profile of MMPI falls within normal limits, although a slight elevation in attention to bodily concerns
e. Coping resources	Family; confidence in mechanical ability; no undue financial worries; has social and church outlets; supportive friends
4. Interests related to employment	Kuder: Scientific—90th percentile, Mechanical—95th percentile, Social Service—65th percentile, Computational—55th percentile, Outdoor—60th percentile. Strong-Campbell: General occupational themes: Investigative theme—high score, S theme—moderately high. Basic interest scales: Mechanical activities—very high, Medical service—high, Nature—moderately high. Occupational scales: Engineer—high, Medical tech—high, Computer programmer—moderately high.
5. Values (interview discussion) a. Physical	Activity, cleanliness, money, location, work with hands
b. Emotional–interpersonal	Stability; challenge; commitment; job security
6. Environmental factors	Family supportive, eager for client to return to work; no serious problems; employer has positive attitude about returning to work; family willing to make, if needed, the house more accessible
7. Special considerations	Limited standing on job; takes medication for back pain; can drive car; no job modifications required

Figure 16.2. (continued)

Step 2: Focusing the Evaluation Results

A. Client Interest(s)   Areas of Competence

Mechanical   Mechanical ability
Scientific   Developed work habits
Outdoor   General level of knowledge
Computational   Numerical abilities high, appears well
                                     organized in work habits

Values   Limitations

Structure   Back condition
Location   Limited standing
Work with hands   Away from school for many years
Challenge   Pain currently may inhibit performance of
Stability   cognitive functions
Job stability

(The information in Step 2 was developed from interpreting the assessment results to the client and obtaining feedback. Client was asked to rank values and interests, and areas of competence were identified from test results.)

B.   Priorities of   Areas of Competence
        Occupational Interest(s)   Related to Interest(s)

1. Medical Technician   Computational ability
2. Computer Programmer   Mechanical conceptual ability
3. Small Engine Repair Mechanic   Developed work habits

        Prioritized Values   Limitations Related
     Related to Interest(s)   to Interest(s)

1. Structure   Back
2. Job security   No specific training in fields
3. Work with hands

C. Occupational Information Related to Interests
    1. Available jobs and career opportunities
        a. Jobs appear to be available in health field technology
        b. Many advertised openings for computer programmers
        c. Client lives near hospital centers and variety of medical facilities
    2. Occupational and entry-level requirements
        a. Medical technician: usually 4-year college degree program
        b. Computer Programmer: 2- or 4-year college program
        c. Small Engine Repairman: Vocational training

Figure 16.2. *(continued)*

**Step 3: Selection of Rehabilitation, Occupational,
or Training Independent Living Goal**

A. Attention was focused on values and competencies in relation to occupational areas of medical technology, computer programming, and small engine repair. Occupational requirements and job availability were also discussed. The client believed that although computer programming would be a satisfying field for him, many health care facilities were located close to his home, and medical technology offered job security, challenging work, advancement, responsibility, and working with his hands. He also stated that he liked the "clean environment" that medical technology offers. Consequently, decisions were made in the perspective of client values and job availability. Also, client believed that he could accomplish a 4-year college program but would have to begin training gradually.

B. Selected Occupational Goal: Medical technologist

Step 4: Formulation of Rehabilitation Plan

A. Major Goal: To obtain employment as a medical technologist

B. Subgoals	1. To visit local 2-year community college and inquire about courses in field related to medical technology
Date of implementation	Immediately
Date of completion	2 weeks
Resource	College
Monitor	Rehabilitation professional
	2. To take two adult education courses offered by community college in liberal arts subjects to develop study skills
Date of implementation	Immediately
Date of completion	6 months
Resource	Continuing education program
Monitor	Rehabilitation professional
	3. To enroll in community college program that is transferable to a BS degree program in medical technology
Date of implementation	6 months
Date of completion	2 years from date of entry

Figure 16.2. *(continued)*

Resource	College
Monitor	Rehabilitation professional
	4. To make inquiries in local area about job openings in small engine repair for temporary, part-time work
Date of implementation	Immediately
Date of completion	2 years
Resource	Local area—employment offices and small shops
Monitor	Rehabilitation professional
	5. To maintain physical therapy appointments and inquire about self-help groups to deal with anger about disability
Date of implementation	Immediately
Date of completion	6 months to 1 year
Resource	Local hospital
Monitor	Rehabilitation professional
	6. Upon successful completion of a 2-year college program, to enroll in 4-year BS degree program in medical technology
Date of implementation	Completion of 2-year program
Date of completion	2 to 3 years after entry
Resource	College
Monitor	Rehabilitation professional

Figure 16.2. (*continued*)

marketable job skills (Vandergoot, 1982a). Planning should also consider the difficulties that might arise after placement in a job. The client may still have many concerns about the integration of work with other life activities.

The importance of occupational information cannot be underemphasized in rehabilitation planning. The professional should have access to reliable information that identifies what job areas are growing or decreasing. Local labor market information must be used sensitively (Vandergoot et al., 1982). When the professional knows about employment and training resources as well as occupational requirements, the planning session is more valuable for the client.

Appendix A:
An Interview Guide
for Difficult Clients

INTERESTS

Everyone likes to do certain types of activities more than others. This is true of hobbies, sports, school subjects, and jobs. Knowing your interests will help you choose a career and succeed in it.

In almost everything people do, there are different activities—some that we like and others that we don't like. Usually, we are more successful when we enjoy things than when we don't.

Most workers prefer activities in 1 or more of 10 interest areas. After you have read over and understand all of the activities, select the one that you think you would like best on a job. Then circle the number next to the activity you have chosen.

1. Activities dealing with things and objects

2. Activities involving business contact with people

3. Activities of a routine, definite, organized nature

4. Activities that involve direct personal contact, to help people or deal with them for other purposes

5. Activities that bring recognition or appreciation by others

6. Activities concerned with people and the communication of ideas

7. Activities of a scientific and technical nature

8. Activities of an unusual, indefinite nature that require creative imagination

9. Activities that are nonsocial and involve the use of machines, processes, or methods

10. Activities that bring personal satisfaction from working on or producing things

© 2000 by PRO-ED, Inc.

GENERAL EDUCATION LEVEL

The things taught in school help us to do better in nearly every part of our lives. Imagine trying to order food in a restaurant if you couldn't read, trying to make change if you couldn't count, or figuring out how a new toy goes together if you couldn't reason the steps!

Most every job requires that you have some of the same general skills that schools teach. Some jobs require many of these skills, whereas others require fewer of them. We will show you a chart and ask you to rate yourself in each of three areas.

Enter your self-rating below:

Reasoning: I can _____

Mathematics: I can _____

Language: I can _____

Comments:

In addition to using general skills learned in school, most people learn specific skills to handle their jobs. They may go to college or trade school, learn on the job, or learn through an apprentice program—which is a combination of school and work. However they learn, they get skills that take time.

How long do you think you are willing and able to train for a job after you leave high school? Circle the number that best answers this question.

1. Short demonstration only
2. Anything beyond short demonstration up to and including 30 days
3. Over 30 days up to and including 3 months
4. Over 3 months up to and including 6 months
5. Over 6 months up to and including 1 year
6. Over 1 year up to and including 2 years
7. Over 2 years up to and including 4 years
8. Over 4 years up to and including 10 years
9. Over 10 years

Comments:

© 2000 by PRO-ED, Inc.

WORK SITUATIONS

Job satisfaction and success require a great many things. One of these is your willingness and ability to adjust to situations on the job. These situations are very different on some jobs than others. Knowing the types of situations that you may find in jobs can help you make the best possible choice.

Here are 12 very common situations found in jobs. How many could you adjust to without hating them? Make sure you understand what they are and then circle the number of each situation you think you could handle.

1. Performing a variety of duties that may often change

2. Repeating activities or tasks of short duration according to a required procedure or sequence

3. Doing things only under specific instructions, allowing little or no room for independent action or judgment in working out job problems

4. Directing, controlling, and planning an entire activity or activities of others

5. Dealing with people in actual job duties beyond giving and receiving instructions

6. Working alone and away from other workers, although the work may be related to work other people are doing

7. Influencing people's opinions, attitudes, or judgments about ideas or things

8. Working well under pressure when faced with critical or unexpected situations or when taking necessary risks

9. Rating information by using personal judgment

10. Rating information using standards that can be measured or checked

11. Interpreting feelings, ideas, or facts from a personal point of view

12. Working within precise limits or standards of accuracy

Comments:

PHYSICAL DEMANDS

Some school and hobby activities make you use your body in different ways. For example, you can run more in basketball, lift more in weight lifting, and crouch more in football. Jobs differ in how much they demand you to use your body, too.

© 2000 by PRO-ED, Inc.

Here are six physical demands that jobs have. After you understand what is required in each, think about your abilities and decide which ones you can do.

1. Lifting. How much? _____ lbs. at most/ _____ lbs. often

2. Climbing and/or balancing: _____

3. Stooping, kneeling, crouching, and/or crawling: _____

4. Reaching, handling, fingering, and/or feeling: _____

5. Talking and/or hearing: _____

6. Seeing: _____

Comments:

WORKING CONDITIONS

Where you do an activity also is important. For example, inside sports are not affected by weather and temperature. Other sports are very much affected by weather—such as mountain climbing.

Jobs are like that, too. If you don't like being indoors, you probably wouldn't like to be a bookkeeper. If you can't stand hot, humid conditions, you probably wouldn't like to be a ship's mechanic.

What conditions would you want, could you stand, in a job? Here are seven conditions frequently found in jobs. Which ones would suit you?

1. Inside, outside, or both
2. Extremes of cold plus temperature changes
3. Extremes of heat plus temperature changes
4. Wetness and humidity
5. Noise and vibration
6. Hazards
7. Fumes, odors, toxic conditions, dust, and poor ventilation

Comments:

© 2000 by PRO-ED, Inc.

APTITUDES

Aptitude is a word you have probably heard before. Usually, it goes with the word *test*. However, aptitude really means the ability to learn something. There are many kinds of aptitude tests because there are many kinds of things to learn.

People who study school subjects and students have found that the ability to learn certain things is important for school. These are the items that they put in their aptitude tests. People who study jobs have found that there are 11 aptitudes that are important for work. Not all aptitudes are needed in any job, and some people succeed in jobs even though they find it difficult to learn some of the things in the job. Nevertheless, the better your aptitude in those areas, the more likely you are to be happy and successful in that job.

Two good ways to find out which areas you have the most aptitude in are by taking job aptitude tests and by looking at what you have already done. Let's start by looking at what you already know about yourself. Here are the 11 aptitude areas. By discussion and looking at yourself, estimate how much of each aptitude you have.

	Little	Below average	Average	Above average	A lot
1. G—General learning ability	____	____	____	____	____
2. V—Verbal	____	____	____	____	____
3. N—Numerical	____	____	____	____	____
4. S—Spatial	____	____	____	____	____
5. P—Form perception	____	____	____	____	____
6. Q—Clerical perception	____	____	____	____	____
7. K—Motor coordination	____	____	____	____	____
8. F—Finger dexterity	____	____	____	____	____
9. M—Manual dexterity	____	____	____	____	____
10. E—Eye/hand/foot coordination	____	____	____	____	____
11. C—Color discrimination	____	____	____	____	____

Comments:

© 2000 by PRO-ED, Inc.

TAKING STOCK OF THE
OPINION OF OTHERS

No one lives in isolation from others. You constantly influence and are influenced by others. Certain persons' opinions and expectations are more important to you than those of others. Sometimes others' opinions are clearly conveyed to you. Often, these opinions may be expressed very indirectly, but they may still be influential.

1. Do you welcome other people's opinions with regard to your vocational planning?

2. Whose opinions do you see as valuable to you in your vocational planning?

3. What two or three persons' opinions are most important to you with regard to your vocational planning (such as mother, father, husband or wife, teacher, friend, etc.)?

   a. _____

   b. _____

   c. _____

4. Do you feel bound to following their advice?

5. What kind of an occupation do you feel these people you have named expect of you? Be careful here. Don't say anything vague such as, "Whatever is best for me." Go beyond this, and consider what kind of job you think they regard as best for you.

6. What alternative kind of occupation might they like to see you enter?

7. In what ways are their expectations similar to or different from your expectations?

8. How would they react if you did something else—that is, did not enter this kind of occupation? Again, be thoughtful in your answer.

9. How would you feel about their reactions, especially if they disagreed with your choice?

10. How would you deal with these feelings?

11. What occupation(s) do you want for yourself?

    a. _____

    b. _____

    c. _____

© 2000 by PRO-ED, Inc.

LEISURE TIME ACTIVITIES

The following questions concern leisure time activities. Please answer them as honestly and completely as possible so you can get a clear picture of what you are like.

1. Describe any hobbies you now have.
   What do you like about them?

2. Describe any hobbies you had when growing up.
   What did you like about them?

3. Describe any hobbies you wish you had tried.
   What might you like about them?
   Why haven't you tried them?

4. How many hours per day do you watch TV?

5. What is your favorite spectator sport?

6. What is your favorite participant sport?

7. Do you spend time at your local pub?

8. To which social, civic, or political organizations do you belong?

9. Do you like to read? What? _____

10. How often do you go to the movies?

11. Do you like to work with your hands? How? _____

12. Do you own any tools or equipment? What? _____

13. Have you built anything for your home? What? _____

14. Have you made any of the decorations in your home? What? _____

15. Do you have the patience to stick with something slow and time-consuming?

16. Are the results of an activity important to you?

17. How do you react when you are unable to finish a task?

18. Have you had experience with animals, or do you have any pets?

19. What is the best way to relax?

20. What have you done in your leisure time that you most enjoy telling others about?

21. What have you learned about yourself from your leisure time activities that might help you in your future vocational planning?

22. What have you learned from these questions?

© 2000 by PRO-ED, Inc.

23. Do you think these questions are relevant to your future vocational planning? Why? _____

24. What else would you like to tell me about your leisure time?

25. Do your leisure time interests have job possibilities?   Yes ☐   No ☐

26. If so, list them:

a. _____

b. _____

c. _____

This guide primarily was developed by Charles Robinson, MS, in 1973. It has been used successfully with many low-verbal persons with a disability. In fact, information can often be solicited by having the client point to the particular response on the guide.

© 2000 by PRO-ED, Inc.

Appendix B: Independent Living Assessment Instrument

I. Independent Living Assessment (Verbal)

Goal: *To discriminate ability for safe independent living within an apartment setting*

A. Hygiene, personal cleanliness, and clothing

1. How did you dress today?

2. Did the weather outside influence your choice of clothes?

3. Do you like to take a bath or a shower?

4. Can you describe your routine for bathing or showering and dressing to me?

5. How do you shop for clothes? Do you like to go by yourself or with a friend?

6. When is it important to wash your hands?

7. How often do you brush your teeth?

8. How often do you wash your hair?

9. How do you handle hygiene when you have your period?

B. Apartment cleanliness and care

1. Do you do all of your own housekeeping? If you need help with it, who do you ask and how?

2. What would you do if your toilet backed up onto the bathroom floor?

3. Where is the garbage kept?

4. What would you do if you saw bugs in your apartment?

5. Who would you call if:

   a. The sink was clogged?

   b. Something was broken?

   c. The heat was not working?

© 2000 by PRO-ED, Inc.

    6. Do you have a special day to do your laundry? Do you do it with assistance or independently?

C. Kitchen skills

    1. What are your favorite meals to cook?

    2. Tell me about the word *nutrition*.

    3. Do you shop for food on your own or with another person?

    4. Can you show me where you keep:

        a. TV dinners?

        b. Hamburger, other meats?

        c. Cheese?

        d. Unopened cans of fruit?

        e. Open cans of food?

        f. Milk?

        g. Cereal?

    5. What happens to food when the refrigerator breaks?

    6. How can you tell if food is spoiled?

    7. Can you show me how you:

        a. Wash dishes?

        b. Broil a steak?

        c. Bake a chicken?

        d. Boil eggs; water?

        e. Clean floor?

        f. Store paper products?

        g. Clean refrigerator?

D. Body care, first aid, emergencies, and safety

    1. What happens when you are sick?

    2. What would you do if you cut your finger and it was bleeding?

    3. When might you need to call the emergency number?

    4. When do you stay home from work because you are not feeling well?

© 2000 by PRO-ED, Inc.

     5. Do you have a doctor whom you see when you are not feeling well? When have you needed to call him or her?

     6. If someone has a seizure, what could you do?

     7. What would you do if you smelled smoke or suspected a fire?

     8. If there were a fire in your building, what would you do?

     9. Are there precautions you can take to avoid having a fire occur in your apartment?

    10. When someone knocks at your door, do you open it right away?

    11. If someone were breaking into your apartment, what would you do?

    12. When someone buzzes your apartment, do you check to see who it is before allowing them to enter the building?

  E. Public Transportation, Community Resources, and Leisure Time

     1. How often do you take the metro bus?

     2. How did you learn the routes that you use?

     3. How do you find out about new activities

     4. Do you travel alone at times? Are there times when you prefer going with a friend?

     5. How do you get to the grocery store? Is there a convenience store nearby for quick trips?

     6. How do you spend evenings home alone when nothing special is going on?

II. Emotional and Behavioral Assessment (Verbal)

Goal: *To assess social coping skills and appropriate ways of handling independent living issues*

  A. Do you have any special friends to whom you feel very close and with whom you spend a lot of time?

  B. How do you handle problems between you and your close friends?

  C. How do you let people know you like them?

  D. How do you handle disagreements between you and your roommate (if applicable)?

  E. Tell me some wrong ways to handle anger.

  F. Do you feel angry at times? How do you handle it?

  G. Have you ever been interested in the same man (woman) as a friend of yours? What did you do?

© 2000 by PRO-ED, Inc.

H. Have you ever had a problem at work because you lost your temper? How did it work out?

I. What is the difference between borrowing and stealing?

III. Financial Responsibility

A. Do you have bills to pay?

B. How do you remember to pay bills?

C. What happens when you forget to pay a bill?

D. Do you have a savings account?

E. Do you have a checking account?

F. What do you do with your check when you get it?

G. Can you show me how you budget your money?

H. Role-play a financial transaction:

1. paying rent

2. going to store

© 2000 by PRO-ED, Inc.

Appendix C:
Employment Readiness Scale

DIRECTIONS

This is a survey used to learn about the many feelings people have toward working. Please fill in the blanks below. Then read the statements on the following pages and circle the number in the column that explains the way you feel about the statement.

Highest grade of education you have completed _____ Age _____

	This is true for me all the time	This is usually true for me	This is usually not true for me	This is not true for me at all
1. When working, I move at a steady pace.	4	3	2	1
2. If I watch someone do something that I know is wrong, I will forget it because it does not affect me.	4	3	2	1
3. I believe that safety is important.	4	3	2	1
4. I like to work around machinery.	4	3	2	1
5. People can depend on me.	4	3	2	1
6. I feel people are against me.	4	3	2	1
7. I feel I could succeed at a job.	4	3	2	1
8. I like to look neat at work and away from work.	4	3	2	1
9. I am willing to study when I am not working in order to learn better how to do my job.	4	3	2	1

Source: Alfano, 1973

	This is true for me all the time	This is usually true for me	This is usually not true for me	This is not true for me at all
10. I am willing to get dirty when I work.	4	3	2	1
11. Once I am given something to do, I want to complete it.	4	3	2	1
12. I respect people in authority.	4	3	2	1
13. I think children should work for their spending money.	4	3	2	1
14. I can get along with people.	4	3	2	1
15. I enjoy taking on more responsibility.	4	3	2	1
16. I dislike most other people.	4	3	2	1
17. I would like to be good at what I do.	4	3	2	1
18. I would like to improve myself.	4	3	2	1
19. I am willing to work a 40-hour week.	4	3	2	1
20. My work is important to my employer.	4	3	2	1
21. I feel like I could develop a feeling of belonging to a company.	4	3	2	1
22. I believe in being on time for work.	4	3	2	1
23. I am willing to get up early in the morning to come to work.	4	3	2	1
24. I want to support myself.	4	3	2	1
25. I am willing to work past my regular hours for more money.	4	3	2	1
26. The kind of job I want is one that pays well for very little work.	4	3	2	1
27. I would hate to live on welfare.	4	3	2	1
28. I am willing to do any work given to me.	4	3	2	1
29. I am not careful in most things that I do.	4	3	2	1

	This is true for me all the time	This is usually true for me	This is usually not true for me	This is not true for me at all
30. Receiving charity from other people does not bother me.	4	3	2	1
31. I am willing to work at night.	4	3	2	1
32. I believe it is important to earn a living.	4	3	2	1
33. I do not worry if I am out of a job.	4	3	2	1
34. I believe money is important.	4	3	2	1
35. I would rather beg than work for money.	4	3	2	1
36. I want to work to keep myself out of debt.	4	3	2	1
37. I do not believe in saving money.	4	3	2	1
38. I always do just what I want to do.	4	3	2	1
39. I never worry about getting food or clothing.	4	3	2	1
40. Work should be avoided if possible.	4	3	2	1
41. The government owes me a living.	4	3	2	1
42. I would rather follow the crowd than start anything by myself.	4	3	2	1
43. If I am working at a job and finish early, I will look for something more to do.	4	3	2	1

References

Acton, N. (1982). The world's response to disability: Evolution of a philosophy. *Arch. Phys. Med. Rehab., 63*, 115–149.

Aero, R., & Weiner, E. (1981). *The mind test*. New York: Morrow.

Aiken, L. R. (1997). *Psychological testing and assessment* (9th ed.) Needham Heights, MA: Allyn & Bacon

American College Testing Program. (1989). *The DISCOVER program*. Hunt Valley, MD: Discover Center.

American College Testing Program. (1993). *Realistic Assessment of Vocational Experiences*. Hunt Valley, MD: Author.

American Counseling Association. (1994). *Code of ethics*. Alexandria, VA: Author.

Americans with Disabilities Act of 1990, 42 U.S.C. § 12101 *et seq.*

Ammons, R. B., & Ammons, C. H. (1950). *Full-Range Picture Vocabulary Test*. Missoula, MT: Psychological Test Specialists.

Ammons, R. B., & Ammons, C. H. (1962). *The Quick-Test*. Missoula, MT: Psychological Tests Specialists.

Anastasi, A. (Ed.). (1982). *Psychological testing*. New York: Macmillan.

Anastasi, A. (1988). *Psychological testing* (6th ed.). New York: Macmillan.

Anastasi, A. (1992). What counselors should know about the use and interpretation of psychological tests. *Journal of Counseling and Development, 70*, 610–615.

Andrew. D. M., Patterson, D. G., & Longstaff, H. P. (1961). *Minnesota Clerical Test*. New York: Psychological Corp.

Anthony, W. A. (1979). *The principles of psychiatric rehabilitation*. Amherst, MA: Human Resource Development Press.

Anthony, W. A. (1980). A rehabilitation model for rehabilitating the psychiatrically disabled. *Rehabilitation Counseling Bulletin, 24*, 6–14.

Anthony, W. A., Howell, J., & Danley, K. S. (1984). Vocational rehabilitation of the psychiatrically disabled. In M. Mirabi (Ed.), *The chronically mentally ill: Research and services* (pp. 215–237). New York: Spectrum Publications.

Atkins, B., Lynch, R., & Pullo, R. (1982). A definition of psychosocial aspects of disability: A synthesis of the literature. *Vocational Evaluation and Work Adjustment Bulletin, 15*, 55–61.

Baxter, R., Cohen, S., & Ylvisaker, M. (1985). Comprehensive cognitive assessment. In M. Ylvisaker (Ed.), *Head injury rehabilitation: Children and adolescents* (pp. 247–274). Austin, TX: PRO-ED.

Becker, R. (1988). *Reading Free Vocational Interest Inventory–Revised*. San Antonio, TX: Psychological Corp.

Beley, W., & Felker, S. (1981). Comprehensive vocational evaluation for clients with psychiatric impairments. *Rehabilitation Literature, 42*, 194–201.

Bennett, G. K. (1968). *Bennett Mechanical Comprehension Test*. New York: Psychological Corp.

Bennett, G. K. (1981). *Hand–Tool Dexterity Test*. San Antonio, TX: Psychological Corp.

Bennett, G. K., Seashore, H. G., & Wesman, A. G. (1990). *Differential Aptitude Tests–Fifth Edition*. New York: Psychological Corp.

Biggs, D., & Keller, K. (1982). A cognitive approach to using tests in counseling. *The Personnel and Guidance Journal, 60*, 528–532.

Bitter, J. A. (1968). Toward a concept of job readiness. *Rehabilitation Literature, 28*, 201–203.

Boland, J. M., & Alonso, G. (1982). A comparison: Independent living rehabilitation and vocational rehabilitation. *Journal of Rehabilitation, 48*, 50–59.

Bolles, R. (1980). *What color is your parachute?* Berkeley, CA: Ten Speed Press.

Bolles, R. (1989). *How to create a picture of your ideal job or next career.* Berkeley, CA: Ten Speed Press.

Bolton, B. (1979). *Rehabilitation counseling research.* Baltimore: University Park Press.

Bolton, B. (Ed.). (1982). *Vocational adjustment of disabled persons.* Austin, TX: PRO-ED.

Bolton, B. (1994). Review of USES General Aptitude Test Battery (GATB) USES Interest Inventory (USES-II). In J. T. Kapes, M. M. Mastie, & E. A. Whitfield (Eds.), *A counselor's guide to career assessment instruments* (pp. 115–123). Alexandria, VA: National Career Development Association.

Bongiorno, P. (1993). Summary of the Rehabilitation Act Amendments of 1992. *Journal of Job Placement, 9,* 26–31.

Bordin, E. D. (1943). A theory of vocational interests as dynamic phenomena. *Educational and Psychological Measurement, 3,* 49–65.

Bray, G. (1980). Team strategies for family involvement in rehabilitation. *Journal of Rehabilitation, 46,* 20–23.

Brolin, D. (1973). Vocational assessment: What can be gained from it. In D. Brolin (Ed.), *Vocational assessment systems.* Des Moines: Iowa Department of Public Instruction.

Brown, D. T. (1991, Winter). Computerized techniques in career assessment. *Career Planning and Adult Development Journal, 6,* 27–34.

Bruyere, S., & O'Keefe, J. (1994). Implications of the Americans with Disabilities Act for psychology. New York: Springer Publishing Co.

Bureau of Labor Statistics. (1998). *Occupational outlook quarterly.* Washington, DC: U.S. Department of Labor.

Burkhead, E. J., & Sampson, J. P. (1985). Computer-assisted assessment in support of the rehabilitation process. *Rehabilitation Counseling Bulletin, 28,* 262–274.

Carkhuff, R. R. (1969). *Helping and human relations.* New York: Holt, Rinehart & Winston.

Carkhuff, R. (1971). *The development of human resources.* New York: Holt, Rinehart & Winston.

Carkhuff, R. R., & Anthony, W. A. (1979). *The skills of helping.* Amherst, MA: Human Resource Development Press.

Cattell, R. B. (1986). *Sixteen Personality Factor Questionnaire.* New York: Psychological Corp.

Chan, F., & Questad, K. (1981, Winter). Microcomputers in vocational evaluation: An application for staff training. *Vocational Evaluation and Work Adjustment Bulletin, 14,* 153–158.

Choppa, A. J., & Shafer, K. (1992). Introduction to personal injury and expert witness work. In J. M. Siefker (Ed.), *Vocational evaluation in private sector rehabilitation* (pp. 135–168). Menomonie: University of Wisconsin–Stout.

Civil Rights Act of 1991 (PL 102-166). Washington, DC: U.S. Government Printing Office.

Clarke, R., Gelatt, H., & Levine, L. (1965). A decision-making paradigm for local guidance research. *The Personnel and Guidance Journal, 44,* 40–51.

Cohen B. F., & Anthony, W. A. (1984). Functional assessment in psychiatric rehabilitation. In A. Halpern & M. Fuhrer (Eds.), *Functional assessment in rehabilitation* (pp. 79–100). Baltimore: Brookes.

Cohen, R. J. (1988). *Situational assessment.* Unpublished manuscript, University of Maryland at College Park.

Cohen, R., Swerdlik, M., & Phillips, S. (1996). *Psychological testing and assessment,* (3rd ed.). Mountain View, CA: Mayfield.

Cohen, S. (1982). Supporting families through respite care. *Rehabilitation Literature, 43,* 7–11.

Cottone, R., & Tarvydas, V. (1998). *Ethical and professional issues in counseling.* Columbus, OH: Merrill.

Crewe, N. M., & Athelstan, G. T. (1978). Functional assessment inventory. In B. Bolton & D. W. Cook (Eds.), *Rehabilitation client assessment* (pp. 389–399). Baltimore: University Park Press,

Crowe, S. (1976). The role of evaluation in the rehabilitative process. In R. Hardy & J. Cull (Eds.), *Vocational evaluation for rehabilitative services* (pp. 29–39). Springfield, IL: Thomas.

Cummings, W. H. (1995). Age group differences and estimated frequencies of the Myers-Briggs Type Indicator preferences. *Measurement and Evaluation in Counseling and Development, 2,* 69–77.

Cutts, C. (1977). Test review—The self-directed search. *Measurement and Evaluation in Guidance, 10,* 117–120.

Dawis, R. V., & Lofquist, L. H. (1984). *A psychological theory of work adjustment: An individual-differences model and its applications.* Minneapolis: University of Minnesota.

DeNour, A. D., & Czaczkes, J. W. (1975). Personality factors influencing vocational rehabilitation. *Archives of General Psychiatry, 32,* 573–577.

Doherty, W., & Baird, M. (1983). *Family therapy and family medicine.* New York: Guilford.

Dolliver, R., & Nelson, R. (1975). Assumptions regarding vocational counseling. *Vocational Guidance Quarterly, 24,* 12–19.

Doppelt, J., & Bennett, G. (1967). Testing job applicants from disadvantaged groups. *Test Service Bulletin, 57,* 1–8.

Dowd, L. R. (1993). *Glossary of terminology for vocational assessment, evaluation, and work adjustment.* Menomonie: University of Wisconsin–Stout.

Dunn, L. M., & Dunn, L. (1997). *Peabody Picture Vocabulary Test–Third Edition.* Circle Pines, MN: American Guidance Service.

Eaton, M. (1979, April/May/June). Obstacles to the vocational rehabilitation of individuals receiving worker's compensation. *Journal of Rehabilitation, 45,* 59–63.

Educational Testing Service. (1980). *System of interactive guidance and information program.* Princeton, NJ: Author.

Edwards, A. L. (1959). *Edwards Personnel Preference Schedule.* San Antonio, TX: Psychological Corp.

Edwards, A. L. (1989). Computers and the rehabilitation field. *American Rehabilitation, 15,* 23–24.

Enright, M., Conyers, L., & Szymanski, E. (1996). Career and career-related educational concerns of college students with disabilities. *Journal of Counseling and Development, 75,* 103–114.

Farley, R. C., & Bolton, B. (1994). *Developing an employability assessment and planning program.* Fayetteville: Arkansas Research and Training Center in Vocational Rehabilitation.

Farley, R. C., Little, N. D., Bolton, B., & Chunn, J. (1993). *Employability assessment and planning in rehabilitation and educational settings.* Fayetteville: Arkansas Research and Training Center in Vocational Rehabilitation.

Farley, R. C., & Rubin, S. E. (1982). The intake interview. In R. T. Roessler & S. E. Rubin, *Case management and rehabilitation counseling* (pp. 33–50). Austin, TX: PRO-ED.

Fayne, L. J. (1989). Vocational evaluation of traumatically head injured individuals: Critical factors for consideration. *Vocational Evaluation and Assessment Bulletin, 3,* 1–2.

Field, T. (1979). The psychological assessment of vocational functioning. *Journal of Applied Rehabilitation Counseling, 10,* 124–129.

Field, T., & Sink, J. (1980). *The employer's manual.* Athens, GA: Udare Service Bureau.

Fisher, G. L., & Harrison, T. C. (1997). *Substance abuse.* Needham Heights, MA: Allyn & Bacon.

Fitts, W. H. (1988). *Tennessee Self-Concept Scale.* Nashville: Counselor Recordings and Tests.

Forrest, J. W. (1963, March 29). *Evaluating job readiness.* Paper presented at the Bi-Regional Institute on Placement, Stillwater, OK.

Foss, G., Bullis, M. D., & Vilhaver, D. A. (1984). Assessment and training of job-related social competence for mentally retarded adolescents and adults. In A. Halpern & M. Fuhrer (Eds.), *Functional assessment in rehabilitation* (pp. 145–158). Baltimore: Brookes.

Foss, G., Cheney, D., & Bullis, M. (1983). *Test of interpersonal competence for employment.* Eugene: University of Oregon, Rehabilitation Research and Training Center in Mental Retardation.

Fouad, N. (1993). Cross-cultural vocational assessment. *The Career Development Quarterly, 42,* 4–13.

Fredrickson, R. (1982). *Career information.* Englewood Cliffs, NJ: Prentice-Hall.

Frey, N. D. (1984). Functional assessment in the 80's: A conceptual enigma, a technical challenge. In A. Halpern & M. Fuhrer (Eds.), *Functional assessment in rehabilitation* (pp. 11–44). Baltimore: Brookes.

Friel, T., & Carkhuff, R. (1974). *The art of developing a career.* Amherst, MA: Human Resource Development Press.

Gati, I. (1994). Computer-assisted career counseling: Dilemmas, problems, and possible solutions. *Journal of Counseling and Development, 73,* 51–56.

Geist, H. J. (1988). *Geist Picture Interest Inventory* (rev. ed.). Los Angeles: Western Psychological Services.

Ginzberg, E. (1972). Restatement of the theory of occupational choice. *Vocational Guidance Quarterly, 20,* 169–176.

Godley, S. (1978). Topical review. *Vocational Evaluation and Work Adjustment Bulletin, 11,* 51–57.

Golden, C. J., Purisch, A. D., & Hammeke, T. A. (1984). *Luria–Nebraska Neuropsychological Battery.* Los Angeles: Western Psychological Services.

Goldman, L. (1971). *Using tests in counseling* (2nd ed.). Santa Monica, CA: Goodyear.

Goldman, L. (1972). Tests and counseling: The marriage that failed. *Measurement and Evaluation in Guidance, 4,* 213–220.

Golter, G. D., & Golter, M. C. (1986). Rehabilitation and computerization. In E. G. Pan, S. S. Newman, T. E. Backer, & C. L. Vash (Eds.), *Annual review of rehabilitation* (Vol. 5, pp. 151–169). New York: Springer.

Gordon, L. V. (1981). *Gordon Occupational Checklist-III.* San Antonio, TX: Psychological Corp.

Gordon, R. P., Stump. K., & Glaser, B. A. (1996). Assessment of individuals with hearing impairments: Equity in testing procedures and accommodations. *Measurement and Evaluation in Counseling and Development, 29,* 111–118.

Gorski, T. T. (1990). The Cenaps model of relapse prevention: Basic principles and procedures. *Journal of Psychoactive Drugs, 22,* 125–133.

Gough, H. G. (1987). *California Psychological Inventory.* San Antonio, TX: Psychological Corp.

Griggs, S. A. (1985). Counseling for individual learning styles. *Journal of Counseling and Development, 64,* 202–205.

Growick, B. (1983). *Computers in vocational rehabilitation: Current trends and future applications.* Washington, DC: National Rehabilitation Information Center.

Growick, B., & Schmidt, P. (1988). Addressing the vocational transitional needs of adolescents and young adults with learning disabilities. Presentation at the Ohio Rehabilitation Association 1988 Fall Conference, Columbus.

Guidubaldi, J., Perry, H. D., & Walker, M. (1989). Assessment strategies for students with disabilities. *Journal of Counseling and Development, 68,* 160–165.

Hahn, H. (1985). Changing perceptions of disability and the future of rehabilitation. In L. G. Perlman & G. F. Austin (Eds.), *Social influences in rehabilitation planning: Blueprint for the 21st century* (pp. 53–66). Alexandria, VA: National Rehabilitation Association.

Halpern, A. S., & Fuhrer, M. J. (1984). *Functional assessment in rehabilitation.* Baltimore: Brookes.

Halstead, W. (1947). *Brain and intelligence.* Chicago: University of Chicago Press.

Harrington, T. F. (1997). Career development theory. In T. G. Harrington (Ed.) *Handbook of career planning* (2nd ed., pp. 3–40). Austin, TX: PRO-ED.

Harrington, T. F., & O'Shea, A. J. (1984). *Guide to occupational exploration* (2nd ed.). Circle Pines, MN: American Guidance Service.

Harrington, T. F., & O'Shea, A. J. (1992). *Career decision making system revised.* Circle Pines, MN: American Guidance Service.

Harris, J. A. (1982). Innovations in vocational evaluations and work adjustment. APTICOM: A computerized multiple aptitude testing instrument for cost and time effective vocational evaluation. *Vocational Evaluation and Work Adjustment Bulletin, 4*, 161–162.

Hathaway, S., & McKinley, C. (1990). *Minnesota Multiphasic Personality Inventory–Second Edition*. Minneapolis, MN: National Computer Systems.

Helms, J. E. (1992). Why is there no study of cultural equivalence in standardized cognitive ability testing? *American Psychologist, 47*, 1083–1101.

Herr, E., & Cramer, S. (1979). *Career guidance through the life span*. Boston: Little, Brown.

Hershenson, D. (1990). A theoretical model for rehabilitation counseling. *Rehabilitation Counseling Bulletin, 33*, 268–278.

Holland, J. (1959). A theory of vocational choice. *Journal of Counseling Psychologists, 6*, 35–45.

Holland, J. (1977). *You and your career*. Odessa, FL: Psychological Assessment Resources.

Holland, J. (1994). *The self-directed search*. San Antonio, TX: Psychological Corp.

Hood, A. B., & Johnson, R. W. (1997). *Assessment in counseling* (2nd ed.). Alexandria, VA: American Counseling Association.

Hoppock, R. (1976). *Occupational information* (4th ed.) New York: McGraw-Hill.

Hursh, N. (1989). *Assessing vocational capacity of learning disabled adults*. Unpublished manuscript, Boston University.

Hursh, N. C., & Kerns, A. F. (1988). *Vocational evaluation in special education*. Austin, TX: PRO-ED.

Interdisciplinary Council on Vocational Evaluation/Assessment. (1994). *A position statement by the vocational evaluation and work adjustment association* (VEWAA). Colorado Springs: Author.

Irvin, L. K., & Halpern, H. S. (1979). A process model of diagnostic assessment. In G. T. Bellamy, G. O'Connor, & O. Karan (Eds.), *Vocational rehabilitation of severely handicapped persons*. Baltimore: University Park Press.

Isaacson, L. E., & Brown, D. (1997). *Career information, career counseling, and career development*. Needham Heights, MA: Allyn & Bacon.

Jastak, J. G., & Jastak, K. S. (1987). *Wide Range Interest–Opinion Test*. Wilmington, DE: Jastak Assessment Systems.

JIST. (1993). *Complete guide for occupational exploration*. Indianapolis, IN: JIST Works.

JIST. (1998a). *Guide for occupational exploration*. Indianapolis, IN: JIST Works.

JIST. (1998b). *Occupational information network*. Indianapolis, IN: JIST Works.

Job Search People. (1983). *Transferable Skills Inventory*. Indianapolis: Author.

Johansson, C. B. (1986). *Career assessment inventory–The enhanced version*. Minneapolis, MN: National Computer Systems.

Kaplan, S., & Questad, L. (1980). Client characteristics in rehabilitation studies: A literature review. *Journal of Applied Rehabilitation Counseling, 11*, 165–168.

Karlsen B., & Gardner, E. F. (1986). *Adult Basic Learning Examination*. New York: Psychological Corp.

Kaufman, A. S., & Kaufman, N. L. (1990). *Kaufman Brief Intelligence Test*. Circle Pines, MN: American Guidance Service.

Kellogg, C. E., & Morton, N. W. (1978). *Revised Beta Examination–Beta II*. New York: Psychological Corp.

Kjos, D. (1995). Linking career information to personality disorders. *Journal of Counseling and Development, 73*, 592–596.

Knapp, L. F., & Knapp, R. R. (1994). *Career Ability Placement Survey*. San Diego: EdITS/Educational and Industrial Testing Service.

Knefelkamp, L. L., & Slepitza, R. (1976). A cognitive-developmental model of career development—An adaptation of the Perry scheme. *Counseling Psychology, 6*, 53–58.

Knoff, H. M., & Prout, T. (1985). *Drawing System for Family and School*. Los Angeles: Western Psychological Services.

Koch, L. (1998, March). *Increasing client involvement in the vocational rehabilitation process: An expectations-based approach*. Paper presented at the meeting of the National Counselor Association (NRCA & ARCA), Vancouver, Washington.

Kolb, D. (1976). *The Learning Style Inventory: Technical manual*. Boston: McBen.

Kolb, D., & Goldman, M. (1973, December). Toward a typology of learning styles and learning environments: An investigation of the impact of learning styles and discipline demands on the academic performance, social adaptation, and career choices of M.I.T. seniors. *M.I.T. Sloan school of management working paper*. Boston: M.I.T.

Krantz, G. (1971). Critical vocational behavior. *Journal of Rehabilitation, 37*, 14–16.

Kroll, L. G. (1984). LD's—What happens when they are no longer children? *Academic Therapist, 20*, 133–148.

Kuder, F. (1960). *Kuder Occupational Interest Survey–Form DD*. Chicago: Science Research Associates.

Lanyon, R. I. (1978). *Psychological Screening Inventory*. Port Huron, MI: Sigma Assessment Systems.

Leung, P. (1974). The use of behavior contracts in employability development planning. *Journal of Employment Counseling, 11*, 150–153.

Levinson, E. M. (1994). Current vocational assessment models for students with disabilities. *Journal of Counseling and Development, 73*, 94–101.

Lock, R. D. (1988). *Taking charge of your career direction*. Pacific Grove, CA: Brooks/Cole.

Lock, R. D. (1992). *Taking charge of your career direction* (2nd ed.). Pacific Grove, CA: Brooks/Cole.

Lofquist, L. H., & Dawes, R. (1969). *Adjustment to work: A psychological view of man's problems in a work-oriented society*. New York: Appleton-Century-Crofts.

Luria, A. R. (1973). *The working brain*. New York: Basic Books.

Lynch, R. (1979). Vocational rehabilitation of worker's compensation clients. *Journal of Applied Rehabilitation Counseling, 9*, 164–167.

MacKay, W. (1975). The decision fallacy: Is it if or when? *Vocational Guidance Quarterly, 23*, 227–231.

Maki, D., Pape, D., & Prout, H. (1979). Personality evaluations: A tool of the rehabilitation counselor. *Journal of Applied Rehabilitation Counseling, 10*, 119–123.

Markwardt, F. C. (1989). *Peabody Individual Achievement Test–Revised*. Circle Pines, MN: American Guidance Service.

Marrone, J., Horgan, J., Scripture, D., & Grossman, M. (1984). Serving the severely psychiatrically disabled client within the VR system. *Psychosocial Rehabilitation Journal, 8*(2), 5–23.

Mastie, M. (1976). Differential aptitude tests, Forms S & T with a career planning program. *Measurement and Evaluation in Guidance, 9*, 87–95.

Matkin, R. (1980). Legal and ethical issues in vocational assessment. *Vocational Evaluation and Work Adjustment Bulletin, 13*, 57–60.

Maze. M. (1984). How to select a computerized guidance system. *Journal of Counseling and Development, 63*, 158–161.

Maze, M., & Mayall, D. (1995). *The enhanced guide for occupational exploration* (2nd ed.). Indianapolis, IN: JIST.

McCarron, L., & Dial, J. (1986). *McCarron-Dial Systems*. Dallas, TX: Authors.

McClelland, D. (1973). Testing for competence rather than for intelligence. *American Psychologist, 28*, 1–14.

McCray, P. (1979a, Spring). Competitive work sample norms and standards: Some consideration. *Vocational Evaluation and Work Adjustment Bulletin*, 24–26.

McCray, P. (1979b). *Learning assessment in vocational evaluation*. Menomonie: University of Wisconsin–Stout.

McCue, M. (1989). The role of assessment in the vocational rehabilitation of adults with specific learning disabilities. *Rehabilitation Counseling Bulletin, 31*(1), 18–35.

Menchetti, B. M., & Rusch, F. R. (1988). Vocational evaluation and eligibility for rehabilitation services. In P. Wehman & E. S. Moon (Eds.), *Vocational rehabilitation and supported employment* (pp. 79–90). Baltimore: Brookes.

Menchetti, B., Rusch, F., & Owens, D. (1983). Vocational training. In J. Matson & S. Breuning (Eds.), *Assessing the mentally retarded* (pp. 247–284). New York: Grune & Stratton.

Menchetti, B., & Uduari-Solner (1990). Supported employment: New challenges for vocational evaluation. *Rehabilitation Education, 4,* 301–317.

Miller, G. M. (1982). Deriving meaning from standardized tests: Interpreting test results to clients. *Measurement and Evaluation in Guidance, 15,* 87–93.

Mischel, W. (1968). *Personality and assessment.* New York: Wiley.

Moore, A., Gartin, B., & Carmack, P. (1981). WRAT or SIT: Tools for assessing handicapped adults. *Vocational Evaluation and Work Adjustment Bulletin, 14,* 60–64.

Moos, R. H. (1986). *Work Environment Scale* (2nd ed.). Palo Alto, CA: Consulting Psychologists Press.

Moseley, C. R. (1988). Job satisfaction research: Implications for supported employment. *The Journal of the Association for Persons with Severe Handicaps, 13,* 211–219.

Murray, H. A. (1943). *Thematic Apperception Test.* Cambridge, MA: Harvard University Press.

Murray, S. (1990, Winter). Role of vocational evaluation in psychiatric rehabilitation. *Vocational Evaluation and Work Adjustment Bulletin,* 149–153.

Musante, S. E. (1983, Spring). Issues relevant to the vocational evaluation of the traumatically head injured client. *Vocational Evaluation and Work Adjustment Bulletin,* 45–68.

Myers, I. B., & Briggs, K. C. (1988). *Myers-Briggs Type Indicator.* Palto Alto, CA: Consulting Psychologists Press.

National Computer Systems. (1989). *Professional assessment services,* Minneapolis, MN: Author.

Neff, W. (1966). Problems of work evaluation. *The Personnel and Guidance Journal, 44,* 682–688.

Neff, W. S. (1971). *Work and human behavior.* Chicago: Atherton Press.

Nester, M., (1994). Psychometric testing and reasonable accommodation for persons with disabilities. In S. M. Bruyere & J. O'Keefe (Eds.), *Implications of the American with Disabilities Act for psychology* (pp. 25–35). New York: Springer Publishing Company.

Okun, B. G. (1987). *Effective helping: Interviewing and counseling techniques.* Monterey, CA: Brooks/Cole.

Olson, L. (1992). Use of vocational evaluation in the workers' compensation system. In J. M. Siefker (Ed.), *Vocational evaluation in private sector rehabilitation* (pp. 99–134). Menomonie: University of Wisconsin–Stout.

Omizo, M. (1980). The differential aptitude tests as predictors of success in a high school for engineering program. *Educational Technology Measurement, 40,* 197–203.

Owings, S. (1992). Using vocational evaluation in determining employability, wage loss, lost earning capacity, and other aspects of expert witness work. In J. M. Siefker, (Ed.), *Vocational evaluation in private sector rehabilitation* (pp. 169–194). Menomonie: University of Wisconsin–Stout.

Owings, S., & Siefker, J. (1991, Fall). Criterion-referenced scoring vs. norming: A critical discussion. *Vocational Evaluation and Work Adjustment Bulletin,* 109–111.

Parker, R. M., & Schaller, J. (1996). Issues in vocational assessment and disability. In E. Szymanski & R. Parker (Eds.), *Work and disability* (pp. 127–164). Austin, TX: PRO-ED.

Parker, R. M., Szymanski, E. M., & Hanley-Maxwell, C. (1989). Ecological assessment in supported employment. *Journal of Applied Rehabilitation Counseling, 2,* 26–33.

Perlman, L. G., & Austin, G. F. (Eds.). (1984). *Technology and rehabilitation of disabled persons in the information age.* Alexandria, VA: National Rehabilitation Association.

Peterson, M. (1984, Winter). Vocational evaluation and work sample development for skilled, technical, managerial, and professional positions. *Vocational Evaluation and Work Adjustment Bulletin,* 144–148.

Phillips, J. (1978). Occupational interest inventories: An often untapped resource. *Journal of Applied Rehabilitation Counseling, 9,* 10–16.

Pickman, A. (1994). *The complete guide to outplacement counseling.* Hillsdale, NJ: Erlbaum.

Pierce, R. M., Cohen, M. R., Anthony, W. A., & Cohen, B. F. (1978). *The skills of career counseling,* Austin, TX: PRO-ED.

Pittenger, D. J. (1993, Fall). Measuring the MBTI and coming up short. *Journal of Career Planning and Employment, 49*–53.

Polinko, R. (1985). Working with the family: The acute phase. In M. Ylvisaker (Ed.), *Head injury rehabilitation: Children and adolescents* (pp. 91–116). Austin, TX: PRO-ED.

Power, P. W. (1988). An assessment approach to family intervention. In P. Power, A. Dell Orto, & M. Gibbons (Eds.), *Family interventions throughout chronic illness and disability* (pp. 5–223). New York: Springer.

Power, P. W., & Dell Orto, A. E. (1986). Families, illness & disability: The roles of the rehabilitation counselor. *Journal of Applied Rehabilitation Counseling, 17,* 41–44.

Power, P. W., Dell Orto, A. E., & Gibbons, M. B. (1988). *Family interventions throughout chronic illness and disability.* New York: Springer.

Prince, J. P., Vemura, A. K., Chao, G. S., & Gonzales, G. M. (1992). Using career interest inventories with multicultural clients. *Chronicle Guidance Publications,* 2–12.

Pruitt, W. A. (1986). *Vocational evaluation.* Menomonie, WI: Walt Pruitt.

Psychological Corporation. (1988). *Stanford Achievement Test* (8th ed.). San Antonio, TX: Author.

Raven, J. C. (1986). *Raven Progressive Matrices.* New York: Psychological Corp.

Rayman, J. R. (1990, April). *Ethics in choosing and using assessment instruments.* Paper presented at the Maryland Career Development Association Conference, Columbia.

Rehabilitation Act of 1973, 29 U.S.C. § 701 *et seq.*

Rehabilitation Act Amendments of 1986, 29 U.S.C. § 701 *et seq.*

Rehabilitation Brief. (1987). *Supported employment, X.* Washington, DC: National Institute on Disability and Rehabilitation Research.

Rehabilitation Research and Training Center Brief. (1988). Richmond: Virginia Commonwealth University.

Reitan, R. M. (1966). A research program on the psychological effects of brain lesions in human beings. In N. R. Ellis (Ed.), *International review of research in mental retardation* (Vol. 1, pp. 153–218). Orlando, FL: Academic.

Reitan, R. M. (1974). *Halstead–Reitan Neuropsychological Test Battery.* Tucson, AZ: Reitan Neuropsychology Laboratory/Press.

Ripley, R., Hudson, K., & Neidert, G. P. M. (1992). *World of Work Inventory.* Tempe, AZ: World of Work, Inc.

Roessler, R. (1982). Vocational planning. In B. Bolton (Ed.), *Vocational adjustment of disabled persons* (pp. 167–180). Austin, TX: PRO-ED.

Roessler, R., & Rubin, S. (1982). *Case management and rehabilitation counseling.* Austin, TX: PRO-ED.

Rogan, P., & Hagner, D. (1990). Vocational evaluation in supported employment. *Journal of Rehabilitation, 56,* 45–51.

Rorschach, H. J. (1942). *Psychodiagnostics: A diagnostic test based on perception* (P. Lemkau & B. Kronenberg, Trans.) Berne: Huber (1st German ed. published 1921; U.S. distributor, Grune & Stratton).

Rosenberg, M. (1979). *Conceiving the self.* New York: Basic Books.

Rotter, J. B., Lah, M. I., & Rafferty, J. E. (1992). *Rotter Incomplete Sentences Blank* (2nd ed.). San Antonio, TX: Psychological Corp.

Rounds, J. B., Jr., Henly, G. A., Dawis, R. V., Lofquist, L. H., & Weiss, D. J. (1981). *Manual for the Minnesota Importance Questionnaire: A measure of vocational needs and values*. Minneapolis: Vocational Psychology Research, University of Minnesota.

Rubin, S. E., & Porter, T. (1979). Rehabilitation counselor and vocational evaluator competencies. *Journal of Rehabilitation, 45*, 42–45.

Rubin, S. E., & Roessler, R. T. (1995). *Foundations of the vocational rehabilitation process* (4th ed.). Austin, TX: PRO-ED.

Rubin, S. W., & Emener, W. G. (1979). Recent rehabilitation counselor role changes and role strain—A pilot investigation. *Journal of Applied Rehabilitation Counseling, 10*, 142–147.

Rusalem, H., & Malikin, D. (Eds.). (1976). *Contemporary vocational rehabilitation*. New York: New York University Press.

Rusch, F., Mithauge, D., & Flexer, R. (1986). Obstacles to competitive employment and traditional program options for overcoming them. In F. Rusch (Ed.), *Competitive employment issues and strategies* (pp. 39–55). Baltimore: Brookes.

Salomone, P. R. (1996). Career counseling and job placement: Theory and practice. In E. M. Szymanski & R. M. Parker (Eds.), *Work and disability* (pp. 365–415). Austin, TX: PRO-ED.

Salvia, J., & Ysseldyke, J. (1995). *Assessment* (6th ed.). Boston: Houghton Mifflin.

Sampson, J. K., McMahon, G., & Burkhead, E. J. (1985). Using computers for career exploration and decision making in vocational rehabilitation. *Rehabilitation Counseling Bulletin, 28*, 242–261.

Sanchez, I. (1981). *The California Workers' Compensation Rehabilitation System*. New York: Macmillan.

Satir, V. (1967). *Conjoint family therapy*. Palo Alto, CA: Science and Behavior Books.

Sax, A. (1981). New VEWAA/Carf standards for work evaluation and adjustment. *Vocational Evaluation and Work Adjustment Bulletin, 14*, 141–142.

Sax, A. B., & Pell, K. C. (1985, Summer). A primer on tools of evaluation. *Vocational Evaluation and Work Adjustment Bulletin*, 57–60.

Saxon, J. P., & Spitznagel, R. J. (1995, Fall). Transferable skills and abilities profile: An economical assessment approach in the vocational placement process. *Vocational Evaluation and Work Adjustment Bulletin*, 61–67.

Schalock, R. C., & Karan, O. C. (1979). Relevant assessment: The interaction between evaluation and training. In G. T. Bellamy, G. O'Connor, & O. Karan (Eds.), *Vocational rehabilitation of severely handicapped persons* (pp. 33–54). Baltimore: University Park Press.

Schlenoff, D. (1979). Obstacles to the rehabilitation of disability benefits recipients. *Journal of Rehabilitation, 45*, 56–58.

Schlenoff, F. (1974). Considerations in administering intelligence tests to the physically disabled. *Rehabilitation Literature, 35*, 362–363.

Schuster, D. & Smith, F. (1994). The Interdisciplinary Council on Vocational Evaluation and Assessment: Building Consensus Through Communication, Advocacy, and Common Goals, *Vocational Evaluation and Work Adjustment Bulletin, 27*(4), 111–114.

Schwab, L. (1981). *Independent living assessment for persons with disabilities*. Lincoln, NE: Department of Human Development and the Family.

Sedlacek, W. (1994). Issues in advancing diversity through assessment. *Journal of Counseling and Development, 72*, 549–553.

Seligman, L. (1994). *Developmental career counseling and assessment* (2nd. ed.). Thousand Oaks, CA: SAGE Publications.

Sherman, J. S., & Robinson, N. (Eds.). (1982). *Ability testing of handicapped people: Dilemma for government, science, and the public*. Washington, DC: National Academy Press.

Shertzer, B., & Linden, J. (1979). *Fundamentals of individual appraisal*. Boston: Houghton Mifflin.

Shipley, W. C. (1986). *Shipley Institute of Living Scale*. Los Angeles: Western Psychological Services.

Shurrager, H. C. (1961). *Haptic Intelligence Scale for the Adult Blind*. Chicago: Illinois Institute of Technology.

Siders, J., & Wharton, J. (1982). The relationship of individual ability and IEP goal statements. *Elementary School Guidance Counseling, 16*, 187–192.

Siefker, J. M. (1992). What is the difference between public and private sector rehabilitation? In J. M. Siefker (Ed.), *Vocational evaluation in private sector rehabilitation*. Menomonie: University of Wisconsin.

Siefker, J. M. (1996). *Tests and test use in vocational evaluation and assessment*. Menomonie: University of Wisconsin–Stout.

Silberberg, M. E., & Silberberg, M. (1978). And the adult who reads poorly? *Journal of Learning Disabilities, 11*, 15–16.

Simon, S. B., Howe, L. W., & Kirschenbaum, H. J. (1972). *Values clarification: A handbook of practical strategies for teachers and students*. New York: Hart.

Simpson, R. G., & Umbach, B. T. (1989, July/August/September). Identifying and providing vocational services for adults with specific learning disabilities. *Journal of Rehabilitation*, 49–54.

Sinick, D. (1969). Training, placement and follow-up. In D. Molikin & H. Rusalem (Eds.), *Vocational rehabilitation of the disabled* (pp. 185–199). New York: New York University Press.

Sink, J., & Field, T. (1981). *Vocational assessment planning and jobs*. Athens, GA: Udare Service Bureau.

Sink, J., & King. W. (1978, July). The vocational specialists: Preparation for court testimony—Fact or fantasy? *Careers*, 28–32.

Skinstad, A. J. (1998). *Substance Abuse Screening and Assessment*. Iowa City: Addiction Technology Transfer Center of Iowa.

Slosson, R. L., Nicholson, C. L., & Hibpshman, T. H. (1990). *Slosson Intelligence Test–R*. East Aurora, NY: Slosson Educational Publications.

Spokane, A. R. (1991). *Career intervention*. Englewood Cliffs, NJ: Prentice-Hall.

Stewart, W. E., & Vander Kolk, C. J. (1989). Instructional model for assessment of injured persons. *Rehabilitation Education, 3*, 123–135.

Strong, E. K., Hansen, J. C., & Campbell, D. P. (1994). *Strong Interest Inventory*. Palo Alto, CA: Consulting Psychologists Press.

Sue, D. W., & Sue, D. (1990). *Counseling the culturally different: Theory and practice*. New York: Wiley.

Sundberg, N. D. (1977). *Assessment of persons*. Englewood Cliffs, NJ: Prentice-Hall.

Super, D. (1970). *Work Value Inventory*. San Antonio, TX: Psychological Corp.

Super, D. E. (1949). *Appraising vocational fitness*. New York: Harper & Row.

Super, D. E. (1957). *The psychology of careers*. New York: Harper & Row.

Sutton, J. (1985). The need for family involvement in client rehabilitation. *Journal of Applied Rehabilitation Counseling, 16*, 42–45.

Suzuki, L. A., & Kugler, J. G. (1995). Intelligence and personality assessment. In J. G. Ponterotto, J. M. Casas, L. A. Suzuki, & C. M. Alexander (Eds.), *Handbook of multicultural counseling* (pp. 493–515). Thousand Oaks, CA: Sage.

Talent Assessment, Inc. (1985). *Talent Assessment Program*. Jacksonville, FL: Author.

Thorndike, R., & Hagen, E. (1969). *Measurement and evaluation in psychology and education*. New York: Wiley.

Thorndike, R. L., Hagen, E. P., & Sattler, J. M. (1986). *Stanford-Binet Intelligence Scale–Fourth Edition*. Chicago, IL: Riverside.

Tiedeman, D. V. (1961). Decision and vocational development: A paradigm and its implications. *The Personnel and Guidance Journal, 40*, 15–20.

Tiffin, R. (1948). *Examiner manual for the Purdue Pegboard.* Chicago: Science Research Associates.

Tyler, L. (1984). What tests don't measure. *Journal of Counseling and Development, 63*, 48–50.

U.S. Congress, House. Rehabilitation Act Amendments of 1986. 99th Congress, 2nd Session, October 2, 1986. Report 99-955.

U.S. Department of Education, Rehabilitation Services Administration. (1985). *Program policy directive* RSA-PPD-85-3, January 24th.

U.S. Department of Labor. (1970). *Manual for the USES General Aptitude Test Battery.* Washington, DC: U.S. Government Printing Office.

U.S. Department of Labor. (1971). *Manual for the USES Nonreading Aptitude Test Battery, Section 1.* Washington, DC: U.S. Government Printing Office.

U.S. Department of Labor. (1972). *Handbook for analyzing jobs.* Washington, DC: U.S. Government Printing Office.

U.S. Department of Labor. (1977). *Dictionary of occupational titles* (4th ed.). Washington, DC: U.S. Government Printing Office.

U.S. Department of Labor. (1981). *Selected characteristics of occupations defined in the* Dictionary of Occupational Titles. Washington, DC: U.S. Government Printing Office.

U.S. Department of Labor. (1982). *Manual for the USES General Aptitude Test Battery.* Washington, DC: U.S. Government Printing Office.

U.S. Department of Labor. (1990). *Occupational outlook handbook.* Washington, DC: U.S. Government Printing Office.

U.S. Department of Labor. (1991). *Dictionary of occupational titles* (4th ed., revised). Washington, DC: U.S. Government Printing Office.

Valpar International Corporation. (1991). Valpar System 2000 [computer software]. Tucson, AZ: Author.

Vandergoot, D. (1982, November). Work readiness assessment. *Rehabilitation Counseling Bulletin*, 84–87.

Vandergoot, D., Jacobsen, R. J., & Worral, J. D. (1979). New direction for placement practice in vocational rehabilitation. In D. Vandergoot & J. D. Worral (Eds.), *Placement in rehabilitation* (pp. 1–42). Austin, TX: PRO-ED.

Vandergoot, D., Swirsky, J., & Rice, K. (1982). Using occupational information in rehabilitation counseling. *Rehabilitation Counseling Bulletin, 26*, 94–100.

Vander Kolk, C. J. (1995). Future methods and practice in vocational assessment. *Journal of Applied Rehabilitation Counseling, 26*(2), 45–50.

Versluys, H. (1980). The remediation of role disorders through focused group work. *American Journal of Occupational Therapy, 34*, 609–614.

Virginia Commonwealth University. (1989). *Return to work following traumatic brain injury.* Richmond, VA: Rehabilitation Research and Training Center on Supported Employment.

Vocational Evaluation and Work Adjustment Association. (1975). *Vocational evaluation project final report.* Washington, DC: Author.

Vocational Psychology Research. (1981). *Minnesota Importance Questionnaire.* Minneapolis: University of Minnesota.

Vocational Research Institute. (1989). *The APTICOM Aptitude Test Battery.* Author: Philadelphia.

Vocational Research Institute. (1992). *Vocational transit.* Philadelphia: Author.

Vogel, S. A. (1989). Adults with language learning disabilities. *Rehabilitation Education, 3*, 77–90.

Walk, T. E. (1985, Spring). A review of commercial vocational evaluation systems and disability groups. *Vocational Evaluation and Work Adjustment Bulletin*, 29–34.

Walker, R. A. (1966, April). *Evaluation*. Paper presented at the Institute on Professional Services, sponsored by the Pennsylvania Association of Sheltered Workshops, Harrisburg.

Walls, R. T., Zane, T., & Werner, T. J. (1979). *The vocational behavior checklist* (experimental ed.). Dunbar: West Virginia Research and Training Center.

Walsh, W. B., & Betz, N. E. (1995). *Tests and assessment* (3rd ed.) Englewood Cliffs, NJ: Prentice-Hall.

Wechsler, D. (1997). *Wechsler Adult Intelligence Scale–Third Edition*. San Antonio, TX: Psychological Corp.

Weinstein, H. (1983). Transferable skills analysis in the rehabilitation process. *Rehabilitation Forum, 9*, 25–27.

Weinstein, M. (1978). The concept of the disability process. *Psychosomatics, 19*, 94–97.

Wheeler, J. D. (1996). *Goodness of fit—A guide to conducting and using functional vocational assessments*. Menomonie: University of Wisconsin–Stout.

Wilkinson, G. S. (1993). *Wide Range Achievement Test–Third Edition*. Wilmington, DE: Wide Range Inc.

Wollack, S., Goodale, J. G., Wijting, J. P., & Smith. P. C. (1976). *Survey of Work Values*. Bowling Green, OH: Bowling Green State University.

Workman, E. (1983). Vocational rehabilitation in the private, profit-making sector. In E. Pan, T. Backer, & C. Vash (Eds.), *Annual review of rehabilitation* (pp. 292–321). New York: Springer.

Wright, B. (1960). *Physical disability—A psychological approach*. New York: Harper & Row.

Wright, G. (1980). *Total rehabilitation*. Boston: Little, Brown.

Wright, G. N., & Fraser, R. T. (1976). *Improving manpower utilization: The rehabilitation task performance evaluation scale*. Madison: University of Wisconsin.

Zadny, J., & James, L. (1977). Time spent on placement. *Rehabilitation Counseling Bulletin, 321*, 31–35.

Zeigler, E. A. (1987, January/February/March). Spouses of persons who are brain injured: Overlooked victims. *Journal of Rehabilitation*, 50–53.

Ziezula, F. R. (Ed.). (1986). *Assessment of hearing-impaired people: A guide for selecting psychological, educational, and vocational tests*. Washington, DC: Gallaudet University Press.

Zytowski, D. G. (1965). Avoidance behavior in vocational motivation. *The Personnel and Guidance Journal, 43*, 746–750.

Author Index

Subject Index

Please remember that this is a library book,
and that it belongs only temporarily to each
person who uses it. Be considerate. Do
not write in this, or any, library book.

WITHDRAWN

DATE DUE

NO 8 '02			
ILL			
796124			
12/12/03			

DEMCO 38-296